The
Bardic Handbook

The Complete Manual for the
Twenty-First Century Bard

To Keith,
May your Awen
flow!

Kevin
23 April
2012

First published by Gothic Image Publications
PO Box 2568 Glastonbury,
Somerset BA6 8XR, England
www.gothicimage.co.uk

ISBN 0 906362 67 9
13-digit ISBN 978 0 906362 67 9

A catalogue record for this book is available
from the British Library

All illustrations are by the author, Kevan Manwaring,
unless otherwise captioned. The author can be
contacted via his website: www.tallyessin.com

Cover design by Peter Woodcock
Book design and artwork by Bernard Chandler
Illustrated borders by Peter Woodcock
Set in Monotype Bulmer
Printed and bound in Slovenia

The
Bardic Handbook

The Complete Manual for the
Twenty-First Century Bard

by

Kevan Manwaring

Gothic Image
PUBLICATIONS

About the Author

Kevan Manwaring is a poet, storyteller, novelist and teacher, holding an MA in the Teaching and Practice of Creative Writing from Cardiff University. Originally from Northampton, England, he studied performance art and film on the Fine Art Degree in Coventry. He has been performing his poetry for over a decade in venues across the Southwest as well as further afield (ie: Rhode Island Festival, USA). In 1998 he was awarded the Bardic Chair of Caer Badon (Bath) for an epic poem based on a local legend. With Fire Springs Storytelling Company he has co-created and performed in several shows (*Arthur's Dream, Robin of the Wildwood, Return to Arcadia*). He has been running creative-writing and performance workshops for all ages since launching himself professionally as Tallyessin in 2000. In 2003 he edited *Writing the Land – an anthology of natural words*, after receiving a Reading Families Millennium Award. He has written to date seven collections of poetry and five novels. His third, *The Long Woman*, was published late 2004, and the Land Song Tour, when readings were given in all the locations featured in the book, took place thanks to a grant from the Arts Council of England. In 2005 he founded the Silver Branch Bardic Network, and currently teaches creative writing for the Open University. He lives in Bath, where he is actively involved with the Bardic Chair, and the monthly Bath Storytelling Circle. His goal is to preserve, promote and develop the Bardic Tradition: training and initiating Bards, running Bardic showcases and Eisteddfodau (eg: Wessex Gathering, Lammas Games), giving talks on the path of a Bard, and unning workshops on the Shining Word. He loves walking the land, the imaginative arts, and celebrating the spirit of place.

Publications by Kevan Manwaring:

Writing the Land: an anthology of natural words,
Edited by Kevan Manwaring. Awen/Reading Families Millennium Award, 2003

Speak Like Rain: letters to a young Bard. Awen, 2004

Fire in the Head: creative process in the Celtic diaspora. Awen, 2004

Green Fire: magical verse for the wheel of the year. Awen, 2004

The Long Woman, a novel. Awen/Arts Council of England, 2004

Thank you to:

Frances Howard Gordon for picking up the Silver Branch.

Adrian Beckingham, the Man from Story Mountain, whose beautifully wise book *Stories That Crafted the Earth* inspired me to get in touch with Gothic Image.

Emma Restall Orr for blessing these pages with her beautiful wisdom.

Robin Williamson for showing me what a truly great Bard can be,
and for allowing the inclusion of his masterful *Dialogue of the Two Sages*, originally published in *Celtic Bards, Celtic Druids* (with RJ Stewart), Blandford Press 1996.

All those who took part in the Way of Awen weekends 2004.
My fellow Bards in Fire Springs, shining brows all.
Claire Hamilton and Blackbird Hollins for the wisdom on harps.
Penbeirdd Taliesin and all those who have contributed to the Bardic Tradition.

All whose wise words I have quoted.

Wendy Andrew (www.paintingdreams.co.uk), Stuart Littlejohn (domusminervae@hotmail.com), Briar (www.mysterium-jewellery.co.uk), Sheila Broun for their divine images,
and to Bernard and Peter for their stunning design and artwork.

Finally, to my partner Cathy, for supporting me through the
writing of this book and my Bardic Path.

Contents

THREE - FIRE

FOUR - WATER

FIVE - EARTH

APPENDICES

Preface

I believe in the power of words to transform, heal and inspire. It is immensely satisfying to communicate what one believes in an eloquent and entertaining way. Taking an audience on a magical journey, creating an enchanting atmosphere, making sacred the air – this is the joy of being a Bard. I love helping people express themselves, hone their talent and shine. I wish there had been a book like this when I started out (it would have improved my learning curve dramatically!) because I think *The Bardic Handbook* will make the road easier for you. Allow me to share my fifteen-plus years of experience and expertise, so that you do not have to reinvent the wheel, hit deadends or learn the harder way.

The Bardic Handbook is designed to awaken the Bard within. It will teach you essential Bardic skills, and support your development as a Bard: either as poet, storyteller, musician, or all three. Whether you take the craft further and begin to remember, record and recite, use your words in a ceremonial way, or simply improve your oral communication skills – that's up to you. *The Bardic Handbook* can only give you the tools and show you the way, describing what you need to learn and how to go about honing your craft – but it is only through practise, dedication and passion that you'll truly become a Bard.

Modern Bards can be male or female, so when I use the word 'Bard' I am referring to both. However, in the text it is sometimes necessary to use a personal pronoun, in which case I will ascribe a particular gender as the Muse takes me, to avoid the tedious and awkward 'he/she, his/her'. If I veer towards the masculine, then it is simply the fault of my sex.

Although I draw upon the Celtic Tradition, I believe Bardic skills can be of benefit to you whatever belief system or background you have. There are equivalents to the Bard all around the world, in cultures equally as valid. I suggest using *The Bardic Handbook* to celebrate your own identity, community and heritage.

Words in **bold** are concepts dealt with in more detail elsewhere in the book, normally in their own chapter (refer to the Contents page) or in the **Appendices**: where **A Brief Bardic Glossary** appears for some definition of terms. Key concepts such as BARD, AWEN, AIR, FIRE, WATER and SPIRIT I have used capitals for, to highlight their importance.

Throughout I use BCE for Before Common Era (instead of BC) and CE for Common Era (instead of AD). This is not to deny Christianity but to accept that there are other paradigms.

A book like this could not come out of thin air. Apart from practical experience and the insights of Awen, I have drawn upon many sources, which are referred to either directly in the text or in the **Bardic Reading List**. Needless to say, any errors within are my own and not my sources'.

A finite publication made by mortal hands can never be completely comprehensive or flawless (and perhaps like the Persian carpetmakers who deliberately include a flaw, maybe we should leave perfection to the Creator) but I have strived my very best to offer an accurate, authentic, thorough, and user-friendly guide for the budding Bard. Yet to err is to be human, so let me know of any omissions or errors and we will endeavour to amend them in future editions.

May we always remember.

Kevan Manwaring,
Bath, Samhain 2005

Foreword

by Emma Restall Orr

From the earliest age, a child held within the embrace of a family, of a community, of a culture, is nourished by stories. When a child is distressed, sleepless and upset – even one we don't know – there is an instinct within us to draw her towards us and read her a story, tell her a tale. Yet it isn't just children who are comforted by stories. Some say language itself is derived from a communal need to know what others are doing, what others have done, to tell of our own experiences, to gossip about people, to dramatise events; language emerged through our inherent need to share stories. Stories ease the soul. They allow us to find ourselves within the currents of an ever-changing world.

It saddens me to see young children now placed in front of television screens, albeit still engrossed in stories, for as a child I knew the delight of having the storyteller there before us, of watching his eyes move over us, provoking and responding to our horror and laughter; the television is so distant in comparison, so dead. And though our culture is blessed with great film makers and novelists, biographers and historians, comic book creators and song writers, there is still nothing quite like a living, breathing and utterly present storyteller.

So do we imagine the Bards of our ancestral heritage. The wild and wind-blessed traveller sat by the hearth in the tavern, reciting tales from distant lands to the amazement of those gathered around: you can almost smell him, glimpse the wide reach of the horizon and the mud of the open road in the folds of his cloak, hear the coins of appreciation clatter in his cup. Or the shuffle and hush of a great feasting hall at some chieftain's court, cold stone and chill draughts, the roar of the centre fire, and the Bard gives another eulogistic remembrance of his lord's blood line and battle glories. Or the one dressed in fripperies, mischief and longing, singing his tawdry and eternal tale to the lyre, words of love lost and bleeding hearts. We can each, I have no doubt, pause for a moment and find a handful more images – Bards of our people.

Of course, not every story moves us, but those we relate to allow us to feel ourselves a part of that ancient flow of human living: the Bard's tales may speak of ancestors long dead, but they have been lived by our grandparents, our parents, ourselves, and these simple human complications will be lived again by our children, in one way or another. Holding the essence of what it is to be human, the greatest tales provoke us to laugh and cry and watch, attentive and wide eyed, enthralled by the storyteller.

The craft of the Bard is in many ways that simple: somewhere inside, we recognize the tale. Yet the mysteries of his skill are not only in the story's words. The true Bard is a magician of sound. While each spoken word holds the sub-linguistic power of music, many a Bard will use an instrument, together with his voice, to intensify the effect of a tale. With melody and cacophony, with rhythms and pauses, with his harp, his guitar, his pipes or drum, the Bard plays with his audience's emotions, evoking empathy, provoking the series of human responses that make up the power of the tale. He observes and criticises human behaviour, crafting communities by declaring what is acceptable and what immoral. His sound magic heals, tears apart, recreates, the mythologies of a people expressed, described, explored and played out in a thousand ways – again and again.

Within my own religious tradition, Druidry, the song is fundamental. Though Bardism is sometimes considered to be an element of Druidry, not all Bards study Druidic religion or philosophy, ancient or modern, but deeper ideas about the song are nonetheless still interesting. On the simplest level, a song is a tale held within the embrace of a melody. Yet to the Druid it is much more: a 'song' is often synonymous with a concept of the soul. Every part of nature shimmers with its own unique song, humming with its energy, expressing its consciousness, its history and potential. Nature's songs playing together create what is both the glorious music and the violent clamour of existence. Indeed, the spiritual practice of the Druid is very much about learning to hear the songs of nature, to express one's own song with clarity and truth, and to add to the music of our world (in its ongoing flow of creativity) most poignantly, relevantly and honourably.

A Druid is a priest, not an entertainer. Yet, in the same way, what distinguishes a Bard from your average performer is perhaps his understanding of the importance of what he does. He isn't simply telling stories to ease the boredom of a gathering, and this is true whether he is telling the old tales of gods and heroes, or modern stories. As Kevan Manwaring says in this very book, the Bard is a keeper of memory. With his words, he gives each one of us an opportunity to experience at least the glimmer of events that have happened before. Battles fought, love lost and won, wisdom gained and lost again, lands claimed and teachings found: he reminds us what it feels like to be proud, to be victorious, to grieve, to discover. As an active bearer of the most valuable lessons of our blood, our land, our heritage, he encourages us to be awake and to live with honour.

But let us not imagine that the Bard is a carrier of pedantry or self-righteousness! He carries too an understanding that we have too often lost in the past few hundred years or more: there is no fact and there is no fiction. The Bard may declare his tale to be absolutely 'true', but his words come from the open and embracing heart of the oral tradition of our British and Celtic heritage. It is an attitude that has been a strong part of the Western philosophical tradition for many centuries: we each can know only what we perceive. The Bard tells his tale as an expression of his experience, without imagining that his perception is indisputable fact anymore than the perception of another who may have seen events very differently. Each individual experiences the world differently. And that's just fine. Furthermore, the Bard knows that each person who hears his tale will hear it differently, and that's just fine too. So do stories find their meandering path through time.

With the children of our culture sat before their television screens, nowadays we may think of the Bard as no more than a part of our lost heritage. Striding into the twenty-first century, those who do commit to learning the Bard's craft are, surely, no more than eccentric idealists playing out a nostalgic role, dressing up and playing games. The Bardic Crafts may be considered replaced by published words, books of poetry and novels, political commentaries and histories, anecdotes and scandals in newspapers and web blogs. Yet the element of performance is a crucial part of what makes a Bard.

Who are the Bards of our century then? A group of punks, with harsh guitars, satirising the government and consumer culture? A primary school teacher telling a fairy story to a group of children? A stand-up comedian, telling tales of his community? It is worth spending a moment considering the question, for in doing so we are forced to wonder what we might imagine to be the true value of a Bard in the twenty-first century Western society. What is his role? Perhaps it is most poignantly, as ever it has been, to remind people about the past, in the most evocative way, and in doing so to question the present.

This is why Kevan's Bardic Handbook is such an important publication. The tradition of the Bard is far too broad for any book to be comprehensive, yet this one is a beautiful wide basket filled with our heritage. For some, these fruits will be enough, while for others they will be like Alice's rabbit hole and that basket will transform into a bottomless black cauldron into which we might journey, exploring beyond the known or knowable, diving into the depths of the mysteries, in search of inspiration and connection, release and wisdom.

The path of the Bard is one of exploration, and like any serious expedition it requires dedication. It may be that you pick up this book, and biting into a few nuts, taking an apple to eat upon the road, you find what you are looking for, quickly and easily. It may be that you pick it up at the wrong time in your life, a time when it is more important to be 'doing' (earning, parenting, working, supporting) than learning how to listen. But the time may well come when the need to commit rises in your soul, when you long to hear more deeply and to sing out more effectively, not only your own song but the songs of your ancestors. When that time comes, this gentle and accessible guide will be a valuable resource.

And it is about listening. We may imagine the Bard to be one exquisitely skilled in the telling of the tale but, if he weren't able to hear the story fully and truthfully, he would have nothing to retell. And what can give us more grounded, integrated and beneficial confidence than a true ability to hear?

May the song of your muse fill you with wonder. May you breathe in that song and, shining with Awen, sing that song, well-blessed that your singing will fill others with wonder...

So must the world be created, day by day.

Emma Restall Orr (bobcat)
January 2006

Introduction

The skills and wisdom of the Bard are as relevant today as they have ever been, in fact, in a world of communication breakdown and collective amnesia – where we fail to honour our geo-cultural heritage, and forget again and again the lessons of the past – possibly more so. The Bard was far more than 'just' a teller of tales or singer of songs: he or she was the remembrancer and chronicler for the tribe – of ancient lore, bloodlines, land rites, battles, geasa, great events, important details… In short, their living memory. And further-more, a celebrant, in an official or unofficial capacity – whose tales and tunes would mark the cycles of life within the circle of the community: the wooings, the weddings, the nativities, comings-of-age, and other thresholds of change. With their words they could bless or blight. Warriors would vie for the honour of being immortalised through their elegies, kings and chiefs would take care to avoid their satire, lords and enemies feared their curses. The system of patronage may no longer be viable, but that also means the Bard is no longer at the behest of a liege. In a world where most forms of communication are monitored, perhaps only the Bard is truly free to speak his or her mind without having to kowtow to so-called 'political correctness', corporate values or media fads. In the age of spin, we need more than ever a re-enchantment of language, where people actually mean what they say, free of Post-Modern irony, and a man is as good as his word. It is not a return to spurious 'old values' but a re-imagining and renewing of what those values are, by learning from the lessons of the past and acknowledging the perspective which history affords. The wisdom of the past is ever-present, if we but listen. It is an insult to our collective ancestors to do otherwise, for it is their countless sacrifices which have enabled us to have come thus far: to be in this relatively privileged, but precarious, position on the cusp of a new millennia.

In an age of Climate Change and global turmoil, the importance of community, of common people helping one another, having a voice, being heard, validating personal 'narratives' outside the hegemony of a grander one, drawing upon their own resources and talents, wealth of experience and motherwit, could never be more imperative. The Bard's ability to express the inexpressible, to celebrate the lives of all that live and have lived, and preserve for posterity the little epiphanies, personal triumphs and tragedies, heroics and hard-won wisdom from extinction, or from being drowned out in the white noise of endless trivia, enables excellence of expression and freedom of information at a grassroots level beyond webs and nets, dishes and boxes. It offers a folk democracy of the tongue and the limitless possibilities of the imagination. The Bard helps us to celebrate being human and enables us to appreciate other cultures, other perspectives, at the same time as being more fully in our own. It praises the universal through the particular: the local and microcosmic, the parts that make up the whole, which make something bigger than their sum – the biodiversity of humanity.

So, I have written this book in the belief that everyone can benefit from Bardic skills: either as a listener or performer, whether you only wish to improve your public speaking, entertain your family and friends, or aspire to be a fully-fledged professional Bard, with 'harp on back', fire in the head and hundreds of stories at your fingertips. I can claim with complete conviction that you will benefit, however far down the path of the Bard you wish to go, because I certainly have. It has transformed my life: improving not just my communication skills (I never had the 'gift of the gab', although I always had a good imagination), but social ones as well (at school I was the introvert wallflower and now, it seems, I can keep most audiences entertained, although everyone has bad days). Becoming a Bard has given me, and is still giving me, so much: it has given me a community and a role to play in it and, perhaps most importantly of all, it has given me a way to live – a true and reliable guide for life.

A disclaimer: this book does not claim to be able to make you a Bard – only *you* can make yourself one, through your belief, dedication and skill. However, this book *will* provide you will all the tools needed to set you on your way, through a structured learning programme, a comprehensive manual of techniques and an essential reference guide.

To summarise: the overall aim of this book is to empower people to find and use their true voice for the good of all. Its objectives are to:

- ❖ offer initiation for the budding Bard
- ❖ provide a practical 12 month training programme
- ❖ teach the art of storytelling
- ❖ teach techniques of poetic inspiration, composition and performance
- ❖ develop the power of the memory
- ❖ widen understanding of Awen
- ❖ develop awareness of the Bardic Tradition
- ❖ explore what it means to be a Bard in the twenty-first century
- ❖ provide resources, such as a reading list, contacts, etc.
- ❖ connect with the wider community
- ❖ encourage respect for diverse global traditions and cultures
- ❖ foster 'mythic literacy' and an understanding of mythic levels in modern life
- ❖ act as a catalyst for new Bardic circles and the re-establishing of Bardic Chairs

I hope you enjoy working with this book as much as I have writing it, especially in revisiting the sources of my inspiration. It has made me take stock of what I know, and what there is still to know – for truly, one never stops learning. I am still on the journey. I hope to see you along the way.

Author performing with Fire Springs in *Robin of the Wildwood*.

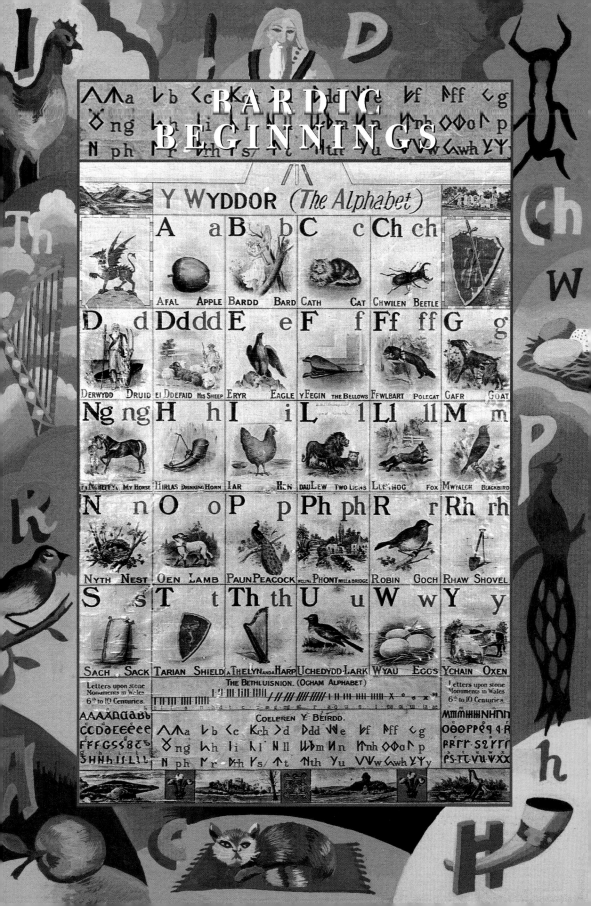

BARDIC BEGINNINGS

Y WYDDOR (The Alphabet)

A a	B b	C c	Ch ch
AFAL **APPLE**	BARDD **BARD**	CATH **CAT**	CHWILEN **BEETLE**
D d	Dd dd	E e	F f	Ff ff	G g
DERWYDD **DRUID**	EI DDEFAID **HIS SHEEP**	ERYR **EAGLE**	Y FEGIN **THE BELLOWS**	FFWLBART **POLECAT**	GAFR **GOAT**
Ng ng	H h	I i	L l	Ll ll	M m
FY NGHEFFYL **MY HORSE**	HIRLAS **DRINKING HORN**	IAR **HEN**	DAU LEW **TWO LIONS**	LLWYNOG **FOX**	MWYALCH **BLACKBIRD**
N n	O o	P p	Ph ph	R r	Rh rh
NYTH **NEST**	OEN **LAMB**	PAUN **PEACOCK**	PONT **MILL & BRIDGE**	ROBIN **GOCH**	RHAW **SHOVEL**
S s	T t	Th th	U u	W w	Y y
SACH **SACK**	TARIAN **SHIELD**	A THELYN AND A HARP	UCHEDYDD **LARK**	WYAU **EGGS**	YCHAIN **OXEN**

Letters upon stone Monuments in Wales 6ᵗʰ to 10 Centuries

THE BETHLUISNION. (OGHAM ALPHABET)

Letters upon stone Monuments in Wales 6ᵗʰ to 10 Centuries

COELEREN Y BEIRDD.

Using *The Bardic Handbook*

This handbook offers a twelve month self-study programme of Bardic development, which aims to be practical, contemporary, user-friendly and inspiring. The book is divided into five parts, corresponding to the elements of the Western Mystery Tradition: Air, Fire, Water and Earth – with Spirit at the centre. This is in effect casting a circle *deosil*, sunwise, and since it is important to work with, rather than against, Nature, I suggest that you follow the programme in sequential order. You can commence it at any time of the year, as long as you dedicate a full year to completing it (see **A Bardic Year**). At what-

Medicine Shield. Oil on canvas frame.

ever point you join the circle you can benefit from fulfilling this circular path of development. *The Bardic Handbook*'s learning cycle is also a holistic one of healing – by working with and balancing these elements within yourself you will find wholeness. It is based on the **Wheel of the Year**, consisting of the Eight Festivals: the four Celtic **fire festivals** (Samhain, Imbolc, Beltane and Lughnasadh), and four **solar festivals** – the equinoxes and solstices, which I have used as way-markers for the Bard's initiatory journey.

The Celtic Bards traditionally spent twelve years mastering their craft. As previously stated, this book does not claim to be able to magically turn you into a fully-fledged Bard in twelve months – there's no quick route, alas – instead it offers an introduction to the Bardic Tradition and the Way of Awen. By following this year-long programme you will become an *Anruth* – a Bardic initiate (in an initiation where you make a vow to what *you* consider sacred, and a commitment that *you* are prepared to make). By dedication and determination, humility and respect, you may build upon this foundation to become a fully-qualified Bard over the next twelve years, if you choose to make such a commitment.

If you have already been pursuing the path of the Bard through music, storytelling, poetry, teaching, or writing for a numbers of years, then this process will serve to consolidate and honour that effort; thus, if you began on your path eleven years ago, then by the end of this book and its twelve months of training, you will have become a full Bard of the **Taliesin grade** (see **The Training of a Bard**). This may seem like a long apprenticeship, but it is based upon the traditional length of study required by the Bardic Colleges. The surviving curriculum (ibid) offers a useful guide to the extent and depth of commitment required to master such a craft. A guide to professional practice it may be, but *The Bardic Handbook* is not seeking to set itself up as the 'voice of authority' (although some kind of peer adjudication system is useful – and the **Eisteddfod** system offers this). However some may rail against any such system, the simple truth is you cannot in all honesty start to call yourself a Bard until others do so: this is the ultimately benchmark – the acknowledgment of your community (see **Bard and Community**). You may wish to avoid the long training, but you cannot avoid this fact.

To become an **ollamh** (a doctor of verse) takes twenty years training (the equivalent to becoming a fully-fledged Druid, which traditionally required the same number of years of study); and to become a true Master Bard (**Penbeirdd**), a lifetime. However, you need not have to be willing to make such a long-term commitment to reap benefit from this book. It will be of use to any who wish to express themselves, celebrate their identity, community and heritage. How far you wish to take it is up to you.

The Bardic Tradition has many national variations (eg: African griot, Anglo-Saxon scop), all with their rich lineages and lore. Essentially, it is about connecting with it in *your* way, with *your* voice. Although the material we will be working with is predominantly Celtic, most of it is transferable to other traditions, or has cultural equivalents. Yet it is equally respectful to honour the Bard's roots in a pan-European Celtic culture, which has lived on largely through the skills of those very same Bards over the centuries. Thanks to the tradition-bearers and scholars we have tantalising glimpses of ancient techniques, and a rigorous framework for training: all of which can be applied or updated as appropriate.

Each of the five sections in this book has material associated with its respective element, and offers monthly topics, thematic essays, stories, techniques, exercises, examples and review. To complete the course you will need to dedicate at least a couple of hours a week to the readings and activities, although a daily commitment is encouraged, through a simple personal ritual – a prayer and journal entry (see **Praise Poems** and **The Leaves of Life**). Every time you work with the Way of Awen, you open a doorway to the Otherworld.

Step through and enter in peace.

Newgrange   Kevan Manwaring '97

A Bardic Year: a Month-by-Month Guide

The Wheel of the Year, as the round of festivals and seasons is known, has its own tides, like the 29.5 day lunar cycle, as the energy ebbs and flows, waxing and waning with the inception, acceleration, culmination, and withdrawal of each 'node' of elemental, spiritual and secular activity. It is wise to work with, rather than against, these currents, like a surfer riding the waves. In Spring begin to manifest projects visioned in the darkness of Winter. In Summer be expansive, travel and socialise at the festival time. From the start of harvest, work hard to gather in what you have sown, and enjoy the fruits of your toil. Then in Winter take stock, reflect and begin to dream again… Of course, we revisit these 'stations' each year – time is not a line but a spiral, as we look over the shoulders of our former selves, slightly higher up the loop…overlapping with the ghosts of the past, walking in the footsteps of ancestors – seeing how far, or little, we've come – how much or how little we have learnt or forgotten. The Wheel of the Year is a seasonal mnemonic, reminding us constantly of our own 'seasons', our own seed-times and harvests, our growing and withdrawing – synchronising with the cycle of life, harmonising with the Earth and all that lives and dies upon it.

- ❖ **Spring Quickening (February – April)**
- ❖ **Summer Shining (May – July)**
- ❖ **Autumn Gathering (August – October)**
- ❖ **Winter Dreaming (November – January)**

Our 12 month programme below is adapted from John Matthews' Shaman's Ladder (*Celtic Shaman*, Element 1991). There are a lot of correspondences between the two paths, as explored in his *Taliesin, the Last Celtic Shaman* (Inner Traditions 2002) and throughout this present book:

SPIRIT
Month 1 - Awakening to Bardic Awareness: "the First Realisation".

AIR
Month 2 - Threshold Guardians: "the difficulties encountered at the beginning of the journey".
Month 3 - Twice-Born: "the first rites of passage in the making of a shaman".

FIRE
Month 4 - Finding the Fire Within: "the discovery of individual potential".
Month 5 - Encountering Faerie: "the first encounter with inner reality".
Month 6 - Entering the Realm of Story: "passing within and exploring the Otherworld".

WATER
Month 7 - Connecting with the Animal Kingdom: "discovering and learning from the totem beasts and power animals".
Month 8 - Calling the Inner Bard: "encountering an Inner Guide or Teacher".
Month 9 - Awenyddion: "learning to move at will through the place of the spirits".

EARTH
Month 10 - Your Bardic Debut: "second rite of passage and the beginning of outer work".
Month 11 - The Tongue That Cannot Lie: "the ability to see into the inner realms and to divine future events".
Month 12 - A Bardic Life: "the integration of inner work into outer life".

Orientation: The Circle of Elements

It is important to find your centre – in life as much as in performance. If you lose your centre you may act out of character or even out of order. Life continually tests us, forcing us to consider what we like, what we think, what we believe. Rather than being persuaded into doing things against our nature, or even worse, Mother Nature; being peer-presured, or seduced by advertising, by hype, by the 'mob mentality', it is best to remain centred, and then you will always do what is right, by being fully present, in the here and the now. Religions and other belief systems offer us maps, nothing more. It is wise to remember this. The writer Alan Moore once said in a short film I made (*My Life as a God*, 1992): "do not mistake the map for the territory."

Below is another 'map', **The Circle of Elements:** a personal *mappa mundi* – as subjective, perhaps, but one that I hope you will find as useful as I have. By balancing the five elements throughout your life you will remain centred. Sometimes you need to be fiery; other times, more earthed – but, generally, it is best to aspire to a harmony and balance between these characteristics, for that is what they represent on a microcosmic, personal, scale. On a macrocosmic scale – local, national, global – they represent the forces of nature that shape our world, our universe. The dance between them is the dance of creation. Of course, other elements shape the cosmos, but these magical elements are rich metaphors for different qualities within all of us. In the Western Mystery Tradition the elements are associated with Quarters (Cardinal Points) and are used for casting a circle for ceremony, for protection, for any magical working, including a **Gorsedd**.

In Britain the correspondences and assignment of elements relates directly to the distinctive climate and lay of the land. Thus, Air is associated with the East because this is where the dawn wind blows from, where we find the vast open Fens and choppy North Sea. In my old home town of Northampton on the edge of the East Midlands the next highest place due East was Russia, and one certainly felt it on a chilly day. It layered that direction for me with an impression of white vastness, of windswept Steppe, of icy clarity. Fire is associated with the South, because in these temperate Northern lands that is where the sun is at its hottest, towards the Equator; as well as the 'hot-blood' of the Mediterranean, the blazing colours of Africa, and, further, to red Uluru and volcanic Aotearoa. In the West we find Water – and it's obvious why when you picture Europe on the Atlantic seaboard. In Britain itself to the West we find the moist mystical lands of Wales and Ireland, and dream of other lost islands towards the setting sun. Finally, in the North we find Earth – because, I think, the great mountain ranges of Scotland are located there, the megalithic islands of the Gael and Norse and, ultimately, the magnetic North Pole – that lodestone of the Earth. And, of course, Spirit is within and without – all around us, all of the time. So, as you can see, these correspondences are not arbitrary and they make sense for those working in the British Isles and most of Western Europe. For those working in different continents, a different set of associations needs to be worked with (ie: the Native American medicine wheel relates to the geo-cosmology of North America, but makes little sense out of context).

By working with these elements you can bring balance and richness to your life. It is akin to the Jungian process of Individuation – by working through and completing the whole wheel you are creating a mandala of the year – a circle of wholeness in which all the aspects of one's personality are balanced. This is a process we repeat each year, hopefully with deepening insight. Each turning brings new teaching. Enjoy your journey around the Wheel.

THE CIRCLE OF ELEMENTS

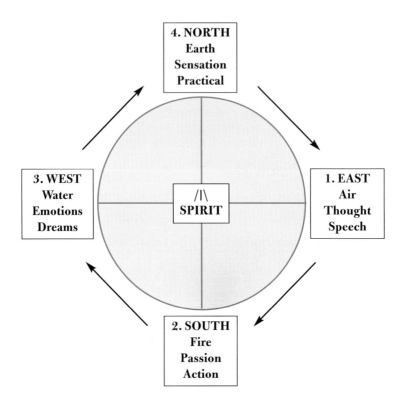

Where to Begin?

I will set out on foot,
to the gate I will come,
I will enter the hall,
my song I will sing,
my verse I will proclaim,
and the king's Bard I will cast down.
In the presence of the Chief,
demands I will make,
and chains I will break –
Elffin will be set at liberty.

The Journey to Deganwy, Taliesin

The longest journey begins with the first step. Becoming a Bard who is booked to perform at festivals, run workshops, even officiate Gorseddau and Eisteddfodau may seem like a million miles from where you are now, but if it – or some variation of it – is what you desire, then it's achievable, in incremental steps, through dedication and practise. By acquiring this book you have already made a statement of intent and taken your first step along the Way of Awen. And by reading it this far you have been introduced to some of the basic principles. But, of course, however much you study the theory, it is about how *you* implement the Bardic lore practically in your life. Throughout this book there are techniques to learn and exercises for you to participate in. I believe that you learn through *doing*. Here are some pointers to get you started and keep you going:

1. Keep reading *The Bardic Handbook* (the **Introduction** and **Spirit** sections).

2. Fill in the **Self-evaluation** now.

3. Start keeping a Bardic journal and notebook (**The Leaves of Life**).

4. As soon as you are ready, announce your intent to become a Bard (**Declaring your Chair**).

5. Compose a **Praise Poem** or song and perform it every day.

6. Try an exercise once a week, starting with **Raising the Awen**.

7. Work through the monthly chapters and sections.

8. Review each 3 months.

9. Start collecting stories, songs and poems to perform.

10. Attend a regular story circle or start one of your own (see **Running a Bardic Circle**).

11. Take your Bardic Vow and choose a Bardic Name (see **The Weir of Twice Born**).

12. Hold a public ceremony/showcase – your first 'gig'. Launch your poetry/story or song collection and yourself as a Bard into the community (**Your Bardic Debut**).

13. After a Year and a Day has elapsed from your initial commitment, claim your Bardic Chair (**A Year and a Day: Accepting Your Chair**) and celebrate the completion of your foundation year of Bardic training. Join the Community of Bards (ie: The **Silver Branch Bardic Network** – see back of book) and keep following the Way of Awen.

Self-Evaluation
START OF THE PATH

Date……/……../……..

1. Describe yourself:

2. Why are you interested in the Bardic Path?

3. What do you know about it?

4. What attracted you to it?

5. What do you hope to gain from it?

6. What experience do you have in creative writing?

7. What experience do you have in performance?

8. What would you like to improve or learn?

9. Do you have any concerns, questions or doubts?

10. What do you think your greatest challenge will be?

11. What do you think your best strength is?

12. How do you feel right now?

The Leaves of Life

From the beginning of your Bardic path I suggest that you keep a journal, to track your development and reflect upon your learning. This does not have to be a day-to-day diary – you don't need to list everything you do in the day (washing, walking the dog, pub, etc.), or chart the trivia of the moment (eg: weather, news and gossip) but to use it to record insights, feelings, poems, prayers, readings, what has been called by Lindsay Clarke (author of *The Chymical Wedding*) a 'mirror of inward process'.

Journals can be beautifully bound or virtual 'blogs'. Image: Shani Hubble.

Handsome leather-bound journals are all well and good, as long as you're not afraid to write in them. Don't get one with gold leaf pages! I suggest a hardback A4 book with good plain paper – ideal for the luxury of writing longhand with your favourite pen, but so you can also draw in it if you have the ability or inclination (include doodles, diagrams, mindmaps, etc.), glue postcards, clippings, feathers, mementoes from interesting places (ie: museums, or heritage sites) – basically anything that relates to your path as a Bard.

A smaller notebook (A5 or A6) would be ideal to carry around with you and have by your bedside: for those sudden bursts of inspiration. Use it to gather fragments of life. Collect choice words and unusual snippets of conversations eavesdropped on the radio, on the bus, in the park. Follow what Canadian writer Margaret Atwood calls the 'Way of the Jackdaw': hoard shiny words and phrases and line your 'nest' notebook or study with them – savour them, and use them as and when appropriate. Sometime in the future that curious title, suggested by a misheard sentence or misread piece of graffiti, may give birth to a poem, a story, or even a book. If you're like me, you'll find it hard to throw anything out – you never know when it may come in useful!

Remember to keep your journal safe, away from prying eyes – this is for you and you alone. Clarke says a journal is: "the individual human voice speaking its own word on its own terms". Promise to be honest to yourself always within its pages. This is your portable place for reflection. The sanctuary of your imagination. Decorate the cover, ask for its protection, keep it somewhere discreet and ask loved ones to respect your privacy. If they are worried, explain to them it's not a diary, but a workbook. I keep several of these on the go for different projects (eg: for novels, poems, ideas and drawings). Enjoy yourself – this is your space to dream: nothing is too ridiculous or outrageous. Don't filter. This is a place for creative play - bearing this in mind should over-ride any 'fear of failure'. No need to 'get it right' first time. This is a first draft no one ever has to see. Let happy accidents happen. The only limit is your imagination.

Starting Out: A Personal Journey

As a child I found paganism in the fields and oak woods near my family's home in Far Cotton, the beginning of my thread. I would take my dog for a walk every day to the nearby ruined abbey, with its rambling wilderness gardens, permeated with the odour of sanctity when nuns paced its grounds in devout contemplation. There I found sanctuary from the difficulties of growing up in a rundown market town, a peace and healing *beyond* words – to begin with. Yet it was there that I discovered the poetry of nature, in my personal Arcadia: for it was seldom visited, except by the ghosts of my imagination. I would make up names for trees, see gypsy lights in the gloaming, and a witch in a ramshackle hut. There I dreamed the summers away, more comfortable with the invisible than with crowds.

Portrait of a Bard as a Young Man.
Photograph of author with dog, Ben,
in Delapre Abbey, Northampton.

My parents are salt-of-the-earth and non-dogmatic, and I have them to thank for not indoctrinating me. Given free rein, I groped my own way towards dialogue with the Divine – finding an outlet initially through the visual arts. Developing a knack for sketching, I began to worship the beauty of the world in silent meditation, finding peace in a pencil, inkpen or paintbrush. I was encouraged to go to Art College and there I began to 'find myself' and come out of my shell.

One day, in my eighteenth year, I walked into a bookshop and the first book I picked up was on the Arthurian Tradition. I opened and read a little about Lancelot, and received a flash of – what, déjà vu? After reading obsessively about the Matter of Britain I made a pilgrimage with friends to Glastonbury Tor, which was haunting me like the Devil's Tower in the Spielberg film *Close Encounters of the Third Kind*. I had passed by it earlier that summer on the way to my first Glastonbury Festival – the strange-shaped hill intrigued me, but my lift did not stop. Similarly, I remember the shock of recognition as we drove through Avebury on the way home. A couple of years before I had drawn Stonehenge, on a Sixth Form field trip: unaware of its significance to me later in life. At Glastonbury, over a number of visits, I was initiated into the mystery tradition of this land.

Back home I set up a Zeitgeist Forum with my friend, as a showcase for different faiths – for we could find no guidance for those starting out on the path. But this creative act summoned to us kindred spirits, and we found our first pagan community, on our doorstep, but hidden to us until now. We had called, and they had come. We were adopted by two unconventional 'mentors': one, a pipe-carrier for the Native American path; the other, a runemaster and novelist. They challenged our arrogant, precocious perceptions, in true Don Juan style, until suddenly terminating our informal apprenticeship. We were on our own.

The initiation had been brief, but it had worked: I had found my natural spirituality, connected to the native tradition of Britain. I had been practising it all along before I knew what it was – Paganism. Nature was my first and foremost teacher and healer – and I began to write praise poems to the wonder I saw around me.

On a trip to the West of Ireland I discovered my Celtic Muse, in the flesh to begin with, until I realised it was within me. Poetry poured out of me, as though a long-capped spring had been unblocked. I had to share this 'treasure' and began to perform my work – painfully improving through trial and error. This was when the Green Man burst out of my subconscious, and provided me with a male face to these mysteries. I have honoured him, and the Goddess he serves, ever since.

For the next few years I was preoccupied with the business of growing up and finding my place in the world. After much experimentation, I finally did, in the city of Bath. Having been drawn down to the 'Summer Country' for the last seven years, I finally moved there, and much to my delight met Druids, a King, minstrels and Celts, becoming Bard of Bath in 1998. I had found my raison d'être. Since then I have been heavily involved with the Bardic Chair of Caer Badon, with the Gorsedd and the annual Eisteddfod, the Bardic Festival of Bath.

Over the last few years I have honed my craft, becoming an author and teacher of creative writing. With friends from the Bath Storytelling Circle, which began in late 1999, Fire Springs was formed, and together we have devised and toured shows about King Arthur, Robin Hood, and other legends from world cultures.

As a solo performer, I appear as Tallyessin – to honour the greatest Bard of Albion and the Bardic Tradition he epitomises. This is my path – the Way of Awen. Through it I celebrate the mysteries, bringing alive the ancient tales and creating new material, to enchant and entertain.

After several collections of poetry I have turned to fiction to preserve my tales. In my novels I explore the interface of time, memory, landscape and imagination (as in my third, *The Long Woman*).

Through my workshops I help people express themselves and awaken the Bard within. A course I ran in 2003 led to the publication of *Writing the Land – an anthology of natural words*, in aid of Friends of the Earth. The Natural Words writers' circle that came out of it is still going. In 2004 I set up the first series of Way of Awen weekends at various locations around the country, where a lot of the material in this current book was 'field-tested', quite literally!

At a local woodland campsite on the borders of Somerset, Wiltshire and South Gloucestershire, I have organised several eco-arts events raising money for green charities, annual bardic gatherings, Spring dressing, the creation of a poetry trail, and the planting of a Celtic Tree Wheel, joining with others to celebrate our sacred land, and finding the Divine beneath my feet – full circle from the green abbey where I began.

EXERCISE: Where did the Bardic Path begin for you?
Describe how you 'started out' in a brief essay – either exclusively for your journal, or perhaps as something you could share with people (ie: at a moot, on a website, or in a magazine). Such reflections often help others just starting out, and it will help you put things in perspective, realise how far you have come, and celebrate what you have achieved so far. It may even help to draw a 'map' of your life, showing the important points along the way.

Declaring your Chair

It is the custom of the Welsh **Eisteddfod** to announce their intent to hold a competition a year and a day before in the place where it is to be held. This is always done in the public eye (what Edward Williams, aka Iolo Morgannwg, called 'the eye of light'). This is to allow any competitors time to enter and prepare. Why a Year and a Day? Because it encompasses the circle of the year, of mortal time. It allows for a full year to have elapsed,

A Way of Awen participant
declaring his Chair, 2004.

but also allows for a day 'outside time', for the Otherworld to speak; and also it creates a sense of movement, as the event moves slowly around the calendar. By the end of the twelve years of Bardic training, your Bard-Day (the day when you began your Bardic training) would have moved twelve days along the calendar, 12 being the number of the sun, of full consciousness, and echoing the twelve days of Christmas (Christ was said, in some traditions, to have grown a year each of his first twelve days so by Epiphany, Twelfth Night, he was twelve years old. Many cultures' heroes, not least **Taliesin**, grow unnaturally rapidly or have wisdom beyond their years). However, this is not always taken literally. Eisteddfodau generally happen at the same time of year (eg: Welsh, beginning of August; Cornish, beginning of September; Bath, midwinter) fixed, as they generally are, to a location and a season or festival.

EXERCISE

I want you to announce your intent to claim your own **Bardic Chair** (a symbol of your graduation as an Anruth – Bardic initiate – of the Hare Grade, and of entering the public domain). For the first year, from the moment you make your declaration, you are an Anruth of the Gwion Grade (see **The Training of a Bard**). Like Gwion Bach, the boy in the **Tale of Taliesin**, you are going to enter into the 'service of Ceridwen' (in effect, the **Goddess of the Bards**) and imbibe the Awen by following the path of the Bard. Go to a suitable spot – a local hill, grove, spring, stone circle, or other numinous place, on an auspicious day (new moon, full moon, solar or fire festival, birthday, New Year's day, etc.) and announce out loud your intent to follow the Way of Awen – whatever that signifies to you (see **Bardic Vow**). You may become a professional performer, or you may just keep honouring and following the Bardic Path in your own way – it does not matter. The main thing is to make your commitment, your act of dedication. Wear some special clothing – a robe, a cloak, a hat, a new dress, shirt, coat, boots etc. – whatever makes you feel special. Prepare your Bardic Vow. Take an offering for the Spirits, Ancestors and Gods – fruit, incense, candles, poems (but remember to clear up after yourself – leave no nitelights, spilt wax, fruit peel etc.). You may want to bring a witness, a friend, loved one, even a pet! Or call upon the spirits, elements, ancestors and gods to be your witness. Remember to ask any landowners, and the site itself, for permission. State your peaceful intent and check that it feels right before proceeding. Stand up and say it loud: you are going to follow the Way of Awen! Visualise the Bardic Chair awaiting you – imagine yourself as a Bardic Graduate of the Hare Grade in a year's time, and vow to

Author, aged 28, winner of the Bardic Chair of Caer Badon (Bath) 1998-9.

return in a year and a day to claim your personal chair. NB: this does not make you a Chaired Bard in the official sense; although if you serve your community well then due recognition will come and maybe it could trigger an actual Eisteddfod (see **Setting up and Running a Bardic Chair**). After you have 'graduated' you could state your intent to claim a chair of that locality if there is one, as Druid Philip Shallcrass, chief of the British Druid Order, suggests: "Those Bards that have laboured through the apprentice stage of mastering their art or craft, and reached a certain proficiency, are entitled to apply to the Council of British Druid Orders for the right to proclaim themselves a Chaired Bard of a particular geographical locale or sacred site location". This initial rite is a way of activating your own Bard within. The chair is a symbol, a metaphor of your empowerment. The 'throne awaits.' Finally, remember such gifts are for the asking, not the taking – and can be taken away if used unwisely, if you act unworthy of it. When dealing with the spirits, ancestors and gods always be polite and respectful. Ask them to grace you with their presence/blessing. NEVER demand, or arrogantly summon them. They are not at the celebrant's beck and call. You can but prepare, request and wait… You have stated your intent, it has been witnessed: that is enough. Now you must be true to your word.

The Bardic Learning Cycle

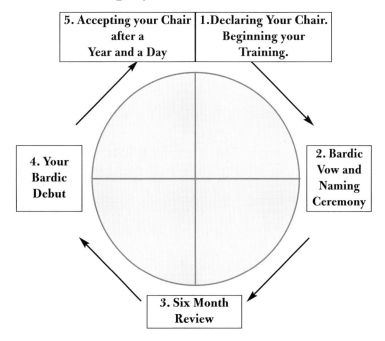

5. Accepting your Chair after a Year and a Day

1. Declaring Your Chair. Beginning your Training.

4. Your Bardic Debut

2. Bardic Vow and Naming Ceremony

3. Six Month Review

THE BARDIC LEARNING CYCLE: YEAR ONE

1. Declaring your Chair. Beginning Your Training
Month 1 and 2 (all of Spirit; first section of Air)

2. Bardic Vow and Naming
Month 3 Anruth Ceremony (Air) Quarterly review. Month 4 and 5 (Fire)

3. Six month Review
Month 6 (Fire). Months 7-9 (Water). Quarterly review.

4. Your Bardic Debut
Month 10 and 11 (Earth)

5. Accepting your Chair after a year and a day.
Month 12 (Earth, Twenty-First Century Bard and Appendices)

A Bardic A-Z

This is just a quick guide to key concepts. Each is worth studying in more depth and all are covered to a lesser or greater extent in this book. With a nod to the Welsh alphabet chart at the start of this chapter and a humorous wink to you, dear reader, here goes:

A BARDIC ALPHABET
by Kevan Manwaring

A	Awen /|\ Bardic Inspiration	N	Names - Essential identity
B	Bard - Remembrancer/wordsmith	O	Ogham - Celtic tree alphabet
C	Community - The circle of the Bard	P	Poetry - Word magic
D	Druid - Priest/ess and MC	Q	Questions - Colloquies and riddles
E	Eloquence - What a Bard aspires to	R	Repertoire - The Bard's 'word-hoard'
F	Filidh - Seer-poets, Gaelic	S	Storytelling - The oldest art
G	Gorsedd - A gathering of Bards	T	Triads - Welsh wisdom in 3s
H	Harp - Stringed instrument	U	Utterance - It's the way you say it
I	Imbas - Inspiration, Gaelic	V	Voice - Most essential instrument
J	Jokes - Sense of humour!	W	Women ...are Bards too!
K	Kerridwen - Initiatorix of Taliesin	X	Excellence - Be the best, and better!
L	Light - Share it, become it *light*	Y	Yell! Stand up and be heard
M	Music - Universal language	Z	Zeitgeist - The spirit of the age

Can you think of your own Bardic associations for each letter?

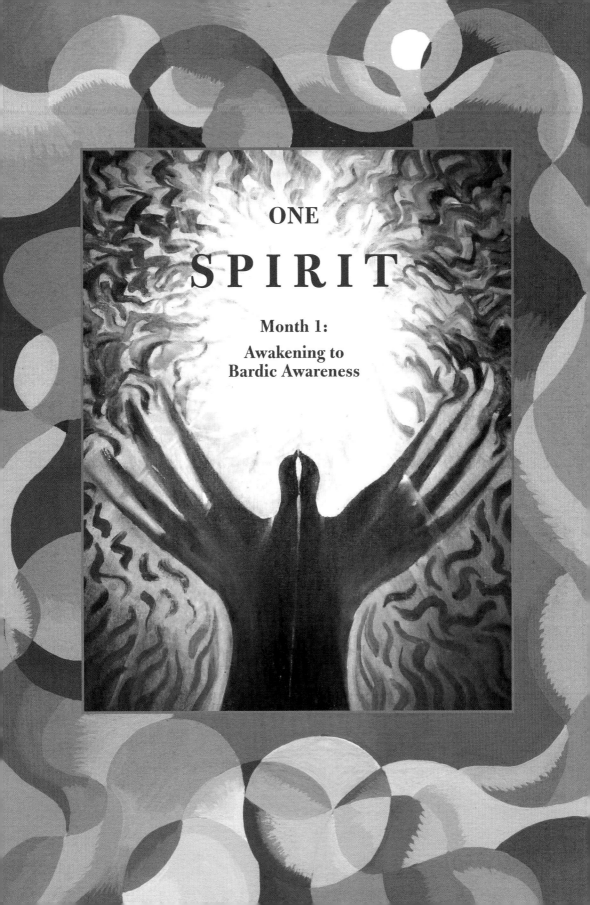

ONE

SPIRIT

Month 1:

Awakening to
Bardic Awareness

Month 1:
Awakening to Bardic Awareness

What in me is dark,
Illumine; what is low,
Raise and support

Milton's Invocation to the Muse at the beginning of *Paradise Lost*.

They say there's a book inside every person. Well, maybe there's a Bard too. But like the former, the latter will only happen if you do something about it. To paraphrase a famous saying, I don't believe 'Bards are born, not made'. We can all become 'a natural': it's simply a matter of becoming comfortable with what you're doing (easier said than done, granted). I was certainly no born performer: I had to teach myself to be eloquent and entertaining (with the help of some good role models) and now, when the Awen is flowing, it does feels like second nature: but I've had to work at it. Of course, there will always be protégés and virtuosos, who start manifesting their talent at an incredibly early age – but who knows how old *their* souls are? Yet we all have to start somewhere. If you haven't already begun (and the **Introductory** section should have helped) then start your path to Bard-dom right *now*. This section is designed as a Bardic Primer. Read through it over a month, allowing yourself time to digest and take on board any concepts you find unfamiliar or challenging; work through any exercises: if you get stuck then move onto the next part, but make a note to return to it later, perhaps asking yourself why you skipped it: obstacles and challenges teach us the most (see **Threshold Guardians** in Month 2). You may come across things you know already, or didn't know you knew. There may be a shock of recognition, a Damascus-like moment that is called the First Realisation in the Shaman's Ladder. This is no religious conversion, however, but an affirmation of what you knew deep down inside all along. We have more wisdom than we realise, if we let our intuition speak: this may be mother-wit, ancestral memory (which could well be the same thing) or lost knowledge (which can be retrieved from the Collective Unconscious). Like the many legends of kings and heroes slumbering under mountains, there is much latent wisdom and talent within you: this is the dormant potential of a Bard. It is time to awaken it.

The Nature of a Bard: Past and Present

When most people think of a Bard today, William Shakespeare comes to mind, the Swan of Avon, who is often referred to as '*The* Bard'. His skills as a playwright and poet were consummate and rightly world-renowned, but less is made of his career as an actor, which is how he learnt his art, by treading the boards with his fellow players. I believe performance ability is a prerequisite of being a Bard. A Bard has the power to enchant with his voice alone. He or she should be able to hold an audience spell-bound, sometimes for hours or even days. Not only could his gramarye stop time, it could make people forget their daily concerns, their fears and doubts, their aches and pains. Lady Gregory, in *Selected Writings,* relates a comment about a famous Irish Bard: "You would stand in the snow to listen to Callinan!" What is it that draws people to such figures? It is their charisma as much as their material, or skill. The audience feed off the energy the performer gives out, like a kind of blessing or healing – and, in some ways, that's exactly what it is, for, at his heart, the Bard is a shaman.

Bard is a Welsh word (n. *Bardd*), and it perhaps evokes the splendid, but outmoded, image of a Cymric Bard, dark-browed, deep-voiced and robed in blue. Thomas Gray's eponymous 18th Century poem conjures up the classic icon of the Celtic Bard, immortalised in oil painting, railing against tyrannical Royalty, in this case Edward the First, before throwing himself off a cliff, the last of his outlawed kind:

> On a rock, whose haughty brow
> Frowns o'er old Conway's foaming flood,
> Robed in the sable garb of woe,
> With haggard eyes the poet stood;
> (Loose his beard and hoary hair
> Streamed, like a meteor, to the troubled air)
> And, with a master's hand and prophet's fire,
> Struck the deep sorrows of his lyre.
>
> Thomas Gray, *The Bard*

A haunting symbol of doomed resistance. One can almost hear Gray's Bard declaim the defiant bardic dictum 'Truth against the world!' (see **Voice of the World**).

The downside of this proud line is what **Taliesin Penbeirdd** called the 'pot-bellied bards' of the Royal court, full of sycophancy and self-importance, entrenched in their tradition and clinging to power and privilege, but lacking the Bright Knowledge, severed from the Source.

Yet, in danger of stating the absurd, you need neither a beard nor a robe, a big-belly or a lord, to be a Bard in the Twenty-First Century! Although the **harp** is the Bardic instrument *par excellence*, even this is not essential – a guitar or even just an awareness of the musicality of words can be enough.

So, where does that leave us? Is a Bard 'just' a poet, a storyteller, or a 'song and dance man'? Often he (it was almost exclusively a male profession, but of course this outdated notion need no longer apply either) was a combination of all three, but far more besides. The Celtic Bards were also genealogists, journalists and historians – recording and remembering the family trees and clan histories, battles and great deeds: in short, the living memory of the tribe. Before the written word Bards were effectively walking libraries, knowing up to a staggering 350 tales (see **The Training of a Bard** and **Repertoire**). Bardic training was traditionally done in the famous Bardic Colleges of Britain, to which students travelled from all over Europe and Ireland and lasted twelve years, and sometimes up to twenty.

For the Twenty-First Century we need to reinvent the tradition and make it relevant. Bardic skills can help us improve our public-speaking and presentation skills. They can help us convey our message, expressing what we believe in, so we can be ambassadors for our path and the planet. With word magic we can entertain and educate, bless, defend, honour and celebrate.

We will explore the nature and role of the Bard, past and present, in three parts:

1 What is a Bard?

2 The Bardic Tradition

3 Why be a Bard Today?

WHAT IS A BARD?

Bard, n 1. A poet, traditionally one reciting epics. 2. the winner of a prize for Welsh verse at an Eisteddfod. *Concise Oxford English Dictionary*

The above definition, however vague and unsatisfactory, at least suggests two things about a Bard relevant to our present purposes, a. A Bard was skilled in poetic language, b. A Bard won prizes with his or her skill, through a public ceremony or competition. Both of these notions are ancient but still hold water. For the Twenty-First Century I think we need to both look back and forward for a suitable definition. As discussed, in the Celtic Tradition, the Bard was recognised as a combination of the following:

❖ Poet
❖ Storyteller
❖ Musician
❖ Remembrancer (chronicler of community/lorekeeper)
❖ Voice of the Tribe/the people/the land/the ancestors

✤ Celebrant/eulogist
✤ Seer-poet (**Awenyddion**/*filidh*)

I think all of these are applicable to the present, yet some imaginative interpretation may be required, indeed essential. A Bard has no need to be archaic in his methods or material. We are not trying to recreate an idealised notion of the past here, but expressing what always needs to be expressed: the eternal truth, the voice of the land, the wisdom of our ancestors, and the soul of the people. His existence should be justified by his relevance to his community. A Bard should never rest on his laurels.

In the modern era, what should a Bard be able to do? The following are only my suggestions, not The Ten Commandments! As was said of the Pirates' Code in the Disney film, *Pirates of the Caribbean*, they are more 'guidelines':

✤ Remember and recite.
✤ Tell stories of old and create new ones.
✤ Compose and perform poems.
✤ Research and disseminate Bardic lore.
✤ Use a musical instrument of some kind.
✤ Use the magic of words for healing and inspiring, in a responsible way.
✤ Teach, either directly (through workshops) or indirectly (through stories).
✤ Raise the Awen.
✤ Have at least a basic understanding of Ogham.
✤ Ideally be able to speak one of the Celtic languages.
✤ If not, at least have a fascination with the mysteries of language.
✤ Have 'mythic literacy' – be steeped in myths, legends, folk tales, etc., and recognise the different characters, common motifs and so on.
✤ Explain Bardic Chairs. Enter or judge Eisteddfodau.
✤ Promote peace, reconciliation, understanding and healing.

THE BARDIC TRADITION

So what is the Bardic Tradition? Is it 'just' a collection of obscure lore and customs from Ireland and Wales? Although that is a very important part of it, one that we'll be looking at primarily in this chapter, I believe the Bardic Tradition is more ancient and more universal than that. It stretches back to the first tales told around the first fires, as Ben Okri describes in his inspiring essay *The Joys of Storytelling* in *A Way of Being Free* (Phoenix 1997): "The earliest storytellers were magi, seers, bards, griots, shamans. They were, it would seem, old as time, and as terrifying to gaze upon as the mysteries with which they wrestled. They wrestled with the mysteries and transformed them into myths which coded the world and helped the community to live through more darkness, with eyes wide open, and with hearts set alight."

Side-by-side with human evolution was the development of language. With humanity's migrations the global Bardic Tradition has evolved in geographical and culturally specific ways across the planet. The root of the Celtic Bardic Tradition, and all such equivalents, is essentially the Oral Tradition: folk wit and wisdom shared by word of mouth for millennia. Whenever a story, song, poem, riddle, anecdote, joke, or fact, is passed from one person to another – something we all do on a daily basis, however sophisticated our jobs – that is the Oral Tradition in action. It is a living thing, by its very nature, and even high-tech communication devices will not kill it out completely. Whenever something dramatic and traumatic happens and is broadcast as 'breaking news', ie: the South-East Asian Tsunami, it's the personal testimonies of the survivors and bereaved that are the most powerful, the most moving. In the era of digital communication, blasted across the Earth by satellites and fibre-optic cables, we are humbled by the 'mere' power of the word, spoken from the heart – reaching out and touching us all. And that is where the Oral Tradition intersects with the Bardic Tradition. Some would say they are inseparable, but if there has to be a difference, it is probably the difference between the amateur and the professional – not to put the Bard on an exalted level, just to acknowledge the skill of their craft, and the size and calibre of their repertoire. The Bard has dedicated his or her life to the Way of Awen (or equivalent thereof). It is their practise, their profession, their spirituality. While most people can utilise the spoken word, the Bard is the expert at it: they have to be – it's their business, and if they're not, they'll soon go hungry.

So, what does the Bardic Tradition actually involve? Generally, the remembering and passing down of stories, songs and poems. This would have been done by ear alone. The Druids forbade the writing down of their wisdom – perhaps to prevent it falling into the wrong hands. This may have been necessary in the past – but one could argue that if they had written down their lore we would have more than fragments to go on now (although much can be reconstructed and inferred from the myths, lore, artefacts, customs, etc. that we do have. And much is stored in the memory of the land, and "in the very cells of our bodies" as Caitlin Matthews puts it) – but for present needs, to disseminate the knowledge to stop it dying out entirely, I think it is time to let their doctrines become public property. This does not cancel out the necessity of Bardic memory – which is essential to performance, to the path of the Bard.

The famous Welsh triads are mnemonic devices, useful ways of remembering lore. The earliest ones recorded were in the 13th Century. Like many of them, this triad from the *Red Book of Hergest* gives us useful Bardic advice: "Three things that enrich the poet: myths, poetic power, a store of ancient verse". Iolo Morgannwg, aka Edward Williams, that great Victorian visionary, reinventor and father of the modern Welsh Eisteddfod, embellished them and incorporated them into his doctrines, as he explains: "From this system, the

Iolo Morgannwg originally created the first Gorsedd circle of the modern era with a pocketful of stones placed on Primrose Hill, 1792. He continued to use them as a portable Gorsedd circle. Solsbury Hill medicine wheel created by Roy Littlesun and group, 1999.

privileges and organised custom, respecting the Bards and Bardism in the Isle of Britain, were first formed". In his Bardic Triads, Morgannwg explains the three Ultimate Intentions of Bardism: "to reform morals and customs; to secure Peace; and to celebrate the praise of all that is good and excellent". Whatever one thinks of Morgannwg's proclamations, these particular aims hold water. Yet some of his work has to be taken with more than a pinch of salt. He suggests the Three Joys of the Bards of Britain to be: "the Increase of Knowledge; the Reformation of Manners; and the Triumph of Peace over the Lawless and Depredators". We can perhaps agree with the first point, but as for moral crusading, we can leave that in the Victorian era; and however admirable the notion of a peace is, we have to be wary about casting judgement over others. As with all archaic Bardic lore, we must re-evaluate, rather than accept blindly. What has withstood the rigours of time, we cherish; what has the germ of truth, we cultivate; and what is no longer acceptable, we jettison. All Morgannwg did was consolidate the disparate threads into a (relatively) coherent system, although one couched in archaic terms and Celtic obscurity to lend it an air of authenticity, mystery and antiquity.

We are in danger of alienating audiences, or even facing cultural extinction, if we stick to the letter of tracts like the *Barddas* (1862), which, after all, was largely the invention of one man, our inimitable Mr Williams. This is how a tradition can die out. We run the risk of being like King Arthur Pendragon's Bards in *The Dream of Rhonabwy*, who no one could understand except the Chief Bard: "At that Arthur's Bards began to chant a song, which no man except Cadyryeith [fair-speech] himself understood, except that it was in praise of Arthur." We need to transcend the esotericism – which may have been necessary in the past (the **Dark Speech**) to preserve the secret Bardic lore – and the obfuscation inherent in a lot of Celtic texts, if we are to disseminate and maintain the tradition. A Bard's *modus operandi* is, in essence, about communication. If the audience do not understand us, then it is our failure, not theirs. How else can the torch be passed on?

Bearing in mind that stories and songs work through Mystery, for therein lies their enchantment, and that things should not be spelled out (or else they would lose their spell) we nevertheless need modern Bards who are willing to innovate and reach out, not just utter gnomic sayings, repeating old saws and stale laws without thought, or just preach to the 'converted' – the cognoscenti or pagan 'homecrowd'. Caitlin Matthews says: "we need such interpreters in the Celtic Tradition, people who honour our sacred heritage and yet who can interface with the predominant culture without loss of respect. The task of the *filidh*, the *Awenydd* or the *drui* descends to such interpreters as these."

WHY BE A BARD TODAY?

Some of the reasons for being a modern Bard have been discussed already: community, communication, celebration. Yet the curious and singular urge to be one (for not everyone is compelled thus) is the same as ever: it is that irresistible creative urge (one that can manifest in many ways but in the Bard mainly through voice and memory); it is a calling in the blood to honour one's ancestors, the spirits of the land, and the gods; and a sense of duty to preserve and pass on the hard-won wisdom and time-forged beauty of the past. It is summed up by the opening of the Finnish epic, *Kalevala*:

> I am driven by my longing,
> And my understanding urges
> That I should commence my singing,
> And begin my recitation.
> I will sing the people's legends,
> And the ballads of the nation.
> To my mouth the words are flowing,
> And the words are gently falling,
> Quickly as my tongue can shape them,
> And between my teeth emerging.

WB Yeats, in his preface to *Gods and Fighting Men* by Lady Gregory, says: "...the ancient storytellers are there to make us remember what mankind would have been like, had not fear and failing will and the laws of nature tripped up its heels". And this fear has not gone away, or the need to assuage it. Ben Okri talks of: "stories that would counter terror with enchantment", a benefit perhaps even more poignant than ever, but a service to humankind since the dawn of time.

In a world of sickness, there is always need of healing. In hearts of sorrow and despair, solace and hope need to be seeded. Souls of individuals, of communities, of countries need to hear their song sung, clearly with love. We need the emancipation and vision of Imagination. We need doorways of possibilities, positive alternatives, and a deeper empathy for others, through the stories of all that share this precious planet.

So, I hope I have answered the question of why we need Bards (for more, see **The Voice of the World - relevance and motivation**). We need now, perhaps more than ever, the wisdom and wonder of the Bards who, as Gaelic filidh Fiona Davidson beautifully phrases it: "made with the heart and voice and harp a lasting beauty to feed the dreaming of the world."

Druid Grove Four Winds suggest the following as modern criteria for a bard:
- ❖ Carry and transmit this material.
- ❖ Be familiar with its history and lore.
- ❖ Be able to support the spiritual community as Bards.
- ❖ Act as spokespeople for the Earth and Spirit pathways.
- ❖ Perform the material unsupported, and use it in a spiritual context and manner.
- ❖ Be able to teach and lead others.
- ❖ Show a commitment to study and practice

The Nature of Awen

An understanding of Awen is fundamental to Bardism: it underpins and influences everything we do. It is deceptively simple and incredibly complex, in fact, like the nature of Deity itself. This similarity is not surprising considering its literal meaning: 'flowing spirit'. It is a Welsh word meaning 'inspiration', but what is it to be inspired but to be in-*spirited*, to be taken over by Spirit; be it in the form of the Muse, Poetic Genius, Goddess, a creative frenzy, a fire in the head. Philip Shallcrass calls it "the Holy Spirit of Druidry", and this is an appropriate analogy for several reasons: on one level, there's the comparison with those faithful who are taken over by the Holy Spirit in a Service and start talking in tongues – there's a Celtic Bardic equivalent to this to be found in the Irish seer-poets and Welsh **Awenyddion**, which we'll look at later. In a mythopoetic sense, the Holy Spirit is the Christian analog for the Goddess, to balance the Father and Son patriarchy – although it is seldom acknowledged as such, except through the Madonna. Finally, I think it is no coincidence that Awen sounds like Amen in pronunciation – certainly in the South West of England, with softer vowels. Awen is pronounced: Aah-OO-Whenn. It punctuates druidic ceremonies in the way 'amen' does in Christian ones, which is an interesting echo. But Awen is neither Christian or Pagan, or any other Faith – it is universal, it is Spirit, on its own terms, whatever our cultural frame of reference. There are equivalents in other traditions, notably Buddhism, with its most famous mantra: Om Mani Padme Hum,

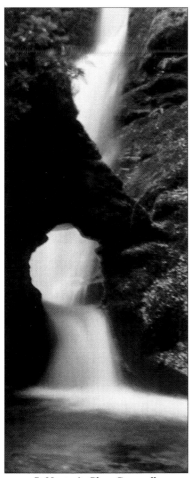

St Nectan's Glen, Cornwall.

(AUM) meaning in essence: 'the Jewel takes its Seat in the Heart of the Lotus' – a symbol worth meditating upon for its own sake. It could be seen as the opening of the Brow Chakra – the centre of Vision. I would argue that is why when Elphin, son of Gwyddno, discovers the **twice-born** Bard at the **weir** on May Eve he declaims: "Behold, the Radiant Brow!" Those filled with Awen shine, because of this 'jewel' of enlightenment, giving Spirit tongue, the voice of Creation. Furthermore, the mantra of AUM has *four* syllables, each letter a distinct sound – an Awen-like Ahh-OO-Mmm – the fourth being the most important: silence. This is what I call the Endless Sound, underpinning everything.

Druids and Bards traditionally chant Awen three times (Celts and Pagans like to do things in threes, ie: Bard, Ovate, Druid; the Threefold Effect; the Welsh Triads – it is the number of the Goddess: maiden, mother, crone… Is that why the feminine Holy Spirit is the third aspect of Christian Deity?) When I chant it, I always include a moment of silence, for it is important to listen if we speak – to sense the impact of our words, of the change in energy. If you get a circle of people to chant Awen, most effectively in an enclosed space (room, marquee, Gorsedd circle), then with each wave of energy the atmosphere within changes significantly as the space is charged up – that is why I like to get the audience or workshop members to help me do this at the start of a performance or workshop. It is a simple and effective way of raising energy, but also it gets everybody contributing straight away, feeling the energy, and being fully present. But why chant Awen? Because it is a way of asking for inspiration – something we can continually benefit from. It is, in effect, asking for guidance and wisdom from Spirit, from Deity, the Creator, the Great Mystery, however you conceive it. Personally, I like to chant the Awen before a Bardic performance, to ask for eloquence, and privately, when writing, to ask for inspiration. It can be done discreetly, or from the top of mountain, verbally, or just through visualisation (see **Raising the Awen**).

The symbol of Awen (/|\) is known as the Three Rays (that magic number again!): three beams of inspiration, of Imbas (the Irish equivalent to Awen) streaming down from the Source, or Sources (as it is normally depicted as coming from three circles – perhaps symbolising the Triple-aspect Deity, normally associated with the phases of the moon and faces of the Goddess (Maiden, Mother, Crone). Ross Nichols, founding father of the Order of Bards, Ovates and Druids describes the Awen as: "the Three Rays of Light or Three Pillars of Wisdom, also called in Brittany the *Tribann*, in India the *Tri-Sul*". However universal this icon seems, the symbol of the three rays, as associated with Awen, was in fact invented by Iolo Morgannwg, although it seems to have been influenced by the Masonic symbol seen on old buildings to this day (the shared roots of Freemasonry and modern Druidry is a book in itself). The Gorsedd of Bards ceremony, as devised by Morgannwg in 1792, shaped the modern Eisteddfod system. In 1907, the Rev J Griffith, in an article in *Nature*, describes a Gorsedd Circle with twelve bards and a ring of stones, outside of which a triad are set out in the pattern of the Three Rays: "the ancient Kymric symbol of Awen, or Holy Wings, the three rays or rods of light signifying the Eye of Light, or radiating light of the Divine Intelligence shed upon the Druidic Circle". The Awen has been central to Druidry ever since.

So, does this invalidate the use of Awen and its symbol in Bardism? No, because the word Awen was mentioned by Bards from at least the Sixth Century, in poems by Taliesin and others. It was used to infer gifted inspiration, possibly from a divine source – especially Ceridwen, initiatorix of Taliesin and Bards in general. The Three Rays itself, whatever its origins, can still be used to signify inspiration received from the Gods, from All That Is, to use a term of Caitlin Matthews. It is as good a symbol as any, and I have grown fond of it, as many have. As elegantly as the White Horse of Uffington, it evokes, in its lean economy, the rays of a sunrise – as seen from a stone circle on solstice morning – a metaphor in itself of the awakening of consciousness, the receiving of inspiration, the flash of revelation. When form and function meet, you have something beautiful and valid.

As for the word 'Awen' – if it did not actually mean anything (which it does), one could just as easily chant another vowel-rich word and it would be equally as effective in opening up to inspiration and opening up the vocal chords, because that is what it is doing. Chanting the Awen, or any mantra, quietens the mind, drowns out the white noise of life, that eternal internal dialogue – the background chatter of trivia and mundane concerns – and helps us to 'tune into a higher frequency', to align with a different, more subtle vibration: perhaps that Field of Potential mentioned earlier; the Platonic Realm of ideal forms, what writer Alan Moore calls 'Idea Space'. It is 'the stuff that dreams are made on', the place where dreams are born perhaps – the æther, where they wait to manifest, to be drawn down by the visionaries, the avant garde. If these ideas pre-exist in the æther, waiting to 'come down to Earth' (a Qabalistic notion) then would that explain simultaneous discovery or invention – when some new invention or innovation is 'discovered' in different parts of the world at the same time, eg: by Think Tanks, Research Teams, etc.? *The Origin of the Species* is the classic example of this, with Charles Darwin getting all the glory at the expense of his contemporary Alfred Russell Wallace, who independently developed a theory of natural selection. Hence that deeply annoying thing occurs when you've had a 'genius brainwave', made notes, drawings, plans, etc., and then discover someone else has pipped you to the post, so that it either becomes redundant, or you are accused of plagiarism, even if it had been years in the pipeline! Maybe this also accords with the notion that 'everything has its season': ideas have their time and if you are tapped into the 'æther' *and* have the resources, connections and wherewithal to make it happen, then you'll be the first to manifest it and to claim the credit.

Some Druids use I-A-O as their chant, most memorably Rollo Maufghlin, Head of the Glastonbury Order of Druids, who at countless public ceremonies described the 'I' as representing the phallus of the God; the 'A' as the open legs of the Goddess, ready to receive Him; and 'O' the sound of their ecstatic love-making, creating the Earth, perhaps even creating the Cosmos – literally, the Big Bang! When hundreds of people chant this (I-A-O) within the inner circle of Stonehenge, for instance, the effect is very impressive: the stones seem to act as resonators, coming alive with sound.

Yet it is wise to remember that, like a lot of things to do with Spirit, the Awen is something we can project whatever we like into. Iolo gave it his own set of associations, as has Rollo. There's nothing wrong with this, as long as we are conscious of doing it. Personally, I see the Awen as a portal to Spirit, and a very portable one at that: chanting the Awen is a very simple technique for tapping into it, for aligning oneself with Spirit, that force of creativity all around us, at the heart of Creation. I think it is the same as what that great Twentieth Century Bard, Dylan Thomas, memorably describes as: "the force that through the green fuse drives the flower." Another master Bard, WB Yeats, captured its essence in the immortal phrase: now known as the 'Fire in the Head', taken from *The Song of Wandering Aengus*: "I went out to a hazel wood, because a fire was in my head…" This poem will be looked at in more detail later, (see **Fire in the Head**) but for now I want to give a brief résumé of the creative process.

The Bard who has the fire in the head – when one is consumed by an idea, that is haunting, disturbing, maddening even – may suffer from insomnia or hyperactivity. You may be restless, distracted, ill-at-ease – perhaps knocking things over, or forgetting/losing things if you're not careful. It is a form of obsession – like falling in love. A storm is brewing – the ions of Awen charging in one's skull. Depression, anxiety, illness may precede it: the Cloud of Unknowing descends – you are in the doldrums, perhaps unable to see the 'way ahead', the solution. A composition may become stagnant. It's the classic writer's block. Then suddenly, boom! Synapses fire across the hemispheres of your mind, you experience literally a brain storm and, in a flash, you have the answer – you experience illumination. It is the famous Eureka moment. You may or may not leap out of the bath like Archimedes, suddenly discovering the solution to a problem that logic alone could not solve, but metaphorically you have reached saturation point - the thunder clouds rumble, there's a flash, and the waters of inspiration break. The Awen flows and you 'speak like rain', as you can't get the ideas down fast enough. You are in the white heat of creativity - the best 'buzz' in the world, I think. The Grail Winner was known as the Freer of the Waters, the waters that heal the wasteland, be it personal, local, or national – after this revelation you are the Rainmaker and Spirit flows through you: wonderful Awen.

The amazing lightness and sense of relief that comes with this revelation may be partly the result of having the pressure of the problem weigh down upon you (see **Stone upon the Belly**). Suddenly it is lifted as the solution presents itself and there's this feeling of euphoria. You have broken through and seen to the heart of the problem, like the Holy Fool, Parsifal, who in his innocence (purity of perception) 'pierces-the-veil' of reality and sees things as they 'really are'. You may have the 'hawk tongue', swift-witted, piercing insight, as was given to a boy who fell asleep on a hillside and dreamt of a 'green-garlanded god' who gave him the gift of 'hawk tongue'. Could this correlation between bard and bird be connected to the notion of the 'language of birds' – the magical language bards were said to speak, and is it echoed in the obscure text of the **Hawk of Achill**? The shining garlanded god could be the Celtic Apollo or Hermes – Ogma, God of Eloquence, who gave his name to Ogham, or Mabon, the ancient Eternal Child. The Celtic God of Love, Angus Mac Og, had four birds fly around his head (his 'kisses') and the Welsh horse Goddess Rhiannon had her Birds of enchantment, whose song could soothe any sorrow. This 'green-garlanded god' could be simply the Green Man himself – and the image of the foliating mouth, common in churches and cathedrals, is perhaps a symbol of eloquence, of a cornucopia of poetry, issuing from the lips of the illumined. The Welsh Awenyddion (the inspired ones) spoke in prophetic utterances in the same way those possessed by the Holy Spirit speak in tongues. They have **The Tongue that Cannot Lie** – the gift of prophecy that 13th Century seer-poet Thomas of Ercildoune was said to have received from the Queen of Elfland herself (aka the Goddess). This is fitting considering Bards believed they received their inspiration from the Cauldron of Ceridwen, like Taliesin. And I believe the poetic genius of Taliesin can be tapped into by all of us: it is an energy – the Field of Potential. A mantle to be assumed, a title to be adopted, in the same way that Merlin was possibly 'The Merlin'. It is common for people to talk of the wisdom of Merlin, and to work with his 'archetype'. I think Taliesin has entered the same realm, as an Inner World Guardian (a concept explored by RJ Stewart in his books, especially *The Underworld Initiation*, Mercury 1998), waiting to guide us when we are ready. The wisdom and Awen of Taliesin can be channelled. The best way to do this is to write a poem as him, which is what I've attempted to do with my poem, *The Creation of Taliesin*, which has become my 'signature' poem: the one I begin my performances with, when I

The Three Rays of Awen.

appear as Tallyessin. I took elements of the *Hanes Taliesin* and rewrote it in my own way, with bardic performance in mind, so it is much abbreviated and simplified. The original still stands, yet some would say this was sacrilegious. I would argue this form of emulation affords us empathy, is a classic learning method, and is a way of accessing the mystery of these gnomic utterances. By imagining his voice flowing through us we can be taken over by his energy and eloquence, by Taliesinic Force, as in South-Wales-based poet Vernon Watkins' visionary poems *Taliesin in the Gower* and *Taliesin and the Spring of Vision*. The Awen is all around us and is for all to tap into and receive the gift of inspiration from.

EXERCISE: Raising the Awen

This simple exercise is the most important in the book. With it you can find inspiration and the means to express it, and from that comes everything. It is the lifeblood of the Bard. The great thing about it is its simplicity: it can be done in front of a PC as you are about to write, or in a public ceremony with hundreds of people. There are many occasions in life when it is handy friend to have around: before an exam or interview; before a performance or public speaking presentation. I use it to ask for inspiration and to give me eloquence. It opens up the Third Eye (the Brow Chakra: thus 'Behold the radiant brow!') and the vocal chords. This is an indispensable technique. Here's how to do it:

- ❖ **Relax:** relax your body. If seated, then assume a meditation posture (straight back, arms loose). If standing, centre yourself, stand with feet shoulder width apart. With each, slowing the breathing is important. Take three deep breaths. On the final one, fill your lungs and on the out-breath make the first of three 'Awens'.
- ❖ **Chant:** This couldn't be simpler. Just repeat 'Awen' three times, very slowly, with

a pause in between (important, see **The Shining Word**). Really emphasise each syllable: 'Aaaah – Ooooo – Wwhhennnnn.' I find the 'A' tunes me into Spirit, the 'Uo' sound opens up my vocal chords, and the 'Nn' my Third Eye – you can feel it resonating within your skull. This is altering your brain waves from the shorter Alpha waves to the slower, flowing Theta frequency, more conducive to creativity.

✣ **Visualize:** As you chant each Awen visualise a white ray of light streaming into your mind, into your heart and entire body from above. This is Spirit, whatever you consider its essence and source to be. By the time you finish you would have created the Three Rays of the Awen.

✣ **Pause:** ensure you pause between each Awen to allow for the Fourth Syllable, the Endless Sound. Listen to the Universe.

Sulis Rising, ink and pastels.

Sense how the silence around you changes, how the atmosphere intensifies. You are raising energy, to use in your show, for ceremony, for the blessing and benefit of everyone present and beyond: for it can be sent out to those that need it, to the planet and all of its denizens.

✣ **Write/Talk:** Again, sense the silence. Listen. Then begin, either to write, speak or act. You have asked for inspiration, now use it. And thank the stars for it. Use what you have been given (a stunning idea, a sudden ability to express yourself with grace and wit, to give thanks, to give something back).

Creating a Bardic Space

There are many examples of artists, writers, composers and painters who have needed a dedicated space in which to create: Virginia Woolf wrote of *A Room of One's Own*; Dylan Thomas famously had his boathouse in Laugharne; Philip Pullman has a shed in his Oxford; Expressionist Jackson Pollock needed an old barn; Pop artist Peter Blake bought a converted chapel when he moved to the West Country as part of the Brotherhood of Ruralists in the 1970s; First World War poets had their côterie in Dymcock, a Cotswold village; Coleridge found his personal Arcadia in Nether Stowey, on the Quantocks; Wordsworth had his Dove Cottage in Grasmere; Chatterton had his garret; Orwell wrote the manuscript for *Down and Out in Paris and London* while living in well-heeled Southwold on the Suffolk coast; film-maker and artist Derek Jarman had his installation-garden near Dungeness... Like the Celtic monks in their beehive cells, creative types throughout history have needed a place to retreat to, to channel the inspiration. We need to make space in our lives for something to manifest. By setting aside a regular period of time each day, be it only half an hour, we are providing a window of opportunity for Awen to come into our lives. In the same way that we can make space in time, we can set aside a space as well. It could be a particular chair, a window seat or alcove, a bookshelf or mantelpiece, corner of the garden, shed, garage, basement, attic, altar or study. In this instance, it's not the size that matters but the intent. You are making room in your life for bardic mysteries. By designating and delineating a place within your living space for the Awen, a place you can commune with it, have visible symbols of it, books, artefacts, talismans, and so on, you are creating a frame-work, what RJ Stewart called: a 'field for imaginative energies to become defined and active'. This is your magical zone, your threshold to the Otherworld. Don't let others invade this space. Ask them to respect your privacy. This is your sacred space, full stop. Put a Do Not Disturb sign on the door if need be, 'Genius at Work', an image of a Threshold Guardian, pentagram...Whatever does the job!

Tips:
- ✤ Ask permission, if necessary, to use a space.
- ✤ Give it a thorough cleaning, then cleanse it with smudging, salt water, prayer, toning, music.
- ✤ Raise the Awen, asking it to bless your space and commune with you there.
- ✤ Light a blue candle (the bardic colour) when you are working there, but take care!
- ✤ Add images, icons and quotes of people, places, aphorisms you find inspiring.
- ✤ Don't clutter, keep clean and sacred. Never drink alcohol or smoke there.
- ✤ Use every day. Set what Julia Cameron calls 'the artist's date' with yourself to be there.

The Celtic Diaspora

Sky-eyed and fiery-haired, tattooed, woaded and adorned with gold, this is the popular image of the Celt of pre-history, yet we have to take these impressions of them from the Roman historians with a sackful of salt – they had their own agenda. It was in the interest of such generals as Seutonius Paulinus to have the natives depicted as savages with brutal customs, (eg: the wicker man) who needed 'liberating' from themselves, to justify the massacres and cutting down of sacred groves, such as took place on Mona (modern day Anglesey) in 60 CE (see Tacitus' famous account and a poetic response in **Using Passion**). The Romans wanted the land and its wealth for themselves. Plus ça change.

That the Celts used human sacrifice of some kind is attested by the evidence of the 'bog bodies', but in what context it took place (ie: were the victims murderers or willing sacrifices?) is unclear. What we know of their culture tells us the *eric* or blood price was high for a death, and if a debt could not be

A stereotypical image of a 'head-hunting' Celtic warrior, naked and daubed with woad. Watercolour by John White, c1590.

paid in this world, it would be paid in the next – so strong was their belief in the Otherworld. Whatever took place it is not necessary to emulate everything without question. We are not seeking to 'recreate the past', but learn from its wisdom where appropriate, innovate when not, and jettison where necessary. Mutatis Mutandis.

Yet some stereotypical traits of the Celts hold-fast, appearing as they do in their own stories: bold, boastful, loyal, land- and horse-loving, bound by their word, hot-headed, great-hearted, steadfast to clan and hearth, but prone to wild abandon. It was this energy that drove them across Eurasia, from the Russian Steppes to the Western Isles, from the Third Millennium BCE, sweeping across the continent over centuries, leaving their trademark knotwork, exquisite metalwork, place-names and gods, eg: in the La Têne culture of Switzerland, or in the magnificent Gundestrup Cauldron found in a Danish bog, an artistic movement reaching its zenith in that 'work of angels', *the Book of Kells* – an exquisite illuminated manuscript that is perhaps the antithesis of a pagan past, but it 'shows its roots', quite literally, in the use of organic knotwork and iconography: the self-same spiral path the monks' ancestors had trod.

Never an empire – it was not in their individualistic nature to be – but the Celts *were* prolific and pro-active, so that: "at the height of their expansion, when they ranged from Ireland and Spain in the west to the Black Sea and Asia Minor in the East, from Northern Italy in the South to (probably) the banks of the Elbe in the North, the Celts owed their cultural cohesion to the language and religion rather than any centralising political institution", according to Alexei Kondratiev (*Celtic Rituals*, New Celtic Publishing 1999). This is an essential point: the Celts were never a race, but a culture.

From the very outset, as the eclectic 'Celts' (a label they were to be given later) scattered they absorbed elements of the cultures they passed through. With the meeting of the stone battle-axes bearers and Beaker people: "two cultures appear to have fused", Kondratiev continues: "A new merging of cultural perspectives would begin, and the crystallisation of a new civilisation".

Ironically, 'Celt' was the one name they probably never called themselves, using instead tribal identities, which remain in placenames, eg: the Parisi: Paris, or regions, Dumnonii: Devon. The ancient Greeks were the first to call them Keltoi or Galatae; the latter related to the Irish word 'gal' for valour – a virtue they valued highly. The warrior caste had great status. The champion's portion was competed for by heroic feats and fearlessness in battle. Vain-glorious, they geared their exploits for Bardic accolade – the ultimate honour of poetic immortality. Cattle raids were a popular diversion in peacetime, yet they were constantly crossing borders – either by invasion or migration. And thus they evolved: adventuring, plundering, trading, mingling, marrying and settling.

Some tribes managed to reach a kind of equilibrium – probably through much trial and error – as the Celts learned to live more harmoniously with each other and the land. Kondratiev suggests: "Celtic civilisation achieved a creative balance between Tribe and Land, between the activities of the human community and the imperatives of its natural environment."

An eco-Celtic consciousness had been created, and the secret was in the myths they lived by. Kondratiev describes how "the balance was maintained by a guiding mythology…stories and images reinforced it on every level". This notion is explored in Anthony Nanson's *Storytelling and Ecology*, (Papyrus, 2005).

Of course, this 'golden age' was not to last and the pages of history are bloodied with reasons why. Ethnically-cleansed "hordes of refugees sought shelter farther and farther west and, in the end, across the sea," Kondratiev explains.

Two 'smoking guns' were the pogroms of the Monarchy and the Industrial Revolution, the apogee of which were the Highland Clearances and Potato Famine. Kondratiev describes how "everywhere the centralised economy, stressing heavy industry and the needs of cities, drove marginal rural areas into depression, and Celtic populations into emigration". The links with the past, with tradition, and with the Land were broken, violently. The despairing flight to America went on and on, generation after generation. Many of those left behind were only sustained by the dream of the boat to the New World and the hope of escaping the stagnation of a land with no apparent future.

And so the six main Celtic nations (Breton, Cornish, Welsh, Irish, Scottish, Manx) were brought to their knees and the tribes were scattered, living on in ragged fragments: "The Cornish, by and large, went to Michigan, and to Australia; the Manx to Ohio; the Bretons to Quebec. After generations of Welshmen had settled in Pennsylvania and parts of the mid-West, an effort was made, beginning in 1865, to establish a full-scale Welsh-speaking colony in Patagonia," so Kondratiev summarises.

Exiles of the Old World, cast beyond the Ninth Wave, this was one 'immram' (wonder voyage) they would not be returning from – and when some descendants did finally make it back to the homeland, centuries later, like Ossian, they would find themselves strangers and speaking a different tongue. The diaspora was complete.

The restless Celt has always been on the move. Perhaps the notion of a Celtic Twilight is in fact a diurnal round – as it seems the Celts have followed dawn and dusk around the world, forever dwelling in the liminal. Like the sun on the hill in Elizabeth Barret Browning's poem *A Musical Instrument*, the 'Dying Gaul' forgot to die.

Yet whatever our ethnicity, it's not where you're born, it's where you belong. Our home is wherever our Spirit calls the strongest. Barry Cunliffe, archaeologist, concluding his excellent survey of Iron Age Europe in *The Ancient Celts*, says: "a Celt is a person who believes him or herself to be Celtic". It's an *attitude*, if anything. The Matthews reinforce this in their *Encyclopaedia of Celtic Wisdom*: "It is time to view the Celtic spiritual tradition as an *international* sacred heritage not bounded by territory or genetics".

It is important to remember whether you consider yourself a Celt or not, we are *all* emigrants, all scattered, from the motherlands of Africa and Asia onwards – all the more reason to connect, with one's roots, with one's cultural heritage and identity. Americans and Canadians of Celtic descent seem to celebrate their heritage more than some of the current residents of these lands, ie: the famous St Patrick's Day Parade in Boston. This is common of 'ex-pats' and emigrants around the world – it is a way of celebrating and re-asserting one's cultural boundary in a permeable environment, ie: a 'melting pot' culture. Yet think how the diversity of Asian and Afro-Caribbean Post-War immigration has brought colour and spice to Britain's shores, from carnival, clothing and cuisine, to Second and Third Generation literature and music. Britain is a 'mongrel' nation, and all the better for it: the English language being the finest example of that hybridisation.

Similarly, those who claim only Celts of 'pure blood' have the right to be Bards and Druids would do well to remember that even 'Sassenach' England itself was once inhabited by Celtic tribes, as ancient maps and place-names prove, because – as has been stated, but it can never be said enough – the Celts were not one race, but a Pan-European culture, stretching from the Black Sea to the Atlantic, the Baltic to the Mediterranean; and now across the world. It was never a 'Civilisation' – though it has perhaps a better claim than some to that title – but more a take on life. The Celtic culture is forever spiralling backwards and inwards on itself, at odds with the myth of Progress. Unlike the phallic roads of the Roman, the archetypal Celt does not move forward, or even think, in straight lines, but in a more lateral, cyclical, *feminine* way. The true border of the so-called Celtic Fringes is the threshold of the imagination. And this is where you find the modern Celt alive and well. Furthest from the centre, closest to the Source.

AND, oil painting depicting an effigy of the triple-aspect goddess found in Bath, Somerset.

The Cauldron-Born

Stories offer us an insight into the mysteries of the land of their origin. Knowing the tales of a place help us to access its *genius locus*, and the psyche of its people. They let us get under their skin, and they get under *our* skin – working on our subconscious with the language of dreams, bypassing logic to access wisdom.

So it is with the Welsh cycle of stories known, erroneously, as the *Mabinogion* (a misnomer by translator, Lady Charlotte Guest, of *Mabingoi*: Tales of Youthful Adventures). Recorded by monks in the 12th or 13th century from oral material dating back far earlier, they are a body of teachings from the native tradition, miraculously surviving the ravages of time and man – by hiding in plain sight as a bunch of 'harmless' tales for the young. Yet within them are contained bizarre and dark images, brutal truths, and archetypes unmitigated by political correctness. Primal and powerful, these stories may at times seem raw, crude or convoluted – but, like Chinese whispers, they have been told many times before being transcribed by monks with perhaps little inkling of their original significance. What we get is a degenerated copy of the original, but by meditating upon the symbolism, it is possible to tap into the inner teachings and consequently enjoy the tales with fresh insight.

The Gundestrup Cauldron (100 BCE), discovered ritually broken in a bog in Denmark.

For me, the tale of Taliesin was the key that unlocked many of the Bardic Mysteries. It was the first tale I told as a storyteller without script, on request, at an Arthurian-themed party. It has become my 'signature tale' – the one I opened with and identified with the most – as I related more and more to the lore and legend of the **Penbeirdd Taliesin**. He was the master Bard and I was, in spirit, his apprentice. I strive to honour his name and what he stands for: the Bardic Tradition of Britain. Although this has druidic roots in Britain, I believe it is non-denominational and of use to people of all paths. It is about speaking with spirit and 'making sacred the air'. It is **gramarye**, word magic. You can use it to cast a spell, a circle, hold a ceremony, celebration, bless, curse, seduce, and heal. But, as with all magic, bear in mind the Three-fold Effect (see **The Voice: Word Magic and the Uses of Gramarye**). Words are powerful things, to be used wisely, carefully, sensitively.

This amazing story offers us an insight into the Bardic mysteries – like all good stories, it works through symbolism and is worth meditating upon for it holds to key to the bardic initiation. Taliesin, as Gwion Bach, is the initiate. Ceridwen, a form of the **Goddess of the Bards**, is the initiator. He drinks of her cauldron, enters her, when she catches and eats him, and becomes 'Twice-Born' (in Christian terms, 'born again'). The awakened Taliesin receives **The Shining Brow** – the star of his opened Third Eye, as we all can: by asking for Awen. Shine and you will be a star!

We can all be Cauldron-Born and sup of its inspiration by reading these old tales, or better still – listening to actual storytellers tell them. Also, by visiting the ancient sites and landscape associated with them, I find the ancient stories come alive – as we behold the backdrop of these mythic dramas, have a first-hand experience that can add authenticity and local colour to our telling, and imbibe the spirit of the place – and in the process of taking such bardic pilgrimages, new stories are often discovered along the way. We take from the pot and add to it anew: this is the circle of Tradition. Like the Three Cauldrons of Plenty, Inspiration and Rebirth, the Cauldron of Story fills us with spiritual nourishment, Awen, and healing. Never has Stone Soup tasted so good!

STONE SOUP

A storyteller's staple: this classic should be in every teller's repertoire. There are many variations, an Eastern European one being especially flavoursome. Below is a version to cut your teeth on, but remember – as with all stories, whatever the raw ingredients, it is how the 'storyteller chef' cooks and serves it up:

Once upon a time a stranger rode his tired horse down a backcountry road on his way home from a long journey. It was late afternoon and the man was tired and hungry. Ahead he saw a small village. "I'll get something to eat there and find a place for the night," he thought.

Suddenly the horse tripped, throwing the stranger to the ground. As he brushed himself off, he saw that the horse had stumbled over a rock sticking out of the ground in the middle of the road. He walked over to it and dug it out of the earth so that it would not trip anyone else. It was a splendid rock, almost perfectly round and smooth. The stranger liked the rock, so rather than throw it away; he put it in his saddlebag, climbed up on his horse, and continued into the village.

As he road past the first houses the village people stopped their work to stare. He waved to several of them, but no one waved back. He got off his horse and approached a woman standing in front of a small house. "Good evening," he said cheerfully, "Could you spare a bit of food for a hungry man?"

The woman began shaking her head almost before he had finished his sentence. "We have had a poor harvest here. We are very worried that there is barely enough food for our family. I am sorry." And she walked into her house and shut the door.

The man continued to the next house where a farmer was working on his wagon.

"Do you have a place at your table for a hungry traveller?" he asked. "It didn't rain during the last month before harvest," the farmer said. "What little we have is needed for our children."

At every home the stranger heard the same sad story: the harvest had been poor, there was not enough food to make it through the winter. Everyone was very worried about themselves and their immediate family.

Completely discouraged and very hungry, the man sat down under a tree in the village square. "Poor people," he thought, "in a few weeks they will be as hungry as I am." Suddenly an idea hit him. He reached into his saddlebag, took out the stone and addressed the villagers. "Gentle folk of the village", he shouted, "Your worries are over! I have in my hand a special stone that will help take you through the long winter. This is a magic stone. With it you can make stone soup."

"Stone soup?" an old man repeated. "I have never heard of stone soup."

"The wonder of stone soup," the stranger continued, "is that it not only feeds hungry people, it also brings people together. Now who has a large empty pot?"

Quickly a huge iron pot was found, and delivered to the stranger in a wheelbarrow. "The kettle is barely large enough, but it will do," the stranger said. "Now we must fill the pot with water and start a fire."

Eager hands carried buckets of water and firewood. Soon the pot was placed over a roaring fire. As the water began to boil the stranger dramatically raised the magic stone above his head, and then he gently placed it in the kettle.

"Stone soup needs salt and pepper," the stranger announced. Two children ran to find salt and pepper. After the water had boiled for a few minutes the stranger sipped the brew. "This stone makes an excellent soup, but it would be better if we had a few carrots." "We have a few carrots that we're willing to share," a farmer replied. Immediately his daughter ran home and returned with an apron full of carrots.

"It's too bad the harvest was so bad," said the stranger. "Stone soup is always much more tasty when we add a cabbage or two."

"I think I know where to find a cabbage," a young mother shouted as she dashed towards her home. When she returned she was carrying three large cabbages.

The stranger was busy slicing carrots and cabbages with his hunting knife. "The last time I made stone soup was at the castle of a rich man. He added a few potatoes and a bit of beef."

Several people talked quietly, "A bit of beef and we can eat like rich people", they whispered. They went home and soon returned not only with beef and potatoes, but some brought milk, onions and barley too.

By the time the soup was ready it was almost dark. It was the most delicious soup that they had ever smelled and to think, it all came from the magic stone. The stranger finally declared that it was done and invited everyone to have as much as they could eat. After everyone had eaten their fill, some folk brought out their fiddles. Everyone began to sing and dance - and they continued till the wee hours of the morning. Never had the village people had such a wonderful party.

The next morning the whole village gathered to say goodbye to the stranger.

As he mounted his horse a small child called out, "You forgot to take your magic stone!"

The stranger smiled. "I am going to leave the stone with you as gift of gratitude for your hospitality," he said. "Remember, as long as you make stone soup, you will never have to worry about being hungry."

The Story of Taliesin

Taliesin walks between the worlds, inhabiting like Arthur both history and myth. There was a 6th Century Welsh Bard called Taliesin, whose praise poems to his Lord are still extant. Then there is the Taliesin of legend, with his own creation myth – the archetypal shaman-Bard, who journeyed with King Arthur into the Underworld to win the fabled Cauldron of Plenty, as recounted in *Preiddu Annwn*. Yet it was from 'another' cauldron (surely all cauldrons are one, in the same way any glass or goblet represents THE Chalice) the Cauldron of Inspiration, that Taliesin received his poetic gift...

It belonged to Ceridwen, the wisest woman in Wales. By her husband, Tegid Foel, she had given birth to a beautiful daughter, Creirwy (Dear One) and an ill-favoured son, called Avagddu (Utter Darkness). To compensate for his ugliness, Ceridwen decided to concoct a potion of inspiration for him. She collected the necessary ingredients and cooked them in her cauldron. She got Gwion Bach, a boy from the nearby village, to stir the cauldron for a year and a day, and an old man called Morda to stoke the fire and keep it burning. Alas, when the task was nearly complete, Gwion became sleepy and dropped in the spoon – splashing his hand in the process. He quickly put his burnt fingers in his mouth and – Eureka! – received the distilled wisdom meant for Avagddu. The rest of the potion was poisonous, and split the cauldron asunder, its contents spilling into a nearby river, killing the horses of Gwyddno, which drank there.

Meanwhile, Gwion knew Ceridwen would have his guts for garters – so he high-tailed it out of there, in the form of a hare. With the potion coursing through his veins he had the power to shape-change! So off he dashed, but when Ceridwen discovered the disaster, she was so furious that she poked out one of Morda's eyes with his own poker. Then she changed herself into a greyhound and gave chase. Soon she was snapping at his heels, so Gwion jumped into a stream, his fur fell away, and he turned into a salmon. Ceridwen would not be outwitted and turned herself into an otter-bitch. She had almost caught him, until he leapt into the air, the scales fell away to reveal feathers – he had become a tiny wren, king of the birds. But the sky would not protect him from Ceridwen, who turned from otter to hawk. In a flash she had him within an inch of his life, so Gwion became smaller – turning into a germ of wheat and falling below, onto the threshing floor of a farmyard. Hawk-eyed Ceridwen dropped down too, and became a black hen. She scratched around until she spotted the suspicious wheat grain. Triumphantly, she plucked Gwion up in her beak and swallowed him. Ceridwen turned back into a woman, but the transformations did not stop there, for nine moons later she gave birth to a baby boy so beautiful she could not kill him – but because of ugly Avagddu she could not keep him, for the boy shone with the wisdom meant for her poor son. So Ceridwen wrapped up the Twice-Born in a leather bundle and cast him out onto the sea in a coracle.

It was May Eve by now and Elphin, son of Gwyddno, was out fishing at his father's weir. He had been granted the rights to catch the salmon there, which returned every year at that time. He was hoping to change their fortunes, but he wasn't having much luck, and was just about to give up when he spotted the sea-battered coracle. He pulled it ashore and was astounded to see something move in it. Gingerly Elphin unwrapped the bundle, saw the baby boy, and cried, 'Behold, the Shining Brow!' And that was how Taliesin got his name…

The boy shone with intelligence beyond his years, and immediately began to prophesy good fortune for Elphin and his family. And so, wisely, Elphin took the child home to show his father. At first, Gwyddno was annoyed to see his son return with nothing but a leather bundle, but when the bundle began to speak, and not only speak, but prophesy he was impressed. They decided to adopt the child and raise him as one of their own flesh and blood. With Taliesin's uncanny knowledge about when to reap and when to sow, Elphin and his father prospered.

One day, thirteen years later, at the court of his Uncle, King Maelgwyn, Elphin drunkenly boasted he had a Bard better than any there. He was clapped in irons for his insolence and the boy-Bard was sent for – now thirteen in body. Taliesin came and pitted his wits against the court Bards, winning the Bardic duel by setting a riddle none could answer. With Elphin's claim vindicated he was released from the dungeon, but he also released Taliesin from his service – he was a Bard too great for one man: he belonged to the nation, and so Taliesin became the Royal Bard of Camelot and the greatest Bard Albion has ever known.

Thus, the legend of Taliesin was born, but the fame of the historical Taliesin was as widespread. His epithet, Lady Guest informs us, was 'Chief of the Bards of the West' and his rank of Penbeirdd was 'the most highest of the exalted class'. It was said "his feats, learning and endowments were found to be so superior that he was created a golden-tongued Knight of the Round Table", in itself an interesting designation. After Arthur, whom he was said to have escorted to Avalon with Merlin (*Vita Merlini*), he became the bard of Lord Urien ap Rheged, on whose demise he would compose famous eulogies. Thus, the legendary figure blurs into the historical, like Thomas of Ercildoune, in a mythically protean way. The Penbeirdd was said to preside over three chairs: Caer Lleon upon Usk (the Chair of Glamorgan); Rheged, at Bangor Terwy; and Gwyddnyw (Gwynedd?). Morgannwg calls him the 'chair-president', suggesting he governed the Chairs and Bardic Colleges of the time. Certainly, he was an important, inspiring figure, who set an exemplary standard with his consummate skill and vast wisdom. His bright shadow looms large after the Bardic Tradition still and, in essence, he is its true founding father. His radiant brow guides all along the Way of Awen.

The Training of a Bard

The transformations of Taliesin. *Cerridwen* by Wendy Andrews.

The Story of Taliesin offers us a grading system for the development of the Bard. In the Celtic Tradition Bardic training took twelve years – this may seem like an inordinately long time by our modern 'three minute culture' standards, but consider how long it takes for a doctor, vet or airline pilot to qualify. The Bard should be equivalent in skill in his or her profession, if they are to truly live up to the name. To become a doctor of verse, an Ollamh, should take twenty years, I believe. It is a lifetime's commitment. I do not want anyone to be under the illusion that you can become a Bard overnight. It is a serious undertaking. Twelve years to become a Bard is not setting unrealistic demands. If a budding Bard began his training on his eighteenth birthday (and I do not recommend it should begin before this: one should have the foundation of a decent rounded education first) then he could 'graduate' as a fully-fledged Bard by his thirtieth. To be a Bard before then seems to me improbable because you need a certain degree of life experience to draw upon. Knowledge is not enough. Of course, these are only my thoughts, and some may disagree. And there are always going to be protégés who excel before their years, as did Taliesin. Yet it took even the Penbeirdd himself twelve years until he was ready to assume his mantle: he was twelve when he went to Maelgwyn's court, to validate his master

Elphin's claim that he was greater than the Bards present, and fully come into his power (twelve was also the age when Christ was said to have first made his 'professional debut', as it were). Thus, I suggest the journey Taliesin took, from Gwion to Penbeirdd, is a suitable format for the Bardic path of development. Each transformation offers a rich metaphor for a state of consciousness or awareness. Meditate and research the significance of each animal/symbol as you come to it. What does it signify for you? Celebrate each 'graduation' on your Bard Day (the day you declared your intent to follow the path of the Bard).

THE JOURNEY OF THE BARD

- ✤ 1-12 Years: *Anruth* initiate
- ✤ 13-19 Years: *Bard* master
- ✤ 20+ Years: *Ollamh* pencerodd (chief of song)
- ✤ Lifetime Achievement: *Penbeirdd*

STUDY PATH

Before you begin your Bardic training, you may have other skills and experience, but as far as the Awen is concerned you are 'unenlightened'. This is the Afagddu stage, so called after Ceridwen's ill-favoured son whose name means 'Utter Darkness' (in some versions he was first known as Morvran, Great or Sea Crow, but this seems to be confused with the old man who stirs the cauldron, Morda. If the two were separate entities, or simply conflated in later texts it is hard to say). It was for his sake she concocted the Potion of Inspiration: this is the wisdom you will imbibe from the Bardic Tradition as you take the Way of Awen.

Yet at the same time, however 'ugly' or 'ignorant' the exterior of a person, their soul is essentially beautiful, ancient and divine: this is symbolised by Ceridwen's other child, her beautiful daughter, Creirwy (Dear One). These are the two sides of the uninitiated, and perhaps all embryonic souls.

As soon as the student begins their Bardic training they become an *Anruth* of the **Gwion** Grade, and thus commence the pattern of transformations, which are theirs to experience if they choose to pursue the path of the Bard. Gwion Bach (Little) is the boy plucked seemingly at random from the nearby village by Ceridwen to stir her cauldron for a year and a day. This is symbolic of the initial 12 months Bardic training the Anruth must undertake. At the end of this period of rigorous study, the *Anruth* (Grade 1) has knowledge: they have sipped from the Cauldron of Inspiration like Gwion Bach. But a little knowledge is a dangerous thing: they must 'flee', through a series of metamorphoses, for their training is not over yet. The pursuit of Ceridwen is another part of the initiation process. The transformations involved in the chase are a powerful rite-of-passage through the cycles of life, evolution, elemental realms and consciousness. With each stage of the *fith-fath* (the druidic art of shape-changing) the Anruth, like Gwion Bach, attunes with and assimilates the wisdom of the respective animal. By identifying deeply with pursued **and** pursuer, the initiate (who remains an *Anruth* throughout this entire stage until their 13th Year) experiences not only the shifting perspectives and Mysteries of masculine and feminine, but also the five magical elements: Air (boy, hare, greyhound); Water (salmon, otter, wren); Fire (hawk, wheat grain, black hen); Earth (Elphin, Gwyddno, Maelgwyn); and finally Spirit (Taliesin).

Thus, the 12 years of this Bardic Training mirrors the 12 month cycle of *The Bardic Handbook*, macrocosm to microcosm.

THE PATH OF THE BARD

- ✤ Before training: Afagddu/Creirwy
- ✤ Beginning of 1st Year: *Anruth*, Gwion Grade
- ✤ 2nd Year (a year and a day after Bard Day): *Anruth*, Hare Grade
- ✤ 3rd Year: *Anruth*, Greyhound Grade
- ✤ 4th Year: *Anruth*, Salmon Grade
- ✤ 5th Year: *Anruth*, Otter Grade
- ✤ 6th Year: *Anruth*, Wren Grade
- ✤ 7th Year: *Anruth*, Hawk Grade
- ✤ 8th Year: *Anruth*, Cian (Wheat of Song) Grade
- ✤ 9th Year: *Anruth*, Black Hen Grade
- ✤ 10th Year: *Anruth*, Elphin Grade
- ✤ 11th Year: *Anruth*, Gwyddno Grade
- ✤ 12th Year: *Anruth*, Maelgwyn Grade
- ✤ 13th Year: Taliesin Grade. *Bard*
- ✤ 21st Year: Pencerodd (chief of song) Grade. *Ollamh*

The Bardic Handbook (and associated workshops) should be sufficient for your training arc up to and including Bard level. **The Silver Branch Bardic Network** will offer courses on other aspects of the Bardic path, which could help in complementary and further development. Further publications will aim to deal more in depth with each respective grade and the Way of Awen in general.

It is no coincidence that there are similarities between Bardic degrees and the modern university system, because they share similar origins: perhaps in the Bardic Colleges the British Isles were rightly famous for. Even to this day universities have 'Chairs', use robes of symbolic hue, and archaic ritual in their award ceremonies. When I accepted my Masters at Cardiff from the University of Wales, the bilingual degree ceremony, partly in Welsh, with the Dean as Master of Ceremonies, chaired staff as the Gorsedd, and young 'priestesses' holding the space, felt very Bardic.

THE TRADITIONAL BARDIC CURRICULUM

- ✤ 1st Year: Fifty oghams or alphabets. Elementary grammar. Twenty tales.
- ✤ 2nd Year: Fifty oghams. Six easy lessons in Philosophy. Certain specified poems. Grammar. Forty poems.
- ✤ 3rd Year: Fifty oghams. Six minor lessons of Philosophy. Certain specified poems. Grammar. Forty poems.
- ✤ 4th year: The *Bretha Nemed* or Law of Privileges. Twenty poems of the species called Eman. Fifty tales. Grammar. Sixty tales.
- ✤ 5th Year: Grammar. Sixty tales.
- ✤ 6th Year: The Secret Language of the Poets. Forty-eight poems of the species called *Nuath*. Seventy or eighty tales.
- ✤ 7th Year: *Brosnacha* (miscellanies). The Laws of Bardism.
- ✤ 8th Year: Prosody. Glosses (the meaning of obscure words). *Teinm Laeghdha. Imbas Forosnai. Dichetal Do Chennibh* (the Three Illuminations). Dindsenchas.
- ✤ 9th Year: A specified number of compositions of the kind called *Sennat, Luasca, Nena, Eochraid, Sruith,* and *Duili Feda*. To master 175 tales in this three year period.

- ❖ 10th Year: A further number of compositions listed above.
- ❖ 11th Year: 100 compositions known as *Ananmuin*.
- ❖ 12th Year: 120 *Cetals* or orations. The Four Arts of Poetry. During the three years to master 175 tales in all, along with the 175 of the *Anruth*, 350 Tales in all.

from *Manners and Customs of the Ancient Irish*, Eugene O'Curry;
and *A Social History of Ancient Ireland*, Patrick Joyce. (quoted in *Taliesin*, Matthews)

Now, this list is illuminating in showing the sheer depth and breadth of learning of the Bardic student, and the size of their repertoire by the time they graduate. It has been calculated that a Bardic student would have needed to have learned 10 lines of poetry a day for twelve years: this is certainly not impossible, although such mindless learning by rote is not appropriate for our more open-minded times. I believe we do not need to follow *to the letter* this curriculum – much of what they refer to has been lost – but we can follow it in spirit, with our 12 year structure. I have found, through following my own studies, that I have amassed Bardic knowledge, composed and performed many poems, developed a repertoire of stories, and explored the mysteries of languages and speech: this seems inevitable if you follow the Bardic path for years. I suggest you pursue your own studies after this first year with its structured programme, but stick to the Anruth/Bard/Ollamh tier system and the year-by-year grades – this will give your studies some structure, acknowledge your progress and give you something to aim towards. As you achieve each grade, celebrate!

The Crane Bag: Bardic Techniques and Exercises

Fionn Mac Cumhail, that great culture hero of Erin, was given a bag made from crane-skin – the crane, or heron, being a divinatory bird sacred to the Druids – its legs in flight were said to have suggested the Ogham alphabet. Fionn obtained it from his father by 'skill and cunning'. As a child Fionn was saved from death by his grandmother, who, in the form of a crane (heron) carried him off to a great tree, where he remained protected (like Odin on the World Tree). The Crane Bag was said to have been made from the skin of the enchantress Aoife, who had been transformed into a crane for two hundred years as punishment by Bov the Red, King of the Tuatha de Danann. She was the childless second wife of Lir (father of the sea-god Manannan) and filled with jealousy for his first wife's four children, planned to slay them, but instead turned them into white swans (the Children of Lir). When her crime was discovered, she herself was enchanted into a 'witch of the air', in the form of a crane.

Is the Crane Bag, in a mythopoeic sense, the Goddess, whose womb contains all life? It originally belonged to Manannan Mac Lir, the Irish God of the Sea, who was said to have a bag filled with treasures – although it emptied and refilled according to the tide, suggesting it was an analogue for the sea itself with all of its myriad riches, as this poem relates:

The shirt of Manannan and his knife,
And Guibne's girdle, altogether:
A smith's hook from the fierce man:
Were the treasures that the Crane Bag held.

The king of Scotland's shears full sure,
And the King of Lochlann's helmet,
These were in it to be told of,
And the bones of Asal's swine.

A girdle of the great whale's back
Was in the shapely Crane-Bag:
I tell thee without harm
Used to be carried in it.

From the *'Dunaire Fionn'*, trans. E Macneill

Mac Lir with his Crane Bag.

In short, the Crane Bag carries anything we can imagine. On one level it is the ocean itself, which is commonly seen as a metaphor of the subconscious. For our purposes, the Crane Bag will be a metaphor of the Bardic 'toolkit', the collection of techniques at the Bard's disposal, which are here gathered together in this book. By all means, make a bag to carry actual 'tools' or props, musical instruments, notes, water, booklets and CDs for sale, etc., in short, everything you need for a performance, but be careful: I have a beautiful suede

A 'Crane Bag' used by the author, made by Lesley Hilton.

satchel, made by a friend, which I took once to Glastonbury Festival filled with my poetry booklets, CDs, wallet, mobile phone, etc., and lost it all on the first day. Amazingly, I received it through the post a couple of weeks later – completely intact, except for one copy of a poem. Apart from restoring my faith in the festival and people in general, this experience told me not to rely too much on such accoutrements. Maybe it was a lesson from the People of Peace!

Another idea is the Story Bag – containing curious artefacts that can trigger tales, either ones in your repertoire, or new ones, invented with the help of your audience. Story Bags are great for children to make: they can place things they collect in the bag, eg: a shell, a feather, stone, or other mementoes, and use them as triggers for new stories or aide memoires for old ones.

Whether you interpret the idea literally or not, the concept of the Crane Bag is an engaging and useful one. I will be using it as a portmanteau term for the Bard's tricks of the trade. Throughout the book, under the aegis of The Crane Bag we'll be exploring traditional Bardic techniques and lore and how they can be used or adapted by the modern Bard.

The Three Illuminations: *Imbas Forosnai* - The Light of Foresight

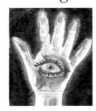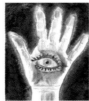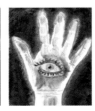

The seer-Bard was said to be adept at three types of divination, *Imbas Forosnai*, *Teinm Laida* and *Dichetal do Chennaib*. Caitlín Matthews (CM), well-respected authority on Oracular Studies, says: "These three techniques were called the Three Illuminations, since they threw light on dark matters. These are the primary shamanic skills employed by the *filidh* poet."

These are deep mysteries, worthy of lengthy study beyond the scope of this book (such as Nora Chadwick's essay on *Imbas Forosnai*), but to summarise:

1. *Imbas Forosnai:* the wisdom that illumines, "the light of foresight" (Robert Holdstock), "inspiration of tradition" (CM)
2. *Teinm Laida:* inspiration by song; "decoding by means of verse" (CM)
3. *Dichetal do Chennaib:* wisdom from the cracking open of hazel nuts; "psychometric composition" (CM).

There is much confusion between the three. Such obscure concepts are difficult to recall or disassociate. A useful mnemonic, though perhaps a gross simplification, would be: vision, voice and vein – symbolised by eye, mouth and hand. Use these as visual keys for meaning and memory.

We will look at **Teinm Laida** and **Dichetal do Chennaib** later. Let us look at the first:

1: *IMBAS FOROSNAI* - The Light of Foresight

Definition: *Imbas* is the Irish word for inspiration: the equivalent of Awen.
Forosnai: bright, burning. The wisdom that illumines, the inspiration of tradition.

Background:

> *Imbas Forosnai* – the inspiration of tradition, the knowledge that discovers whatever the poet wishes to know. It is done like this: the poet chews a piece of flesh from the red pig, or of cat or dog and after so chewing puts it on the flagstone behind the door. He pronounces an invocation over it and offers it to his spirits. He calls his spirits to him and if they do not reveal the matter immediately he sings incantations over his two palms and calls the spirits again to keep his sleep undisturbed. Then he lays his palms over his cheeks and so falls asleep in this posture. He is watched over to ensure nothing interrupts him until the matter is revealed to him: this may be a minute or two or three, or as long as necessary. Patrick abolished this practice along with *tenm laegda*, for he judged that those that practised these methods should merit neither heaven nor earth, because it renounced one's baptismal vows. The practice of *dichetal do chennaib* he alone allowed, since it was not necessary to make offerings to spirits, for the revelations come straight away from the poet's fingers.

> *The Yellow Book of Lecan*, from the *Encyclopaedia of Celtic Wisdom*,
> Caitlin & John Matthews

Modern seer Caitlin Matthews describes it as 'a wholly interior act', as opposed to divination by wand, or by fingers. It has echoes in the story of both **Taliesin** and the Caudron; and **Fionn and the Salmon**. Both young heroes burn their fingers while responsible for the cooking of a magical brew or food, and both place their scolded digits into their mouth to soothe them and so inadvertently received the distilled wisdom instead of the intended recipient. Whenever Fionn wishes to know something he places his thumb (with which he burst the blisters on the cooking salmon) into his mouth and chews on its skin.

I would argue this is a symbolic act and can be interpreted in a metaphorical way: that we can 'chew things over' without having to kill and eat animals, especially pets! You are welcome to try it with meat if you are so inclined but I believe it is not necessary to follow this technique so literally. The imbibing of an animal as part of a divinatory process is brought to its maximum extreme with the *Tarbh Feis*, the Bull Feast – a form of prophecy to find a king – when a bull would be ritually slain, a broth made for the Bard to glut himself on, and wrapped in the Bull's Hide, he would sleep it off, to reveal the candidate upon waking. Fortunately, these days there's a vegetarian alternative!

The covering of the face with one's hands is interesting – for this is a form of sensory deprivation, as used in the Bardic colleges (see **Stone on the Belly**).

The offering to the spirits, of the threshold, and of a ritual guardian – holding the space while the Bard 'journeys' – are all ingredients we can adapt easily to the present.

EXERCISE: Chewing it Over

Choose a problem that is frustrating you – one you have 'hit a wall' with, or 'drawn a blank'.

Write it on a piece of plain paper. Find a quiet space where you will not be disturbed (ie: your Bardic Space). Make sure you have a glass of water handy. Clear the space, using incense, rattle, water, salt, sound. Prepare offerings on the threshold (doorstep, windowsill) such as a candle (on a saucer, or in a jar), incense, fruit, flowers, etc. Leave the candle/incense unlit for now – remember to leave some matches or a lighter handy. Ask for a Guardian to watch over the space while you work. Sit down with the paper in front of you and the glass of water at hand. Relax your body and ask for Awen (see **Raising the Awen**). Read the paper and meditate upon the problem, then place the paper in your mouth and 'chew it over' slowly, unless it is edible paper be careful not to swallow (if so take the paper out of your mouth and place it at the edge of your space/circle – on a doorstep or windowsill if possible). With this problem in mind, light the candle asking for enlightenment. In thanks burn incense, leave an 'offering' of fruit or flowers to the Spirits. Make sure the flame is safe, away from curtains, breezes, etc. Close your eyes, or cover them with a blindfold or hood. Clear your mind. Then let the answer come. Don't filter or censor anything at this stage, however impractical or strange. Remember the 'answer' you have received. Slowly return to everyday consciousness. Get up slowly, stamp your feet, return into your body. Now, thank your guardian and bid them hail and farewell – extinguishing the candle to 'banish' them. Tidy the threshold 'altar' and dispose of chewed paper. Make yourself a hot drink and a snack to ground yourself and use your journal to write down your answer and experience. Did you find your solution?

Imbolc: The Poet's Festival

Imbolc, falling on the eve of February, is one of the four main Celtic Fire Festivals and is sacred to Brighid, Goddess of poetry, smithcraft and healing (see **Goddess of the Bards**). The name comes from 'ewe's milk' (*oi melc* in Gaelic) for the festival was designed to coincide with the birth of the spring lambs and the lactating of the ewes. White is the colour of Imbolc, in the ewes' milk, in the thawing snow and frost that lingers, and in the snowdrops – the first flowers of the year, that make a welcome appearance – the first signs of life, or rebirth, after the dead of Winter.

Although Winter can often maintain a stubborn grip upon the land for weeks to come, Imbolc heralds the first inklings of Spring, which will have manifested fully (depending on Climate Change) by the Spring Equinox (21st March) and be in its glory by May Day. Before those exuberant joys to come, Imbolc is a quieter, more 'introvert' festival: a time for us to peacefully light the candle of the year, listen to the Silence, and envision what the Awen wants us to manifest in the coming months.

It is a good time for beginnings, for initiating things and for initiations. If you are interested in embarking upon the Bardic Path, then you could pick no better time than Imbolc, for you have the blessing of Brighid and the energy of the year behind you. If you are serious, then compose and take a **Bardic Vow**, (making a commitment of your choosing in your own words to what you deem sacred, ie: 'to write twelve poems over the coming year in honour of the Goddess') choose a **Bardic Name** and begin your journey along the Way of Awen in earnest (see **Twice-Born**). For now, it is not the details which are important, but the intent, to make your first tentative steps along the Way. Imbolc is an appropriate time of year for this, not only because it marks the rebirth of Spring, (an auspicious time to become 'Twice-Born') but because mythopæically it is connected with Ceridwen and the Tale of Taliesin: for Ceridwen is a kind of Welsh Brighid and **Taliesin** is the greatest Celtic poet.

Brighid is connected to springs, in the way that Sulis (of *Aquae Sulis*, Bath) is associated with the hot springs there. They were believed to be heated by an undying flame, rather like the Flame of Brighid in her temple at Kildare, tended by the priestesses. The hot springs of Sulis were also said to be heated by 'brass tuns' beneath the water – an echo of the cauldron of Ceridwen tended for a year and a day by Morvran, and stirred by Gwion Bach, who, of course, splashes three drops of the potion of inspiration on his fingers and receives the distilled wisdom of the world meant for Afagddu. After the culprit is caught and 'devoured' by Ceridwen, he is Twice-Born with a shining brow and given the name Taliesin. In this tale we have a brilliant example of a Bardic initiation and naming.

So, Imbolc, being sacred to poets and associated with these legends is the ideal time for a poetic initiation – more than, I would argue, Samhain, the Celtic New Year and traditional time associated with death and rebirth. I feel the Bard's year begins at Imbolc, for after the busy winter circuit (Harvest, Hallowe'en, Yuletide) it is time to replenish the Awen and rededicate oneself to one's path. Therefore, even if you have already been initiated and named, I would suggest you use Imbolc to 'renew your vows' to the Goddess – for this is a kind of sacred marriage, with you as the Goddess's (or Horned God's) consort on earth.

A mild echo of this is found in the medieval courts, with the winning of a woman's 'favour'. A troubadour would have his Lady, to whom he would compose and sing songs – she would be his earthly muse. And the idea of the Muse is a direct legacy of this notion of divine patronage. In Greece, poets actually received their inspiration from the Nine Muses, who lived on Mount Parnassus above Delphi. The fabled Cauldron of Plenty that King Arthur plunders in the ancient Welsh epic *Preiddu Annwn* was 'warmed by the breath of muses'.

Imbolc is the festival to ask for inspiration from the Goddess herself, to receive her favour for the coming year, in exchange for your loyal service (for non-pagans, for 'Goddess' read Planet Earth). The main thing is to serve something bigger than your self (ie: Gaia, Mother Earth) and to realise the Awen is not to be taken for granted: it is a boon that can be withdrawn if you are deemed unworthy (writer's block, losing your voice, etc.). Imbolc is the taper that lights you. Christianised as Candlemas, it is time for lighting candles and making wishes, visualising what you want to manifest in the coming year. But this is a covenant that comes at a price. We have to be willing to put in the work, and walk our talk. The Goddess may decide to help us, but only if we prove our integrity and intent. She has no truck with fools, only those who are true at heart.

I think it is important to renew this 'pact' with the Muse-Goddess every year, like the renewal of hand-fasting vows. It is an interesting coincidence that only a fortnight later than Imbolc we have St Valentine's Day, when we are 'encouraged' by the media and expected by our partners to do the same. We express our love to our beloved with poetry (or the stuff that passes for it in cards), floral tributes and a ritual meal. However spurious this tradition, it serves a healthy purpose if it makes us think about our feelings, the object of desire and our commitment to them. And in this respect, as well as its superficial trappings, it echoes the older Fire Festival. Imbolc is especially focussed on feminine mysteries, but should not be seen as a 'women only' festival. It has a lot to offer men (and ultimately it is about the dance and the balance of both).

So Imbolc is a very 'feminine' festival (a term I use in respect of energy rather than gender), one which is of especial resonance to Bards dedicated to honouring the Goddess, but it has wider significance for all of us. It is time to clear and bless our own springs of creativity, to nurture the tender shoots of our dreams seeded in deepest winter, and to celebrate the renewal of life.

Sacred spring overflow, Roman Baths, *Aquae Sulis.*

EXERCISE: Rite of Spring

Create a ceremony to honour the return of Spring. Compose and recite a poem, in situ if possible: in a grove, by water. Make offerings to the Spring Goddess with flowers, white candles, incense, and song. Clean, dress and bless a local spring or well. Visualise what you want to bear fruit in the coming year, and what you are willing to give in return.

Spring Goddess

The Bride of Spring

In darkest hour of the year
she arises,
casting off her shadowy gown
as she steps over the horizon –
by sun king kissed,
borne by his golden down.

A dress of frosted cobwebs
veils maiden skin.
Within a seasons turning
the crone has become virgin.

Snowdrops touch her and turn into flowers,
as the slumbering land stirs
in these formative hours.

The earth softens at her feet
where buds shake free their winter bed.
Newborn lambs begin to bleat –
insistent mouths by ewes milk fed.

Rooster heralds her on the ground.
Above, the feathered chorus
makes naked trees resound.

We awake to a changing world.
Her white magic revealed -
a petal uncurled.

Stone bound man
let your proud bells ring,
for we are welcomed into her garden
as she stands at the gates of spring.

The infant year she presents,
placing the future in our hands.
A gift of renewed innocence,
restoring the egg timer sands…

Kevan Manwaring

Brighid: Goddess of the Bards

Brighid (pronounced *breed*) looms large over the Celtic world as its most important Goddess. She has been worshipped across the lands of the Celt, changing form like the cloak of seasons over the landscape. She seems to embody the Triple-aspect Goddess herself, being the Celtic goddess of poetry, healing and smithcraft: an interesting combination echoing the Greek Athena/Roman Minerva – Goddess of poetry and warfare. She is indeed a double-edged sword, not to be dealt with disrespectfully. She is no 'bimbo' of male fantasy, although many poets have written about her, trying to capture her ethereal beauty. As befitting a Goddess, she alters her shape and guise – her very elusiveness maddening poets. Robert Graves calls her 'the White Goddess': 'with leper pale brow, rowan berry lips, hair, honey-coloured to white hips'. Yet she is certainly not all 'sweetness and light'. Graves warns, perhaps prejudiced by his own encounters, that 'jaw bones and entrails of poets litter her lair', the Mare's Nest. She is Keats' *La Belle Dame Sans Merci*, leaving unwary knights 'alone and palely loitering'. The Wandering Aengus of WB Yeats' famous poem, caught a glimpse of 'a glimmering girl' with apple blossom in her hair' and spent the rest of his life looking for her: 'Though I am old with wandering through hilly lands and hollow lands I will find out where she has gone…' The Muse is elusive and seemingly fickle, although actually only bestowing her favours on those worthy to receive – she is sister to the Goddess Sovereignty, who can make – and break – Kings.

Brighid: Stuart Littlejohn's brilliant vision of the Goddess, showing her attributes and associations.

Brighid is connected to springs, and she manifests in subtly different forms around the country. Clues can be found in place names or street names. Bridewell Lane is a giveaway. In Dorset, above Bridport, there are the verdant moist valleys of Little Bredy and Long Bredy, overlooked by the long barrow of Long Meg and her Daughter nearby. Not far away is the Abbotsbury Swannery, swans being sacred to Brighid, and a ruined chapel dedicated to St Catherine, of the burning wheel (flame also being connected with her), is situated on a hill with fine views over Chesil Beach. St Catherine, patron saint of widows and spinsters, is strongly associated with Bath, Somerset: St Catherine's Chapel is the 'mother church' of the city, and has one of the many sacred springs in the area. But most famous of all are the geothermal springs of the so-called Roman Baths. The hot springs which emerge in the centre of Bath from a 4km fault in the Cotswold limestone (*Aquae Sulis*: waters of the gap) are sacred to the Celtic Goddess Sulis – her cult was assimilated by the invading Romans who established their temple-city there, and she became known as Sulis-Minerva.

The hot springs were believed to be heated by an undying flame, rather like the Flame of Brighid in her temple at Kildare, tended by the priestesses. The geothermal springs of Sulis were also said to be heated by 'brass tuns' beneath the water – an echo of the cauldron of Ceridwen tended for a year and a day by Morda, and stirred by Gwion Bach, who, of course, splashes three drops of the potion of inspiration on his fingers and receives the distilled wisdom of the world meant for Afagddu. After the culprit is caught and 'devoured' by Ceridwen he is Twice-Born with a shining brow and given the name Taliesin – in this tale we have a brilliant example of a Bardic initiation and naming. Again and again Brighid, and her sisters, act as initiatorix to the fledgling bard. As the saying goes, when the pupil is ready, the teacher will appear.

I believe I found my Muse, or rather, She found me, when I visited Ireland for the first time in 1991 on a Lughnasadh pilgrimage to Croagh Patrick, Newgrange and other sites, including Thoor Ballylee and Coole Park, Yeats' old haunts. I returned home and started writing poetry in praise of the Goddess. She has changed Her face many times, but has been with me ever since.

The equivalent to the Muse, for women, is 'the Daemon Lover', the incubus/animus opposite of the men's suc-

Sulis, oil on wood.

cubus/anima – the idealised 'other'. He crops up in numerous ballads, poems, stories, paintings and novels (Dion Fortune's *The Demon Lover*, and Caitlin Matthews' non-fiction book on the subject). Perhaps the stereotype of the 'tall, dark, handsome stranger' comes from this – if he is an archetypal figure that haunts women's dreams. Is the popularity of elven Orlando Bloom-types, especially with younger women, because they are feminised 'non-threatening' males: the classic Prince Charming fantasy figure, the stuff that girls' dreams are made of?

And, in the similar way, perhaps the Muse is so common a figure with male poets because she is *his* female half... Yet the Goddess is, generally speaking, the idealised feminine, for both males and females – in her gentler aspects at least. Of course, she has many faces, and seems to become darker and fiercer as the year progresses, so that by the time the wheel has turned to Samhain, she has become the hag Cailleach, the fierce mountain mother of the north: a kind of Celtic Kali, stripping away all that is unnecessary and false. And as Crone she has much to teach us, through her catabolism and wisdom. But at Imbolc we can enjoy her Maiden aspects, although Brighid is no 'foolish virgin'! We must honour her fully, in all her aspects, or suffer the consequences. The Goddess inspires us and bestows the sovereignty of her love: we must prove ourselves worthy of it, or her favours will be removed.

EXERCISE: Finding Brighid
This brief introduction has only touched the tip of the iceberg. It is important that you make your own connection with Her: by visiting the sacred sites; meditating, visualising and communing; researching the legends and customs; and writing your own poems and songs about Her. Her story is waiting to be told.

Praise Poems

One function of the Bard is that of Praise-singer. At one time this may have been as the 'Royal Sycophant', but fortunately times have changed (although the official Poet Laureate's role may still retain vestiges of this). Bards still have to sing for their supper but their very lives no longer depend upon whether their latest ode pleases their Lord or Lady patrons. The Bards may have been the spin-doctors of medieval Britain, when persecution forced them to toe the official line or starve. Of course, some Bards must have subverted this role through veiled criticisms of the Court couched in obscure Bardic references, (the **Dark Speech**) but the Bard's **satire** was greatly feared, and their curses were said to raise blisters on the faces of their enemies, in much the same way that to be lampooned or lambasted in the modern press must feel.

Moon Nymph.

However, the positive side to the Bard's role was to give praise where praise was due, to celebrate brave and noble deeds, generous hosts, beautiful ladies, and more importantly, to praise the wonder and mystery of nature. The very first recorded songs and poems do this, ie: in the earliest recorded English poem, about Spring: "Sumer is icumen in". Much earlier than this, hunter gatherer chants, preserved in the traditions of Native America, Africa and Australia, celebrate the power of the animal-prey in an act of propitiation and mimicry known as sympathetic magic. By identifying with the animal it was a way of foreseeing its moves, of successfully hunting it, and honouring its spirit. It was the oral equivalent to the cave paintings of bison, gazelle, and so on. Real effort had been made. It was a sign of respect. And in its personification, rhythm and metaphor, it was the first poetry.

The need to honour and value the riches of life bestowed upon us by nature is perhaps more relevant and urgent than ever. A restored reconnection with and sustainable relationship with Nature is essential to survival of life on Earth. And on a personal level we should always be grateful for what we have, not in a 'humble pie' way, but because as Westerners we are generally incredibly privileged compared to the Developing Nations. A simple way of remembering to appreciate what riches we have is to say thank you for them every morning. This could be seen as a statement of intent, as well: for the day, and for your life as a Bard, to walk in beauty and truth.

EXERCISE: Writing a 'Thank You' Poem or Song
I have written my Thank You poem based upon a Praise Song by Seneca Native Americans. I changed the words, beautiful though they are – because it has to be in your own words to truly have power. I suggest you draught your own, either using this simple format, or by doing it in your own distinct way. The important thing is to use your voice. It has to come from the heart. If it is not genuine, just a technical exercise, it will mean nothing. What do you need/want to give thanks for in your life? Write a poem or song to sing every day.

Sunrise Praise

Thank you,
Mother Earth,
For holding me in your arms all night
And bringing me back to a world of light.

Thank you, Father Sun,
For returning to brighten our day,
May you shine for us
And show us the way.

Thank you, Brothers and Sisters,
Of water, earth, wood and air.
I shall tread lightly
on this planet we share.

Thank you, Great Mystery.
May we live this day with the wisdom of love,
Guided by the blessings of
below and above.

May peace prevail on Earth
And in all our hearts.
Love and light to our loved ones
Wherever they may be.

So Mote It Be

End of Month Review

By now you should have reached the end of your first month as an *Anruth*. If you have read and worked through the **Bardic Beginnings** and **Spirit** sections you should be able to:

❖ Describe what a Bard is, does and where he came from (the Bardic Tradition).
❖ Understand Awen and be able to raise it.
❖ Regularly use your own Bardic Space.
❖ Reflect upon how you started out and where you are now.
❖ Relate the Story of Taliesin.
❖ Understand the Training of a Bard.
❖ Know what the Crane Bag is.
❖ Summarise the Three Illuminations.
❖ Explain the significance of Imbolc.
❖ Reflect upon your Bardic development, ideas, etc., in a journal.
❖ Describe Brighid.
❖ Compose and recite a Praise Poem.

If you can manage all of these things, firstly – well done! You have mastered the Basic Principles and have all you need to know to begin your bardic training in earnest, starting in the East of our circle of the year, with **Air**.

NB: After this critical first month, it will only be necessary to review every quarter, although it is always healthy to reflect on one's practice, development and experiences in your Bardic Journal throughout the year.

TWO
A I R

Month 2:
Threshold Guardians

Month 3:
Twice-Born

Spirits of Air

Let us consider the magical element of air. In the Western Mystery Tradition it is associated for reasons I have already discussed with the East, with the time of dawn, the break of day, and the beginning of Spring – the time from Imbolc to the Spring Equinox. Air is of course the Kingdom of the Birds, and many birds feature significantly in Celtic lore and tales: King of the Birds, the tiny Wren; bold Cock-Robin; flower-faced Owl; the lovely Swan-maidens; Ogham-legged Crane; Pendragon's Chough; Morrigan's Raven; the Eagle of Gwernabwy and Lleu Llaw Gyffes; the Hawk of May, Gwalchmai; the Birds of Rhiannon; the Starling on a Kneading-Trough; the Ravens of Bran; Merlin, Kestrels and Kingfishers… So many, in fact, to make you wonder whether Britain at one point was divided into bird-tribes. This is explored in Moyra Caldecott's book *The Winged Man*, which recounts the story of Bladud of Bath, (see **The Swineherd Prince and Flying King**) one of a number of legends of flying magicians and holy men, including Daedalus, the Druid Mogh Ruith, Simon Magus, and William of Malmesbury. Throughout history man has aspired to the heights, as though to break the yoke of his mortality and steal the fire of the Gods. And many actual aviators have paid the price for their ambition, including American pioneer of the skies Amelia Earhart and Antoine de St-Exupéry, visionary author and pilot. Writer Richard Bach, of *Jonathan Livingstone Seagull* fame, continues the tradition of wordsmiths of the sky.

It is not surprising that the element of Air has inspired so much poetry and sublime prose, since it corresponds to intelligence and eloquence, to clarity and reason in an Apollonian sense: the clarity one gets in the morning, after the Cloud of Unknowing has descended and one has experienced the Dark Night of the Soul. Yet in a very Celtic sense, it is the Awen, whispered on the morning breeze, in the shivering of trees, the susurration of the surf. It is what we hear when we fully listen, with all our mind, body and spirit. It is the 'Holy Word' Blake's Bard hears when he walks among the ancient trees. The Holy Spirit is often equated with wind – and this is one of the many places where Christianity overlaps with Druidry. When devotees are filled with the Holy Spirit they are said to 'speak-in-tongues.' This is like the **Awenydddion**, who we'll look at later. But on a very fundamental level wind, or air, is connected with speaking – air is the conveyor of speech, even in a recording it turns back into sound waves before entering the ear. Air fills our lungs and the voicebox turns it into speech – in terms of oxygen we literally do get our words from the trees, and return them to carbon dioxide to be absorbed and recycled. All sound based communication boils down to vibration – and we'll look at that in the chapter on The Harp.

Air is the original and most universal medium of language – in an oral and aural sense. It is the element of true conversation (not emails or texts!). The Chief Bards often used **colloquy** in teaching (aka the Socratic Method), most famously and beautifully in *The Colloquy of the Two Sages*. These poetic Q&A sessions are reduced to their quintessence in **Riddles**, which the Anglo-Saxons *Scops* mastered above all. A question is like a baited fish-hook, pulling the answer out of the depths of the pupil: it is empowering, for it encourages them to find the solution themselves. The Truth is far more effective when come to by one's own resources. When realisation dawns from within, it stays.

The genius loci of air are the sylphs. The Faerie were sometimes referred to as the Folk of the Air (euphemisms were always safer when referring to these easily offended 'People of Peace'). And, while we're mentioning magical beings, we must not forgot Griffins, Pegasi (winged horses), Rocs (giant eagles), and Dragons. The Summer Country's Lord of the Underworld, Gwynn ap Nudd, resident of Ynys Witryn, was said to ride through the air with his Wish-Hounds in winter, collecting the souls of the dead. The Wish-Hounds seem to echo the Nordic Valkyries and the Egyptian Anubis, and Gwynn seems to be similar to Thoth, who in turn is related to Hermes, wing-heeled messenger of the Greek pantheon (Mercury in the Roman pantheon) – who was said to be accompanied by Wind-Dogs. There's meant to be a natural pause in the conversation every twenty minutes known as the 'Hermes Pause' (worth checking out next time you're having a good chat with friends). The Lord of the Winds was known in the Hellenic tradition as Aeolus, and each of the four Cardinal winds of the world had a name: commonly, Eurus for the East Wind; Notus, South; Zephyrus, West; and Boreas, North – hence, Hyperborea: The Land Beyond the North Wind (the classical Greek name for the British Isles). In fact, according to the Greeks there were eight directions, each with its corresponding deity, whileas in the Celtic Tradition there are references to twelve winds with associated colours (the 'Wheel of the Winds' is referred to in an Irish cosmological poem, *Saltair Na Ran;* and also in the 10th Century *Hibernica Minora*).

Air is symbolised by the sword, which in this context represents the intellect – think of precision and discernment, as epitomised by Occam's Razor, once belonging to the eponymous monk and now a cipher for critical choices. Legend is rife with magical blades, from Excalibur to the Answerer, Manannan Mac Lir's sword. The Sword of Nuadu is one of the **Four Treasures** of the Tuatha de Danann, originating in the Otherworldly city of Findias, the Place of Brightness. Interestingly enough, its guardian was the poet Uscias, the Praiser. The hallow of the Sword bestows sovereignty, via a Goddess-figure such as the Lady of the Lake. And the Sword, of course, signifies Justice (as seen in the icon of Justice still there above Law Courts – blind-folded, with scales in one hand and a sword in the other). Yet, on a deeper mythic level, the Sword is the *Glaive*, the Celtic Sword of Light, one of the Four Hallows. The same Sword of Nuadu – it is said no man could escape its blade when it was drawn from its scabbard – so it is wise to think before you speak, before you give someone the sharp end of your tongue! Interestingly, there's a 'Bard' in scabbard. When King Arthur was offered Caliburn (or Caladvwlch, the Welsh name for Excalibur) from the Lady of the Lake, he was given two choices – the sword or the scabbard. He chose the sword – naturally thinking he would need its magic to defend his people – but he chose 'unwisely', for he who lives by the sword dies by the sword, as Arthur does at the hands of his own son, Mordred. If he had chosen the scabbard, Merlin explained, no harm would have come to him in battle:

> And Merlin said unto Arthur
> you have chosen unwisely,
> for the scabbard is worth
> a thousand of the sword
> for the scabbard symbolises true enchantment.

In the TH White version of the story, Arthur has to learn to use 'Right, not Might' – and we know what it feels like to be living in a world where those in charge use the opposite. The Bard, in effect, has to *be* the scabbard – the peacemaker, the one who heals with his words, for he has chosen the path of words, not swords. In the Welsh Eisteddfod the Chief Bard would traditionally hold up a scabbarded sword and threaten to unsheave it, crying out: "A oes Heddwch!" (Is there peace?), to which the Gorsedd replies "Heddwch!"(Peace). And to this day, no blade is meant to be drawn in a Gorsedd, because it is a gathering of peace. Yet, there is a power and beauty in the symbolism of the sword that transcends its mundane use: apart from their legitimate use of defending what is worth defending, swords are still used ceremonially, for casting circles and knighting people – it can be empowering, as when I was knighted on Solsbury Hill by our modern King Arthur Pendragon.

Words can heal or harm, curse or bless – they are a double-edged weapon and have to be wielded wisely and carefully. And, similarly, air is essential to life on earth. It is one of the planet's most precious resources – so obvious, yet taken for granted. We must do all we can to stop it being polluted, by chemicals and excessive air traffic on a global level, and by excessive noise (noise pollution) and ugly words on a personal level. We should, as Bards, always be conscientious about what we say. The Buddhist's advise 'Right Speech':

> One's speech is like a treasure,
> Speech should be at the right moment in the right place
> Accompanied by arguments, moderation and common sense
> Unless one can say something useful, one should keep a 'noble silence'

If we are to speak, then the first thing we must do is *listen*. I believe the Bard's duty is to 'make sacred the air':

The Poet's Prayer

In silence can poetry be found.
At peace can you listen to the world's sound.
In stillness can you sense its motion.
In humility offer devotion.
To honour creation,
Make sacred the air.
This is the poet's prayer.

Kevan Manwaring

EXERCISES:

1: Active listening. Have a pen and paper handy. What can you hear right now? Don't censor anything. Jot everything down. A list will do, but if you want to include a phrase, or a description then do – try to be observant and precise. We filter out so much, and often hear only what we want to. Listen to your immediate surroundings, to your body, and to far off.

2: Windwalking. Go for a walk on a windy hill top or along a coast and listen to the wind, feel it on your skin, in your hair, blowing through your soul. What is it telling you? What do you hear whispered or roared on the wind? Take mental notes. Write it down as soon as you can.

3: Carving Air. Be aware of different winds and how they affect people, eg: Sou'westerly, Sirocco, Mistral, East Wind, North Wind. It was once believed different diseases and qualities were carried by different winds (as related in the *Hibernica Minora*). There are many sayings about the wind and weather, ie: 'It is an ill wind that blows…' Write a poem evoking a particular wind, choosing one of the directions or seasons. Recite it back to the wind.

4: Castle in the Air. Using your imagination, build your own 'castle' with words: what would it be? See this is a day-dreaming exercise if you like, or as positive visualisation. The Celtic seers used a form of divination known as neladoracht, **Cloud-Scrying**. Gaze up at the sky on a cloudy day. What shapes do you see? What shape are your dreams? Imagine. The clouds are a neutral cipher for your subconscious – a Rorschach test in the sky. Use it for 'imagineering', for envisioning your Utopia and bringing it down to Earth…

Cloud-Scrying

Dathi, King of Erin, was at his residence, Croc-na-Druad [Druid's hill] one Samhain Eve, when he demanded his Druid to forecast events for the next year:

> The Druid went to the top of the hill, where he remained the night, returning at sunrise. He then addressed the king with these words: 'Are you asleep, O King of Erin and Alban?' 'Why the addition to my title?' asked the King, 'I am not the King of Alban.' To which the Druid answered: 'I have consulted the clouds of the men of Erin, and have discovered that you shall make a conquest of Alban, Britain and Gaul, which accordingly he did soon afterwards.

Manuscript Mat. 285, Dublin, quoted in *Taliesin* by John Matthews

Month 2: Threshold Guardians

You should have been using *The Bardic Handbook* for at least a month now. How have you got on? Have you found it easy, challenging, disturbing, reassuring, inspiring? Have you found inspiration? Have you awakened to Bardic consciousness? Does it feel like you have come home to yourself, or an ill-fitting skin? Have your studies been constantly disrupted by one thing or another? This is perfectly natural – when you are trying to cross to a new place in your life (ie: a new job, house, relationship, etc.) you always encounter obstacles: these are known as 'Threshold Guardians'. It could be in the form of an old boss, an interview panel, a school board, your bank manager, your partner, your family…but the worst threshold guardian is yourself. Your own fear or doubts may be holding you back. This is the 'inner policeman' – that voice of authority, of mockery, of failure – perhaps 'programmed' into you from school, from home, from work, from a relationship. Fear not! In New Age parlance, you can change your script. Tear up the old one if it has established negative patterns inhibiting your full potential. You may have been given 'signals' at school that you were no good at writing, or making music, or playing sport. Time to dump those bad messages from the past and move on.

We all have the capacity to learn anything, if we put our mind to it – it is mainly a matter of practise, of dedication, of belief. If you don't believe in yourself, no one else will. It is time to start. As the surfers say: "feel the fear and do it anyway!" You are hereby given permission to succeed, but also the freedom to fail – you don't have to get it right the first time. Make a mess! Play! From our capacity to play we not only stay young at heart, but discover new ways of doing things – while enjoying the process. Play is about being in the moment, being fully present and forgetting one's worries and responsibilities for a while. Don't worry – they'll still be there when you've finished, but you'll feel more refreshed, light-hearted and able to tackle them in a better state of mind. Play frees up stagnant energy – shakes things up a bit, stops us from being a 'stick in the mud' – scrub that: a Sword in the Stone (a powerful symbol of unused potential). It's all about how you look at things.

Throughout the following section you'll be focussing on the Element of Air, associated with the sword, as has been discussed in the introduction (**Spirits of Air**). In the Celtic Mysteries, the Sword of Air is associated with Battle, as referred to in *The Settling of the Manors of Tara,* an old text referring to the divisions of Ireland's five 'quarters'. It's appropriate here in the context of Threshold Guardians. Those that seem to oppose us are perhaps just testing our resolve, our true intentions. Think of interviewers, for instance, the classic contemporary threshold guardians, standing between us and our desire: that dream job, that improved income. Sometimes these Threshold Guardians seem frightening, even hostile, as anyone can be who is protecting what is important to them (ie: a mother bear and her cubs), but if we are 'worthy' (ie: right for the job/of pure intent) then we have nothing to fear. Come from the heart, be adept at what you do, and doors will open. Orpheus was able to negotiate past three-headed Cerebus and walk right into Hades because of his consummate skill.

There is a saying: when the student is ready, the teacher will appear. When you are ready, doors *will* open, ie: you will get phone calls offering you gigs, talks, workshops, commissions.

It is just a case of sticking at it until people start to take interest. Tenacity does pay off.

There are two famous examples of Threshold Guardians from the Irish Sagas. In the first, the hero is not ready, in the second, he is. The first tells of how Cuchullain, the Hound of Ulster, got his name. He was originally known as Setanta. His uncle, Cullan the Smith, was hosting a feast for the Ard-Ri, Cormac Mac Art. Young Setanta, away at a hurley-match, didn't find out about this until it had started. He rushed to Cullan's dun, but his way was barred from entering by the smith's fiercesome wolfhound. With his typical short temper the hot-headed hero killed the guard-dog with one blow of his hurley stick and entered the feast hall. When Setanta discovered he had slain the host's favourite hound he offered to make amends by becoming his 'guard-dog' instead. His uncle declined, but gave him the name Cuchullain, the Hound of Cullan. In time, through his exploits and deeds, he became known as the Hound of Ulster.

This tales shows what happens when you are not ready to cross a threshold. In this case, Cuchullain forced an entry, (normally you would be refused entry, or forcibly ejected) and in doing so became the new Threshold Guardian, not only of Cullan's dun, but of his country. This is echoed by the action of King Arthur, who supposedly dug up the head of Bran the Blessed from the White Mount in London where it was buried facing the coast, in one of the Three Unfortunate Disclosures. He was, in effect, becoming the new Guardian of the Land.

The next story deserves to be told in full from TW Rolleston's classic collection, *Celtic Myths and Legends*, because of the excellent exchange, which emulates a **colloquy**:

Lugh the Many-Skilled and the Gatekeeper

He came, it is told, to take service with Nuada of the Silver Hand, and when the doorkeeper at the royal palace of Tara asked him what he could do, he answered that he was a carpenter.

'We are in no need of a carpenter,' said the doorkeeper; 'we have an excellent one in Luchta son of Luchad.'

'I am a smith too,' said Lugh.

'We have a master-smith,' said the doorkeeper, 'already.'

'Then I am a warrior,' said Lugh.

'We do not need one,' said the doorkeeper, 'while we have Ogma.'

Lugh goes on to name all the occupations and arts he can think of – he is a poet, a harper, a man of science, a physician, a spencer, and so forth, always receiving the answer that a man of supreme accomplishment in that art is already installed at the court of Nuada.

'Then ask the King,' said Lugh, ' if he has in his service any one man who is accomplished in every one of these arts, and if he have, I shall stay here no longer, nor seek to enter his palace.'

Upon this Lugh is received and the surname Ildanach is conferred upon him, meaning 'The All-Craftsman', prince of all the sciences.

It is interesting to note that Ogma, Celtic God of Eloquence, was thought of as their mightiest warrior. Perhaps in his case, the tongue was mightier than the sword.

Threshold Guardians come in all shapes and sizes. You may be having doubts or finding things that interrupt or disrupt your study, the job, the children, the relatives, the washing up, the shopping, the dog… These are what the Buddhists call the 'Ten Thousand Things' that get in between us and Enlightenment – well, in this case, we are not trying to leave the World but fully engage with it, but through following the Way of Awen. Observe what happens when you go to sit down to write, and to read a section of this book, or to work on one of the exercises. Does the phone ring, does the dog need walking, does the kitchen need cleaning, or do all of your pencils need sharpening? These are all displacement activities: be mindful of them. But remember: being a Bard does not exempt you from your responsibilities, domestic or otherwise – in fact it is about living your life responsibly in every way, not least what you say, but how you act, how you 'walk your talk'. If you feel threatened, undermined in your resolve, in belief in your path, then take heart from this wonderful poem. Say it out loud in defiance to all that opposes you:

Quiet

There is a flame within me
That has stood
Unmoved, untroubled through
A mist of years…
I fear no fate nor fashion,
Cause nor creed,
I shall outdream the slumber
Of the hills.

John Spencer Muirhead

Gods of the Threshold

Gabriel, to thee thy course by lot hath given
Charge and strict watch, that to this happy place
No evil thing approach or enter in.

Milton, *Paradise Lost*

Throughout myth and legend there have been numerous Threshold Guardians, some more obvious than others: St Peter at the gates of Heaven; Heimdall guarding Bi-Frost, the rainbow bridge to Valhalla; Bran the Blessed, who said 'let him who is chief be a bridge'; Archangel Gabriel, standing sentinel at the gates of Eden with flaming sword; Charon, the spectral ferryman of the Styx; Barinthus, the boatman of Avalon...although any figure who warns against transgression is, in essence one too, ie: Tam Lin, chiding Janet for pulling a rose at Carterhaugh. Yet not all such guardians are conscientious of their duties. Seithennin is the drunken steward who causes the inundation of Cantred Gwaelod in Cardigan Bay (as immortalised in the poem by Taliesin). He is echoed by the drunken porter in the famous scene from Shakespeare's *Macbeth*, but Threshold Guardians are, by the nature of their role, seldom comical. A sense of humour doesn't come with the job description.

It will be productive to look at the figurehead of Janus, the Roman god of thresholds – perhaps an odd choice for a Celtic-based system, but there have been several stone-heads discovered at Celtic sites, although carved with three faces, rather than two. Illustrative, perhaps, of the Celtic obsession with trinities – but also of their broader, less binary, view of things? This is in direct contrast to, and indeed was at odds with, the rigid, linear culture of the Romans, who conquered by 'divide and rule'. This polarised mindset is called the Law of the Excluded Middle, which denies a third alternative between the polarities of 'yes' and 'no', 'right' and 'wrong', 'good' and 'evil', 'rich' and 'poor', and so on. Our whole (virtual) world is built upon bits of information constructed from this Binary System of ones and noughts. Yet nothing in life is so black and white. It is healthier to go beyond the deadlock of duality, as ex-hostage turned author, Brian Keenan, who more than most knows what it is to suffer under the extremist logic of Threshold Guardians, explored in his novel *Turlough*, about the blind 17th Century Irish harper O'Carolan, triggered by his harrowing experience:

> Janus is the spirit of the threshold, of things both inner and outer, of all beginnings. In its centre is a purifying pool of water where Turlough dips his hands. Those same hands that gave us his music. I think our friend was like his idol. Standing between two worlds looking backwards and forwards, but always looking into the light. And perhaps that is where he is standing now – somewhere between us and the light.

The Roman God Janus gave his name to the month of January, when his festival was celebrated, as the entry in *The New Larousse Encyclopaedia of Mythology* (Hamlyn 1982) explains: "He was honoured on the first day of every month and the first month of the year (*Januarius*) bore his name," consequently he is associated with beginnings and endings as the god who stands at the threshold of the year. He is the perfect icon I think for this moment in history: as the century turns we look back and look forward. This epitomises the Twenty-First Century Bard's ethos of remembering and honouring the wisdom of the past, but keeping an eye on the future, our impact on it, and what we can do to pass on the planet in better shape.

So, for me, Janus represents an awareness of the past, a prescience of the future, and the need to be fully present in this critical moment in history. We are, like the Janus, the threshold guardians – for future generations. It's up to us – so Janus incorporates a sense of moral responsibility and accountability lacking in Post-Modernism. After that movement, and now Post-post-Modernism, there is nowhere that impasse can lead us –

unless we look 'back to the future' - aware of the cyclical nature of Time - and how history repeats itself, and can become a tragedy and a farce, unless we learn from the past.

Here's what the *Larousse* has to say about Janus:

Janus was first the god of all doorways; of public gates (*jani*) through which roads passed, and of private doors. His insignia were thus the key which opens and closes the door, and the stick (*virga*) which porters employed to drive away those who had no right to cross the threshold. His two faces (*Janus bifrons*) allowed him to observe both the exterior and interior of the house, and the entrance and exit of public buildings.

Being god of the gates he was naturally the god of departure and return and, by extension, the god of all means of communication. Under the name Portunus he was god of all harbours; and since travel can be by either land or sea, he was supposed to have invented navigation.

Janus was the god of 'beginnings'. As a solar god he presided over daybreak (*Matutinus Pater*). He was soon considered as the promoter of all initiative and, in a general way, he was placed at the head of all human enterprises. For this reason the Romans ascribed to him an essential role in the creation of the world. He was the god of gods, Janus Pater. Ovid relates that Janus was called Chaos at the time when air, fire, water and earth were all a formless mass. When the elements were separated, Chaos took on the form of Janus; his two faces representing the confusion of his original state.

Most significant of all is this topical resonance, again from *Larousse*: "In the Forum he had a temple whose gates were open in times of war and closed in times of peace...The gates of the temple were rarely closed..." It would seem we live in similar times. Our appointed Threshold Guardians have let us down:

It was told of this temple how, during an attack on Rome by the Sabine Tatius, a Roman woman was bribed by jewels to show the enemy the path to the citadel. But Janus – whose function it was to open a channel for fountains – caused a jet of boiling water to gush forth which stopped Tatius short. On the spot where the water spurted the temple of Janus was erected...

Fire Springs, the storytelling company I'm in, named themselves after the geo-thermal springs that flow up into the Roman Baths of *Aquae Sulis*, modern day Bath in Somerset. And as performers they are not only the conduits for this hot energy (Awen) but also channelling it for others to receive – to be fired up in return.

The Bard is the 'thresholder', channelling the voices of the ancestors and performing a similar function to the head of Bran the Blessed, which continued to speak and sing to his surviving host, and for eighty years entertained them in a Hall with a Forbidden Door on 'Gwales'. The Cult of the Severed Head was widespread across Celtic Europe - not that they were headhunters, although some may have taken heads as trophies, but because they believed the spirit resided in the head. Ancestors' heads were revered and brought out at such times as Samhain, the Celtic Feast of the Dead, so that the tribe could honour and commune with them.

There is an interesting echo of this in the tale of Orpheus, the greatest Bard of Greece, who famously went to Hades and back to win back his beloved Eurydice, only to lose her at the threshold because he turned back to check she was still there... Orpheus, who retired to the mountains to commune with Apollo, Lord of Light, rejecting Dionysus and the delights of women – whose head still sang, after the Bard had been ripped apart by Maenaeds – it floated down the river Hebron to the sea, and was swept up onto the shore of Lesbos, where its voice was finally silenced. In a way the Maeneads were just trying to bring him back into his body: one extreme created another – his rejection of earthly delights led him to being torn apart by women. It is not healthy to deny the body's needs, or spiritual ones. Balance is the answer in all things. Lao Tsu says: "Wise ones seek to avoid extremes and excess," speaking of the Middle Way of Taoism, where all things are equalled in the dance of Yin and Yang. Realising this "subtle interplay", the Master says, is "vital to evolution". Humanity needs to find a balance between its needs and the needs of the planet if it is to survive and preserve the Earth's resources for future generations.

EXERCISES: An Eye to the Future

❖ Research an issue with long-term consequences, ie: Global Warming, and write a song, story or poem about it to raise awareness.

❖ Imagine a future scenario based upon contemporary trends and science, ie: cloning. Create future 'legends' – compose them in verse as if they have already happened.

❖ Use a divination method, ie: Tarot, to look into your immediate future, by gaining a perspective on your current situation and options through the guidance of the subconscious.

The Harp

The harp is the Bardic instrument *par excellence*. For many the Bard and the harp are inextricably entwined, and for some, the Bard's ability to play it is their badge of office. However old-fashioned and even elitist these views now are (see **Being a Twenty-First Century Bard**), we have to recognise the importance of stringed instruments, especially the harp, in the **Bardic Tradition**. The origins of music and the origins of poetry, storytelling and song are closely linked and throughout the history of the oral tradition music has complemented Bardic utterance and vice versa. Now is not the place to go into a full-blooded history of the harp – all that is needed is a brief acknowledgment of its importance, discussion of its musical significance and practical application.

Roman historian Diodorus Siculus spoke of the Celtic Bards as 'lyric poets' who "sing to the accompaniment of instruments resembling lyres sometimes a eulogy and sometimes a satire". He refers to the harp, of course, but his frame of reference was the lyre, the most popular instrument of the Mediterranean – and when one thinks of

The Lamont Harp, West Highland, c1500. Museum of Scotland.

the modern equivalent, pop stars with guitars, it still is today. All popular songs have memorable *lyrics*, which stem from the genre of lyric poetry, which itself originates in the distant past, from songs sung accompanied by the lyre, as was used in Homeric storytelling. The great Classical epics of *The Odyssey*, *The Iliad*, *The Aeneid* and *Jason and the Argonauts* were chanted or sung accompanied by the lyre, as explored in depth in Albert J Lord's seminal study, *Singer of Tales*.

The greatest Bard of the Classical World, Orpheus, was the Son of Apollo, God of Poetry and Music, and was given him the lyre, made out of tortoise-shell. His songs could soothe the beasts and make the trees bend near – it was even powerful enough to allow him entry to Hades' realm and back, and to persuade the Lord of the Dead to let Eurydice, his beloved, return with him – providing Orpheus did not look back as she followed on the long walk out of the Underworld.

Harps are thought to have derived from the hunting bow, which makes a twang as it is fired. Egyptian harps were bow-shaped and strung with eighteen strings. Some were lain flat and plucked, or hammered (as the dulcimer is). Yet their enchantment continues to shoot arrows (of sound) into the hearts of the listener, so they become enamoured, sorrowful, sleepy or 'slain by spirit'. It is a powerful tool in the Bard's 'arsenal'.

In the Celtic Bardic Tradition there were traditionally three main categories or styles of music, known as The Three Noble Strains: the strain of Joy, Sorrow and Sleep. You can use any of these, or a combination in your performances – but maybe save the sleep one until the end!

Goltai; the bitter or sorrow mode (Irish)/*Bragod-gywair*; bitter-sweet (Welsh)
Geantrai; the joy mode (Irish)/*Gan*; song (Welsh)
Suantrai; the sleep mode (Irish)/*Suogan*; lullaby (Welsh)

These mirror the patterns of life, and were connected to the cycle of seasons (*Goltai*, Winter; *Geantrai*, Spring/Summer; *Suantrai*, Autumn). The Three Strains were said to have received their names from the Irish Goddess Boann who – by Uaithnem, the Dagda's harper – gave birth to three musically-gifted children: the first birth was difficult (*Goltrai*); the second was easier (*Geantrai*); and the third brought her weariness and sleep (*Suantrai*).

The Great God Dagda himself once overcame his enemies by playing these modes on his harp, what he called 'The Four Angled Frame of Harmony', one after the other, thereby throwing them into an uncontrollable state of emotion (rather like the scientist Duran Duran's orgasmatron in the movie *Barbarella*!). It is claimed that the *goltrai*, or sorrowful strain, was once played and so stirred the listeners that twelve men afterwards died of grief. In the Welsh tradition, there is the 'bragod-gywair' or bittersweet mode, composed for the funeral of Ivan the Smith. And music has been used in a psychopompic way for centuries, helping souls to pass on (ie: Buddhist Dirges, as in their Book of the Dead, *The Bardo*; or *The Lyke Wake Dirge*). Gaelic harper and contemporary Culdee priestess Fiona Davidson sings one haunting song that is supposed to help someone who has died suddenly to 'cross over': it is meant to emulate the sound of a shoreline bird, a bird of the threshold, and so is suitable for helping someone pass over the borderlands of life and death.

Bardic harper and author Claire Hamilton says: "According to Celtic myth, locked into the harp was the powerful music of the Faerie people, the Tuatha De Danaan". Perhaps that is why musicians talk of the 'soul' of the instrument, although perhaps that spirit originates in the original material, in the wood – could that soul be its dryad? Dartmoor-based musical maestro Nigel Shaw (partner of multi-talented diva Caroline Hillyer) has over the last few years been making flutes out of different native hardwoods, each with its own distinct sound. I heard him play his yew flute at a festival and it was as though the soul of the tree was speaking – he had released its 'soul-sound', its quintessence, or unique 'acoustic signature', the key-note. This relates directly to a deep Bardic mystery: the 'secret name of things', the idea that all things have a secret name, including God, and to know is to have power over it – that is why one has to be careful about revealing one's magical name. It is one's Bardic DNA. This secret name of things is echoed in the story of Adam naming all the animals in Eden. In doing so he was the 'first' Bard (in the Christian cosmology). Adam was pin-pointing their *isness*, and I think it is the duty of all true poets to do this, to find new names for things, new ways of describing things, so we can see things afresh, so we don't become blasé or blind to the beauty around us. Instead of referring to a tree just as deciduous or coniferous, as oak or pine etc., try to describe it as you really see/sense it. What is unique about it? What is its *isness*? Blake said in *The Crystal Cabinet*: "I [strive] to seize the inmost form". This is akin to the idea that Michelangelo's *David* was already dormant within the block of marble, and it took the sculptor to see it and 'release' it. This is connected to the idea of Awen, of drawing something down from the aether, from the Platonic Realm of ideal form, helping it to manifest. Could this be related to the Pythagorean notion of the 'Music of the Spheres' as reprised by Plato, that a Siren sits on each planet: "who carols a most sweet song, agreeing to the motion of her own particular planet" (*Brewers*). Perhaps the universe was once united in Divine symphony, but with the creation of humanity became discordant, so that we must strive for that original harmony, for those first songs, whose distant echo we can sometimes glean…

Music essentially comes down to scales and chords, made of notes, and notes are essentially different frequencies, a spectrum if you like – and identical, in an auditory way, to colour. The scale is a musical rainbow.

Colours 'vibrate' to our eyes in a similar way a musical instrument's strings vibrate when plucked – the only difference is the sense with which it is picked up by, although in certain states of consciousness (ie: under the influence of psychotropics) synaesthesia occurs, when one sense is 'explained' by another. This is a remarkable thing to experience: to be able to 'taste' colours, 'see' sounds; 'hear' smells (maybe that's why strong offensive smells are described as 'noisome'), etc. Sensing the world in this way helps us to experience it in a new way, it helps to reawaken jaded senses and stagnant expectations about life. Poets sometimes use synaesthesia in their poetry, to make an image seem especially fresh and vivid, eg: 'the tang of winter sunlight'; 'the slow glowing of her voice' etc.…

Returning to the rainbow of sound: it relates very directly to the Tantric system of Chakras (Sanskrit for 'wheel') – the seven energy centres of the body, each with a corresponding colour. From top to bottom, Purple: Crown; Indigo: Third Eye; Blue: Throat; Green: Heart; Yellow: Solar Plexus; Orange: Spleen; Red: Base or Root Chakra. Each Chakra has a vibration at which it operates, a note, as it were. That is why we can feel music in different parts of our body during live performance, why it 'plucks our heart strings', makes us 'tap our feet', nod our head, sway our hips and so on – a powerful base you can certainly feel in your very bones, sometimes through the soles of your feet on a dance floor. Such music changes, by increasing or slowing, our personal vibration. It releases endorphins, frees up stagnant energy and 'tunes us up' as well – that's why music is so healing, why we feel so much better after listening to music, be it in a concert, gig, or even just on the radio – in the car, or dancing around our kitchen or living room. And of course this is partly why it is so spell-binding, but also because it can open up gateways, as RJ Stewart explores in his book on magical British ballads; *Where is Saint George?* and in his seminal classic, *The Underworld Initiation.* He explains about how certain notes open certain gateways, and can help us access the Otherworld – perhaps explaining why so many musicians end up there, tragically prematurely, ie: Nick Drake, who wishes: 'not to be tied to an old stone grave in your land of never' in his haunting masterpiece, *Magic.*

Music is at its root, shamanic. The very first music most probably was some kind of percussive instrument, which became the shaman's drum, his 'horse' with which he journeys to the Otherworld in the same way that Thomas the Rhymer journeys on the back of the Queen of Elfland's white steed after she had shaken her 'bridle of fifty silver bells and nine' (many shaman staves and costumes have bells on them – and, of course, rattles perform the same rhythmic trance-inducing function). While True Thomas and his Queen travelled on 'saw they neither sun nor moon but heard the roaring of the sea.' This sea could be the amniotic fluid of the womb, or the roaring could be the sound of blood rushing in one's ear – while in a trance-state. So, music is a powerful enchantment – it can transport us to other worlds, it can 'move' us, excite us, and heal us (see **Ballads**, for tips on song-craft).

EXERCISES:
1. Listening in the Dark
Listen to some harp music, ideally played live by a master, or from a recording in a darkened room. Close your eyes and savour every note – feel it in your body. What images does it conjure up? Write down any impressions immediately afterwards in your journal. Inspired? Recommended: Alan Stivell, Robin Williamson, Fiona Davidson, Claire Hamilton.

2. Combining Words and Music
Try reciting a poem to harp music – if you can't play, then just play a recording and read over the top, trying to fit in with the harmony, the rhythm, the timbre of the music. Now try telling a story over some harp music. If you can play, use at certain points of the story for dramatic effect. Try different moods (The Three Strains). Use it to punctuate and emphasise. Alternatively, work with a musician who can complement your skills as a poet or storyteller. See **Using Music and Sound Effects**.

3. Learning to Play the Harp
Nothing can substitute having direct tuition from an experienced harper, but to get going you could do worse than buying a cheap practise harp and a book or instruction tape. Harper and singer Blackbird Hollins told me how she got started: "I got a tutor

book from the library and took it from there." She says you can 'just experiment' to begin with, discovering and enjoying the sounds the harp can make – almost anything sounds heavenly on a harp (once it's in tune). Try finding different sounds to express various moods. If you know the basics of music, start picking out notes, finding chords, and so on. Here's what she suggests: Take the red strings as a starting point - these are the Cs. Put your third finger on the C string, your second finger on the next but one (E) and your thumb on the next but one again (G). Pluck all together, and you have a basic C major chord. Move your hand up to the black strings, which are Fs. Repeat the same pattern, and you'll find yourself with your fingers on F, A and C - F major chord. Move all your fingers up by one string, and you will be playing G major, with your fingers on G, B and D. Now, the big secret is that almost all songs use that chord pattern. Basically, you've got the chord which is the chord for the key the song is in. This is called the 'tonic'. (If the song is in C, C is the tonic chord. If the song is in Eb, Eb is the tonic chord etc.) If you are playing in C, F is called the 'subdominant' ie: four up from the tonic. G is then the 'dominant', five up from the tonic. Most tunes use tonic, dominant and subdominant predominantly, so if you can find those three chords, you can improvise an accompaniment to almost anything. Actual technique is hard to explain, but I wouldn't worry too much about it. The main thing is that you should enjoy playing. But do try to get hold of a tutor book, which will explain hand position, finger placement, etc. Generally, imagine that you're holding a tea cup – thumbs up, fingers down and the little finger not used! Finally, vary how you play those chords – you can miss one note out, add an extra one in, play one an octave higher, play them as 'broken' (rippled) chords, generally play about with them and let your imagination have a field day.

Master harper Robin Williamson
plays his harp to participants of the first Silver Branch weekend, Bath 2006.

Perpetual Choirs of Song

In the Celtic tradition Three Perpetual Choirs were said to exist in the British Isles, maintaining harmony throughout the land. The location of one of these was in Glastonbury, Somerset, which is widely claimed to be the Isle of Avalon. By telling the stories, singing the songs, reciting poety, we are maintaining these 'choirs' and most importantly our harmony with the land, its spirits and ancestors. Music helps us to attune the Chakras of our body (ie: the healing effects of music if one is 'out of sorts' or 'off-kilter') but also, potentially, the chakras of the land. This is one of the main reasons why the Aborigines of Australia walked and sang the Songlines – to maintain their harmony with the land. By singing something's 'song' you are attuning yourself to its 'vibration' or frequency, its isness, or soul. We need more than ever to live in harmony with the Earth. The songs of the wild and of the world need ever to be sung anew.

EXERCISE: Join a Choir

Join (or start) a community choir, ie: Avalonian Free State Choir. The regular rehearsals and occasional performances are ideal for vocal exercises and experiencing the power of the unadorned voice. See famous choirs and singing groups perform live (eg: The Trio Bulgaria; Welsh Male Voice Choir; King's College Choir, Cambridge; etc.).

Ballads

The ballad form is a 'design classic' of the Oral Tradition, which is easy to use and highly adaptable. Think of it as those old blue jeans, comfortable and long lasting. It is a form so familiar to us – from nursery rhymes to pop songs – that we can slip easily into it, almost like a steady walking gait. This is not surprising considering its been with us a long time and originated in movement: "the word **ballad** comes from the Latin word 'ballare', meaning 'to dance', and was originally a song which served to accompany a dance" (*The Forms of Poetry*, Peter Abbs and John Richardson, Cambridge 1990). Its easy iambic (limping) rhythm is such that anyone could sway to it, and its simple alternating rhyme scheme (usually AB, AB) makes the ballad exceptionally memorable: good news for Bards!

Ballads came out of the Oral Tradition and many were originally composed by ear, before being written down by collectors and poets, who often 'corrected' their rough and ready rhyme schemes and spelling. Abbs and Richardson tell us: "A Scottish peasant woman once protested against a collector of song:

Girl with guitar.
Linocut by Skip Palmer.

> They were made for singing and no for reading
> but ye hae broken the charm now and they'll never
> be sung mair. And the worst thing o' a', they're
> neither right spell'd, nor right setten down."

The reference to the charm being broken is intriguing indeed, and suggests the spell-like quality of song. The ironic truth of the matter is without the diligent efforts of collectors, most famously Cecil Sharp, many of the songs would have been lost to us altogether. Fortunately, many singers and folk musicians have managed to re-enchant the old songs, bringing them alive off the page, or from a crackling recording, once more.

The ballad is a narrative form and many are folk tales in verse, based upon some historical incident – preserved, shared and perhaps sensationalised by the ballad singers. Ballads were, in a way, the tabloids of the day, certainly in terms of their common popularity, (they reached their heyday with the broadside ballads, sold on street corners from the 16th Century to the 1920s) but this does them a gross injustice, for many have true poetry in them, and even enchantment (as singer and author RJ Stewart explores in his books *Where is St George?*, *Magical Tales* and *The Underworld Initiation*). Some of the older ballads are full of magical symbolism and contain deep wisdom.

Hunt down collections, both in book form and audio recordings. Listen to and read *Thomas the Rhymer*, *Tam Lin*, *The Unquiet Grave*, *Down in Yon Forest*, etc. Study their symbolism, use of language, rhyme scheme, metre, structure and tone, and let them work their magic upon you. Nothing is better than listening to a great folk musician live work their spell with the power of their voice and music (ballads are traditionally unaccompanied, but there are masterful exceptions by the likes of Martin Carthy, Ewan McColl, Christy Moore, Kate Rusby, etc.). Try writing your own using the same poetic form, making sure it scans (ie: with the same number of syllables or stresses in each line).

The wind doth blow today, my love,	A	8 syllables,	4 beats or stresses
and a few small drops of rain;	B	7 syllables,	3 beats or stresses
I never had but one true-love,	A	8 syllables,	4 beats or stresses
In cold grave she was lain.	B	6 syllables,	3 beats or stresses

Opening verse of *The Unquiet Grave*, Anon.

The Crane Bag: *Senchus* – Bardic Memory

Long is the path of the sun. Longer my memories.

The Lament of Heledd

Memory is primary to the Bard – as remembrancer of the tribe, it is his raison d'être. In this chapter we will explore this key skill. Its title is taken from the Irish Law Tracts known collectively as *Senchus Mor*, a vast body of texts, many gnomically referring to Bardic lore, such as **The Three Illuminations**. Relevant to our purposes here, it extrapolates upon the oral tradition, in which the ability to recall what one hears is critical, "for hearing is conveying". In a section devoted to *Senchus*, it defines it as: "the storehouse in which this famous knowledge was arranged and treasured up for preservation".

This 'storehouse of memory' seems an early example of the mnemonic technique of 'memory mansions', whereby one can store and retrieve large amounts of information by visualising it being positioned about a house you know inside out, ie: one's childhood home. I continue to have dreams about the house I grew up in. I mention it here because of one memorable dream: there was a cavity under the stairs that was walled up for some reason – ever since, I speculated what must have been there, and began to imagine hidden rooms, secret doors and stairs, in fact an entire 'other side' to the house. It always appeared neglected in my dreams – the furniture was old and covered in cobwebs, the walls were damp, and the rooms were dark. Yet one time I ventured further and further into this labyrinth, which seemed to go on far beyond the confines of our semi-detached red brick house. I passed stone statues festooned with cobwebs. Then I noticed other people (fleeting impressions of people out of the corner of my eye) moving in a 'sleepwalking' way around this maze of rooms. I was not alone. Then, suddenly, the point of view switched to 'God's Eye' and zoomed out to reveal a vast 'dream maze', which, in fact, covered the entire planet!

Now, I interpret this in the following way: the 'hidden half' of the house is my sub-conscious, which I visit in my dreams. But more, my subconscious links up with everyone else's (Collective Unconscious): my 'memory mansion' is annexed to the rest of humanity's, thus suggesting *all* knowledge is retrievable, an idea suggested by the Akashic Record. If this may seem far-fetched, consider how we only use a fraction of our brains. There are whole swathes of our cranium which don't seem to be accessed on a regular basis. Not only is this tantalising in itself (like an unexplored continent – maybe the dream-maze I walked was the grey labyrinth of my own mind) but if we can use a computer analogy for something so organic, it's as though we have a massive hard-drive, with untold gigabytes of unused memory. In theory we could use an awful lot more of it, and I think our ances-tors probably did (thus the vast repertoire of the Bard). In a modern world where we are continually bombarded by trivia and 'info-tainment' it may be more difficult, but not impossible. Life seems more complicated – we have to remember a lot more (more peo-ple, more passwords and user names, pin numbers and protocols), which clogs up our short term memory. However, we can train our brains to retain the information *we* choose, rather than what is imposed upon us by modern life. It's as if Consensus Reality is trying to colonise our consciousness, in the way multinationals wish to control the 'real estate' of Virtual Reality. Our minds are perhaps the last place we can truly be free, where we are only limited by our imaginations. I think Bards have a duty to emancipate people's imag-inations and to show the humble, simple 'power' of the human mind, memory and voice.

The *Senchus Mor* describes what it calls Bright Knowledge: "Tradition from ear to ear, ie: the transmission of bright knowledge to preserve it". The Bright Knowledge, the collective wisdom of the Bards, is like a candle flame or torch, which is passed from teller to listener, teacher to pupil, or 'one master to another'. Our job as Bards is not to let that flame die out. We must be 'torch bearers' and kindlers of the fire in the head in others, so their Afagddu (Utter Darkness) meets its Taliesin (Radiant Brow). This is not about making people 'see the light' but about helping them to find their own light within and to shine. Penbeirdd Taliesin, in *The Hostile Confederacy* says: "The inspiration that I sing I have brought up from the depths". I believe that dormant potential is in everyone: ances-tral knowledge and the body's own wisdom are there to be accessed by all of us. A Bard, in being true to himself, gives people permission to be more fully themselves.

In his modern Bardic epic *Five Denials on Merlin's Grave* (the performance of which is, in itself, an impressive feat of memory) master harper and storyteller Robin Williamson incants the haunting lines: "And I will not forget..." Why should we remember? So we don't make the same mistakes: that we learn from the past, that we honour those who have come before us and endeavour that their lives haven't been lived in vain, that their existence and legacy will not be forgotten. Of course, memory is a way of preserving wisdom, but perhaps it is a form of afterlife – we live on in the memory of our loved ones. A man's life will be weighed against how he is remembered. That is why the Celts were so keen to be seen as generous, hospitable, brave, etc. – they sought renown but by doing so acted to the benefit of the rest of the tribe. Lords hired Bards to compose eulogies upon their deaths, so they would be remembered well. But the Bards were the remembrancer for all of the tribe – their duty was to bring 'healing and alignment', what the Matthews call: "the Celtic shamanic task of the seanachie, the chronicler and the storyteller, as guardian of memory". Before written records it was their duty to know the genealogies of the tribe – out of practical reasons connected to land ownership as much as anything. If the Bard forgets, who will be around to remember the deeds of the fallen, of those who have lived, loved, added to the community? It is our sacred duty to remember.

The story of Mabon and the Oldest of Animals is a brilliant memory tale – about the value of memory, but also a great one to learn, as a feat of memory. I remember the first time I did it, unrehearsed, at a festival. I hadn't planned to do so, and I wasn't sure if I knew it all, but the window of opportunity was there and I plunged in: storytelling is an act of faith, as summed up by the Fool card of the Tarot – the raggle-taggle chancer stepping off the cliff into the void, hoping his blind faith will stop him from falling flat on his face. And almost without fail, it does: your tongue remembers what to do. And the less you 'think' or worry about it, the easier it is. The more you are in the moment the better. If you get wound up, you lose your centre and stumble, so the more relaxed you are the better you'll be. It's not about being 'prepared' but present. Interestingly enough in my first telling of the Mabon it seemed to come back to me as I went on* – I couldn't recall the entirety of the story to begin with, but with each step another 'stepping stone' appeared, another part of the story. This is disconcerting, but thrilling – real 'seat of the pants' storytelling that makes you think on your feet, rather than do something off pat. It's an adrenalin rush, and when it works, it's the best buzz.

*I believe this is an instance of ancestral memory: it felt as though I was drawing upon some vast data-bank, what Jung called the Collective Unconsciousness, where the sum of human experience is stored within the World Mind, aka the Akashic Record. Brian Keenan experienced a powerful instance of ancestral memory (see **Stone Upon the Belly**).

Modern culture diminishes the power of our memory, ie: films, however wonderful are generally fast food for the imagination (certainly the popcorn-selling blockbusters are).

As soon as we leave the cinema we forget what we've seen: the hype and glamour fades and it doesn't leave you fulfilled.

Memory is a muscle which, if not used, atrophies. It is a mysterious and largely uncharted 'zone', but for general purposes is divided into short and long term memory.

The former is for things we only need to remember that day, ie: shopping, washing, etc. – the triviality of modern life. The latter is for precious memories, powerful experiences, painful lessons, tales, song, poems and is akin to the Hard Drive of a computer. We have a vast unused capacity for 'storage'. When we prepare for a show, we 'download' from the long-term memory. The lists and triads Bards used were the menus and file names of their repertoire – allowing retrieval. The title or name acts as a mnemonic trigger for the whole piece. I find I can remember long complicated stories but forget people's names – that's because so much of your short-term memory is taken up before a performance. Being able to remember things is not something exclusive to Bards: we all have a repertoire of hundreds of stories, or anecdotes. We all remember so much, not only personal memories which make us who we are, but all the 'life skills' we need to get by on a day-to-day basis, ie: how to tie our shoe laces, how to boil a kettle, how to cross the road – things we take for granted (unless we are disabled in some way), things that are 'hard-wired' into us, in exactly the same way a poem, song or story can be, until it becomes second nature and you can virtually perform it in your sleep. And these days we are forced to remember so much more. Our memories are cluttered up with brain-numbing trivia: names of celebrities, movies, pop songs, ad nauseam. Quiz Shows test our memory of such trivia, placing a greater value on it than actual wisdom and real knowledge. It's as if they want us to be saturated by it, to not take our eye from the ball, to keep watching, keep consuming... But we can control our diet of trivia or cut it out entirely by not having a TV or buying tabloid newspapers, by not always having the radio blaring, tuned into a pop station – by turning down the white noise of the world... Then we are able to listen, then we are able to remember.

The repertoire and memory of the Bards was legendary. Some stories lasted several nights, ie: "*Sgeul Coise Cein*, the lost story of the foot of Cian...was in twenty-four parts, each part occupying a night in telling", so the *Carmina Gaedelica* tells us: a vast collection of Gaelic material gathered by Victorian folklorists Iain F Campbell and Alexander Carmichael. Carmichael, in an account of one of their field trips, remarks: "The stories and poems which Hector Macisaac went over during our visits to him would have filled several volumes. Mr Campbell now and then put a leading question which brought out the storyteller's marvellous memory and extensive knowledge of folklore." Modern day Scottish Bard, Duncan Williamson, now in his eighties, is said to have a repertoire of thousands of stories. He grew up without formal education, is semi-literate, but the Bright Knowledge runs deep in his veins and he has a vast inherited knowledge of his people.

Retrieving Lost Knowledge

A fascinating anecdote, recorded by John Matthews in his *Taliesin*, relates how it is possible, through a form of ancestral memory to retrieve lost knowledge. In 598 CE Senchan Torpeist, the Chief Poet of Ireland, called a meeting of Bards and storytellers to see who could remember the whole of the great epic *Tain Bo Cualigne* (The Cattle Raid of Cooley). Only fragments could be remembered between them – no one knew the whole epic. Senchan sent two young poets on a quest to find a 'long lost book' said to contain the whole of The Tain. Apparently it had been exchanged for another rare book, but:

> On their way they reached the tomb of Fergus Mac Roith at Magh Aei in Roscommon, and
> there one of the young Bards recited a poem of his own. At once he found himself enveloped

in a thick mist, in which the figure of Mac Roith himself appeared and proceeded to recite the entire Tain over a period of three days and nights.

Presumably the young poets were able to remember this incredible recitation verbatim, and relate it to their peers and master upon their return. It is interesting that it is one of the poet's own compositions which trigger the manifestation of Mac Roith (perhaps suggesting the poet who taps into the Awen is able to channel wisdom beyond his years). Also, the 'thick mist' which enveloped him suggests a kind of sensory deprivation.

In a similar incident, *The Poet's Curse*, a warrior returns from the dead to end a dispute about the way of a battle between liege and Bard.

Perhaps a method of retrieval akin to the one used by the two young poets could be used to recover the lost tales mentioned in ancient Celtic manuscripts? Here are some, listed in Matthews' *Celtic Shaman*, to work with:

- The Fosterage of the House of the Two Vessels
- The Enchanted Hall of the Rowan Tree
- Hound, Son of the Smith
- The Adventure with the Naked Savage
- The Bird of Sweet Music
- How Cormac Got His Branch
- The Wandering of the Empress
- The Quest of the Rock Scarlet

Another approach would be to simply use such titles as a catalyst for one's own imagination and invent new stories. Meditate upon the symbolism, by all means, or simply see where your pen and Muse will take you.

A similar inspiring list is the *Thirteen Treasures of Britain*, first recorded by Giraldus Cambrensis (Gerald of Wales) in the 12th Century. They could actually refer to lost artefacts, and they *do* allude to figures and lore from myth and legend, which can be researched. However, they can also serve as triggers for the imagination:

1. Dyrnwyn (White Hilt) the sword of Rhydderch the Generous
2. The Horn of Bran
3. The Hamper of Gwyddno Garanhir
4. The Chariot of Morgan the Wealthy
5. The Halter of Clydno Eiddyn
6. The Knife of Llawfronedd the Horseman
7. The Cauldron of Dyrnwch the Giant
8. The Whetstone of Tudwal Tyddglyd
9. The Coat of Padaen Red-Coat
10, 11 The Crock and Dish of Rhygendydd the Clerk
12 The Chessboard of Gwenddolau ap Ceidio
13 The Mantle of Arthur of Cornwall

Whether these artefacts actually existed or not is a matter of speculation for scholars. They may all refer to tales or lore lost in the mists of time. However, we can make use of this amazing list as practicing Bards, either to inspire new stories, or as a memory test, and here's how:

- ❖ Find objects to represent the 13 Treasures.
- ❖ Memorise the name of each while staring/handling the object.
- ❖ Place the objects inside a large dark bag or chest.
- ❖ At random, pull the objects, one at a time, from the chest or bag and name them from memory.

Another memory game you can play is placing all of the objects on a table or spread out over the floor on a cloth or rug. Then get a friend to take one away at random while you close your eyes. When you look you have to guess which one and name it properly.

A list is a mnemonic device, but you may want to make it easier to remember such a complicated and obscure list of artefacts by crafting a song around them. This will make it far easier to remember. Think of *The 12 Days of Christmas*. Maybe use that as a framework to build your song around. Alternatively, you may want to construct a larger narrative that weaves them all together (ie: a show with 13 episodes, rather like Heracles' 12 Labours). This could lead to some amusing invention!

A similarly inspiring list is the Four Treasures of the Tuatha De Dannan, mentioned previously:

- ❖ Sword of Nuadu
- ❖ Spear of Lugh
- ❖ Cauldron of Dagda
- ❖ Stone of Fal

These are powerful hallows, and perhaps unlike the Treasures of Britain, *do* exist in a mythic sense (see *Hallowquest*, Matthews, Aquarian 1990). They are there to be restored and worked with. The Druid Network's annual Lammas Games has reinstated the Spear of Lugh as the prize of the Eisteddfod. Will others take up the challenge to restore the others?

Ritual Phrases

Learning something off by heart and performing it from memory may seem a scary insurmountable obstacle to some people, but it is possible for anyone to do it if you know the technique. Here are some devices. The first is described in *Celtic Heritage* by the Rees Brothers: "An interesting feature of the storyteller's art, and a mark of its high antiquity, is the use of stereotyped descriptive passages or rhetorical 'runs'. Archaic and obscure in diction, they are introduced when it is required to describe a hero setting out on his adventures, a battle being fought, or other recognised scenes. They serve to embellish the story and to impress the listeners while affording the narrator an opportunity to be ready with the next step of the story." These stock phrases, such as the Homeric poets used, are linguistic breathing spaces, and provide 'safe ground' between the wilder improvised waters, the more organic extempore sections. These ritual phrases can be incantatory and trance-inducing to both listener and performer – hypnotic in effect, they can send the audience into a different state of consciousness and bring them back again. Also, the use of epithets, ie: 'Swift-heeled Hermes, messenger of the Gods', help to introduce and fix a character in the audience's mind's eye, flagging them up and setting the scene very efficiently. Repeated patterns of actions, or 'chains' (as in the Russian story of *The Maiden Czar* explored by Robert Bly and Marion Woodman in *The Maiden King*, Element 1999) and other mnemonic devices all help to make the Bard's job easier and the tales more memorable to the audience – remember, some may be hearing this 'cold' (for the first time) and need all the help/clues they can get. Reoccurring motifs help to make the story sink in and emphasise certain points. They also allow for audience participation, as the audience becomes familiar with the 'runs' and join in.

My Bardic path started when I began to write and perform poems – especially when I began learning them. A copy of a text (ie: a copy of the poem) can be a barrier between the performer and audience, although some use it as a prop, and there are a few who can carry it off (rehearsed readings help). However, reading seems like a private activity one should be doing in an armchair, not on stage! If you make the effort to learn something *by heart* then the audience is more likely to make an effort to listen – for it is far more impressive than just reading something out. Anyone can do that (disabilities aside – in fact, learning from memory helped a visually impaired Anruth overcome this obstacle). Also, it creates a certain frisson of tension as the audience wonder whether you are going to remember it all, especially if it's obviously your first time and you pause. It's a bit like a tight-rope walk. The audience, generally speaking, is sympathetic – they don't want you to fall, they want you to succeed because it makes a far more enjoyable performance, less painful and embarrassing for all concerned. The other main advantage in actually remembering your words is that you can establish and maintain eye contact with the audience, rather than your page, and it frees up your hands for gestures.

So, how do you learn a poem by heart? By rote, basically – just like in old fashioned schools, and more appropriately, Bardic Colleges – by repetition. There's no short-cut to this, but it's easier than it may at first appear:

> The master first repeated a line, or a quatrain, or whatever was regarded as the unit of verse. The students repeated it after him till they were perfect in pronunciation and intonation. The master then analysed it, explaining its grammatical structure word by word, and setting forth its meaning and the truths which it was intended to convey. When he was satisfied that the pupils had assimilated his teaching, he proceeded to the next section of the composition. In this slow, laborious way we may suppose the sacred canon to have passed from generation to generation.
>
> *RAS Macalister*

This may conjure up the worst aspects of old-fashioned teaching methods in some older readers who can still remember how this was used up until quite recently in schools. Now with the use of calculators and anthologies in exams, it seems the use of memory is no longer being valued as it once was: it has gone from one extreme to the other. Yet there is still mileage to be had from this methodical technique, especially in the idea that: "The students repeated it after him till they were perfect in pronunciation and intonation" (ibid). This is exactly the method I use when learning poems, but I repeat it to myself, not after a teacher – and I have to see it on the page before me to 'fix' it in my mind. Some have the equivalent of photographic memories in terms of hearing – so if they hear something, a word, a phrase, a conversation, they can repeat it word for word. This is a skill which possibly can be developed (like lucid dreaming) although it seems to come more naturally in some than others.

Unlike poetry, which is learned verbatim, stories are learnt in a different way, and we'll look at them later (see **Checklist** and **Climbing the Beanstalk**). Poems have to be learned by heart. 'By heart' is a telling phrase – remember, you are not just learning a poem parrot fashion. No one wants a 'Speaking Clock' version of a poem. So, consider the core emotions of the poem. What is the poet trying to convey? What is the overall mood of the poem? Sometimes it's in the title, ie: *Futility* by Wilfred Owen. Remember this when you perform it. To begin with, you may have to recite it in a mechanical fashion as you learn it, line-by-line, but when you perform it in its reconstructed form, let the Awen come through – the ghost in the machine, the spirit of the piece.

The Stone on the Emperor's Hand: Mnemonic Devices

In *The Dream of Rhonabwy* from *The Mabinogion*, the protagonist lies upon a yellow ox-hide (an echo of the *Tarbh–Feis*, the divinatory bull feast) and receives a prophetic dream. It is incredibly detailed and convoluted and, Rhonabwy himself declares, if not for 'the stone on the emperor's hand' he would have forgotten the lot. This is a mnemonic device, akin to that used in the technique of lucid dreaming, when one visualises one's hands to remind oneself one is dreaming – at which point, one becomes conscious of dreaming and is able, to some extent, to control it, ie: flying, or astral travelling. There is an interesting caveat to *The Dream*…: "This story is called the Dream of Rhonabwy, and the reason is that no one, neither Bard nor storyteller knows the Dream without a book, because of the many colours of the horses and variety of strange colours of armour and equipment and precious mantles and powerful stones" (trans. J Gantz). This tells us a couple of things: firstly, Bards obviously did learn other stories *without a book* and secondly, it is best to avoid complicated stories – for the audience's sake, if not your own. Excessive detail eventually bores an audience: they can't keep track, and it doesn't further the narrative – the pace drops and people nod off! However, there are techniques you can use to help you remember. Some are listed below:

- Alliteration, common in Anglo Saxon poetry, notably *Beowulf*.
- Rhythm, eg: Classic beats, such as a 3 or 4-beat are 'hardwired' into our bodies. As my Native American friend says: 'earthbeat, heartbeat, drumbeat.'
- Rhyme, a classic device. Certain rhyme schemes, ie: the ballad form, are ingrained into the folk consciousness and become the default setting when composing verse.
- Lists, triads etc., ie: The Three Unfortunate Disclosures.
- Images – using vivid imagery helps you to visualise it, ie: "Tyger, Tyger burning bright, In the forests of the night…", "A host of golden daffodils", etc… The more memorable to image, the more easily you'll remember your poem.
- Refrains, a repeated phrase punctuating the verses, ie: "Of those who sailed to Annwn, only seven returned" *Preiddu Annwn*.
- Chorus, a classic song device – but one you can use in poetry.
- Music always makes it easier to remember lyrics as the words are fitted to the melody – remember the tune and it often triggers the words.
- Movement, ie: set hand gestures, postures for different parts of the poem.
- Repetition, ie: "Do you remember the Inn, Miranda? Do you remember the Inn?"
- Visualisation. Visualise the poem and it'll come alive to you (see *Real Property* below)

- Chains of causality, ie: "There was a tree, and on the tree, there was a limb, and on the limb, there was a bird...' (Shaffer, *The Wicker Man*)
- Epithets, ie: 'corn-haired Demeter' (Kirsty Hartsiotis, Fire Springs)
- Stock phrases, ie: 'wine dark sea'; 'rosy-fingered dawn' (Homer, *The Odyssey*).

EXERCISE: Learning a Poem by Heart

1 Choose a poem you want to learn by heart. A great poem is provided below for you to practise with. The first one is also a story (narrative poem) so it could give you a taste of telling one in verse form – which is the way Bards used to recite epics (eg: *The Mahabharata, The Iliad, The Gesar of Ling*).

2 Have a blank piece of paper or card handy, big enough to obscure the poem. Find a quiet space to practise in where you'll be undisturbed.

3 Keeping the first two lines exposed, cover up the rest of the poem.

4 Read out loud the first two lines several times until they sink in. Close your eyes and recite them back to yourself. You have memorised the first two lines.

5 Repeat for the next two or three lines, depending on the rhyme scheme and lineation (sentence breaks). If the poem is in rhyming couplets then recite two lines at a time, finishing on the end-rhyme (the word that rhymes at the end of a sentence).

6 Repeat, until you have worked your way through the first stanza (ie: four, six or eight line verse). Now, without looking at the printed poem, try reciting the first stanza. This may take two or three attempts to run smoothly without stumbling or pausing. When it's set in your memory, proceed to the next stanza and repeat the process 3-6.

7 Half-way through the poem try reciting the first half unaided.

8 When you have reached the end, try reciting the whole poem. Practise.

9 Stand up and recite without the text in front of you. By holding the text, it acts as a crutch which you are more likely to resort to (because you know it's there) than if you put it out of reach. Try it without the 'stabilisers' and you'll find you can do it anyway.

10 When you feel confident that you know the poem – perhaps after at least a day of running through it in your head (although the initial learning of it by rote can only take 30 minutes, depending on the length of the poem) try performing it for a friend or two. It always feels different doing it in front of people, but it's a way of getting used to it, of becoming comfortable being in that space. If it goes down well, try it out at the next public opportunity, ie: an 'open mic' night, storytelling circle, Bardic cabaret. Learn more this way and start to build up a set, and a repertoire.

THE FORM HAS PATTERNED IN MY HEAD

This great poem by Harold Munro sums up the pleasure of Bardic memory for me – it's a great one to learn by heart. And it is an excellent one to visualise.

Real Property

Tell me about that harvest field!
Oh, fifty acres of living bread,
The colour has painted itself in my heart,
The form has patterned in my head.

So now I take it everywhere,
See it whenever I look around.
Hearing it growing through every sound,
Knowing exactly the sound it makes –
Remembering, as one must all day,
Under the pavement the live earth aches.

Trees are at the farther end,
Limes are full of the mumbling bee,
So there must be a harvest field
Whenever one thinks of a linden tree.

A hedge is about it, very tall,
Hazy and cool and breathing sweet,
Around Paradise there must be such a wall.
And all the day, in such a way,
In Paradise the wild birds call.

You only need to close your eyes
And go within your secret mind
And you'll be into Paradise:
I've learnt quite easily to find
Some linden trees and drowsy bees
And a tall, sweet hedge with corn behind.

I will not have that harvest moon,
I'll keep the corn and leave the bread.
I've bought the field, it is my own –
I've fifty acres in my head.
I take it as a dream to bed,
I carry it about all the day…

Sometimes, when I have found a friend,
I give a blade of corn away.

Harold Munro

The House of the Storyteller

The house of the story-teller is already full, and it is difficult to get inside and away from the cold wind and soft sleet without. But with that politeness native to the people, the stranger is pressed to come forward and occupy the seat vacated for him beside the houseman. The house is roomy and clean, if homely, with its bright peat fire in the middle of the floor. There are many present - men and women, boys and girls. All the women are seated, and most of the men. Girls are crouched between the knees of fathers or brothers or friends, while boys are perched wherever - boy-like - they can climb.

The houseman is twisting twigs of heather into ropes to hold down thatch, a neighbour crofter is twining quicken roots into cords to tie cows, while another is plaiting bent grass into baskets to hold meal.

'Ith aran, sniamh muran,
Is bi thu am bliadhn mar bha thu'n uraidh.'
(Eat bread and twist bent,
And thou this year shalt be as thou wert last.)

The housewife is spinning, a daughter is carding, another daughter is teazing, while a third daughter, supposed to be working, is away in the background conversing in low whispers with the son of a neighbouring crofter. Neighbour wives and neighbour daughters are knitting, sewing, or embroidering. The conversation is general: the local news, the weather, the price of cattle, these leading up to higher themes - the clearing of the glens (a sore subject), the war, the parliament, the effects of the sun upon the earth and the moon upon the tides. The speaker is eagerly listened to, and is urged to tell more. But he pleads that he came to hear and not to speak, saying:-

'A chiad sgial air fear an taighe,
Sgial gu la air an aoidh.'
(The first story from the host,
Story till day from the guest.)

The stranger asks the houseman to tell a story, and after a pause the man complies. The tale is full of incident, action, and pathos. It is told simply yet graphically, and at times dramatically - compelling the undivided attention of the listener. At the pathetic scenes and distressful events the bosoms of the women may be seen to heave and their silent tears to fall. Truth overcomes craft, skill conquers strength, and bravery is rewarded. Occasionally a momentary excitement occurs when heat and sleep overpower a boy and he tumbles down among the people below, to be trounced out and sent home. When the story is ended it is discussed and commented upon, and the different characters praised or blamed according to their merits and the views of the critics.

Extract from the *Carmina Gaedelica*, trans. Carmichael

Month 3: Twice-Born

Taking your Bardic Vow and Name

A Way of Awen participant receiving her
bardic name by Glastonbury Tor, 2004.

So far, you have declared your intent to claim your Chair, awoken to Bardic consciousness and overcome Threshold Guardians. Now it is time to make serious your commitment to the Way of Awen. This month you are going to undertake your Bardic initiation, if you so wish. Fear not, this is entirely voluntary and self-led: you are going to choose your own Bardic name and make a vow in your own words, to that which *you* deem sacred. The commitment you choose to make will be exactly that. If you are wary of any such commitments, take heed: for an undertaking to have any real significance and to truly make progress you need to make a commitment, in the same way that unless you 'commit yourself' in a performance it will come across as half-hearted, as in life. If you are serious about becoming a Bard then you need to dedicate yourself, for this is the only way it is going to happen. No one else is going to make it happen for you; they can only help or hinder you along the path. At the end of the day: it is only the hours *you* put in that will pay off, like learning to play an instrument. What you get out of it will be directly correlated to the effort you put into it. It is like making an offering. Yourself. What are you willing to give to the gods?

If you wish to be reborn as a Bard, then you must experience a ritual 'death', which isn't as scary as it sounds, although it is as serious. We are talking about rites of passage here, which normally constitute three parts: 1. Separation or Severance, 2. Initiation or Threshold, and 3. Return or Reincorporation. Such a structure can be seen in everything from a vision quest, first day at school, puberty, examinations, marriage, elderhood, etc. It is also echoed by the threefold structure of Bardic validation as mooted by Iolo

Morgannwg: the Gorseddau of Greeting, Claim and Efficiency. These normally have to take place within an established Gorsedd, (and I certainly believe this should be so when you have reached Bard level) but at Anruth level, I suggest these are equally as valid if done for oneself, either with human or nonhuman witnesses (elementals, spirits, ancestors, gods). Within the format of the 12-month training programme as taught by this book, the three Gorseddau are symbolised by:

1. **Declaring Your Chair** (1st month)
2. **Taking Your Bardic Name and Vow** (3rd month) and
3. **Your Bardic Debut and Accepting Your Bardic Chair** (10-12th month).

In this section, we are going to look at the second stage, the Gorsedd of Claim (see **Anruth Ceremony**).

Anruth Ceremony

This ceremony, the second part of your learning cycle, involves a Bardic initiation and dedication in three parts:
1. **Bardic Vow**
2. **Bardic Name**
3. **Ceremony**

1. BARDIC VOW

When you are initiated in the following ceremony you will take your Bardic vow: to do so start by listing what you hold most sacred; gods, family, planet Earth, etc. Now include them in your vow, starting with your real name, ie: "I, Kevan Manwaring, do solemnly swear in the presence of this Gorsedd on all the gods of the four directions..." Then state your

Bardic ceremony in The Circus, Bath, hosted by the Gorsedd of the Bards of Caer Badon with guests Gorseth Ynys Witrin. Tim Hall, their first Chaired Bard, performs. Summer 2005.

intent, ie: "To honour the Earth, the Goddess, the Muse, to let the Awen flow, to speak with truth and beauty, to follow the path of the Bard..." Practise speaking it out loud. Learn by heart if you can – you should certainly take it into your heart. The more you believe in what you say, the more power it will have.

Bardic Vow [example]

I,.....................................(real name), do swear in the presence of the God and the Goddess, Mother Earth and Father Sun, spirits and elements, and this Gorsedd, to dedicate myself to the Bardic path, using my words to heal, bless, inspire and enchant to the best of my ability, while there is breath in my body. So may it be!
(NB alter to initiate's own words)

---

2. BARDIC NAME

After you have taken your Bardic Vow, you will receive your Bardic Name, as a Twice-Born initiate. It is important that you choose your own. Dream on this; let it come to you from deep within. Is there a deity you closely relate to? A hero or heroine? An animal? Otherwise, be observant – look for signs, often signals from the subconscious, ie: hearing an owl, and noticing the way a willow tree sways in the breeze, may inspire you to use the name 'Owlwillow.' It should sound and feel right – it should reflect the colour of your soul. This is the name of your Bard within. By giving he or she a name, you can awaken and call them to you. See it on one level as a 'stage persona' – imagine yourself as that eloquent, inspired Bard and you will be. It is a kind of confidence trick upon yourself, but will not fool others, unless it truly comes from the heart. Believe in yourself and others will. Take your path seriously, but with a sense of humour and your own fallibility, and if you stick at it, your efforts will be rewarded. There are several famous examples of stars that adopted 'show-biz' names and changed their fortunes. Norma Jean became Marilyn Monroe; Bob Dylan, born as Robert Zimmerman, adopted the first names of Bobby Vee and Dylan Thomas. He started out by playing Woody Guthrie material until he found his own voice. NB: in the ceremony to come, you must use your real (birth) name in the Bardic Vow, *before* being given your Bardic name by the MC.

Finding a Bardic Name

Use a list of gods, goddesses, heroes, etc. (see **British and Irish Gods and Goddesses**) for ideas, but please do not feel constrained by the Celtic pantheon. Choose any culture hero or heroine you can relate to, whether from your own heritage, or the one you most feel drawn to/identify with. Choose with modesty and humility. Living up to legendary names is not easy, although many people are named after saints and prophets, virtues and qualities (as well as cultural icons) – perhaps in the parental hope they will be inspired by the name they possess to embody something of its quality or forebearer. When you have chosen a first name (and I would suggest either questing for it, see **Sitting Out**, sleeping on it, perhaps dreaming it, as in the **Stone upon the Belly** chapter) combine it with favourite colour. And finally, if it does not already feature it, add your power animal (see **Connecting with the Animal Kingdom**), ie: Tallyessin 'Silverwolf'. This is your Bardic name – either keep it private, or use it as a 'stage name', but only when you are ready to launch yourself (see **Your Bardic Debut**).

3. ANRUTH INITIATION CEREMONY

Having composed your Bardic Vow and chosen a Bardic Name you are ready to take the Anruth Initiation Ceremony. Carefully read through the following, so you know what to expect and how to conduct it. In summary it will consist of the following:

- ❖ Preparing Space, eg: ask permission, check for litter, smudge, drum.
- ❖ Casting and Opening Circle.
- ❖ Invoking the Awen.
- ❖ Vow of Kinship.
- ❖ Constituting Gorsedd.
- ❖ Gorsedd Prayer.

- ❧ Taking Bardic Vow.
- ❧ Receiving Bardic blessing and Name.
- ❧ Open Gorsedd (talking stick).
- ❧ Bread and Mead.
- ❧ Closing circle.
- ❧ Tidying up/Grounding.
- ❧ Review – Journal.

Alter the following details, if you wish, but keep to the spirit and general structure of the rite. **NB to participant.** Remember, the following initiation ceremony will make you an *Anruth* (Bardic initiate) not a fully-fledged Bard (See **The Training of a Bard**). It should take place at least 3 months after **Declaring your Chair**, to allow you time to prepare for this serious commitment and symbolic 'rebirth'.

Intent: to form the Gorsedd of...(name of local 'Gorsedd mound'); initiate candidates into the Bardic Tradition; honour the Gods, Ancestors and Spirits of the Place.

Bring: appropriate clothing for the time of year and terrain (eg: sunhat or waterproofs), something blue to wear (eg: scarf, hat, shawl, cloak, or armbands), something to represent each element (eg: candle, incense, spring water, crystal), drinking water, bread or cake, mead or ale, platter and drinking vessel, drum or other musical instrument, talking stick (see **The Silver Branch**), Bardic Vow, camera, First Aid kit, plastic bags for any litter, seasonal flowers for Brighid, ceremony script in transparent sheets or laminated (in case of rain), compass, picnic.

Ideally, you should get a local Druid or Bard to be master (or mistress) of ceremonies. Ask politely, and an offer of a pub lunch, pint, cream tea or other gift always helps (to show respect and reciprocate energy)! Failing that, select an Acting Chief Bard (ACB).

If you wish to, you can incorporate ritual body or face paint into the ceremony. Use blue as the Bardic colour, connecting you to your Throat Chakra and the woad used by Celtic ancestors. Even a couple of dabs of fairy glitter can get people into a different frame of mind and add 'sparkle' to your event. Remember to bring a couple of brushes, bottles of water and maybe a small mirror for this, and wetwipes or tissues for afterwards – or you may get funny looks as you return to everyday reality!

Another staple of the Gorsedd, according to Morgannwg and adopted by Druids ever since, is the Hirlas Horn: "The Hirlas bore three attributes, viz authority or might, the loud voice of the sun and its beneficent effects of causing abundance upon the earth. The Hirlas was the chief emblem of the strength of the Creator through the sun…" Philip Shallcrass, of the British Druid Order, says: "The Hirlas Horn was used by the Druids as a sacramental vessel, out of which they drank the first fruits of the sacred Apples", aka cider, although I prefer mead – the taste of Summer, of the honeymoon. I have used a drinking horn for many years for such occasions and it works excellently.

When candidates have gathered, prepared the space, put on any blue/woad and take off shoes (optional!), the Acting Chief Bard (ACB) begins with an introduction to the site and intent of the ceremony.

The Elements

This is a good warm-up exercise and will help you create the invocations used when casting a circle. You will need pen and paper. Starting with Air, think of all the qualities and correspondences associated with this element. Use word-association, writing down the first thing that comes to you. Write down ten things. Now turn to Fire and repeat, followed by Water, Earth and ending with Spirit. Now choose one that you are most drawn to, that you most need at the moment. If you're a naturally fiery person you may need to invoke water, or vice versa. Write an invocation to this element, starting with the direction. In the Western Mystery Tradition, the cardinal points connected to each element are East (air), South (fire), West (water), North (earth), and the Centre of the circle, above and below for Spirit (see **Orientation: the circle of elements**). Visualise what you are invoking. Do so in a humble and respectful manner – you are not commanding these mighty forces, but asking politely, though you still have to do so with gusto. Include some of the qualities you have listed, and any creatures, places, and gods. End with "Hail and Welcome!" Practise speaking your invocation out loud. Always make sure you banish what you invoke, otherwise you may end up burning your house down, getting flooded, etc. Once I ran a 5 day festival, with each day dedicated to a different element, and sure enough, we got drenched in heavy downpours, a marquee nearly blew away, the site got swamped in mud, and the forest nearly caught fire! These are dragons not to be invited in lightly! Close the circle by thanking the elements and bidding them adieu; "Spirits of the East, thank you for gracing us with your presence and filling us with your power. Go in peace. Hail and farewell!" Join together with four others and practise invoking your respective elements, as a rehearsal for the Gorsedd.

ANRUTH CEREMONY

Introduction

The ACB welcomes everyone and gives a brief introduction to the significance of the site and the purpose of the ceremony. A horn is blown to begin the ceremony, and then he/she says the following:

> ACB: *In the name of Taliesin Penbeirdd, Primary Chief Bard of the West, I, ..., hold this Gorsedd. Let those who wish to be initiated into the Bardic Path, to receive the spirit of inspiration that we call Awen, the Flowing Spirit, step forward to the centre of the circle.*

Align to directions, form circle, join hands.

> ACB: *Let us take the vow of kinship. Repeat after me. We swear by peace and love to stand…*

Vow of Kinship

> ALL: *We swear by peace and love to stand, heart to heart and hand in hand. Mark, O Spirit, and hear us now, confirming this, our sacred vow.*

> ACB: *We have formed a circle with our hands and hearts. Let us now ask for the blessing and protection of the Gods, Ancestors and Spirits of this place by Calling the Quarters.*

Designated participants invoke their direction:

(All face East) Invocation of Air...
(All face South) Invocation of Fire...
(All face West) Invocation of Water...
(All face North) Invocation of Earth...
(Turning to Centre) Invocation of Spirit...(ACB may wish to call upon the Spirits of above, below and centre, or simply invoke the Awen with group)

Invoking the Awen

ACB: *Let us now invoke the Awen, the holy flowing spirit of the Bardic Tradition towards all those here gathered, that they may receive its glowing gifts of clear sight, wisdom and strength of spirit. Visualise the white stream of inspiration flowing into yourself and through you, to energise and inspire not only you personally, but also the* (name of place and region), *the British Isles, and the entire world beyond.* (see **Raising the Awen**)

ACB: *Our circle is cast. Now we will constitute this Gorsedd, witnessed by all those here present, both seen and unseen. Turn and face outwards.*

Constituting the Gorsedd:

ACB: *Repeat after me. We assemble here on this day, the*........(day, month and year).
ALL: *We assemble here on this day, the*............. (day, month and year).
(Continue to repeat with ACB leading)
We assemble in the face of the sun, the Eye of Enlightenment.
We assemble here to constitute ourselves the Gorsedd of.............................(name of local site).

ACB: *In the tradition of the ancient lineage of Bards of this land, and by the authority of those here present, both seen and unseen, I hereby proclaim this sacred Gorsedd of*................. *alive! May it be a meeting place of love and truth and light.*

Let us now proclaim the **Gorsedd Prayer**. *Repeat after me:*

Grant O God and Goddess thy protection...

ALL: *Grant O God and Goddess thy protection,*
(Repeating after ACB)
And in thy protection, strength,
And in strength, understanding,
And in understanding, knowledge,
And in knowledge, the knowledge of justice,
And in the knowledge of justice, the love of it,
And in that love, the love of all existences,
And in the love of all existences,

the love of the God and Goddess, and all goodness.
For Everything that lives is Holy.
So may it be.

ACB: *Now it is time for those amongst you who wish to take your Bardic vows and be initiated as an Anruth on the Way of Awen to step forward, starting from the East of the circle.*

Each candidate stand forward (starting with any in the Eastern quarter, going sunwise) and declares intent to take Bardic vow:

Candidate: *Gorsedd of*.................................., *by your witness I wish to take my Bardic Vow.*

Chief Bard: *Then step onto the sacred Gorsedd mound and speak.*

Candidate steps forward and declaims **Bardic Vow**:

Bardic Vow [example]

I,.................................(real name), *do swear in the presence of the God and the Goddess, Mother Earth and Father Sun, spirits and elements, and this Gorsedd, to dedicate myself to the Bardic path, using my words to heal, bless, inspire and enchant to the best of my ability, while there is breath in my body. So may it be!*
(NB in initiate's own words)

ACB: *You have made this vow before all gathered here, both seen and unseen. Now receive your Bardic name, as Bard of the Gorsedd of*.............................., *and initiate of the Way of Awen.*

ACB: *Bardic initiate, Anruth of the Way of Awen, kneel to the sacred earth and receive your Bardic blessing.*

Candidate kneels.

Receiving Bardic Blessing and Name

ACB with **Silver Branch**:
Wisdom of the serpent be thine.
Wisdom of raven be thine.
Wisdom of valiant eagle.
Voice of swan be thine.
Voice of honey be thine.
Voice of the son of stars.
Bounty of the sea be thine.
Bounty of the land be thine.
Bounty of the boundless heavens.
ACB: *Arise,* ....(Bardic Name). *May the Awen always be with you!*

Step forward now, Bard of (Gorsedd Name), *and take your place within the circle of initiates.*

Initiate joins outer circle. The next candidate steps forward and so on, until all initiated who wish to be.

ACB: *Three Cheers for the Twice-Born. Hip, hip, hooray!*

ACB: *Our circle is now open for bardic contributions.*

Open Gorsedd for poems, stories or songs. Prayers and wishes. Remember to honour Brighid, Goddess of the Bards, the season/festival and any important anniversaries.

Bread and Mead passed around in a clockwise direction, on a platter and in a horn respectively, with the wish *May you never hunger* and *May you never thirst.*

Closing the Quarters:

Maintaining the Circle, all gathered stand facing the directions in reverse order, as those that invoke the elements send them respectfully on their way, ie: *Spirits of the West, in peace you have come, in peace depart. Hail and Farewell*!

1. (N) Earth
2. (W) Water
3. (S) Fire
4. (E) Air
5. (Centre) Spirit

ACB: *Our Gorsedd has ended, but your membership to it does not as long as you so wish. Our Circle is Open but Unbroken Peace to the Spirits of this Place May the Gods Watch Over It.*

ALL: *Long Live the Gorsedd of* ....*!*

Gorsedd of the Bards of Caer Badon,
Wildwood Camp, 2003.

Celebrate! Photographs may now be taken of the celebrants (with permission). Enjoy a picnic if weather clement or retire to a local hostelry, making sure to tidy the site before you go. It should be completely clear of litter, including offerings, and left in a peaceful, cleansed state. Ground yourself with a hot drink and a snack, and write up your experience in your journal as soon as possible.

(With acknowledgements to the British Druid Order and Four Winds)

Voice of the Wind

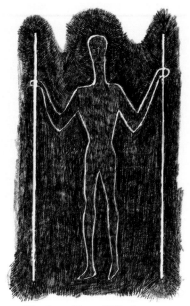

The Long Man of Wilmington.

What is it to speak with the voice of the wind? It is to speak with spirit, or, rather, to let spirit speak through you; it is to have an awareness of breath, of the power of the voice, in silence and strength; it is to make sacred the air, to enchant with your words, to conjure **gramarye**. By mastering the subtlety and power of sound, to be able to make your voice soar to the gods or hold an amphitheatre spell-bound with a whisper: this it is to speak with the voice of the wind.

It is symbiotic with the element of air, and synonymous with the Awen — the flowing spirit of inspiration. Although it is all around us and within we find it initially to the East of our circle, and at the East of the Year – the Spring Equinox, the noon of Spring, after Imbolc's dawn.

We awaken it through meditation, through chanting, intoning and prayer. We feel it caressing our skin, tousling our hair. Let it flow through your fingers as you dance on a hillside. Watch it cat's paw a field of golden wheat, or groom the manes of white waves.

What better place to find it than Windover Hill, overlooking the Long Man of Wilmington, as he strides into the Sussex Weald, or guards the way between the worlds? He keeps the worlds in balance, Spirit and Matter, Gods and Ancestors, as we must do, taking the middle way, the Faerie path – like Thomas of Ercildoune, so we can gain the **Tongue That Cannot Lie**, the gift of prophecy, and become Thomas the Rhymer — the Twice-Born, initiated by the Goddess, as Taliesin was by Ceridwen.

Within our centre we find the truth, as symbolised also by the Vesica Pisces of sacred geometry, famously rendered in iron on the cover of Chalice Well in Glastonbury. We must open up the mandorla to allow spirit to speak. And to speak from the heart. We warm up the breath with exercises so we do not strain our voices, remembering how the Cauldron of Annwn, that would cook food for no coward, was warmed by the breath of nine muses. So, if we are to be bold, as we must as Bards, then we can prepare ourselves by focussing on the breath before a performance, opening up the vocal chords, and invoking the Awen.

With the Voice of the Wind we remember how breath is considered sacred in many cultures, as is the word. It is not to be squandered, or abused. Magically speaking, it is not wise to blow out a candle, or to curse – we should use our gifts to sanctify, heal, enchant and inspire.

Speak with the Voice of the Wind and your whispers shall have as much power as your Sirocco's — why scorch when we can soothe? We must take responsibilities for the vibrations we create with sound and the energy we raise. If we 'sow the wind, we reap the whirlwind.' By becoming masters of our craft we can become Wind Smiths, and forge beauty from thin air. With poetry, story and song we can take our listeners on a magical journey — but their attention is an act of trust – and we have a duty to bring them back safely and satisfied. For without our audience, we are voices in the void. Hone your words with care and people will listen with care, and even delight. What gifts does the wind carry for you?

EXERCISES:

1. Warming up the Voice

The voice is like any other muscle in your body: it needs warming up if you are to use it intensively; otherwise you run the risk of straining it. This exercise, designed to warm-up your voice before a Bardic performance, should be run in tandem with warming up the body (see **The Warm-up**) but try it by itself to begin with. Sit or stand upright but relaxed. Posture is critical – any tension in your body will show in your voice. Make sure your back is straight, chest is out, shoulders are swept back (imagine a 'smile' across your shoulders), your chin lifted up and your arms hanging loosely by your side, hands unclenched. First, take three deep breaths, each one getting deeper and deeper into your diaphragm, in your belly – this is the powerhouse for your breath. If you project from the throat it will severely strain it, and the voice will be weak, but if you project from below, from the belly, then it will be far more powerful – like using bellows to fan a fire. To check you are breathing from the diaphragm, place your hands across your stomach so that the tips of your fingers are touching. When you breathe in, the finger tips should part – when you exhale, they should touch again. Now, on the third deep outbreath, just let out a sound – a sigh, a moan, anything. Take another deep breath, this time, on the outbreath begin to intone – sustain a sound as long as possible. It doesn't have to be in tune to begin with. Slowly modulate the sound, like **Raising the Awen**. You may want to start as low as possible and go higher, or vice versa. See how low you can take it, and how high. You may want to move your arms while you are doing this, ie: raising them upwards as you raise your voice. Now try articulating vowel sounds: A, E, I, O, U. Get those nashers working! Loosen up your chops, by stretching your mouth. Pretend to yawn. You want your mouth to be as supple as possible for the coming performance. Put those dentures in! Make some 'tock-tock' noises, and some 'pops'. Now let's try some consonants, done in tandem to differentiate them in your mouth – this is to help your articulation: 'B D', 'C G', 'P T', 'M N' 'S Z' 'F Th' also practise rolling your R's. You could try a tongue twister at this point. Always fun! Your voice should be getting warmed up by now. Now recite a nursery rhyme, limerick, poem or song – ideally in the space you are performing as a 'sound check', to test the acoustics. NB: remember the acoustics can change with a lot of people present, as I found out once at a medieval banquet – I could be clearly heard in an empty hall, but with 300 diners present it was a different story! This leads us nicely onto projecting…

2. Projection

You want your Bardic words to be heard and to do this you need to *project*! It's a real shame when someone fails to do their lovingly crafted words justice by mumbling them into the page (by not memorising them) or by stumbling on them (by being nervous). Imagine your words as arrows of sound – you want to shoot them across the auditorium, into the hearts of your audience. This can be done in a number of ways – certainly you want to 'throw' your voice, but also use the essential eye contact and body movement (a gesture, such as pointing) to strike your message home. If you don't do this – if you fail to connect with your audience directly, then your words will go 'astray', and just drift off into the aether. It is up to you to make sure your 'message' is received and understood. After you have warmed up your voice using the previous exercise, try a few 'barbaric yawps' (a line of Walt Whitman's, as used in *Dead Poets Society*: see his poem *One Hour of Madness and Joy* – a great one to stretch your lungs to and get you fired up) to get to the top end of your register. Vocally, you need to take command of your space – you want what I call your 'energy footprint' to expand and encompass the entire space. In the next exercise we'll be looking at varying that 'footprint', but for now, fill the space with sound – you want to be heard from the back. Try 'throwing' sounds to the back of the auditorium – imagine them bouncing off the walls. One exercise is to cast a spear of breath as far as possible: stand with one foot forward, take a deep inhalation and, on the out-breath, throw your spear into the distance, letting your whole body follow through, slowly lowering your arms as your breath expires. Another thing you can try is the repetition of a phrase, changing the intonation each time. Now practise a poem or song – with a fellow performer or friend being a test audience for your 'sound check'. Could they hear it alright? Performing a practise number in the space also serves to make you feel at home in it and to boost your confidence before the show. Remember, by breathing from the belly you have the power to project your words. Watch opera singers and notice their posture – how they open up their lungs. Go to the theatre and check out how the actors use their voice. Watch some Shakespeare in the park and observe how the wind and background noise affects audibility and, thus, enjoyment. Notice how some actors (in Amateur Dramatics) can be better heard than others. Voices have different registers – what's yours and how can you vary it? Watch a Town Crier at work. Have a go.

3. Uses of the Voice

As an unaccompanied storyteller all you have to recreate different characters, different landscapes, different times and cultures is the 'unadorned voice.' The voice is an amazingly versatile instrument, and incredibly portable: have tongue, will travel! The Troubadours of Medieval France were known as 'juglares de boca': jugglers of the

mouth, or tongue. You can use your voice to seduce, to impress, to flatter – but be careful not to become a sycophant. Remember the sacredness of words, and as a Bard, if you are not a man of your word, you are nothing. Once you have warmed-up your voice and 'claimed' the space, confident that everyone in the audience will be able to hear you (although test this at the beginning with a quick warm-up routine, an introductory preamble, basic housekeeping, a joke, etc.) it is time to play! You want to modulate the tone of your voice – otherwise it will be monotonous. In your voice you want to echo the peaks and troughs of the story, the arc of your main character(s), the rise and fall of their fortunes, the vicissitudes of fate and the vacillation of their emotions. In this way you are a 'conductor' of the audience's emotions – to a certain degree – and your voice is the equivalent of the conductor's baton and the whole orchestra altogether. It is providing the main 'mood music' for the show. It will signal to the audience when to be sad, when to

The author performing at Priddy.

be happy, when to be frightened, when to be wistful –

it gives them auditory clues, but of course, you have to respect the audience's autonomy. They may not react in the way you expect, and the Bard's position is not one to be exploited. No one likes to be manipulated. However, there is an initial willingness in the audience at least to 'play ball' to begin with — although this honeymoon of good will may not last long if you insult, alienate, mock, or bore them. You need to 'coax' them over to your side – your voice can be coercive, but the great thing about storytelling is its empowering nature: it is asking the audience to make this adventure come alive in their imagination – only they can make it happen in their mind's eye. Stories have 'space' for the audience – and that is why we need to use our 'energy footprint' as performers sensi-

An audience at Rocks East Woodland listen to *Robin of the Wildwood* by Fire Springs, 2002.

tively. We may need to expand it at the beginning to make an impact, to 'net' everyone to take them along with us on our magical healing journey – and at 'check-ins' along the way (see **Audience Participation**) – but then we need to contract it, by quietening our voice. You don't want to bludgeon the audience with your voice and presence – if you shout at people they have a tendency to get offended or stop listening, while if you whisper they are more likely to lean forward, to 'listen in'. Once you have caught the audience's attention you can focus in on smaller details and gestures. You can use the stage whisper, asides, and other tools in the performer's **Crane Bag**.

It makes the audience feel good when they pick up on these subtle things, for it credits them with intelligence and astuteness. At the end of the day, your voice is the 'hook'. It's up to them to bite.

The Voice: Word Magic and the Uses of Gramarye

> She is not of any common earth,
> Wood, water or air,
> But Merlin's Isle of Gramarye,
> Where you and I will fare.
>
> *Puck of Pook's Hill*, Rudyard Kipling

From the day we are born we learn the power of language to summon what we need, to prevent what we find unpleasant, and to express our delight or disgust. This may seem like magic to us as babies – the world bending to our will, until reality bursts our solipsistic bubble – as it must have done to our distant ancestors down the evolutionary tree.

Words and magic have always been linked. Since the dawn of mankind the voice has been considered sacred and has been used shamanically, magically and ceremonially in incantations, cantrips, chants, conjurings, invocations, curses, geasas, blessings and oaths.

The development of language occurred side-by-side with the evolution of mankind.

Those who controlled words had power. Druids forbade the writing down of their mysteries, thus maintaining their control over them, although in doing so they increased the importance and power of memory. Literacy was, until the Education Act of the late Nineteenth Century came in, the preserve of the lettered few, the wealthy elite, or cognoscenti. No wonder, then, that the magical art of 'spells' directly relates to spelling, and gramarye and grimoire to grammar. Paper was not widely available – the *scriptorium* of the monastery was out of bounds to the layman – and books were rare and expensive, as the famous Chained Library of Hereford Cathedral illustrates. Words, and therefore knowledge, was controlled and censored – yet if it weren't for those monks, many of the tales and lore would have been lost all together. The story of the world, how it worked and our place in it, was told to us by the 'Religions of the Book', whose holy texts were the Gospel truth: the actual word of the Divine. The Christian God brought the world into existence through the Word of his will (later Jesus Christ was to become the embodiment of the Word, as God's messenger on Earth): "In the Beginning there was the Word, and the Word was God and the Word was with God." This is mirrored in the Qabala, where the name of God is the DNA of the universe – if anyone could pronounce it, it would unravel. And in Genesis God moves his breath upon the waters, creating life (echoed by the Cauldron of Plenty, said to be 'warmed by the breath of nine muses'). In Egyptian mythology breath is sacred – as were names. Without a name in the afterlife you ceased to exist and so the deceased name was placed upon their mouths – ready for the 'opening of the mouth' ceremony. The gods of communication have carried the torch through history – symbolic wisdom-carriers for humanity: Ptah, Thoth, Hermes, Mercury, to Ogma, Celtic God of Eloquence, who is depicted with listeners chained to his tongue by their ears, a powerful symbol of eloquence, of a captivating performer/speaker, of the spell-binding properties of enchantment, and of a performer with the audience in the palm of his hand, hanging on every word. The voice is the chief vehicle of the Bard's 'message', although there are non-verbal means of communication at their disposal as well (see **Checklist** for **Using Movement** and others). Yet, above all, words can heal and harm, bless, celebrate, transport, defend and satirise. They are powerful things and need to be used responsibly. With this in mind Fire Springs defined the term **Eco-Bardic** in 2005 and draughted this set of guiding principles to work by, a kind of code of practice for Bards (See **Appendices**).

Curses were rightly feared by wielder and target alike. In Wiccan tradition there is the notion of the Threefold Effect, which states that whatever you send out you will receive back three times as much – thus, it is not a good idea to curse anyone or anything. Besides which it goes against the Wiccan Rede: "And it harm none, do what thou will." There have been some colourful and amusing curses through the centuries, perhaps the most amusingly bizarre or disturbing being an Arabic one: "May your left ear wither and fall into your right pocket"! Perhaps the most famous one in history is the enigmatic Chinese curse: "May you live in interesting times." The Celtic equivalent is: "May the sky fall on your head, may the ground swallow you up and may your spirit never find rest!" In his poem, *Journey to Deganwy*, Taliesin utters this curse:

May his life be short,
May his lands be wasted,
May his exile be long
this upon Maelgwyn Gwynedd!

Blessings, like curses, have to be thorough to be effective. The Native American chant *I Walk in Beauty* provides the singer with a kind of fully-covered life insurance: "I walk in beauty, beauty before me, beauty beside me, beauty all around me". Reciting such blessings, or loricas, bestows the protection of the Gods, spirits, ancestors and all good things upon the recipient. One of the most famous blessings is known as St Patrick's Breastplate:

Lorica: St Patrick's Breastplate

I bind unto myself this day
The virtues of the starlit Heavens,
The glorious sun's life-giving ray,
The whiteness of the moon at even,
The flashing of the lightning's free,
The swirling wind's tempestuous shocks,
The stable earth, the deep salt sea
Around the eternal rocks.

Another is this beautiful valediction (see **The Crane Bag: Walking** for the second part):

A Celtic Blessing

Deep peace of the running wave to you,
Deep peace of the flowing air to you,
Deep peace of the quiet earth to you,
Deep peace of the shining stars to you,
Deep peace of the Son of Peace to you.

EXERCISE: Write your own Lorica

Write a protection for you or a loved one or place. Transcribe it or print it onto some good paper (use calligraphy if you can) and frame it.

Colloquy

And long before the tower of Babel fell
and language cracked
there was interchange and colloquy and
conversation upon this world

Five Denials on Merlin's Grave, Robin Williamson

The ritual exchange between two Bards, often in the form of **riddles**, as they try to outwit one another, prove their knowledge, or worthiness for a Bardic Chair is known as Colloquy, meaning: **1.** A formal conference or conversation **2.** a gathering for discussion of theological questions. The classic of this form is *The Colloquy of the Two Sages* between Nechterne and Nede (see Robin Williamson's version, **The Dialogue of the Two Sages**, in the Appendices). These question and answer dialogues are similar to the Socratic Method, of 'dialogues with a master'. One can sometimes channel the wisdom of guides or mentors in this way, by opening up, asking for Awen, putting your question to them and see what comes through – recording it as it happens, either with Dictaphone or writing.

Colloquy played an important part in Bardic training. John Matthews talks of the Bardic Duels when a *Pencerodd* (Chief of Song) won their Bardic Chairs of office through disputation of this kind, as illustrated in Taliesin's poem, *The Contention of Bards*. The Penbeirdd phrases it thus: "With discretion I try the vain poems of the British bards, in contentious competitions, careful as the smith's skilled hammer". One wouldn't want to have gone up against such as Taliesin in contest, although to listen to him in action would have been incredible.

Yet colloquy can be used to restore meaning, as well as deconstruct and debate. Once, the Penbeirdd used his Bardic skills to help heal war-traumatised Myrddin (Merlin), who had been driven mad by a terrible and bloody Battle and had fled into the wildwood of Caledon to live as a wild hermit (*Vita Merlini*). Taliesin talked with the old wizard about the mysteries of the Universe, the great cycles of life and patterns of human existence, thus restoring Myrddin's cosmology and state of mind. This is one of the most memorable examples of the power of Bardic skill – to help heal people. The Bard reminds the listener(s) about the underlying patterns and meanings of life, thus restoring a sense of balance and perspective.

As a Bard the art of conversation should be fostered and honed. All manner of problems are solved simply by being able to talk about them. Sometimes it is enough just to voice one's concerns to somebody, to 'get it off your chest' (**Stone upon the Belly**) and be heard. As Bards we should encourage good conversation firstly by being good listeners. It is not about being witty, but sincere and supportive, although Oscar Wilde honed his wit to a fine art, and left many memorable epigrams or sayings. We can spice up a conversation with quotes, sayings, poems, anecdotes, songs – and even leaven in a little Bardic wisdom, but people don't want to be preached to. You are more likely to be remembered and appreciated if you simply are 'entertaining' in a genuine, natural way: being good with words, but more importantly, good to be around. Erudition and pedantry soon become wearying unless balanced with humility, humour and sincerity.

In this era of emailing and texting, when we are more likely to be talking to our mobile, or staring at a laptop on a train, or a PC in an internet café – talking to someone in a chatroom than the person next to us, the art of conversation may be dying out, so encourage when you can with Bardic soirées, dinner parties, informal gathering, speaking circles, Bardic cabarets and 'open mics'. Strike up a conversation with the person next to you on a bus or in a queue, but be careful not to be annoying or intrusive. Sometimes it is a pleasure just to 'listen in' on a public conversation if it's not too private. Listen to how different people speak, their accents, dialects and cadences – and how much non-verbal communication takes place, how much is conveyed by facial expressions, body language, gestures, etc. Notice those who listen, and those who never do – who talk *at* people, rather than *with* them. Some talk over people, try to drown them out, not letting them have a word in edgeways. Notice how people hear what they expect to hear rather than what is actually said. Notice how some people are never heard and some who don't shut up! Enjoy the babble of human conversation, but don't be drowned out by it. As a contrast, go and sit by a stream or in a wood, and listen to its conversation. Sleep in a forest and be awoken by the dawn chorus. Climb a hill and listen to the wind, stare up at the stars and hear their song – the music of the spheres. And in the quiet of your own room, listen to your heart – what does it tell you? Meditate and channel the wisdom of Elders and Ancestors. Colloquy is still to be found if you have the ears to hear it.

> Dearest friend, and much-loved brother,
> Best beloved of all companions!
> Come and let us sing together,
> Let us now begin our converse,
> since at length we meet together,
> From two widely sundered regions.
> Rarely can we meet together,
> Rarely one can meet the other,
> In these dismal Northern regions,
> In the dreary land of Phoja.

Kalevala, translated by WF Kirby

EXERCISE: Colloquy questions

The questions of Nechterne constitute a kind of Bardic *viva voce*. They can be used for Bardic training in a similar way to establish one's methodology and depth of knowledge.

Write poetic responses to each of these questions, then recite out loud, with a friend or Bardic acquaintance asking the questions, starting with: "Who is this poet, wrapped in the splendid robe, Who shows himself before he has chanted poetry?" Reply in the formal way with the responses "not hard to answer", then continue with your poem.

- ❖ Origins: "Whence have you come?"
- ❖ Identity: "What is you name?"
- ❖ Craft: "What art do you practise?"
- ❖ Practice: "What are your tasks?"
- ❖ Methodology: "By what paths are you come?"
- ❖ Chain of causality: "Whose son are you?"
- ❖ Perspective: "Who is greater than you?"

from *The Colloquy of the Two Sages*

These questions are worth meditating upon. The process of finding your answers to them will prove most illuminating to your path as a Bard. They will help you to reflect upon your practise in a conscious, critical way and possibly provide you with material for a performance.

Riddles

The word 'riddle' comes from the Old English *redan*: to guide, to explain. Riddles are found in the Bible, the Koran and the Sanskrit Rig Veda, and have an equivalent in the paradoxes of the Buddhist koan: the defining difference being a riddle has an answer – often an obscure one, albeit obfuscated by the cryptic description, and sometimes sounding like a double entendre. They seem especially suited to the Anglo-Saxon mind, and became something of a high art form in the Saxon heyday. They are directly related to the Saxon penchant for *kenning*: a kind of Danish equivalent of Cockney rhyming slang, whereby the 'thing itself' is referred to in an elliptical, poetic way, eg: Whale's Road, for sea. They provide an ancient and excellent form of **audience participation**, which works upon ambiguity. Riddles often sound ruder than they actually are – which always provides a source of amusement! They also flourish upon the imagination and wit of the listener. They credit the audience with intelligence and draws people in, from a passive to active state. A question is a great hook to start a story with, to reel the listener in. Hence the perennial popularity of quiz shows! *Storm and other Old English Riddles*, translated by Kevin Crossley-Holland, (Macmillan 1970) has many excellent riddles to draw upon, eg:

> I watched four fair creatures
> Travelling together; they left black tracks
> Behind them. The support of the bird
> Moved swiftly; it flew in the sky,
> Dived under the waves. The struggling warrior
> Continuously toiled, pointing out the paths
> To all four over the fine gold.*

EXERCISE: Write your own Riddle

Writing a riddle is like writing a poem – and the two are closely related – because both avoid stating the obvious, and brilliance shines through the vividness of the imagery and originality of metaphor, because riddles are essentially extended metaphors, where one thing is not just likened to something else (a simile, ie: 'the harvest moon was like a knob of butter in the sky') but actually conflated with it (ie: 'the harvest moon was a knob of butter in the sky'). A metaphor is more intimate, immediate and powerful. Its primal ancestor was the sympathetic magic of the first hunter-gatherers. The painting of the bison on the cave wall wasn't just a likeness of the animal; it was, for the purposes of the ritual, the animal. Try it out on a few friends. If they guess it too quickly then make the metaphor more obscure. Incorporate a riddle or a riddling game into a story, as Tolkien famously did in *The Hobbit*. TA Shippey's superb scholarly book, *The Road to Middle Earth*, explores this famous exchange in great detail. I use a riddle in my version of Taliesin, when the young Bard is tested in Maelgwyn's court and must prove his mettle. It gets the audience involved, and when they guess it they feel smarter than Maelgwyn's court, who did not!

*Answer: *Pen and Fingers*. The 'bird' is the quill, the 'waves' the ink, and the 'fine gold' the manuscript.

Tips for Writing Riddles:
1. List attributes of the subject/answer.
2. Describe as poetically/imaginatively as possible. Be lateral. Check classic riddles for ideas.
3. Choose the best descriptions. Rewrite as a poem. Be economical and cryptic. Try out on people. Do they get the answer straight away or not at all? Adjust accordingly: add/remove clues.

Solar Festivals: The Equinoxes

As we move around the wheel of the year, we will look at the eight festivals of the modern Bardic calendar and explore their associations and meaning: for the themes of each can provide ideas for material, either through the traditional corpus, or by inspiring you to write a new poem, song or story for it. And by working with, rather than against, the tides of the year we can harmonise with the forces of creation and capitalise upon the cyclical energies of ebb and flow inherent in the land and in the aether. Everything has its season and it is wise to attune to the window of opportunities that each affords.

Solar Festivals (the solstices and equinoxes) are astronomical rather than agriculturally-linked celebrations (although the latter, the **Fire Festivals**, are obviously influenced by the orbit and tilt of the Earth as well), fixed to the movements of the Earth about the Sun. The summer and winter solstices are respectively, the longest and shortest days, (and correspondingly the shortest and longest nights) while the equinoxes are times of equal night and day, as the name suggests.

In this chapter we shall look at equinoxes. For me, the equinoxes symbolise relationships and balance: they are the two points of the year of equal night (equi-nox) and day, although the Spring Equinox in the Northern Hemisphere is the *turning point*, not the start of Spring (**Imbolc** signifies the beginning) after which the days will start getting longer and the evenings brighter. At the Autumn Equinox the opposite occurs: from then on the nights will become longer in duration than the day, the evenings draw in and winter is in the wings. Both epitomise a still-point of equilibrium before the shifting of emphasis.

The balance of the equinox is embodied for me by the enigmatic figure of the Long Man of Wilmington overlooking the Sussex Weald. The 231ft chalk giant wields what look like two staves – possibly the sighting poles of a Neolithic surveyor, as has been suggested by Ley-pioneer Alfred Watkins – although he could also be holding open a doorway. The figure is cut out of the side of Windover Hill, part of the barrow-pocked South Downs – which form a barrier between the Weald and the English Channel. Could the Long Man be guarding the threshold of England, or perhaps even the threshold between life and death itself? However, the Long Man's power resides in his ambiguity – he acts as a cipher for whatever we project onto it – and androgyny. Unlike his ithyphallic counterpart, the Cerne Abbas giant in Dorset, the Long Man is sexless and featureless. Of course, this may not have always been the case – details may have been eroded or altered. But we have to work with what is there. It seems a good icon of balance and tolerance – for if it wasn't for the goodwill of the monks of Wilmington Priory over the centuries it wouldn't be there. Indeed, a local folktale (Dru the Windsmith) suggests it was the monks who cut the figure out of the chalk in the first place. Another local legend associated with it suggests there was once possibly a female counterpart to the Long Man, an 'Eve' to his 'Adam'. This tantalising idea inspired me to write my Earth Mystery novel *The Long Woman*.

Harmony needs to be established between the sexes. The relationship between the genders should be one of equality, trust and respect. We should endeavour to manifest this in microcosm in our 'marriages' (with partners, girlfriends, boyfriends, wife, husband, significant other) and in a macrocosmic way in the world – equality in the workplace, etc. But in an internal way the work goes on – whether you have a partner or not. We should aspire towards a Chymical Wedding within ourselves: the marriage of the feminine and masculine sides of our personality.

There are so many wonderful stories, songs and poems about relationships it's almost too obvious to mention. You could say *all* stories are about relationships: between families, strangers, lovers, allies and enemies, different cultures, places, animals, the real world and otherworld, the living and the dead, good and evil, young and old...and all the myriad dualities of the universe.

At the time of the equinoxes it is good to be mindful about relationships of all kinds in your life. Explore and express them through your stories, songs and poems. Research classic myths and legends, or write your own – reflecting upon and honouring the relationships in your life.

If you are experiencing extremes at the moment now is the time to find balance, ie: overwork, overeating, overdrinking, and so on. Meditate upon the image of the Long 'Man' of Wilmington, or even better visit it – or another appropriate spot like Watersmeet in North Devon for instance – where two rivers flowing off of Exmoor meet in a beautiful wooded gorge. Become this figure of balance – if you are feeling buffeted by opposing forces, it is essential to find your centre. To be at one with yourself. The alchemical process of the Chymical Wedding is explored in the brilliant Whitbread Prize winning book of the same name by Lindsay Clarke, and also in the books on alchemy by Jay Ramsay (*The Alchemy of Love*, O Books, 2005). There are an awful lot of self-help books out there about relationships – because an awful lot of healing needs to occur. But the best thing of all to do is to talk. I see the equinox as a perfect time for communication, for agreements and partnerships of all kinds. Energetically, the equinox is a 'level playing field.' Use its evenness to establish a firm foundation in unstable times.

VESICA PISCIS

Another symbol of the equinox and of balance between the worlds is the *vesica piscis*, a form of sacred geometry created by two circles overlapping creating a third space, an almond-shaped interstice called a mandorla. It appears in sacred architecture all over the world, but most famously appears in the beautifully designed wrought-iron cover for Chalice Well, Glastonbury – a liminal zone, perhaps leading to Avalon. The symbol is worth meditating 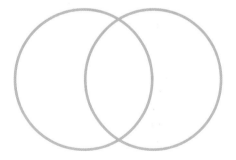 upon, because it is in itself a gateway. Lindsay Clarke sees it as a perfect symbol of the imagination: the mandorla representing the space where the outer and inner worlds overlap. Bards can access this zone through the Awen, and can create it in performances through the enchantment of their words and music. Holy days such as the eight festivals are threshold times when the veil is thinner between this and the Otherworld, so more conducive for this journeying. Shows at such times are especially powerful.

Although the equinoxes are similar, being the extreme swings of the pendulum of the year – both create the neap tide, responsible for the Severn Bore and other tidal anomalies – there are differences, apart from the obvious seasonal ones. The Spring Equinox signifies turning outward, the Autumn, one of turning inward (see **A Bardic Year**: Quickening and Gathering). Work with these tides, rather than against them, in your Bardic activities and you will have the energy of the season behind you.

Quarterly Review

Time to take stock and look back over what you have learnt so far. Browse your journal and reflect on what you have experienced, what skills you have gained. You are an Anruth! Do you feel different? By now you should have a good understanding of the Bardic Tradition and what a Bard is, understand and be able to raise the Awen, have at least one poem and know one tale (Taliesin) – although if you have composed or know more, excellent. You should aim to write one poem and learn one tale a month to develop a repertoire. You reviewed the first month, focussing on Spirit, already. In months 2 and 3 you should have looked at:

- ❖ Spirits of Air – exercises: active listening; windwalking; carving air; castle in the air.
- ❖ Cloud-scrying.
- ❖ Threshold Guardians: Gods of the Threshold.
- ❖ The Harp: exercises.
- ❖ Perpetual Choirs of Song.
- ❖ The Crane Bag: Senchus – Bardic Memory.
- ❖ The House of the Storyteller.
- ❖ Retrieving lost knowledge; Lost Tales; Mnemonic Devices; Ritual Phrases.
- ❖ Learning a poem by heart.
- ❖ Twice-born: Anruth ceremony. Bardic Vow and Naming.
- ❖ Invoking the Elements.

- ❖ Voice of the Wind.
- ❖ Exercises: warming up the voice; projection; uses of the voice.
- ❖ The Voice: word magic and the uses of gramarye.
- ❖ Loricas and curses.
- ❖ Riddles.
- ❖ Colloquy.
- ❖ Solar Festivals: Equinoxes.

Celebrate! You have come a quarter of the way around the **Wheel of the Year**, along your path to becoming a Bard. Well done! May the Awen keep flowing.

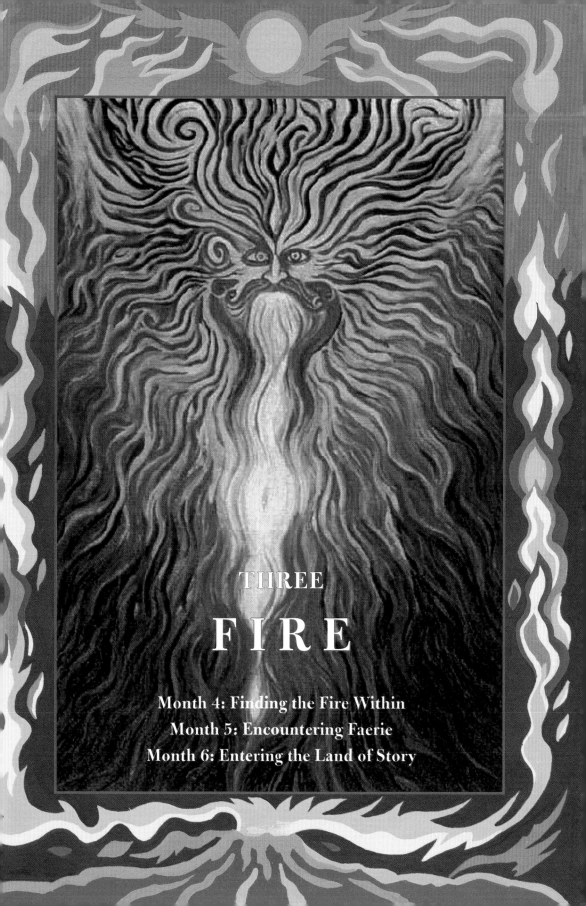

THREE

FIRE

Month 4: Finding the Fire Within
Month 5: Encountering Faerie
Month 6: Entering the Land of Story

Spirits of Fire

We now turn to the South in our circle of the year and invoke its spirits. This direction is traditionally associated with fire, the element of passion, of transformation, of spontaneity and light. It is inhabited by wild creatures of myth: Djinns and Efreets from the Arabian Nights, the resurrecting Phoenix, fierce fire-breathing Dragons…It is an element associated through fire with Bel, the Bright One of the Beltane fires; with Lugh the Long-Armed, the Many-skilled, with his deadly spear that would always find its target, and with his Welsh counterpart, Lleu Llaw Gyffes, Lion of the Steady Hand, who was himself killed by a spear made over a year and a day. The Sun God must die in his prime like the first sheaf of wheat, to be turned into bread and beer – his goodness shared amongst his people in a pagan communion, an annual cycle embodied in the birth and death of Sir John Barleycorn. His tale is mirrored in the rise and fall of all Solar Deities, of Apollo, Christ, Balder and Bladud – a local version of a universal hero. Yet also, when we turn South, we think of the warmer Southern hemisphere, of the hot spice-laden sirocco, blowing across Spain from Africa, of that vast continent's myriad riches; and, furthest South, of the Dreamtime of Australia and the songlines of the Rainbow Serpent – mirrored in the dragon lines of St Michael – shining across the land, from St Michael's Mount to Glastonbury Tor and beyond. All high places dedicated to the light are connected with the Spirit of Fire: the beacon hills and churches, the tors, May Hills and holy mountains. Climb high and commune with the light.

Fire is sacred to many cultures. Imagine the power of the first fires flickering in the primal darkness, holding the night at bay. No wonder it was held in awe and thought of as coming from the gods – certainly it did, in a sense, through lightning, probably the cause of the first fires and the inspiration to the first fire-makers. Watching a tree hit by lightning explode with superheated sap, or burst into flames, must have put the fear of God into early man. Whoever knew the mysteries of firemaking would have been held in deep awe. Promethean-like, they were the first magicians, for magic is about transformation and fire transforms: dark to light, cold to hot. It can turn a cheerless night into a merry one, cook food, scare predators, clear forest, bake clay, create glass, smelt and temper metal. Yet it fosters spiritual transformation as well – either by the insight gained gazing into the flames, the purging heat of a sweat-lodge, or the cathartic ritual of a fire-walk.

The Celts considered fire so sacred they based their ritual calendar upon it: the four **Fire Festivals** of Samhain, Imbolc, Beltane and Lughnasadh, as explored throughout this book. Each of these festivals was based around a sacred fire.

Fire can be one's ally or enemy. It must be treated with respect, for the devastation it can cause is terrible, from a house fire to the fire bombings of Dresden. Like all powerful things, in itself it is neither good nor ill – it is how it is used or abused. That is why it's essential to initiate the young into the mystery of fire, so they know how to use it wisely. In certain tribes the young men would be taken away and shown how to make fire. These rites of passage would probably involve fear and pain of some kind – not that I'm advocating either, but it did serve to teach the young men a healthy respect for something which could inflict fear and pain: it taught them empathy.

Fire and its light are often seen as a symbol of consciousness, illumination or revelation – the burning bush through which God communicates with Moses being the most famous example. However, in Celtic mythology there are numerous instances of mystical fire, such as the 'flaming wheel' given to Cuchullain to guide him through the Land of Shadows from a mysterious stranger who turns out to be his father, Lugh, the sun god. He had given his son his own sun to guide him through the darkness. Yet not all symbolism

Sacred Spring overflow, Roman Baths, *Aquae Sulis*.

is as straightforward as this. In the *Mabinogion*, in the tale of Peredur, there is the startling image of a 'tree half aflame and half in leaf', a dreamlike image that perhaps symbolises conscious and subconscious, or the two hemispheres of our brain, or perhaps the paradoxical duality at the heart of Celtic culture, a visual koan. In Bath, Somerset, the hot springs sacred to the goddess Sulis were said to be heated by 'fires beneath the water', the idea of which inspired my troupe of storytellers to call themselves Fire Springs. We aspire to draw up this fire from within and light it in others. In Kildare there was the famous perpetual flame of St Brighid, kept alight by the priestesses. In a similar way, Bards must be torch-bearers – keeping the ancient fires alight and passing on their mystery.

The Fire Festivals

The Celts had four great festivals, marking the agricultural year. Although the majority of us do not live in the countryside, work with livestock, or work on the land, we can still relate to these agrarian festivals by considering our own harvests: what do we wish to sow, to reap; what have we gained, what do we need to let go of? Attune to these life-patterns along the Way of Awen. Once tapped into soon you will not be able to deny these physical and psychic tides. They are galvanising, nourishing and inspiring.

The Celtic day started at dusk the night before – with midnight being considered the centre of the day, which illustrates the mindset of the Celts: the time of magic and dreams, midnight, being the axis of their day, like ever-present Annwn – and the threshold time was paramount, when the veil was said to be thin between the worlds. These festivals are powerful threshold times. They celebrated each festival for three days, if not longer! Here's a brief précis of each festival, but it is best if you find your own correspondences and significances, by research and observation:

Imbolc, January 31st- 2nd February
The Beginning of Spring. Now the first inklings of your winter dreams will start to show, like the snowdrops emerging from the thawing ground. A time of peaceful meditation and cleansing, preparing the ground for the coming year. Exorcise those winter blues with candle light, flowers, Spring blessing and dressing. Go on walks. Time to get out into the land once more.

Beltane, April 30th-May 2nd
The Beginning of Summer. Celebrate the joy of nature's bounty with rites of fertility and merry-making in the greenwood. Leap the Bel-fire with your beloved. What was seeded in the depths of Winter should now manifest in all its glory. Time to shine in the sun.

Lughnasadh, July 31st-August 2nd
The Beginning of Harvest. The cutting of the first sheaf and the baking and dedicating of a symbolic loaf or cake to the spirit of the grain. Work collectively to gather in your harvest. Enjoy the shortening golden days and reflect upon what you have learnt. Time to take stock and raise a glass to Sir John Barleycorn.

Samhain, October 31st- November 2nd
The Beginning of Winter. The end of the agricultural year, yet in its ashes the birth of the new. Cattle were driven between two bonfires to ward off evil spirits, as they were taken from their summer to winter pasture. A nervously critical time, when livestock was culled, meat salted and harvests carefully stored. Winter suffers no fools – you must be ready for the darker, harder months ahead. Stay indoors. Turn to the hearth. A time to commune with the ancestors and dream of the coming year.

There are many **stories** and **ballads** based around these High Days in Celtic literature – not surprising considering they were popular opportunities for tale-telling, being important tribal gatherings. Research and collect stories for each, as well as devising your own poems and songs, to build up a year-round repertoire. (See **The Wheel of the Year**)

Month 4:
Finding the Fire Within

Bright King Awake Within…
From a gleam in the eye of night
to a star on the brow of day.
Rise and shine,
spark to pyre.
Pentagram, man,
breath to fire!

Awakening the King, Kevan Manwaring

We all have a fire within us. It is the Divine Spark we are all born with, that fragment of Creation – literally, if you consider that, as carbon-based life forms, we are made from the ashes of dead stars – that gives us the power of what Tolkien called 'Sub-Creation': 'we can make in the image in which we're made.'

What is it that fires you up? What are you passionate about? These 'favourite things' should act as catalysts for your poetry, stories and songs – by using them as themes, starting points, subjects – because by sharing what we are enthusiastic about we really shine. Not surprising when you consider the word enthusiasm comes from the Greek *en Theos*: the god within. When we are inspired we become in-spirited, filled with Awen. Enthusiasm can carry us along in a performance – and it's infectious. It will rub off on the audience, as they imbibe your energy when you talk about/perform what you are into in an animated way. When people are in their power, and speak from the heart, they really shine. They are taken over by the radiant brow of Taliesinic energy.

Passion transcends ability. It is better to be coming from somewhere sincere and authentic, speaking about something with integrity and honesty, rather than just doing something off pat, technically perfect, but soulless. Of course, crafting your words and making them shine is better than muddling them, presenting something half-prepared and not doing them justice. We should all aspire towards excellence, towards fulfilling our potential. But the fire has to start with the first spark, and it is important to retain that, to remember the core emotion – of wonder, anger, sadness, joy, etc. – when we rekindle it each performance. It becomes painfully obvious when the 'spark has died'. We need to cherish it like the sacred flame it is. Never put out another's flame, but always nurture your own. As a Bard you should be able to 'fire people up' with your passion, and set their spark aflame. In this section we will be looking at ways of speaking with the voice of the fire and using the element of fire in different ways.

EXERCISE: Write a Fire Poem
Compose a poem or song with 'fire' as the theme, be it about a candle flame, bonfire or inferno, the cold fire of distant stars, a warm hearth's glow or the passion of the heart.

The Wicker Man

Fire in the heart, fire in the head –
Our wick is so short,
Long live the dead...
Torch my tinder, set me ablaze.
Divining sparks skyward rise.
Turn my lead into gold,
Alchemical treasures untold.
Tribal warmth, selfless light,
Dancing the darkness, waking the night.

I am the Wicker Man,
Burning up inside.
Hollow shell,
Nothing to hide.

I am the fuel of my own bonfire,

Let my life be my pyre.
Not to have lived fully
Is the only death.

I want to burn brighter
With my every breath.
Leave these wooden bones in a heap,
With wild flames I want to leap.

I am the wicker man,
Raise my cage to the ground,
Energy is never lost, it goes around.
Losing my skin, the infinite within.
Turning on the inside sun.
Shining brighter in the shadows,
And basking in the glow of the burning now.

Kevan Manwaring

Voice of the Fire

What is it to speak with the voice of the fire? In the *Colloquy of the Two Sages* the young Nede's reply suggests an answer:

> Not hard:
> Very small, very great, very bright, very hard.
> Angriness of fire,
> Fire of speech,
> Noise of knowledge,
> Well of wisdom,
> Sword of song,
> I sing straight from the heart of the fire.

So, it is to speak with passion, from the heart, with enthusiasm, to be overflowing with Awen, to be 'on fire' – in a Christian sense to be filled with the Holy Spirit, to be even speaking in tongues? By speaking with fire we shine, and by giving off bright energy (the 'shining brow' of Taliesin – a fully-opened third eye) we make the audience feel good, as they bask in our joy. This relates back to the shaman's healing dance not only for his patient but for the good of the tribe.

Often, in our performances we find ourselves 'heating up', perspiring and becoming breathless. Sometimes, we get carried away as we are consumed by our own performance – not in an egotistical way, but rather an egoless way – as we are taken over by the story, song or poem. Our material transports and transforms us (in a similar way to how a shaman's chant induces a trance and carries him between worlds). It's exhilarating, and all we can do is hold on and enjoy the ride, the rush – it's like holding onto the dragon's tail as it flies up into the air, or down into its lair. Wild and breathtaking! This is the magic moment when the tale tells and reinvents itself. New phrases spring into our mouths. We are caught up in the moment and find ourselves saying witty or even inspired things off the 'top of our head'. This contrasts with the painful times when one feels thick-tongued and leaden. It's akin to being the logs before they have caught fire – wooden. Yet one spark can set them alight – if the 'kindling' of material is prepared.

So, go in with a bang – do a favourite, something you are confident with, to get the energy going, and to relax you into the role, so you feel comfortable on stage. You've got to warm yourself up, as well as your audience. Try breathing and body exercises – **warm up** those vocal chords. Then on stage get the audience to raise energy by clapping, stamping, cheering, laughing, jumping, and so forth. Call-and-response works wonders – the 'crick? crack!' of Caribbean storytellers is the classic, electrifying the air before the story-storm breaks (see **Audience Participation**). Of course, **riddles** were the Anglo-Saxon stock-in-trade and are excellent ways of engaging an audience. Alternatively, start with a bold statement, rhetorical question or paradox, which you then set out to explore or explain, eg: "It is said the world would end if a day goes by without mentioning the hero Fionn Mac Cumhail's name," or "What do women want?", or "There once was a god of love who could not love."

When we speak with fire we are in our power. We say what we mean and mean what we say. We speak with integrity and passion. We don't mince words. We speak our truth.

We use short sentences, assonance, alliteration and rhythm to speed up the lines, with jaunty metres and snappy rhymes like bass guitar and drums to accompany our lyrics. Our delivery becomes fast and furious, with staccato pulse – hard consonants like gunshots. Pow! Pow! Pow! Our metaphors are fiery, and our message is punchy. We speak with fury – yet don't be a hellfire preacher, be careful not to scorch. Balance this passion with compassion (see the **Shining Word**). Our presence exudes *duende*, the magnetism of the flamenco dancer or matador, as we declaim with utmost determination and poise. Let rip! Blow people off their feet. But remember to breathe deep – the air feeds those flames, those tongues of fire. Build slowly to the point of combustion and then 'erupt', a volcano of bright and flickering words that hypnotise and energise: rise to a crescendo like an inferno and leave your listeners dazzled and panting for more. That is how to speak with the voice of the fire.

EXERCISES:

1. Raising Chi

This is a good way of raising energy for a performance as well as keeping warm! It can be done sitting down or standing up. You just need to be relaxed: roll your shoulders, stamp your feet, etc. You may want to jump up and down or shake your limbs to free up any stagnant energy. Place your hands on your stomach, tip to tip (as before in the 'breathing from below' exercise). Take a deep breath from the diaphragm. Imagine it blowing fire onto the 'coals' of your Chi until they glow. Your Chi – the powerhouse of your body – is located around the centre of your stomach, just below your belly button. It is connected with the Solar Plexus, so visualise it as a yellow ball of energy. Take another deep breath and 'fan the flames' again, feeling the glow spread through your body. Finally, one more deep breath, picturing your Chi glowing bright yellow. You should be feeling warmer now and charged with Chi! If you're ever bitterly cold, (ie: standing on an icy platform waiting for a train) this can really help!

2. Fire Magic

Light a real fire: in your hearth, if you're lucky enough to have one, in a brazier, chimanea, log burner, or in nature – if you have permission from the landowner/abiding by byelaws, and you know what you're doing. There's nothing more magical than a real fire. It is utterly spellbinding, soothing, romantic and inspiring. Gather the necessary materials with care. If you collect firewood from a local woodland, then gather only dead wood, and always ask the dryads. A good folk saying is: "Old lady of the Woods, may I have some of your goods, so that when I become a tree, you may have some from me." Pay attention to the type of tree you are gathering wood from. Different woods burn differently, as the famous 'firewood' poem explains, listing the characteristics of each in a useful mnemonic of rhyme. Coniferous firewood generally spits, and greenwood, which you shouldn't be picking, also creates lots of smoke. Prepare the fire pit/hearth scrupulously. Make sure you have some water nearby in case of emergencies (and some lavender oil for burns). Build a small nest of kindling; then place on top a pyramid of thin sticks. Have larger branches at hand. Then light the kindling. Respectfully invoke a fire god as you light the fire (but remember to thank it and banish it afterwards!). Making a successful fire is an act of sustained will. You have to give it your utmost attention. It can raise a sweat. As the saying goes about firewood, it warms you twice, if not thrice: once in the chopping, then in the carrying, finally in the burning. Gaze into the flames. Consider how long it took for these trees to grow. How many seasons, how many years? The wood is stored time – in a fire it releases it very rapidly and lets out tremendous light and heat, in the same way that as a Bard you spend many months researching, developing and practising material, to let it out in performances in one 'burst', shining with Awen. Scry the flames. What do you see in the different colours, the flickering shapes, the glowing embers? And what do the crackling, hisses and spitting tell you? If you are outdoors at night you'll be very aware of the vast night around you, the forest coming alive…What spirits do you feel are present? Start trying to vocalise them, with a low chant. It does not have to have words at first – just express how you are feeling. Use instruments if you can, or hand claps, clicking, movement. Mirror the dance of the fire in your body, your voice. Feel the fire rise within you. If you are with friends, then raise the energy – run around the fire, leap it (carefully!), make love by it, sleep and dream by it (but not too close!). Tell stories by it, communing with your ancestors, with the first storytellers around the first fires. In the morning write down what you sang, how you felt and how you feel. Try to capture the memory in poem or song. Prepare a good story to tell for next time. If you made a fire outdoors then dowse the embers, scatter the ashes (when cold) and restore the turf – leaving the site as you found it or better, without litter. Thank the spirits of the fire and the grove. Leave a little bio-degradable offering (some bread, nuts or fruit) that the local denizens will appreciate!

3. Protest Poem

What fires you up? Write a list of things that make you angry, and ones that you are passionate about. It may be a cause you particularly relate to, one you wish to defend, or protest about. It could be a local tree being cut down, a motorway bypass destroying a beauty spot or ancient monument, racism, exploitation of immigrant workers, abuse of asylum seekers, famine, conflict, globalisation, etc. Unfortunately, it's likely to be a long list. Choose one and research it thoroughly. Get your facts right before sounding off. If you still feel the same, then compose a protest poem or song about it. Try to express something of the complexities of the situation. Nothing is ever purely black or white. Practise it and perform it at any suitable opportunity – a protest rally, demonstration, open mic night, or eisteddfod. Remember, the power of your message will depend upon the inspiration of your words: the better/more amusing/clever/satirical your lyrics and polished your delivery the more people would be willing to listen to your performance and heed what you have to say. For ideas, listen to some of the classic protest songs of the Sixties (Dylan, The Doors, Joni Mitchell, et al) as well as more recent ones by The Levellers or Seize the Day, among others. Here's my anti-GMO poem:

The Child of Everything

I am the Child of Everything -
do not play with my fire!
I defy your modifications -
mutations not in isolation -
their consequences will be dire…

I am as old as creation,
I am the genius of genesis,
I am the seed of paradise,
I am the dancing serpent-twin,
I am the fruit of knowledge,
I am the sap of the world tree,
I am the pulse of the planet's heart,
I am in everything under the sun.

I am the Child of Everything -
do not play with my fire!
I defy your modifications -
mutations not in isolation -
their consequences will be dire…

I am the grit in the oyster,
I am the gleam in your ancestor's eye,
I am the quick of the dead,
I am the dew on the divine web,
I am the spawn in the gene pool,
I am the fingerprints of parents,
I am the pollen on the breeze,
I am the eye of the storm.

I am the Child of Everything -
do not play with my fire!
I defy your modifications -
mutations not in isolation –
Their consequences will be dire.

Using Passion

Passion transcends ability. It is better to stand up there in your truth, saying what you mean and meaning what you say from the heart, in the heat of the moment, than presenting a technically perfect, but lifeless, performance. Always remember: what is the core emotion of your piece? Tap into it throughout your performance. Sid Vicious sang: "Anger is an energy!"

Use it to defend what you believe in. Seize the **Spear of Lugh** and be a firebrand! Here's a fine example below, from ancient history, (the Druidesses' 'frantic rage of the furies') to the passionate response of Hemans, a Victorian female poet.

THE LAST STAND OF THE DRUIDS
Tacitus reporting on the destruction of the Druid sanctuary at Ynys Môn ('Mother of Wales', modern-day Anglesey,) by a legion led by Seutonius Paulinus, 61 CE:

> Women were seen rushing through the ranks of soldiers in wild disorder, dressed in black, with their hair dishevelled and brandishing flaming torches. Their whole appearance resembled the frantic rage of the furies. The Druids were ranged in order, calling down terrible curses. The soldiers, paralysed by this strange spectacle, stood still and offered them-selves as a target for wounds. But at last the promptings of the general - and their own rallying of each other - urged them not to be frightened of a mob of women and fanatics. They

advanced the standards, cut down all who met them and swallowed them up in their own fires. After this a garrison was placed over their conquered islands, and the groves sacred to savage rites were cut down.

Druid Chorus on the Landing of the Romans

By the dread and viewless powers
Whom the storms and seas obey,
From the Dark Isle's mystic bowers,
Romans! o'er the deep away!
Think ye, 'tis but nature's gloom
O'er our shadowy coast which broods?
By the altar and the tomb,
Shun these haunted solitudes!

Know ye Mona's awful spells?
She the rolling orbs can stay!
She the mighty grave compels
Back to yield its fettered prey!
Fear ye not the lightning-stroke?
Mark ye not the fiery sky?
Hence! - around our central oak
Gods are gathering-Romans, fly!

Hemans

The Crane Bag: The Three Illuminations - *Teinm Laida*

DEFINITION:
- ✤ Chewing of the Pith
- ✤ Illumination by Song
- ✤ Decoding by means of Verse

DESCRIPTION:

The chief poet, ie: the learned poet who explains or exhibits the great extent of his knowledge by composing a quatrain without thinking…[extempore composition] At this day it is by the ends of his bones he effects it… And the way in which it is done is this: When the poet sees the person or thing before him he makes a verse at once with the ends of his fingers, or in his mind without studying, and he composes and repeats at the same time…but this is not the way it was done before Patrick's time…[then] the poet placed his staff upon the person's body or upon his head, and found out his name, and the name of his father and

125

mother, and discovered every unknown thing that was proposed to him, in a minute or two or three; and this is Teinm Laegha… (sic)

Senchus Mor

Practise reciting this fiery poem out loud and put passion into your performance:

One Hour of Madness and Joy

One hour to madness and joy! O furious! O confine me not!
(What is this that frees me so in storms?
What do my shouts amid lightnings and raging winds mean?)
O to drink the mystic deliria deeper than any other man!
O savage and tender achings! (I bequeath them to you, my children,
I tell them to you, for reasons, O bridegroom and bride.)
O to be yielded to you whoever you are, and you to be yielded to me in
      defiance of the world!
O to return to Paradise! O bashful and feminine!
O to draw you to me, to plant on you for the first time the lips of a
determined man.
O the puzzle, the thrice-tied knot, the deep and dark pool, all untied
      and illumin'd!
O to speed where there is space enough and air enough at last!
To be absolved from previous ties and conventions, I from mine and
      you from yours!
To find a new unthought-of nonchalance with the best of Nature!
To have the gag remov'd from one's mouth!
To have the feeling to-day or any day I am sufficient as I am.
O something unprov'd! something in a trance!
To escape utterly from others' anchors and holds!
To drive free! to love free! to dash reckless and dangerous!
To court destruction with taunts, with invitations!
To ascend, to leap to the heavens of the love indicated to me!
To rise thither with my inebriate soul!
To be lost if it must be so!
To feed the remainder of life with one hour of fullness and freedom!
With one brief hour of madness and joy.

Walt Whitman

The second of the Three Illuminations is often confused with the first, **imbas forosnai**, but whereas that is a "wholly interior act", according to Caitlin Matthews, **teinm laida** requires a staff or wand, or some other external prop or mnemonic device. However, it is related etymologically: both *forosnai* and *teinm* allude to 'bright', or 'burning'. Perhaps this is not surprising when we are dealing with two methods for tapping into the Awen to find answers. Both are "shamanic methods for the recovery of lost knowledge" (CM). They both bring light to an endarkened subject, hence their collective name, The Three

Illuminations. What is interesting and challenging to a Bard is the idea of extempore com-position – one of the trickiest things to pull off well, although HipHop artistes excel at it. The Awen really does have to be with you to make improvised composition work, but as we have been exploring, Awen is something that can be summoned and channelled. These prophetic utterances are identical to those chanted by the sibyls and oracles of ancient Greece and Rome to pilgrims or heroes keen to discover their destiny, eg: at Delphi or Dumae. These oracles often worked in shady, enclosed spaces, and sensory deprivation is another technique associated with this method, eg: when the head of the poet DonnBo fulfils his obligation to his liege even after death and sings for the hall when placed facing the wall, 'so that it might be dark for him.' This has echoes of that famous singing head of Celtic myth, Bran the Blessed, which entertain his surviving company for eighty years in a darkened chamber. Of course, the head of that chief Bard of the Mediterranean, Orpheus, continued to sing as it floated down the River Hebron, all the way to the shores of Lesbos, until finally silenced by the Gods. The cult of the severed head is particularly strong in the Celtic lands, with many blank-eyed stone heads staring enigmatically at us from the ancient past. One can imagine the heads of enemies or ancestors being brought out at sacred times for consultation or propitiation (ie: Samhain) and perhaps the custom of carving pumpkins into grinning skulls and illuminating them with candles is a legacy of this, albeit one that migrated to America (with Celtic emigrants?) When Hamlet famous-ly picks up the skull of Yoric, the Royal Fool, in Shakespeare's play and utters those immortal lines, maybe we have an echo of the ancient ritual practise of **teinm laida**. The use of a wand or staff is interesting – rather like a doctor's forceps, feeling the chest of his patient. Could the custom of using a Stang, a Y-shaped staff, for divination – by placing the tip on the earth, and one's brow between the Y be another legacy of this method of Bardic detection?

EXAMPLES:

1. The blind poet Lugaid arrived in Bangor, North Wales, one day and was shown an unknown skull, and was asked whose head it was. Lugaid laid the end of his poet's wand upon it and declaimed: 'The tempestuous water, the waters of the whirlpool destroyed Breccan. This is the head of Breccan's dog; and…Breccan was drowned with his people in that whirlpool.'

2. Finn was brought the headless body of a warrior. To identify who it was, he 'put his thumb into his mouth, and he chanted by tenm laido (sic), 'illumination by song', and he said:

> He has not been killed by people –
> He has not been killed by the people of Laighne –
> He has not been killed by a wild boar –
> He has not been killed by a fall –
> He has not died on his bed – Lomna!

> Cormac's *Glossary*

Finn correctly identifies the body as belonging to his Fool, Lomna the Coward, who had been murdered under orders from Finn's wife, who did not want her infidelity revealed.

EXERCISE: Hot Penning

Apart from being a literary **teinm laida**, this exercise has a lineage in artist Paul Klee's method of 'taking a line for a walk', and the 'automatic writing' devised by the Surrealists as a way of tapping into the subconscious. More recently it has been called 'hot-penning'. It is about enjoying the journey, not just the destination. This philosophy frees us from goal-driven activity and 'getting it right' first time. Masterpieces never arrive fully-formed. The true master is the perfectionist who is never satisfied with initial efforts, realising they are just part of the creative process. Often one does not know what to write until one begins writing, as E M Forster expresses when he says: "How do I know what I think, until I see what I say?" The activity creates the framework for the Awen to manifest. In this way, writing is a divinatory exercise – a kind of teinm laida as we place our 'poet's wand' on the blank page and begin to scry the sub-conscious. Writing is a good way of getting a perspective on things, and working out our feelings and thoughts. Hot-penning overcomes the dreaded Writer's Block, and the fear of failure generated by the expectation to produce something of merit immediately. To be a writer, write! Just make marks on the page – it will loosen you up, and allow the Awen to flow. Creative play gets the synapses firing and allows 'happy accidents' to happen.

As with the voice and body, it is essential to warm up first. This exercise also serves as a good 'palette cleanser', before you begin in earnest. It gets the creative juices flowing and exorcises all that 'white noise.' You'll need a watch or clock handy, a pen and several sheets of blank paper. Make sure you are comfortable and you're holding your pen in a supported position. Now, for twenty minutes, write – without lifting your pen from the page and without pausing. Don't censor, don't edit what comes out: just write, and keep on writing, no matter what gobbledigook comes out. You're not aiming for quality here, but quantity (bearing in mind Julia Cameron's affirmation from *The Artist's Way*: "Great Creator, I will take care of the quantity. You take care of the quality"). Just keep writing and fill page after page. The idea is to free up your subconscious. At first you may just be writing down the stuff floating around in the front of your brain (shopping, lunch, sex, TV, traffic jams, the boss walking in, boyfriend walking out, feeling embarrassed, etc.). This is the white noise that drowns out the Awen most of the time. Download it onto the page and it frees up space for good stuff to come through. As you reach deeper into your sub-conscious interesting, vivid, bizarre, disturbing and arresting images or phrases may emerge, as they do unwarranted, unbidden, in dreams every night (whether you remember them or not, we all dream. We have to, to keep us sane, as researchers into sleep deprivation have discovered – it's not  the lack of sleep that disturbs your mental state, but lack of dreaming). In a way, the mind 'hot-pens' every night, so in theory we all should be 'naturals' at it. It's just about letting go. After twenty minutes are up, relax. If your wrist is hurting give it a little rub, and make yourself a cup of tea. Now scan through your hot-penned pages. Amongst all that 'garbage' there may be gems, an image or expression, the diamond in the coal. Even if at the end of this exercise you have only one good phrase it will be worth it.

Month 5:
Encountering Faerie

Rhiannon, by Briar.

The Faerie of Celtic Tradition are not the saccharine creations of Victorian whimsy, but the Lordly Ones, said to be the Tuatha de Danaan of Ireland who literally went 'underground', into the hollow hills, as their mythic culture was overwhelmed by actual history. Yet the people of Faerie are still to be found everywhere, wherever the spirit of place is alive – and perhaps this is what they embody, the elementals of tree and spring, flower and hill; or maybe there is an order of creation, from the tiniest plant deva to the 'angels', or genius loci, of region and planet. Whether they are the old gods, ancestors of the land (as in the aboriginal Picts) or anthropomorphisms of place, there are many who vouch for their reality. Only the most insensitive would disagree that a sun-dappled bluebell wood has distinct enchantment about it, or a rainbowed waterfall a certain magic.

Following the example of Yeats' Wandering Aengus, who "…went for a walk in a hazel wood" we are going to do the same in the hope of an encounter with Faerie; bearing in mind they are notoriously elusive and more likely to come when you are not looking, than when you are! Once, as a young poet, I journeyed to the Scottish Borders, to the Eildon Hills made famous by the ballad of Thomas the Rhymer, and slept out on them – but did not have as much luck as he! Thomas of Ercildoune lay on Huntlie Bank, on the Eildon Hills, and spied a 'lady both bold and bright' come 'a-riding down by the Eildon Tree' – the Queen of Elfland herself. He accepts her summons to Elfland, agrees to a geas that he utter no word of what he sees and journeys with her there for seven years, receiving the Tongue That Cannot Lie: the gift of prophecy. After this shamanic initiation he returned to the Scottish Borders where his prophecies made him famous and his poems are still known, centuries later.

In the same way as True Thomas's initiation by the goddess, Pwyll, Lord of Dyfed first beheld Rhiannon on her white horse, while sitting on the sacred mound of Gorsedd Arbeth. Contact with Faerie often is associated with being in threshold places (springs, groves, hills) at threshold times (dawn, dusk, full moon, solstices, May Eve, Samhain Eve) and in threshold states of mind (ie: the hypnagogic state between waking and sleeping). This is no coincidence, for at such times the veil between the worlds is thin, the subconscious can burst through into the conscious and Faerie can appear and summon us.

As a young child I remember being told not to be out after dark. I was playing on a neatly turf-covered reservoir, which to my overactive imagination looked like a fairies' rath with its little ventilation chimneys! I still recall the frisson of fear and delight as I found myself still playing there at twilight. And in that littoral moment, when I half-expected the People of Peace to appear and snatch me away, I felt something *did* open up – a little doorway into Sidhe, which hasn't closed since. Perhaps entertaining the possibility is enough to make it exist in a quantum way: each fork along the road of our lives creates another world where some part of us takes that 'road less travelled'.

And, later on, as a wistful art student on a field trip to Bogglehole, Robin Hood's Bay, along the dramatic North Yorkshire coast, I remember going for a walk in the woods that surrounded the hostel, finding a quiet spot and sitting in a meditative state as it grew dark. At the time I was practising TM, so I sat legs crossed, back straight, eyes closed, hands laid gently on my knees. After several minutes in this position, in absolute stillness and silence, I sensed movement in front of me. Returning to consciousness, I slowly opened my eyes to behold a badger staring me right in the face. It had been sniffing me curiously, perhaps wondering if I was a threat. As soon as it sensed my sentience, it ambled off into the undergrowth. I felt blessed.

I suggest we can encounter Faerie in an everyday way, by sensing the numinous in the mundane. Blake famously saw angels crowding the crown of a London tree, and was able to "see a world in a grain of sand, and heaven in a wild flower". Poets, artists and naturalists are able to see the awe and wonder of nature more accurately than most by training their perceptions, but you too can 'see things as they truly are' by opening your senses and sensing fully without preconception, by sensitizing yourself to your surroundings and walking lightly on this Earth. It becomes painfully obvious when a place has lost its spirit, through environmental damage of some kind (industrial or domestic pollution, tourist erosion, over-exploitation of resources, etc.). We can re-enchant many of these places by simple acts of conservation – stream-clearing, litter-picking, tree-planting – and Bardism, such as story walks. Respect the spirits of the place and they will return their blessings manifold.

EXERCISE: Waiting for Faerie

Go to a quiet spot in nature, in a bluebell wood, by a spring, a waterfall, a grove of hawthorn, a sacred hill; meditate and see what emerges, taking care to let someone know where you are (or choose a 'buddy'/sentinel and have them watch over you/hold the space). Be respectful and ready for surprises: the Otherworld may make its presence felt in unexpected ways. Faerie is a notoriously perilous realm, as indeed it has been called in medieval times. Make sure you have a sure way of getting there and back again, a ritual gateway saying, such as:

"By the spirits of this place I ask for safe passage. I come in peace. May I return in peace."

Drumming, rattle, the shaking of the silver branch, can all act as triggers – to send you on your way, and to call you back. This exercise is about preparedness: it's about being in a certain state of mind, rather than expecting too much. Be fully present, use all of your senses and simply pay attention. Faerie may appear in unexpected ways: a robin may alight on your rucksack, a damselfly may rest upon your hand, a fox may skulk past, a stag may suddenly appear. A bird song may break the silence; or a feral bark in the gloaming. Listen to the messages of nature. What is it showing or telling you? Remain still and calm and simply listen and observe. Do not respond unless prompted. Stay with the energy as long as possible – hold the gaze – and wait until the encounter has definitely concluded before you do anything. When you leave, thank the spirits of the place.

Touch base with yourself and your buddy: how are you feeling? Write down first impressions immediately into your journal. It has been mentioned previously, but this cannot be emphasised enough: after such experiences it is essential to ground yourself, literally by stamping your feet, and by some kind of refreshments to bring yourself back fully into your body. Otherwise you run the risk of having an accident, by not returning your consciousness fully to present awareness, thereby not synchronising with this reality. I have often found things missing after a rite or a visit to a sacred site if I have not made an offering. There's an old warning: Never Test the Crew that Never Rest!

Fire in the Head: Inspiration and Composition in Poetry

As Bards we should engage with the mysteries of poetry, so we can not only recite but also compose it, and use poetic techniques in song-writing and in storytelling. The process of creating poetry may seem complex or esoteric to some – and like Bardism, the further you go in, the more there is to find – but it is possible to pen a poem knowing only the simplest elements of the craft. Although I don't believe you can 'write-by-numbers', I do believe that, like dance, drama or music, poetry skills *can* be taught. The scope of this book will not allow me to go into this in depth, but I shall use a famous example to explore the creation of poetry, an example which serves as an extended metaphor of the Bardic path itself.

The Song of Wandering Aengus by William Butler Yeats remains, like many of the poems of this master bard, a perennial classic. It gives us a model for the creative process, and gave birth to the immortal phrase that sums it up so

Green Man, symbol of creativity.

well: 'fire in the head'. This is the moment when we are filled with Awen, a flash of inspiration, and *have* to write it down. It has its literary antecedent in a phrase from the Song of Amairgen: "I am a god who forms fire for a head" (Graves), or "I am a God who fashions fire in the mind" (Matthews, after Macalister, Hull, Cross and Slover). This, I think, is a cipher for inspiration, or even the creative impulse itself: the spark of creation. Dylan Thomas echoes this in his memorable phrase: "the force that through the green fuse drives the flower". It is the primal procreative urge of life, as embodied in the Green Man. It is salient that Aengus/Yeats, possessed with 'the fire' (be it Awen, anger or amour, he does not specify), communes with nature, finding, if not solace, then, at the very least, release and transformation for this powerful force:

> I went out to the hazel wood,
> Because a fire was in my head.

So, in the first sentence, the poet gives us a clue as to the poem's origin. Even though the 'first person' is Aengus himself, we can surmise this is a persona of Yeats', one of his many masks. Crossing the threshold is a significant act – entering the primal wood is akin to entering the subconscious. Welsh poet David Jones explores these "…vast, densely wooded, inherited and entailed domains":

> It is in that 'sacred wood' that the spoor of those 'forms' is to be tracked. The 'specific factor' to be captured will be pungent with the smell of, asperged with the dew of, those thickets. The venator poeta cannot escape that tangled brake.

Going for walks is a common way of finding inspiration; it clears the head and gets oxygen to the brain. It was an approach popular with the Romantics, eg: Wordsworth and Coleridge wandering lonely as clouds over the Somerset Quantocks or the Lake District (see **Walking**).

We may be 'fired up' by an idea, or reached an impasse – we can't see the woods for the trees. At a loss as to how to proceed, rather than face the problem full-on, we do displacement activity, hoping the subconscious will do its work.

I see the brewing of ideas as a necessary fermentation process. Another way of looking at it is like a storm cloud building to a 'thunderhead' charged with ions – usually the harbinger of a migraine. After intensive research we reach saturation point, the brain feels like it cannot fit any more in, you feel weighed down with information and unable to make any leaps, to see above the subject. We brood and become bad tempered, like Nordic storm giants. As the Welsh poet Vernon Watkins, we wonder: "How shall I loosen this music/To the listening, eavesdropping sea?" Then, suddenly: BOOM! Crack! Inspiration strikes – the Eureka moment – and the waters are freed. The writer picks up her pen and the ink begins to flow. In his *Ballad for Gloom* Ezra Pound says, with Wagnerian aplomb: "I have drawn my black where the lightnings meet". Liminality is key to creativity. It is in the locus of the crossing place that boundaries become permeable and something new emerges. Encounter with Faerie is said to occur in the praeternatural nimbus before dawn or at dusk. Twilight is a threshold. In the Celtic Tradition it is one of the times when the 'veil is thinnest' between the worlds and Elves and Men can cross-over each others borders:

> …when white moths were on the wing,
> And moth-like stars were flickering out.

To return to the opening line again, I would like to highlight some of its technical elements, for these are means by which Yeats' creates such haunting phrases. Each line consists of eight syllables of four beats or metric 'feet'. This provides the bass-line rhythm of the poem. Its metre is iambic, which simply means the stress is on the second syllable, thus: I-*am*, I-*am*, I-*am*, I-*am*, I-*am*. This is known as a limping rhythm and it's interesting that Yeats chose it, because it emulates a walking gait, albeit a wounded one – and Aengus does become 'wounded', in the heart. The word 'iambic' originates in the Greek character of Iambe, a clowning figure who tries to cheer up the grieving Demeter, who mourns her lost daughter, Kore. Aengus was perhaps motivated by a desire to find solace:

> I went out to the hazel wood,
> Because a fire was in my head.

Going for a walk is a soothing act, and the walking rhythm of the poem makes it seem more reassuring, like a pleasant stroll. Thus form mirrors content in a marriage pleasing to the eye and ear. Yeats continues this metre throughout the poem, thereby making it 'scan'. It becomes painfully obvious when a poem does not scan, because its lines are of irregular length: words jar on the ear. This can be used to effect, but one should know what one's doing first. I advise steering clear of rhyme until you know the ropes. The common misconception is that a poem has to rhyme and therefore beginners often end up writing doggerel. For an excellent guide, you could do no better than *An Introduction to English Poetry* by James Fenton (Faber & Faber 2002). Although it is not necessary to write in traditional poetic forms, it is certainly advisable to learn the different approaches so that you can make a conscious choice. The poet has a wide and wonderful palette of techniques at his disposal, and rhyme is only one of them. Traditional forms, such as sonnets, are like carafes, into which we decant the wine of our poetry. They provide a 'strong container' for spirit, as poet Rose Flint puts it. You may choose to write in blank verse (metred, but unrhyming) or free verse (unmetred, un/rhyming) but whatever form you use, choose an appropriate one – one that chimes so well with the theme and the words that it becomes invisible to the reader or listener. It doesn't draw attention to itself, but just does what it is supposed to: delivers the 'message' in a medium elegant and apt.

Back to Aengus. He's gone fishing – for inspiration:

> I dropped the berry in a stream
> And caught a little silver trout.

Intuition tugs – you have a line: what's called 'the given line', a gift. You pull. The fish/phrase is caught. Although Aengus's fish is a trout, its silvery quality connects it to the "silver apples of the moon" – even more elusive, and the fact he is in a hazel wood, connects the whole affair to salmon. Let Celtic Tradition expert Caitlin Matthews explain:

> The Well of Nine Hazels, also known as the Well of Segais, is the abode of the Salmon of Wisdom. It is mystically linked with the source of (the river) Boyne, which poets believed to be the wellspring of poetic inspiration. The Salmon of the Well imbibed the nuts that fell into the water from the nine Hazel trees. Whoever caught and ate the salmon would be imbued with its wisdom and filled with imbas or inspiration.

So Aengus, by wandering into the *hazel* wood, is at the source of wisdom. And by catching the Otherworldly fish he is echoing the initiation of that greatest of Irish heroes, Fionn mac Cumhail (see **Fionn and the Salmon**). Aengus' trout is not just a trout, in the same way a salmon is not simply a salmon in the iconography of the Celtic Tradition. Like Taliesin, it slips through your fingers just when you think you've got a handle on it – it metamorphoses into a "glimmering girl with apple blossoms in her hair". The fish has become the Muse, here in her aspect of spring maiden, the desire of many male poets. The apple is the Celtic fruit of the Otherworld – Avalon, where King Arthur sails for healing – is the Isle of Apples, and to this day orchards grow on the side of Glastonbury Tor, popularly believed to be its earthly threshold. The Muse is Robert Graves 'Single Poetic

Theme'; whom he calls the White Goddess:

> Whose broad high brow was white as any leper's,
> Whose eyes were blue, with rowan-berry lips,
> With hair curled honey-coloured to white hips

She has haunted the imagination of writers around the world. After lecturing in America for many years, writing his distinctive novels with the "inkblood of home", author John Cowper Powys settled in North Wales for the last 29 years of his life. His poetry and prose are Celtic in character in terms of their 'hardness', their density and cosmic sensibility, sense of place and mythic present. In his epic novel of 1932 *A Glastonbury Romance* he describes the Muse on the final page: "For She whom the ancients named Cybele is in reality that beautiful and terrible Force by which the Lies of great creative Nature give birth to Truth that is to be". In *A Poet to his Beloved* Yeats brings her the offering of his verse: "White woman with numberless dreams, I bring you my passionate rhyme".

Like the Queen of Elfland in *Thomas the Rhymer* Aengus is summoned to the Otherworld by name, but she "faded in the brightening air" before he could follow – he wasn't quick enough to catch her. Inspiration can slip through your fingers… Alas, the Muse can be a fickle mistress – she can cast you out of her favour as both Blake and Keats found. In *La Belle Dame Sans Merci* the poet-knight meets:

> …a lady in the meads,
> Full beautiful – a faery's child;
> Her hair was long, her foot was light,
> And her eyes were wild.

After a grotesque vision of her former victims, the knight is cast out:

> And I awoke, and found me here
> On the cold hill side.

In an almost identical manner, Blake is cast out of his faerie-like *Crystal Cabinet* where he saw 'another London', after he tries to:

> …seize the inmost form
> With ardour fierce and hands of flame.

and is left:

> A weeping Babe upon the wild,
> And weeping Woman pale reclin'd,
> And in the outward air again
> I fill'd with woes the passing wind.

Anyone who has been abandoned by the Muse knows what it feels like to be "alone and palely loitering". Prosaically it is the dreaded Writer's Block, to name the beast. After the maddening taste of her Grace we have to woo her back with hard work. As the saying goes: first the inspiration, then the perspiration. Wandering Aengus vows to find her again and it becomes his life's work. The poet becomes "old with wandering through (the) hollow lands and hilly lands" of the internal and actual landscapes, imagination and experience. Yet his reward awaits him in the Land of the Ever Young, Tir nan Og: to be her lover, taste divine food, and encompass the cosmic dualities of the:

> The silver apples of the moon,
> The golden apples of the sun.

One could interpret the solar 'golden apples' as masculine, and the lunar 'silver apples' as feminine, and their union as the Chymical Wedding, but we must be careful not to project or prescribe. Yet, by juxtaposing such magical images Yeats creates a loop of enchantment. Within their polarity is found balance: the yin and yang of Tao, the dance of Shiva and Shakti, the God and the Goddess, creating the universe. The symbolism of apples seeds mythic echoes in the reader or listener: of Eden's Tree of Knowledge, Aphrodite's golden apple, the magical orchards of the Hesperides, and Avalon, the Isle of Apples (Afallach). Such Otherworldly icons tantalise us, like Thomas of Ercildoune, who was enchanted to Elfland by the chiming together of its Queen's bridle-rein, which hung "fifty-silver-bells-and-nine". It is this Otherworldly quest that underlies much of the yearning in Celtic myth, legend and music: the promise of Paradise earned through honour, bravery and excellence in skill. To create in music, poetry or art is to honour the Muse, who in the Celtic Tradition is widely called Brighid, **Goddess of the Bards**.

Yeats employed a range of techniques to make his poem worthy of the Goddess: vivid imagery, rhythm, rhyme, metaphor, alliteration, assonance, tone, voice, point of view... The important thing to remember is not to use such devices for the sake of it, but only discerningly – like a master musician would a particular instrument or scale.

And so from Yeats' poem and the Irish legends, the Welsh story of Taliesin, and the ballad of Thomas the Rhymer from the Scottish borders, we can derive common motifs of Bardic inspiration:

- ✤ **Threshold** eg: woodland, stream, bridge, weir or time of day, ie: midnight.
- ✤ **Twilight** eg: Yeats "and moth-like stars were flickering out".
- ✤ **Tree** eg: the Eildon Tree from Thomas the Rhymer.
- ✤ **Hazel** used for divining water: a metaphor of intuition.
- ✤ **Fruit** eg: the fruit of Elfland forbidden to mortals: "all the plagues of Hell dwell in the fruit of this country"; Aengus' berry on a thread; the silver and golden apples.
- ✤ **Fire** eg: 'fire in the head', and for cooking/transformation.
- ✤ **Fish** trout or salmon, the cipher for wisdom.
- ✤ **Metamorphoses** eg: "it had become a glimmering girl", or Taliesin/Ceridwen's chase.
- ✤ **Path** eg: "And see not ye that bonny road, That winds about the fernie brae?"
- ✤ **Hollow Lands** eg: the Faerie Raths ("the earth is full of cavities and cells" R Kirk)
- ✤ **Hilly Lands** eg: the Eildon Hills, the Hill of Vision, Cader Idris, Tara.
- ✤ **Time** eg: Yeats' "though I am old with wandering" and "til time and times are done".
- ✤ **Water/Well/Weir** eg: the Well of Segais, or Boann's well.

These symbols provide us with familiar landmarks in the uncertain territory of Faerie to navigate by: a psycho-geography similar to psychopompic books of the dead, which help souls to journey to 'the other shore'. But, as shaman-bards, we must walk between worlds and return with our vision, and ourselves, intact.

I hope you have found this brief excursion into the sacred wood of poetry interesting. After the Yeats poem in full (which I recommend reciting out loud) I have included **Tips for Writing Poetry** and **Performing Poetry** (also refer to **Ballads**, bearing in mind poetry techniques feed into song-craft). Do not be daunted by the task of crafting poetry. The main thing is to write from the heart. You can hone your words and perfect your craft the more you find out – I sometimes find poems take years to 'mature' into their perfect form, like vintage wines. But, to begin with, forget the technical stuff and just express the fire in the head.

The Willow Tree Man

The Song of Wandering Aengus

I went out to the hazel wood,
Because a fire was in my head,
And cut and peeled a hazel wand,
And hooked a berry to a thread;
And when white moths were on the wing,
And moth-like stars were flickering out,
I dropped the berry in a stream
And caught a little silver trout.

When I had laid it on the floor
I went to blow the fire aflame,
But something rustle on the floor,
And some one called me by my name:
It had become a glimmering girl
With apple blossom in her hair
Who called me by my name and ran
And faded through the brightening air.

Though I am old with wandering
Through hollow lands and hilly lands
I will find out where she has gone,
And kiss her lips and take her hands;
And walk among long dappled grass,
And pluck till time and times are done
The silver apples of the moon,
The golden apples of the sun.

William Butler Yeats

Tips for Writing Poetry

Waking
the
Night

Poems
Kevan Manwaring

❧ Write from the heart. What moves or inspires you? How are you feeling right now?

❧ Look around you. Keep your senses alert. Notice the small details. Experience!

❧ Keep a notebook for ideas/sensations/sound-bites/words/phrases.

❧ Don't wait for a poem to strike – go looking for it.

❧ Try to record emotion as you're experiencing it, if possible, or immediately afterwards.

❧ Fill the page. Keep going until the 'fire in the head' burns out.

❧ Brainstorm, mindmap, word associate, 'run' with your idea. Play!

❧ Try saying each line in as many different ways as possible. Select the best.

❧ Use rhyme as a last resort, and then only with a strict metre.

❧ Stick to one metaphor and pursue it relentlessly.

❧ What are you trying to say – will the reader understand?

❧ Write the poem beside the poem – what have you left out?

❧ Try to find the music of the piece. Fine tune. Let it flow.

❧ Find fresh ways of saying things – avoid cliché 'like the plague.'

❧ Don't try to sound like a poet. Use your own voice.

❧ Be as truthful to the original experience as possible.

❧ Be honest in thought, feeling and expression. Sincerity shines!

❧ Read as much poetry as possible. Study. Don't reinvent the wheel.

❧ Use poetic techniques consciously and discerningly.

❧ With each draft 'prune' your poem until you get to its essence.

❧ Read it out loud several times, playing with order and variation.

❧ Play with lineation – the length of the lines and their arrangement.

❧ Use the space of the page – spread the poem out. Let it breathe.

❧ Print copies. Share with friends/group for feedback. Listen.

❧ Save the title until last. Make it part of the poem – subtle, curious, ironic, subversive

Seize the Pen! Have fun!

Tips for Performing Poetry

❖ What's burning in your breast at the moment? Perform your latest, or the poem you're proudest of.

❖ Start with one you know well to boost your confidence.

❖ Share what you are passionate about. Your enthusiasm will be infectious.

❖ Use rhyme, rhythm, imagery and alliteration as mnemonic devices.

❖ Say it out loud until it 'scans to the ear.'

❖ Consider what is the core emotion or message. Does it come across?

❖ Keep it simple – complication leads to alienation. Be clever between the lines. Communication is about being understood – it's up to you.

❖ Listen to the audience. Let the silences speak.

❖ Remember the effort spent crafting your words – don't throw them away. Speak them with respect. Say them like they're newly-minted.

❖ Don't undersell yourself, apologise or mumble your words.

❖ Keep pre-ambles to a minimum. Cut out altogether if possible. Go in with a bang!

❖ Look sharp and sound sharp. Dress to impress. Wear your 'confidence overcoat'.

❖ Remember to breathe! Don't speak too fast… Pause… Let the audience in.

❖ Make eye contact as much as possible.

❖ Learn your words off by heart – it's more entertaining and more impressive. Audiences appreciate the time and effort spent learning your words.

❖ Passion transcends ability, but honing your craft can only help.

❖ Sincerity shines through. Take your efforts seriously and others will too. Humour wins over an audience, circumvents the hecklers and criticisms of pretension.

❖ Use body language consciously. Practise your stage presence.

❖ If you use a persona still be fully present and real.

❖ Get there early. Practise in the space if possible. Warm-up the voice beforehand.

❖ Practise with the microphone if using a PA, or projecting if not. Do a sound-check.

❖ Use the performance space. Be aware of the energy of the room/audience.

❖ Performing poetry is a buzz – enjoy it. Have a good time and your audience will too.

Stand up there and shine!

Voice of the Sun

What is it to speak with the Voice of the Sun? It is to shine, to give out light and energy to your audience, as epitomised by the Summer Solstice, that most extrovert of the festivals – an expansive time, when the seeds of winter manifest in all their glory. Creative folk share their talents at festivals and fêtes, having prepared through the darker months and dreamed their vision into reality: be it a new show, new craft, new technique, new range or new workshop. It is the time to be out there 'strutting your stuff', and basking in the exuberance of others. And it is the most popular time of gathering at the sacred sites, at the great tribal rings of Stonehenge and Avebury. At these Gorseddau and at the countless marquees and campfires it is a chance to perform in the round – to use the circle. You must learn to shine from all directions – with your body, with your voice, with your eyes, with your clothes. Radiate equally – do not neglect one 'corner' of the circle – keep circling, keep making eye contact and projecting your voice in each direction. This is the real test of a performer. Hopefully by now you would have practised at the Imbolc hearth and performed around the Belfire. You have built up confidence. You have developed your material and should have at least two or three songs, stories or poems. Aim to have something topical, something special for the solstice – a new poem for the sunrise, for the noon of the year.

The summer solstice is also the time of the oak moon – the king of the wood, the protector. The oak guards life – it is a guardian of thresholds, in doors and man-o'-wars. Within its bower can be sheltered and sustained up to 500 species. At the summer solstice it is time to expand your consciousness – to think of the wider community (**Bard and Community**). It may be a friend's wedding, your village summer fair, school fête, or it may be a street party, festival or Gorsedd. Try to reflect this in your subject matter, in your performance. You want to be bolder and brighter. To perform in such spaces you cannot be a shrinking violet. You must radiate confidence – put on your sparkliest clothes, daub yourself with face paint, glitter, jewellery, a feathered hat if you like, but remain genuine and centred. Inauthenticity is easily revealed on a stage, in the glare of the spotlight. The cracks begin to show in the greasepaint. Be confident, but don't be over the top, don't overdo it. Most people love the sun, but not sunburn. If the day is hot, folk don't have the concentration for something long and complicated. It is not the time for esoteric epics – save those for the winter nights. Now is the time for humour and good cheer, as in the druidic Music Hall song: 'the sun has got his hat on, hip hip hip hooray, the sun has got his hat on and he's coming out to play!' It is the time for mad dogs and Englishmen going out in the midday sun. It is the time for great sporting occasions, such as Wimbledon and Ascot. And it is the Silly Season. A merry festival audience want to be amused, not depressed. Morris dancers and Druids are out in their whites. Everyone is shining and Nature smiles down upon all. It is easy to feel good; the crowd are more inclined to indulge you than if they were freezing in the rain! It is the holy-day season – folk want a break from the treadmill of work. Take them on a magical journey with your voice, like sunlight through the leaves – enchanting, seductive and playful.

EXERCISES:

1. Contemplate the sun
What does the sun signify to you? Reflect upon its symbolism. Spend a day watching it – get up before dawn or stay up all night: watch the sun rise, follow its path through the day; and witness it setting. How does it change in terms of light, heat, energy, mood? How does it feel at different times of day? Does its 'voice' change? Try simulating its voice at these 'stations' of the day – have a sunrise voice, a noon voice, a sunset voice. Tell its story. Use movement, music, costume, mask. Consider how the sun is thought of differently in different cultures, ie: in some it is thought of as female. In some it is a tyrant – hot-headed and overbearing. In others it is weak and distant, like a wounded king. Personify it. Give it a character. Draw, paint, sculpt, or dance it. Look at sun icons/images in museums/temples.

2. Sun Story
Find sun poems/stories/songs. Look for solar sites and associated legends, ie: the story of Bladud of Bath (**The Swineherd Prince and the Flying King**) is probably a solar myth. Research one yourself – it could be literally about the sun, ie: how Raven brought back the sun (Native American), or it could be about a Sun God (Apollo – Greek), a Solar Hero (Heracles), concerning the sun (Helios – riding the chariot of the sun), or simply a story from a hot country (eg: Egypt, Africa, Australia).

3. Sun Costume
Make a sun head-dress or solar/solstice mask. Or what about a suncloak, golden and dazzling (add bright feathers, sequins, gold ribbon)? Use gold face- or body-paint. Incorporate into a performance or sun-rite.

4. Telling in the Round
Form a circle with friends. In turn try telling your story to the circle, standing in the middle. Playing word association, use a yellow tennis ball – as you speak, throw the ball/your word at the same time – directing your energy/voice and making eye contact. Visit The Globe Theatre in London and see professional actors performing in the round. Or watch buskers in action, ie: at Covent Garden. See how they work the crowd, and work in a circle. Try this in a Gorsedd at a stone circle, ie: Avebury at festival time.

5. Performance
Devise a solar performance, bringing together your research – perform it in the round. Use a group. Prepare the space. Tell 'the Story of the Sun'. Include poetry, music and dance.

6. Casting your circle

Performance is ceremony. You need to establish and hold your space. Choreograph the crowd to sit or stand where you want them to. Walk around the performance space to define it. Get everyone to hold hands. Use sound to cast your circle (chanting, toning, gongs, drums), or ritual theatrics (robed 'acolytes', torch-bearers, fire-dancers).

Run around inside and outside of the circle to raise the energy. Stake your territory. You are making sacred space, and letting people experience sacred time. Of course, if it is a Gorsedd the Druids would already be doing this. Work with them. Don't reinvent the circle!

THE SWINEHERD PRINCE AND THE FLYING KING

Bladud, with his sky-blue eyes and fiery-red hair was a striking young man – and so he should be, for was he not the son of the High king of Britain, Lud Hudibras – who lived in Lud's Town, London?

The prince was sent to Athens to study with the finest scholars – for even in those days, many centuries before Christ, there was trade between the wine-dark Mediterranean and Hyperborea, the Land beyond the North Wind, as Britain was known in the Ancient World. Baltic amber was traded with Cornish tin, and so were ideas and stories.

When Bladud returned across mainland Europe it appears he contracted leprosy – for when he finally arrived back at his father's court after the arduous journey he was not welcomed with open arms, but shunned in disgust. He

Bladud. Oil painting.

was exiled from court – for the King and the land are one, and if the King was infected, so would the land be, and in those times people feared lepers.

Poor Bladud wandered far into the West, and the only work he could get was as a lowly swineherd, around the area of Swinford, near Bath. Every morning he would take out his pigs to graze – and their favourite breakfast was the beechmast found on Beechen Cliff. Bladud took them there one day, and as they grazed contentedly amongst the trees he gazed out over the misty forest below – for in those days Bath was no more than that.

He daydreamed about his days back at court, when everyone wanted to know him – now no-one wanted to, not even his pigs – for they had run off while he reveried!

Bladud searched around in a panic, calling out, but his words fell dead in the air. With a sinking feeling, the swineherd prince realised they had disappeared into the misty forest. It was shunned by locals for it was said to be haunted by an evil spirit that lured men to their doom in the pits and pools of that foetid fastness. Yet Bladud had to go in there – he had to get his pigs back; they were his livelihood. And so he ventured deeper and deeper into the dark wood, weaving his way between creeper-tangled branches, calling out for his pigs – yet there was not a sound except his own. The silence was disturbing, and his heart beat faster.

Finally, out of breath, he came to a clearing where a green pool swirled with steaming mist. Around its edges, in the black mud, wallowed his pigs. Relieved and annoyed at finding them, he gave them a good telling off and told them to get out of that mud immediately – but they just grunted back at him.

Bladud and the Swine.
Oil painting.

Losing his patience, Bladud waded into the mud and tried to pull one out by its little corkscrew tail, but his hands slipped and he fell – kerploosh! – into the mud. The swineherd prince was about to give those pigs a piece of his mind. He was covered from head to toe in the stinking stuff, but to Bladud's astonishment it was warm! It soothed his leprous skin – and then the penny dropped. His pigs, being intelligent animals – legend has it they were a gift from the Annwn – knew what was good for them. They had caught Bladud's condition and had made a beeline to the magic mud as soon as they could.

And so Bladud, once prince, wallowed with his swine…

When he had finished his treatment, he swam out into the middle of the pool and floated in the blood-warm waters, looking up dreamily at the steam as the eddies of wind made shapes in the mist. Then before him appeared a vision in white – a woman, veiled and mysterious. She hovered above him and spoke these words:

"I am Sulis, Goddess of the Springs. You bathe in my sacred waters and they heal you. Remember this, when you become King, Bladud – or forget at your peril!"

And she vanished, like a dream on waking. But Bladud was determined not to forget. He quickly swam ashore and, as he emerged, he could see his leprosy had gone.

With new-found wisdom he plucked acorns from a nearby oak tree and left a trail that lured the pigs out one by one. Then he led his charge back to the farmstead that had been his home for the last year. Bidding the farmer and his family a fond farewell, he wended his way, with a spring in his step, back to the Lud's town.

This time he was welcomed back as everyone could see he was healthy and whole once more. Yet his father was now ill, having pined for his son, and asking for Bladud's forgiveness, passed away.

And so his father's mantle fell on his shoulders. Bladud claimed his birthright, and was crowned High King of Britain, tenth in line from Brutus. The first thing Bladud did was decree a temple should be built at Bath to honour Sulis – for he had not forgotten her, yet. This was done, and when word got out about how their liege had been healed by those miraculous hot springs, people travelled from far and wide to take the waters. Pilgrims poured into Bath, and they had to be fed, and sheltered, and they all wanted souvenirs of that special place – so business boomed and the city of Bath began, thanks to Bladud, its founding father.

Bladud's reign was a golden one; his was a time of peace and plenty. He invited scholars over from Athens to found four universities in the four corners of Britain. There they shared their ancient knowledge along with the Druids, who taught the inner mysteries.

Bladud was a philosopher king, renowned for his wisdom – but his life ended in folly, or so it seemed to some.

Towards the end of his reign he got into his head the foolish notion that he wanted to fly. Perhaps, while a student in Athens, he had heard of the genius mazemaker Daedalus, who had made wings to escape from the court of Minos.

Yet it seems he had not heard about his son, Icarus, who had escaped with him – but in his youthful arrogance had flown too close to the sun, melting the wax that bound his feather wings together, and falling to his death in the sea below.

Whether he knew of this or not, nothing could dissuade King Bladud from his plan – and so, on a bright midsummer morning the monarch stood on the brow of Solsbury hill, overlooking Bath. His subjects watched with concern and amusement from below.

King Bladud spread out his magnificent wings and leapt, plummeting down surely to perish – but at the last moment a thermal swept him into the sky, and he was flying!

His people cheered as he soared above them, circling around like a buzzard. Far below, they looked like ants, and the fields like a patchwork blanket. He was King Bladud and he was flying!

He flew over the city he had founded, looking down on it with pride. And there, in its centre, was the temple of Sulis – he circled closer and closer to this, thinking if how far he had come since wallowing in the mud with the pigs. There was something he had to remember, but the exhilaration of flying drowned out all concerns. He was like a god!

Then he thought he heard an eery singing coming from the temple baths – he flew closer, hypnotised by its spell…

Perhaps it was the steam from the hot springs, or perhaps it was something else, but suddenly his wings broke and he fell down, down, down, landing with a sickening crunch – his neck broken on the altar stone of Sulis' temple.

And so King Bladud died – though some say it was in the Temple of the Sun God – Stonehenge – where he met his fate. Yet in the way he rose and fell like the sun perhaps he was the sun himself, and his falling was not that of a fool, but of a golden sun setting – for his reign lasted nineteen years, the Great Year of the sun and the moon's dance around the heavens, remembered in The Circus and Crescent of Bath, built by the druidic architect John Wood the Elder, and son.

And Bladud himself can be seen to this day in the Roman Baths, with his sky-blue eyes and fiery red hair, winged-browed and snaked with steam, overlooking the temple he had established in honour of Sulis – and that is what the city became known as by the Romans when they arrived: *Aquae Sulis.*

Adapted from Geoffrey of Monmouth's *History of the Kings of Britain* and Pierce's *memoires*, 1697 (source: *The British King Who Tried to Fly, Levis,* West Country Editions, 1973).

The Shining Ones

Mask for Summer Solstice, by Sheila Broun.

Solar heroes and heroines abound throughout myth – their universal popularity triggered by the ubiquity of the sun as Source of Life, of Light and Heat. It has been argued that worship of the sun is the root of all religions (in *Caves of the Sun* by Adrian Bailey, Jonathan Cape 1997) and, even if this is not so (moon, night, ocean and Earth deities are just as common, just as venerated) it is little wonder considering how essential the sun is to life on Earth. Since sunrise was first beheld by our most ancient ancestors we, as a species, have held that particular celestial object in awe. Too vast, remote and powerful to relate to on its own terms, we have anthropomorphised it, giving it gender, names, attributes according to what we observe and what we project onto it. Worthy of veneration in its own right (as powerhouse of all life on the planet) the sun is also a supreme metaphor for Deity, and its light has been associated with intelligence, with reason, with good. As white light is splintered through a prism, so too has the light of the sun inspired myriad manifestations of the Divine, coloured by the cultural perceptions, parameters and preoccupations of different civilisations throughout the millennia. From the fierce Ra of Egypt, championed by his priest, Akhenaten, as the only one true God; to lightning bolt-wielding Zeus on Olympus; Lord of Light, Apollo, God of Poetry, Music and Reason; his Christian equivalent, the Archangel St Michael; Christ, of course, the Divine Son; Lucifer, the Lightbringer with the Stone of Heaven on his brow; Helios with his chariot pulled by fiery horses, usurped by his wayward son; One-eyed Odin, runebringer; Ogma SunFace, inventor of the **Ogham** tree alphabet; Baldur, who dies at midwinter, slain by the golden bough, mistletoe; Balor of the Baleful Eye, slain by the Spear of **Lugh** Lamfhada, of the Long-Arm, Many-skilled; Lleu Llaw Gyffes, Lion of the Steady Hand, slain by the spear of Gronw Pebr; 'solar knights' Llwch Lleminawg, Lancelot, Galahad and Parsifal; **Taliesin** of the Shining Brow; fiery-haired **Bladud**, the flying king; **Sulis** of the hot springs; **Brighid** of the Undying Flame; St Catherine of the fiery wheel... The list goes on and on. Plenty of material to choose from, plenty of inspiration.

It is the light of consciousness, the light of Awen. We can invoke solar deities to give us the light we need to shine; when we need illumination and guidance, like Cuchullain lost in the Land of Shadows, who is given a 'fiery wheel' by a mysterious stranger (who turns out to be his father Lugh) to guide him across to his destination and destiny. We can use (respectfully) the energy and piercing wisdom of these solar deities, heroes and heroines, to help us through the Dark Nights of the Soul, the moments of doubt and despair that we encounter in our lives: that's why modern equivalents of solar heroes (such as Superman, Spiderman, James Bond) as well as old ones (King Arthur, with his Round Table, golden Camelot and rise and fall) are so perennially popular. The sun will never go out of fashion, although many have used its shining garment to justify all manner of evils (i.e. the blood sacrifices of the Aztecs, the burnings of the Inquisition). Humanity's relationship with monotheistic religion has been a tumultuous one over the centuries: such monomania often creates a harsh God. Too much of the sun can be bad for you. The brightest sun casts the darkest shadow. We must be careful not to scorch (i.e. preach), or be scorched (see **The Shining Word**). We are all equal in the light of sun.

Month 6: Entering the Land of Story

And see not ye that bonny road,
that winds about the fernie brae?
That is the road to fair Elfland,
Where thou and I this night maun gae.
               Thomas the Rhymer, Anon.

Fire drakes at Boscawen-Ûn Stone Circle, West Penwith.
by Sarah Vivian: vivianat.farwest@supanet.com

There are many ways into the Otherworld – although fewer out, as some have found to their peril! A salutary warning can be found in several tales where mortals encounter Faerie. One of the most haunting is the legend of Ossian, son of Fionn Mac Cumhail, poet of the Fianna, who is lured to the Land of the Ever-Young, Tir nan Og, by a beautiful Faerie bride. Upon return to his beloved Erin, he breaks the geasa she has set upon him – not to touch the earth – and withers away, three hundred years catching up with him in the snap of a saddle-strap. After relating his adventures to St Patrick, whose monks record them on vellum for posterity, the super-annuated traveller perishes.

Be careful when returning into the here and now from Faerie that you don't sound off or boast about it and expect everyone to believe you. You may become disappointed with day-to-day life. People who have tasted Faerie grow fey and dissatisfied with the mundane, longing to return to Tir nan Og. Some even commit suicide to get there, unable to bear living in this world.

Yeats' Wandering Aengus spent the rest of life searching for that 'glimmering girl' he had glimpsed once in his youth. Having had a taste of the Otherworld you may become obsessed, forgetting your daily responsibilities to your loved ones, your work, yourself. Robert Kirk, 17th Century Scottish minister and author of *The Secret Commonwealth of Elves, Fauns and Fairies*, ended up taking his antiquarian interests too far – or they took him. He was supposed to have stepped into a Faerie ring once on a walk upon the hills near his Parish of Aberfoyle, in the Lowlands of Scotland, and was spirited away into Faerie, to be replaced by a changeling. He is said to be there still.

There have been numerous changeling incidents recorded in folklore: children, mid-wives, even livestock have been abducted and replaced. These 'shadows of former selves' are perhaps poor souls who have experienced 'soul-loss', who are not entirely in the land of the living. The Sidhe were said to have hollow bodies when seen from behind, and this is what you are in danger of becoming, living off 'thin air', if you end up away with the Faeries… Throughout myth and literature there are various taboos about eating Faerie fruit, most famously in the Greek myth of Kore – the maiden who is abducted by Hades, Lord of the Dead, to become his bride, taking the new name of Persephone – forced to live a third of the year below the Earth after she eats three pomegranate seeds. In *Thomas the Rhymer* the poet errant is warned not to eat the fruit of the otherworldly tree "for all the plagues that are in Hell, dwell in the fruit of this country". Again and again this motif reoccurs: in Rossetti's *Goblin Market*, in Lewis Carrol's *Alice in Wonderland*, and Hope Mirrlees' *Lud-in-the-Mist*. This trope may be an echo of the Christian Eden myth, with the taboo of eating the fruit of the Tree of Knowledge of Good and Evil, but it signifies more than guilt about Original Sin. It is about an exchange of energies: basically, you can't get something for nothing. There's no such thing as a free lunch, or a fey one. If you eat of the Faerie fruit, then you owe something back.

Within these and many other Faerie stories there dwells a wise warning: respect the riches of the Otherworld – don't exploit them, or they'll find a way to exploit you. Remember we are dealing with 'a separate reality' here, as Carlos Castenada called it. The Otherworld is real, and exists autonomously, whether we believe in it or not. Yet, as Bards, we should be heightening people's awareness of the different layers of life, that "there are more things in Heaven and Earth than are dreamt of in most people's philosophy"; that there is magic in the mundane, that divinity is immanent and the divine spark is in all of us. The Celts did not believe in an Otherworldly paradise being 'up in the sky', or beyond life, but in parallel with it and ever present. The utopias of Tir nan Og, Avalon and the like, may be 'over the Westering Sea', but we can be summoned there in an instant. Sometimes the Sidhe comes and snatches you from a hillside in the blink of an eye. It is best to tread carefully in the Land of Story and make sure you make it there and back again in one piece.

A sojourn in the Land of Story *can* be immensely rewarding: inspiring, refreshing, healing, guiding. Stories provide useful maps of the human soul, and perhaps maps for life. They can be used for personal development, to enhance one's relationships, community, even country: think of the national myths such as the legend of King Arthur, the Matter of Britain. Yet we have to be careful not to misappropriate them, as the Nazis did, corrupting their own hoard of culture. Myths are not good or evil in themselves – only what we project onto them or use them to justify – but they *are* powerful things. Treat them with the respect due to these gifts from our ancestors; wisdom from the Otherworld that can help us all to live as one.

As Bards we can explore the Land of Story, which is an aspect of the Otherworld, through the imagination, the storyteller's richest resource. Storytelling is a key skill for the Bard. The relating of myths, legends, folk tales and faerie tales are his or her stock-in-trade. These tales are always happening, outside time, and can be accessed, as a living reality. If you are to tell these stories they must become real to you. You must live and breathe them. You must inhabit them, as they must inhabit you (see **Inhabiting the Story**). This is the only way to understand them fully (ie: the rich obscurities of *The Mabinogion*, which require deep journeying to untangle and engage with) and can be achieved through creative visualisation techniques, sometimes called pathworking. To a lesser extent you employ this faculty of the 'mind's eye' every time you read a book – a story we tell ourselves. The story comes alive only through your imagination, as you not only 'enter the world' of the novel, but you co-create it with a mixture of your **visualisation** and memories. The reader pictures the scenes, more or less vividly, but may also 'cast' the characters with family, friends or even film stars, and emotionally invigorate the action with similar personal experiences that are triggered by it. All the time the reading takes place, there is this dialogue between our inner world and the world of the story, as it stirs memories, feelings, and opinions. This is akin to the experience of live storytelling, which is a similar co-creative act (see **Checklist** for various storytelling techniques).

As a Bard reading a source text, it is not enough to be simply led through a story by the narrator, only seeing and hearing things *they* want you to: you have to imagine the story from different narrative perspectives (view-point); you have to 'see' or experience the story in three dimensions, as if you have stepped into a scene in the story and can walk around unobserved, checking out details. And this is exactly what I want you to try and do.

EXERCISE: Storyscape

Pick a scene from a favourite story, eg: Cuchullain at the gates of Scathach's castle; Fionn cooking the salmon; Taliesin being chased by Ceridwen; Janet pulling the rose at Carterhaugh; young Arthur pulling the sword from the stone, etc. Imagine it as vividly as possible. Find images of it – there are several excellent themed Tarot sets, based on different traditions and story cycles (eg: Arthurian, Celtic, Nordic, Hellenic, Native American), which could help focus your visualisation and meditation. Alternatively, you may want to draw your own scenes, or make your own story cards. Returning to your chosen scene, create an approximate life-size diorama of it with improvised props. Make costumes, masks, sets and act it out with friends – anything that will make it come alive. I want you to live and breathe this story for a month, to 'sleep on it', as if in a Bardic cell, with a stone on the chest (see **Stone upon the Belly**). Visualise a different scene every night (in chronological sequence), and 'enter' into it. 'Record' with the mini-cam of your mind's eye all that you see: focus on the details, the unexpected textures and angles. Reach out and touch, taste, smell things around you. Savour the sensations: the more vivid it is for you – the more vivid it will be for your audience. When you are telling your story it should be like you are describing a personal experience, a place you know well. Each time you perform your tale it should be like a movie running in your head, as though you've just put a DVD on and pressed 'play'. All you need to do is describe what is happening in 'front' of you – on the plasma screen of your imagination. But remember – this is a kind of virtual reality and you are 'in' the story as you are telling it: you are experiencing what your characters are experiencing – but with one eye on the audience at all times.

The Lore of the Storyteller

> The storyteller was originally a seer and a teacher who guided the souls of his hearers through the world of 'mystery.'
>
> Rees Bros., *Celtic Heritage*

Here is a miscellany of useful lore and interesting snippets for and about storytellers:

Some names for storytellers/musicians/poets:

- ❖ Bard (Celtic)
- ❖ Scop (Anglo Saxon)
- ❖ Scald (Nordic)
- ❖ Meistersinger (German)
- ❖ Seanachie (Irish)
- ❖ Troubadour (France)
- ❖ Cantastorie (Italian)
- ❖ Griot (African)
- ❖ Drut'syla (Yiddish)
- ❖ Cyfarwydd (Welsh)
- ❖ El Hablador (Latin American)
- ❖ Runonlaulajat (Finnish)

PRACTISE

Practise makes perfect, as they say, and this is especially the case for storytellers. It may seem obvious, but the fact is: the more you do it, the better you'll get. Tell stories at every occasion, because no matter how thorough your rehearsals, nothing can replace performing to a live audience. The Rees Brothers in *Celtic Heritage* say: "The storytellers are people who from early youth have availed themselves of every opportunity to add to their repertoire and to perfect the manner of their delivery". The actual experience of live performance is the equivalent of flying hours for a pilot. I believe a Bard needs to maintain his 'poetic license' by performing a certain number of times a year. Simply put, to be a storyteller, you have to tell stories! By doing so on a regular basis also maintains one's repertoire. This was said of the seanachie, Sean O'Canaill's youth: "Lest he should lose command over the tales he loved, he used to repeat them aloud when he thought no one was near, using the gesticulations and the emphasis, and all the other tricks of narration, as if he were once again the centre of a fireside storytelling." (see **Rehearsal**)

Categories of Stories
- ✤ *Coimperta* (births)
- ✤ *Tochmarca* (weddings)
- ✤ *Dindsenchas* (stories of place)
- ✤ *Immrama* (voyages)
- ✤ *Echtrai* (adventures)

Customary Occasions for a Tale (based upon traditional lists):
"Storytelling had a recognised place in certain ceremonial occasions"
(Rees Bros., *Celtic Heritage*)

- ✤ Wedding night: tales of wooings
- ✤ 'Warming' of a new house
- ✤ The eve of battle
- ✤ The bringing out of ale
- ✤ Feasts
- ✤ Taking over of inheritance
- ✤ Stories of place are told at every session
- ✤ Wakes: death tales and tales of remembrance
- ✤ Samhain: ghost stories
- ✤ Cattle raids: before undertaking a cattle raid!
- ✤ Voyages: on setting out to sea or on a long journey
- ✤ Conceptions and Births

Modern Occasions
- ✤ Hallowe'en
- ✤ Bonfire Night (November 5th)
- ✤ Fête
- ✤ Festival
- ✤ Dinner party
- ✤ Birthday party
- ✤ Graduation
- ✤ Business launch
- ✤ Street party
- ✤ Protest rally
- ✤ National or Global Events, eg: Elections, Coronation, Olympics, total eclipses, etc.
- ✤ Important Anniversaries, eg: VE Day, Remembrance Sunday, Holocaust Day, etc.
- ✤ Add your own…

HEARTH SIDE AND HIGH STYLE
There are generally considered to be two main styles of storytelling – hearth-side and high style – although within these broad categories there are many variations, and even within one show there could be overlap and a switching of modes as the type of tale, or shift of narrative, dictates. These are working definitions, but by no means definitive. There are always exceptions that prove the rule:

Hearth Side: literally, stories told at the hearth, at your 'grandmother's knee'. These are usually informal folk tales and wisdom, told in an avuncular, 'salt of the earth' way. The teller is seated, body language is limited, but more emphasis is placed on subtler gestures and expressions. Hearthside tales are often, but not always, 'quieter', and ideal for long dark nights and a small gatherings. A whispered voice against the crackle and glow of the fire works deep enchantment.

High Style: this approach is more theatrical, 'louder', with wider gesticulation, and more pronounced movement (ie: mime or dance) and body language. So overall, more visual. Not just focussed on the voice, although greater projection will be required. Perhaps backdrops, props, stagecraft will be used. Ideal for group shows. Good for large gatherings, halls, festivals. This style is excellent for epics. It can be very physical and high energy.

EXERCISE: Hearth Side, High Style
Tell a story in two ways: first in a hearthside manner, then again in high style. Which one works best? Test on different audiences (eg: family, friends, story circle, etc.).

The Storyteller's Season

"Old people speak of storytellers who could recite a different story every night the whole winter through" Rees Bros.

Storytelling took place from Samhain to Beltane – from the beginning of winter to the beginning of summer. In the times when all hands were needed on the land, the brighter months were not the time to be inside listening to tales, and for a modern storyteller the summer season is often the busiest time of year, with all the festivals – it is the time to be out and about, enjoying the fruits of the summer, sharing and gathering tales – to replenish the stock of experiences, to make the tales come alive.

Story Blessings

Stories bless us in many ways: both the teller and listener share in its magic, and may receive from it healing. Wonder tales literally were thought to perform wonders, or small miracles, if recited – in exactly the same way as shamanic performances did to those who experienced them. And in a modern more mundane way this is how a good movie makes you feel: it gives you a 'buzz'; you forget yourself and afterwards there's a feelgood factor, a closeness to friends and loved ones who shared the tale, and the wider community who have tapped into this collective dreaming. This 'chicken soup' effect possibly relates to the ancient idea that particular stories had a healing quality or blessing. Some stories have a built-in **Story Blessing** to preserve the integrity of the tale. Of *The Tain*, of which was said 'a year's protection to him who recited it', the 12th century MS, *Book of Leinster* says: "a blessing on everyone who will memorise the Tain with fidelity in this form and will not put any other form on it". Even St Patrick himself ordered of the story *The Fosterage of the Houses of the Two Mothers*: "that there should be no sleep or conversation during this story, and not to tell it except to a few good people so that it might be the better listened to…" This tale came with some incredible claims, as if it had the power of miracles encoded within it:

If you tell this story
to the captives of Ireland,
it will be the same as if were opened
their locks and their bonds.

This emancipation echoes Taliesin's Bardic Lore:

I am a Bard,
I do not vouchsafe my secrets to slaves.
I am a guide, I am a judge.
As you sow, you labour.

I would suggest that 'slaves' in this context means those entrapped by what Blake calls "mind forg'd manacles": those that are prisoners of consensus reality, of materialism, of trivia, of the status quo. The Bardic arts offer a gateway to deeper levels of living – the key is the imagination – all we need to enter, is to use it.

GREAT STORY CYCLES

- ❖ Dreamtime stories
- ❖ African stories, ie: Anansi
- ❖ Native American stories, ie: Coyote
- ❖ Gilgamesh
- ❖ The Descent of Inaana
- ❖ Monkey (Chinese legend overlapping with the monkey god Hanuman)
- ❖ The Mahabharata
- ❖ A Thousand and One Nights
- ❖ The Odyssey
- ❖ The Iliad
- ❖ The Aeneid
- ❖ Ovid's Metamorphoses
- ❖ The Bible
- ❖ Nasrudin parables
- ❖ The Gesar of Ling
- ❖ The Elder Eddas
- ❖ Kalevala
- ❖ Baba Yaga tales
- ❖ Beowulf
- ❖ The Ulster Cycle
- ❖ The Tain
- ❖ The Four Branches of the Mabinogion
- ❖ Aesop's Fables
- ❖ Grimm's Fairy Tales
- ❖ Hans Christian Anderson's Fairy Tales
- ❖ Arthurian Saga
- ❖ Robin Hood
- ❖ Add to the list…

ENDING YOUR STORY

Always end with a bang, a flourish – people generally remember the first and last thing you say most of all: these are the 'points of power', the thresholds of your performance. You have to take the audience with you – entice them in with a suitable hook – and bring them firmly back again into the here and now. In this cynical age saying they 'all lived happily ever after' won't wash with most, but you could find a way to twist this corny ending, ie: 'And if they happily or long, well that is another story for another night'. Think of a witty and wise way to end. This is an Irish seanachie's caveat or valediction: "That is my story! If there be a lie in it, be it so! It is not I who made or invented it."

Climbing the Beanstalk - Storytelling in easy stages

1 Choose a favourite story, myth, legend, folktale, fairy story or fable.

2 Break it down to the 9 key incidents, 'the bones', ie: Jack went to market with a cow, Jack sold the cow in exchange for some beans, etc.

3 Try to visualise each scene as vividly as possible. Imagine it as a 'room' – walk around it, see it in 3D, touch, taste, listen and smell!

4 Speaking aloud, describe each scene as if it was happening right in front of you.

5 Create a storyboard, or invent a symbol for each scene, ie: cow, bean, stalk, giant.

6 Use these on 'prompt cards'. Tell the story to a friend. Then try without cards.

7 Try telling the story as simply and clearly as possible. Does the listener follow?

8 Sticking to the structure, improvise details, jokes, and spontaneous innovations.

9 Practise in front of a full-length mirror. Be aware of your gestures and expressions.

10 Record your story as you tell it, live, to friends. Listen: does your voice vary? Modulate the tone, exaggerate the expression, and then 'turn down the volume'.

11 Summarise each 'bone' in one line. What happens? Now divide the 9 into 3 'acts'. What is the theme or moral of each act? Now 3 into 1 – what is the overall theme of the tale? What message are you trying to convey? It could be silly (shaggy dog story) or serious. Be aware of it, but don't say directly – don't preach. Let any wisdom speak through the story itself, like the language of dreams. Symbolism speaks volumes.

12 Forgetting all your notes, retell the story – say it as if it was happening for the first time, describe it as though it was happening right in front of you and the audience.

13 Find a group of people (dinner party, story circle, open mic night). Tell it!

14 Trust in the tale – let the tale tell itself. Your tongue will remember what to do.

15 Be aware of the audience. Make eye contact with people as you speak – direct the energy of the story to them. Beam – smile with your eyes too! Be positive, passionate and sincere. A good attitude wins over a crowd more than gilded speech.

16 Project your voice. Breathe from the belly. Do warm-up vocal exercises before.

17 Use your whole body to tell the tale. Move around. Use the space. Improvise with props.

18 Observe the audience's reaction. Monitor and feedback into performance. Listen!

19 Use musical instruments to create atmosphere, for sound effects, or contrast.

20 Use costume if appropriate, ie: Hallowe'en, Heritage Venue, themed event.

21 Listen to as many storytellers as possible, at festivals, circles and on tape.

22 Practise new material at the local story circle, a supportive space amongst friends!

23 Try telling the story several times, in slightly different ways to different audiences.

24 Write down or record your best version. Track its 'success'. Use a logbook or journal.

25 Use your strengths, eg: dance, music, poetry, history, humour, local knowledge, dialect.

26 Try 'hearthside' tales – off the cuff, informal tales, as often as possible. Anywhere!

27 Collect story collections from around the world. Expand your repertoire. Be adventurous, but be respectful of other cultures. Spread multicultural understanding.

28 Look out for stories on holiday. Talk to locals. Uncover the story of a place. Record.

29 Have fun. Enjoy the journey of the story and your audience will too.

Worlds of the Storyteller

An irrepressible sadness came over me at the thought that this society scattered in the depths of the damp and boundless forests, for whom a few tellers of tale acted as circulating sap, was doomed to disappear.

How many times in those twenty-three years had I thought of the Machiguengas? How many times had I tried to understand them, intuitively, to write about them; how many plans had I made to journey to their lands? Because of them, all the people or institutions everywhere in the world that might resemble or in any way be associated with the Machiguenga storytellers held an immediate fascination for me. The wandering troubadours of the Bahia pampas, for instance, who, to the basso continuo of their guitars, weave together medieval romances of chivalry and local gossip in the dusty villages of northeastern Brazil. Seeing one of them that afternoon, in the market square of Uaua, was enough for me to glimpse, superimposed on the figure of the caboclo, in a leather vest and hat, recounting and singing, to an amused audience, the story of Princess Magalona and the twelve peers of France, the greenish-yellow skin, decorated with symmetrical red stripes and dark spots, of the half-naked storyteller who, far, far from there, on a little beach hidden beneath the jungle foliage of Madre de Dios, was telling an attentive family squatting on their heels about the breathing contest between Tasurinchi and Kientibakori that was the origin of all the good and bad beings in the world.

But even more than the Bahian troubadour, it was the Irish *seanchaí* who had reminded me, so forcefully, of the Machiguenga storytellers. *Seanchaí*: "teller of ancient stories," "the one who knows things," as someone in a Dublin bar had off-handedly translated the word into English. How to explain, if it was not because of the Machiguengas, the rush of emotion, the sudden quickening of my heartbeat that impelled me to intrude, to ask questions, and later on to pester and infuriate Irish friends and acquaintances until they finally sat me down front of a *seanchaí*? A living relic of the ancient Bards of Hibernia, like those ancestors of his whose faint outline blends, in the night of time, with the Celtic myths and legends that are the intellectual foundations of Ireland, the *seanchaí* still recounts, in our own day, old legends, epic deeds, terrible loves, and disturbing miracles, in the smoky warmth of pubs; at festive gatherings where the magic of his words calls forth a sudden silence; in friendly houses, next to the hearth, as outside the rain falls or the storm rages. He can be a tavernkeeper, a truck driver, a parson, a beggar, someone mysteriously touched by magic wand of wisdom and the art of reciting, of remembering, of reinventing and enriching tales told and retold down through the centuries; a messenger from the times of myth and magic, older than history, to whom Irishmen of today listen spellbound for hours on end. I always knew that the intense emotion I felt on that trip to Ireland, thanks to the *seanchai*, was metaphorical, a way of hearing, through him, the storyteller, of living the illusion that, sitting there squeezed in among listeners, I was part of a Machiguenga audience.

Mario Vargas Llosa, *The Storyteller*, trans. Helen Lane. Faber & Faber, 1990

The Crane Bag: Using Archetypes

DEFINITION:
ARCHETYPES – primordial images, from Greek: *arkhe* 'primitive' and *tupos* 'a model': "(in Jungian theory) a primitive mental image inherited from the earliest human ancestors and supposed to be present in the collective unconscious; A recurrent theme in literature or art." *Concise OED.* See *Archetypes and the Collective Unconscious,* Carl Jung.

All stories reflect upon the human condition, in whatever form they appear, and are populated with characters and situations 'hard-wired' into our psyches. These Jung deemed archetypal. Many archetypes appear in their 'raw' form in Fairy Tales and subsequently, movies, as screenwriters consciously employ them for maximum impact:

- ❖ Good Mother (Fairy Godmother)
- ❖ Bad Mother (Wicked Stepmother)
- ❖ Good Father (King Arthur)
- ❖ Bad Father (evil king, Darth Vader); or Absent Father (Richard Lionheart)
- ❖ Golden Child (*puer eternus*, ie: Peter Pan)
- ❖ Prince/Princess (anima/animus, feminine/masculine aspect, Mr/Ms Right)
- ❖ The Big Bad Wolf or Beast.
- ❖ Wild Man (Green Man, Iron John, Enkidu from 'Gilgamesh', Robin Hood)
- ❖ List more…

In our stories we should attempt to veil and subvert these – but be aware they are primal energies within us all, so each one can certainly 'push the button' of the reader (we all have primal/subconscious responses to them, depending on our childhood and beliefs).

In *The Writer's Journey*, Christopher Vogler identified the following as "the archetypes that occur most frequently in stories, and seem to be the most useful for the writer to understand":

- ❖ HERO
- ❖ MENTOR (Wise old man or woman)
- ❖ THRESHOLD GUARDIAN
- ❖ HERALD
- ❖ SHAPESHIFTER
- ❖ SHADOW
- ❖ TRICKSTER

What archetypes can you identify in *your* story? Vogler suggests two questions useful for identifying them:

1 What psychological function or part of the personality does it represent?
2 What is its dramatic function in a story?

Images of Archetypes from Greek Myths

From left to right, top to bottom:
Asklepios (healer/magician); *Minerva/Athena* (priestess); *Zeus* (Father);
Lover; Unknown philosopher (hermit); *Kleobis* and *Biton* (twins).

To a lesser or greater extent *all* characters in a story are aspects of the teller's personality. Often what you least like about yourself, or your worst fears, are portrayed as a villain. The plot could be seen as a process of individuation (a wholeness of self) whereby the teller reconciles sundered aspects of his/her personality, eg: the Golden Child, the Wounded King, the Absent Father, etc. In this way narrative can help us to, in New Age parlance, 'rewrite our own script', ie: give ourselves a happy ending, or at least deal with repressed sides of our personality. Use this 'soul-mining' to give authenticity and emotional energy to your characters, and enrich your stories.

Andy Letcher, in his article *So You Wanna Be a Bard?* concludes: "These archetypes are an energy for us to use so we can recreate Bardism for our modern needs in this crazy, crazy world and still be embedded in the Bardic Tradition."

Lughnasadh: A Harvest of Tales

Lughnasadh is the Celtic **Fire Festival** marking the beginning of harvest. The English equivalent is Lammas, from the Saxon word for 'Loaf-Mass', when a ritual loaf was made from the first sheaf cut and dedicated to the Corn Goddess. Named after the Celtic sun god Lugh, who was known by his epithets Lugh-Lamfhada, the long-armed, or Lugh-Samildanach, the many-skilled, the Funeral Games of Lugh (Lugh-nasadh) were dedicated to the fertility Goddess Tailte. Corn dollies are traditionally made at harvest's inception, although they have a cousin in **Imbolc**'s *dealbh Bride* (icon of Bride) made from an oatsheaf.

Lleu Llaw Gyffes slain by Gronw Pebr's spear.

Sir John Barleycorn is the ballad that sums up this time of year best of all, describing the death, dismemberment and communion of the Barley King. The Story of Lleu Llaw Gyffes epitomises this ancient leitmotif, the Death of the Corn King. In this tale from *The Mabinogion* there are several references to the sea. Lleu's brother is called Dylan, son of the sea, because at the first opportunity he scuttles off into the waves and is never seen again. It is ironic that Wales' greatest Bard of the modern era, Dylan Thomas, more or less drowned himself in the same way (with drink), ending his life tragically early. A notoriously formidable drinker, he was a veritable John Barleycorn – a name Jack London appropriated for his memoirs as an alcoholic. Man's relationship with barley is a treacherous one. Its power is not to be underestimated, as is the power of the Bard.

In the tale, Lleu, Gwydion's nephew, is given three geas by Arianrhod – who was humiliated by his birth at the court of Math: firstly, to have no name except the one she gives him; secondly, to bear no arms except the ones she bestows upon him; and thirdly, to never know the love of a mortal wife. Wily Gwydion uses his Bardic skill to overcome these conditions, rising to the challenges set by his sister-goddess, acting here as initiatorix. So firstly, Gwydion must get his nephew a name from the lips of the woman who bore him – for, as in many societies, a name is fundamental. Without a name you do not exist – in Egyptian belief your soul will perish without one, so it is placed across the mouth at burial. Gwydion takes Lleu to the coast and transforms a pile of seaweed into the finest cordovan, then disguising themselves as shoemakers they set off for Caer Arianrhod in a boat. Gwydion tricks Arianrhod down to his vessel after making exquisite shoes for her that don't quite fit: so that she has to come in person for an accurate fitting. As she places her foot upon the boat, Lleu shoots a wren alighted on the rudder with his shoemaking needle between thighbone and sinew and so gains a name from Arianrhod – the name Lleu Llaw Gyffes, meaning the Lion (or Fair-haired One) of the Steady Hand.

Straight after, Gwydion dispels the illusion of their disguise and the boat, much to his sister's annoyance, who places the second geas upon her son: never to receive arms (armour) except from herself. But Gwydion will not be outwitted. He returns to Caer Arianrhod with Lleu, this time in the guise of Bards. As is the custom they are welcomed in, in exchange for entertainment. But overnight Gwydion conjures a mass enchantment (**gramarye**) of an enemy fleet attacking. In the extreme circumstances of the attack even the Bards are expected to bear arms: Arianrhod herself asks them to help defend her castle. Gwydion equips himself, but asks the Queen to arm the boy. No sooner does she do this than Gwydion banishes the illusory enemy host. It was all a ruse and he has beguiled his sister again into overcoming her second geas. This scene shows the power of the Bard.

The ability to create mass panic by words alone is not improbable – Orson Welles caused mass hysteria when his version of HG Wells' *War of the Worlds* was broadcast on the radio in the Thirties. Listeners thought it was really happening and panicked: rioting in the street broke out. And now we live in an age of spin doctors and a culture of fear, when we go to war under the spurious threat of Weapons of Mass Destruction.

The word is a powerful weapon and has to be used wisely, with responsibility and with respect for one's audience and fellow human beings.

Through his foolhardiness Lleu Llaw Gyffes revealed to his adulterous wife Blodeuwedd, the amoral flower-bride that Gwydion and Math make for him out of the blooms of "oak and broom and meadow-sweet", the only highly improbable way he could be slain: "Neither inside or outside, neither on horse nor on foot…" but by a spear made for a year and a day on the Sabbaths. By entrusting his inhuman wife with his 'Achilles' heel' Llew condemns himself to death. Blodeuwedd uses the knowledge to orchestrate his assassination by her secret lover, Gronw Pebr. Struck by the magical spear, Lleu turns into an eagle and flies away.

This shows how, on one level, like the World War II slogan 'careless talk costs lives', we *do* have to be careful what we say. This is not to be paranoid, but to choose carefully who we divulge secrets of the heart, or our path, to. Not everyone will be sympathetic, or ready. Reveal your true colours in the wrong crowd and you may have them mocked. Yeats so beautifully conveys this sense of vulnerability in his poem *He Wishes for the Cloths of Heaven*: "tread softly because you tread upon my dreams".

However, Blodeuwedd's treachery may be interpreted in a different light, not as the unfaithfulness of a wife (who wasn't human and so didn't live by human laws) but as the ritual slaying of the Oak King by the Holly King: as the Lord of Winter takes over from Summer to be consort of the (Spring) goddess.

This is an archetypal situation, the Eternal Triangle that reappears throughout history and fuels many great myths and legends, from the Osiris-Isis-Set trinity to Orpheus-Eurydice-Hades, onto Arthur-Guinevere-Lancelot and endless variants. It is featured in its mythopoeic essence in the tale of Culhwch and Olwen, which contains within it the mini-narrative of Gwythyr, Creiddylad and Gwynn ap Nudd. King Arthur decrees that this flower maiden's love-rivals must fight each other for her hand every May Eve until the end of time.

Six Month Review

Well Done. You have reached the end of the second quarter and should be half-way through your first year as Anruth. So far you should have studied the teachings of **Spirit** and **Air**, and now you have the wisdom of **Fire** to add to your Bardic development. Time to take stock again, and reflect upon what you have learnt in the last three months, and overall. You should have meditated upon the significance of fire, found the fire within, written and performed poetry, encountered Faerie, explored sun symbolism, entered the Land of Story, and climbed the beanstalk! You should know some storyteller's lore – you may even be able to tell a tale or two yourself. Your range of skills and knowledge as a Bardic initiate is expanding, but your training is not yet complete. You need to assimilate the qualities of **Water** and **Earth** to be a fully-rounded and grounded Bard-in-the-making. Keep up the good work and in six months you will be able to claim your Chair as an Anruth of the Hare Grade and take your place in the Gorsedd of Bards. Remember, you are not alone and you may want to take advantage of **The Silver Branch Bardic Network** Yahoo! Group for peer support (*see back of book*). Write in your journal how you feel now compared to how you did at the start of your Bardic training (refer back to your **self-evaluation form**). How do you feel it is going? What have you enjoyed and what you have found difficult, if anything? Read through any poems, songs or stories you have written and see if there's any noticeable progression or path developing. Look ahead at the next six months training and express any concerns you have, or anything you are especially looking forward to.

Tick when you have completed the following:

* Spirit of Fire
* The Fire Festivals
* Month 4: Finding the Fire Within
* Voice of the Fire
* Raising Chi
* Fire Magic
* Protest Poem
* Using Passion
* Fire in the Head
* Write a Fire Poem.
* Tips for Writing Poetry.
* Tips for Performing Poetry.
* The Three Illuminations: *teinmlaida*
* Hot Penning
* Month 5: Encountering Faerie
* Waiting for Faerie

* Voice of the Sun
* Contemplate the Sun
* Sun Story
* Sun Costume
* Telling in the Round
* Casting a Circle in Performance
* Bladud Story
* Solar Hero Tales
* The Shining Ones
* Month 6: Entering the Land of Story
* Storyscape
* Lore of the Storyteller
* Climbing the Beanstalk
* Using Archetypes
* Lughnasadh: A Harvest of Tales
* 6 Month Review

FOUR
WATER

Month 7: Connecting with
the Animal Kingdom

Month 8: Calling the Inner Bard

Month 9: Awenyddion

Spirits of Water

Hail now to the Spirits of the West, the element of water, of emotion. Think of the vast volatile oceans of the world, covering 70% of our blue planet, and in a microcosmic way each one of us is similar in the way our bodies consist largely of water. Small wonder then that we are affected by the cycles of the moon, as the tides of the ocean are. Exactly like our subconscious, it is a part of ourselves we cannot control – but which affects us nevertheless. The more we subdue or deny our real feelings, the stronger they become, emerging in a twisted form unless we let them breathe, unless we give them voice. The waters of the West are treacherous, but full of delights, like the realm of love itself. We are lured in, like unwary sailors by sirens. Yet without love life is too dry: you cry, but not all of your tears, and laugh, but not all of your laughter. Love, like water, restores the Wasteland. Without it, the world is barren. There is the salutary story of King Amangons, who coveted the gold cup offered by the maidens of the wells to passing travellers. He wanted the refreshing draught and the vessel that carried it, for himself. He seized the cup, and his knights defiled the maidens. The wells ran dry and the land became wasted. Amangons himself becomes a Fisher King, unable to die, but not fully alive. If we keep feelings to ourselves they stagnate, turn foetid, as epitomised by the flowing spirit of Awen – Life is Flow, Stasis is Death.

The springs, wells, streams, rivers, lakes, seas and oceans of this water-filled world are populated by a plethora of elementals: undines, nymphs, naiads, rusalka – goddesses of the waves, of the ocean's wealth. The cruel, generous, fickle and beautiful sea itself is universally seen as a woman. Within her oceanic womb is contained a plenitude of life: fish, dolphins, whales, coral, still being charted and constantly under threat from pollution and exploitation. Global Warming heats the oceans, which kills plankton – photo-synthesisers of the oceans and an important food source for whales. Remove a keystone species and a whole ecosystem collapses.

Water is the fundamental element of life. It is the world's most precious resource, the one that sets it apart from the majority of planets in the solar system. Without it, life cannot exist – in the same way that without love we may as well not be alive, because we are not fully alive if we do not feel, deeply.

Being on the Atlantic seaboard has influenced our orientation – because the sun sets in the West, across the wide Atlantic Ocean – the West has come to be associated with the place we go to when we die – and perhaps are reborn. Thus, King Arthur, mortally wounded after the final battle at Camlann with his son, Mordred, is carried into the

West by the Goddess (usually depicted here in her Triple Aspect; or in another tradition, Taliesin, Merlin and Barinthus) to Avalon, the Undying Lands. Ossian, Bard of the Fianna, son of Fionn Mac Cumhail, is tempted to go to Tir Nan Og, the Land of the Ever Young, by Niamh of the Golden-hair. Bran and Brendan set sail on immrama, wonder voyages, to the Isle of Women, The Isle of the Blessed, the Fortunate Isles, and other idealised places. The Westering Sea is the collective location for the utopias of the Celtic imagination: the fabled lost kingdoms of Ys, Kêr-Ys, Lyonesse, Atlantis... Interesting, the susurration in those words – their sibilance echoing the sound of the ceaseless sea, temptingly echoing the hiss of foamy waves upon a distant, paradisal shore. This is the place our heart is called to by enchanting songs, the place of peace our soul yearns for at death, or sometimes, before our time, as in *The Stolen Child*, by WB Yeats:

> Come away, O human child, to the water,
> Come away, O human child, to the water and the wild.
> For the world's more full of weeping,
> Than you can understand.

On the altar and in ritual, the chalice represents, on a literal level, the element of water. And its antecedent is the cauldron, that proto-Grail of the Celts, which appears in many forms, in many stories: the Cauldron of Inspiration, of Plenty, of Rebirth. It could be a silver bowl, as in *The Countess of the Fountain*, or an otherworldly cauldron "rimmed with pearl and warmed by the breath of nine Muses" as in the *Preiddu Annwn*, when Arthur harrows Annwn itself to win it. The Pendragon and his crew aboard the ship Prydwen, must pass through Nine Gates, or Castles to reach it – the final one being the Revolving Seat of Arianrhod herself, the Chair of Awen, Caer Sidi (place of Bardic initiation, which we'll return to when we consider the **Voice of the Stars**). One of the four hallows of the Tuatha De Danann, the Cauldron of the Dagda, which would never go empty, was kept in the City of Muirias, guarded by Semias. It is the place we must go to in our imaginations, when we need to 'replenish the well'. Although it can be reached by pathworking, sometimes we need to go to a physical location, by the sea, to help us recuperate. In West Wales, on Cardigan Bay, in Borth, there is a youth hostel called 'Morlais', **Voice of the Sea**, where the first Way of Awen weekend was held. It overlooks the legendary Lowest Hundred of the 'Bottom Cantreth', Cantreth Gwaelod, which was inundated by the sea. Remains of the fossilised forest can still be picked up on the shore at low-tide (although watch the mud-flats, they are perilous!) Here, Maelgwyn managed to lay claim to it by setting a challenge to his rivals – they all were asked to sit in the estuary – whoever stayed there the longest kept the land. Cunning Maelgwyn had a throne made of wax and feathers, which floated – so he didn't drown. And now, every year, a festival is held where fools sit on thrones, trying to stay afloat as the tide comes in. Maelgwyn's arrogance is the exact opposite of Canute's on the East Coast, who famously sat facing the waves on his throne, commanding them to turn them back, not out of hubris, but to prove that even a king's power is finite and must submit to the greater one of Nature.

In this era of accelerated Climate Change, of ever-frequent disasters, such as the Indian Ocean Tsunami, our perception of the sea is shifting. Many coastal areas are feeling increasingly vulnerable, at the mercy of even small rises in sea level. Some places are decimated by drought whilst others are flooded. As a species, humankind needs to balance its relationship with water. We need to learn how to value it, respect it and share it equally. It has been said the water will be the most important and fought over resource of the Twenty-First Century. The time to find ways of preserving it is now. Everything helps. Make sure you have no leaking taps. Don't use hosepipes. Have a shower instead of a bath. Only boil as much water as you need for a drink. Use rainwater to water the garden, and so on. Petty, prosaic, but practical things that collectively make a difference – in the way the little raindrops make the ocean.

EXERCISE:

1. Spring Blessings
Find a spring, pool or stream. Sit by it, close your eyes and listen in silence. If you know the spring-water is pure, drink some and savour its cool refreshing draught. How does it make you feel? What thoughts or feelings bubble up? Write them down in your journal.

2. Write a Praise Poem or Lorica to a Spring or Stream
Is there a local legend associated with your local well, spring, spout, pool or brook? Recite it at a Spring Blessing or Dressing. Organise a stream or pond clearing day. Create a wildlife haven. Put on a fund-raising benefit for Water Aid. Protect, maintain and celebrate these important resources. This poem (*Heather's Spring*, opposite) is based upon a beautiful spring in a verdant churchyard, and was written for the friend who took me there, while she was suffering from cancer in hospital:

Month 7:
Connecting with the Animal Kingdom

As Bards we should aspire to be connected to the natural world. This month I want you to focus on your relationship with animals. Do you have any pets? Did you grow up with any around the house? Are you drawn to a particular animal? Do you have affinity with, for instance, horses? Dogs? Cats? Dolphins? Do you like to support a particular charity protecting animals or wildlife? At the other extreme, do you eat animals? Are you a meat-eater, a vegetarian or a vegan? If you eat meat, do you care how the animal was treated? Do you buy organic, free range, 'cruelty free' products? Or do you go to animal circuses? Fox-hunting events? Bull-fights? Whatever you do, I merely suggest you do it with awareness and respect. Native Americans famously used every part of the buffalo – and they honoured its spirit, like the majority of hunter-gatherer tribes, whose lives depend upon a respectful and sustainable relationship with nature. Their nomadic lifestyles allow wildlife populations to replenish, and because they have to carry everything they own, they will not hoard more than they need, while our materialistic culture encourages us to consume and discon-nects us from the source of our food, the resources we use. We flick on a switch for light or heat. We buy pre-packaged, pre-cooked foods

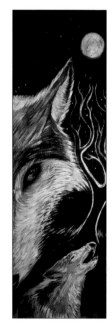

Heather's Spring

There is a spring where hope does flow
– it's nearer than you think.
A place of peace and beauty
Where you can go to drink.

Upon a mossy bank
by a weeping bough
sit and spend some time
in the sacred now.

Listen to the gentle song,
which the waters sing.
Hearken to your heart,
the pulse of its beating.

Immerse and let the music
wash your woes away.
Heed the endless melody,
which the undines play.

Healing rings around you,
for all your ills a balm.
Waves of love enfold you
in an embrace so warm.

Let the love flow through you,
pouring from every pore.
Purifying you with truth,
the beauty that you are.

Thirsty, soul? Come taste
a draught of the infinite.
Baptise this body of water –
let it become light.

Pilgrim, this eternal source
shall always replenish.
Blessings of the circle,
return when you so wish.

Remember, all life flows
and will ever renew.
There is a spring where hope does flow
and it is inside you.

                       Kevan Manwaring

in supermarkets – divorced from the realities of growing and harvesting or rearing and slaughtering. It is about connection.

In the Celtic Tradition, as in many native cultures, animals are not only seen as sources of food, but as repositories of wisdom. It was believed animals were 'older' than mankind, had longer memories and knew more. This is summed up in the ancient Gaelic saying below:

The Memory of Animals

Three ages of a dog,
The ages of a horse,
Three ages of a horse,
The age of a man,
Three ages of man,
The age of a deer,
Three ages of a deer,
The age of an eagle,
Three ages of an eagle,
The age of an oak tree.

Sacred animals populate the tales of Celtic myth and legend: wise salmon, white stags, swine from the Underworld or monstrous boars, loyal hounds, supernaturally swift horses, magical foals, fecund cows, mischievous mice, and birds of every description.

This belief in the wisdom and longevity of animals is best illustrated in the tale of Mabon and the Oldest of Animals from *The Mabinogion* (from *Culhwch and Olwen*). Culhwch wishes to wed Olwen flowerfoot, daughter of the dread giant Ysbaddaden (hawthorn head). The giant sets the suitor thirty nine nigh impossible tasks, which he must accomplish if he is to have Olwen's hand in marriage, the strangest and most difficult of which is to give his future father-in-law a haircut. Now, this is no ordinary trim: for the only tools up for the job are the comb and shears stuck between the ears of the fiercesome boar, Twrch Trwyth. To catch this gigantic boar, a gigantic hound was needed, Drudwyn, and the only person in the world who was capable of handling such a hound was Mabon, son of Modron, who had not been seen since being "stolen from between his mother and the wall" aged only three years old. But this was a long time ago – perhaps at the beginning of mythic time itself, and nobody knew where to find this elusive child, not even his cousin. Culhwch gets the help of Arthur's knights, and the use of his Bard, Gwyrhyr, who knows the language of animals. They track down Mabon's cousin Oiddoel, who doesn't know his whereabouts, but he suggests asking the Elder Beasts, for they had the longest memories – if anyone would remember, they would. So, the five of them set off – Culhwch, Kai, Bedwyr, Oiddoel and Gwyrhyr – on the quest to find the oldest of animals. First they talk to the Blackbird of Cilgwyry, then the Owl of Cwm Cawlwyd, the Stag of Fernbrake Hill, the Eagle of Gwernabwy and, finally, the Salmon of Llyn Llyw – who is the oldest of them all and knows where Mabon, the ancient child, is hidden. The Salmon takes them there, to the Walls of Gloucester, where they find the ancient child imprisoned. Mabon is released and in return helps Culhwch with his quest: Drudwyn is summoned and used to hunt Twrch Trwth across the British Isles – the comb and shears snatched from the Boar just before it disappears beneath the sea off the tip of Cornwall, taking Mabon with it. With the necessary implements in hand Culhwch gives the giant a haircut, completing his incredible set of tasks, and so wins the hand of Olwen.

This rich tale is one of my favourites and this brief retelling does not do it full justice (see various translations of *The Mabinogion* for the full version) but it serves to illustrate the importance of animals, of their wisdom and memory (and telling the tale itself is a feat of **Bardic memory**). It is worth meditating upon, visualising and exploring. The best analysis of it, and the other Branches of the Mabinogion, is found in Caitlin Matthews' *Mabon and the Mysteries of Britain* (Arkana 1987).

Gwyrhyr, the Bard who knows the Language of Animals, is an interesting figure – illustrative of the overlap between the Bard and the shaman (see: *Taliesin, the Last Celtic Shaman,* and *The Celtic Shaman* by John Matthews). Such a figure crops up throughout mythic history in various forms: from Adam naming the animals in Eden; Enkidu, He-Who-Runs-With-the-Wild-Beasts in the Epic of Gilgamesh; green-skinned Osiris, Pan in Arcadia; Diana and Artemis, wild huntresses; Cernunnos, Robin Hood to Herne the Hunter in the Great Windsor Forest, Tarzan, Earl of Greystoke; Mowgli in *The Jungle Book*; numerous feral children, and the equally mythologised Mountain Men of America, such as Davy Crockett. He is, in essence, the Green Man: the human face of Nature, a symbol of creativity with his foliating mouth, like a Bard speaking flowery words, or with Awen pouring out of him; but also of humanity's connection to the natural world. In one way he is Nature anthropomorphised – but, if by giving the wild a human face and qualities, we can relate to it and respect it more, all the better, eg: as Sir John Barleycorn, the spirit of the harvest slain every year to rise again. He beams from the corbels, pews and boss-stones of churches across Britain, symbolic of the Spirit of Nature that not even Christianity could subdue – in fact, there is common ground to be found with their own 'man on a tree'. In his annual Death-and-Resurrection the Green Man mirrors the world myths of the **Solar Hero**: Baldur, Osiris, Tammuz, Jesus, Odin, Lleu Llaw Gyffes, and the like, who are often sacrificed on a tree.

We encounter him in his fiercest aspect in the tale of Owein, or *The Countess of the Fountain*, again from *The Mabinogion*, as the Wild Herdsman:

…take the road that brought you to this valley until you reach the wood which you passed through, and a short distance into that wood you will find a fork: take the right hand path and continue until you come to a great cleared field with a mound in the centre, and on that mound you will see a great black man, no smaller than two men of this world. He has one foot, and one eye in the middle of his forehead, and he carries an iron spear which you can be certain would be a burden for any two men. Though ugly, he is not an unpleasant man. He is keeper of the forest, and you will see a thousand wild animals grazing about him. Ask him where to go from the clearing: he will be cross with you, but nevertheless he will show you how to find what you seek.

trans. Gantz. Penguin

This amazing, frightening figure is perhaps a chthonic deity leftover from a shamanic worldview. With his one eye, one foot and one club he seems to embody the World Tree itself, but perhaps also symbolises the unity of a pure vision, unsullied by the prism of civilisation. He brings with him an air of menace, like the fierce Green Knight in the Gawain story – of a reckoning with nature that needs resolving. If nature is denied, it bursts through in unexpected ways, as in the story of Herne the Hunter, where the enigmatic shamanic Urswick who heals Herne by cutting off the head of a stag and placing it upon him, 'bursts through in flames' when he appears out of the wildwood. The image of the Wild Herdsman sitting upon his mound is echoed in the iconic image of Cernunnos upon the Gundestrup Cauldron, who sits cross-legged, with antlers upon his head, a staff-like snake in one hand, a ram-headed torc in the other.

This is a man who has brought the opposing forces of nature into balance, within himself – he has found harmony, and it is not surprising if he appears in an almost identical posture to the Buddha, who sat under the Bodhi Tree until he found enlightenment and was protected from the rain by a giant cobra – rising from behind him to cover his head.

Cernunnos. Oil on wood.

Could this be the *kundalini*, the sexual serpent energy which rises up the spine in Tantric practice and can be released in ecstasy, yet, if subdued unnaturally can become twisted and is dangerous, manifesting in perversions and obsessions?

Nature will out, so it is essential to work with its rhythms and tides. We are part of Nature, not apart from it. By connecting with the wild, we are connecting with the wild within ourselves. Whatever the ethics of keeping pets at all, they help us to stay in touch with Nature and empathise with it. A dog will make us go for a walk, even when it's raining, and will do what it needs without anxiety – for it is instinct embodied. When I go for a walk in the woods, I go for a walk with my wolf, my **totem animal**. My senses sharpen slightly and I am reminded of the larger Web of Life beyond my own petty concerns. Communing with the natural world helps us to get a perspective on life and reminds us of the natural cycle, which we are part of, and the bigger picture.

EXERCISE: Find your Totem Animal

Everyone has a totem animal. This is the belief of the Native American people and Aboriginal Australians and one shared by many British pagans, especially in the Druid community. Aboriginal Tradition states you are born into a certain animal 'clan' and have a taboo against hunting and eating it, coupled with a right to protect it and know its song – connected with a specific locale, related to the movements of the Rainbow Serpent at the beginning of time. This sense of connection with the animal kingdom is a healthy attitude. By associating with one species in particular, it fosters a sense of stewardship and fellowship – on both the human's and animal's part – and it connects the individual to the larger Web of Life.

Personally speaking, finding my totem animal has helped to not only maintain my sense of connection with the natural world, it has provided a source of guidance and support through the vicissitudes of the human kingdom. My wolf has help me through 'the woods' both literally and metaphorically. I found my wolf at a time I thought I was lost – physically lost in the deepest wildwood, drenched in the pouring rain. Using the wolf within me, its instincts and senses, I found my way out. Since then, he has been my guide and loyal companion. I grew up in a dog-mad family, and have always got on well with canines – but felt less tame, less domesticated, less obedient than Man's Best Friend. The wolf has a wild side, but also is an incredible socially-minded animal, loyal to the pack, mating for life. In the Native American Tradition the wolf is seen as the Teacher – and that is certainly something I can relate to, but we have to be careful not to anthropomorphise as Barry Lopez, author of *Of Wolves and Men*, warns. We should relate to our totem on its own terms. I just appreciate, deeply, the wolf's spirit, its unvain magnificence. Whenever I am faced with a difficult decision or situation, which cannot necessarily by solved rationally, I seek guidance from my 'wolf' – he knows, when I do not.

Your totem is always there to help you to trust your instincts, to stay true to yourself, to defend what is precious to you, to act with the purest motives. Your totem helps you to stay centred, when you feel challenged or threatened. It is your quintessence, your wild soul, when the veneer of civilisation has been stripped away, but not to reveal brutality, but truthfulness, in the way that only nature can be true to itself, nothing other than what it is. As Polonius says to Hamlet, "This above all, to thine own self by true", which echoes the classic dictum of the Athenian lawgiver Solon carved above Apollonian Temples:

Know Thyself

I believe we only have one totem animal, which is 'ours' for life, but Companion Animals may come into our life as and when we need them. The famous example is of the mother, who finds the strength of the bear to lift the overturned car to rescue her baby. In different situations we need different skills – as embodied by the animals: the discretion of a mouse, the wisdom of an owl, the eyes of a hawk, the ears of a bat, the claws of a cat, the roar of a lion, the memory of an elephant, and so on. At times of duress you may find an animal suddenly making an appearance in your life. Watch for clues. Observe nature and read its 'messages.' Robert the Bruce famously found wisdom in the persistence of the spider spinning its web in the cave he was hiding in. By detailed observation of the natural world we can find many suggestions as to how to lead our lives in harmony with the greater web.

So, in this exercise you are going to find your totem. It will normally be a native mammal, although there may be the odd exception, eg: spider, snake, salmon. It must be an animal from your own country, so even if you are living in Britain now, if you grew up in South Africa, say, it will be a species found there. Otherwise, if you are British, then it will be an animal found here only (not a moose, penguin, kangaroo, etc.) and a real, rather than mythic animal (no dragons, unicorns or pegasi!).

This may take two or three attempts. Do not be discouraged. If you are uncertain at first as to whether an animal is really your totem, or merely wish-fulfilment, then sleep on it. You'll know if you are truly connected to this animal in your very bones, your very soul. You may well resemble the animal, either physically, in movement, demeanour or spirit. You may have always been fascinated by that animal, may even have a phobia about it – which suggests how divorced you are from your own nature. Now is the time to come to terms with it, with your 'animal side'. Do you lash out, or snarl when provoked? Are you catty, or dog-tired, sheepish or bear-like? If unreconciled your animal nature may manifest in a Shadow form, erupting through in subconscious mannerisms (eg: this dual nature and unhealthy schism is explored in Herman Hesse's *Steppenwolf*).

1   Meditate. Relax your body: sit in an upright position, or lie down in a darkened room, with a blanket to cover you. Make sure you won't be disturbed.

2   Visualise your favourite natural place. It could be a garden, woodland, a cliff top, a mountainside – anywhere you feel safe, somewhere you know well. 'Sense' your surroundings; 'feel' the grass/sand/rock beneath your feet; smell the flowers; feel the wind or salt spray on your face, etc. Make it vivid in your mind's eye. You can always return to this place at any point of the Pathworking. Be careful not to jump from the Realm of the Totems straight into Daily Consciousness because it can be disorientating and possibly dangerous. If you want to return simply visualise your favourite place, then slowly open your eyes, stretch and get yourself a snack. Try again another time.

3   In your favourite place, find a tree and sit with your back against it. Feel its strength, its longevity. Gaze up into its canopy and see its branches extend into the sky, into the stars. Imagine its roots reaching into the bowels of the Earth and beyond – into the Underworld, for this is your *Axis Mundi*, the World Tree. You will journey down its roots into the Realm of the Totems.

4   Get a friend to start drumming, or to turn on a drumming tape. (Tapes are available from Hallowquest, Dreampower, Kenneth Meadows, etc. See **Contacts**). The drumming will alter your brain waves and send you into a different state of consciousness. On the drumbeat you will journey into the Underworld (that is why it's known as the Shaman's Horse).

5   Listening to the rapid drumbeat, journey down the World Tree – a long dark shaft, until finally emerging into the Underworld, the realm of the totems.

6   Let the drumming slow and stop. Let your heartbeat adjust. Observe your surroundings: you should be in an otherworldly paradise, where nature is especially lush. The leaves and flowers seem to shine with their own light. Everything is 'more so' than in the Middle World. This is the Realm of Faerie – be careful not to eat any fruit, or to offend any of its denizens. Slowly get up and explore, watching where you tread. If anything appears greet it politely. Act with respect towards everything there.

7   Walk along a forest track to a clear pool surrounded by overhanging trees. A light like sunlight dapples the translucent water fed by a spring bubbling from a mossy vulva-like rock. Observe at the Pool of the Beasts. Here all the animals of the forest come to quench their thirst. Wait in silence and stillness and see what emerges from the wildwood. Whenever an animal appears do not be alarmed. Gently announce your presence and ask the animal if it is your totem beast. If it nods then follow it into the woods and 'run with it' before returning to the tree. Unless you get a clear signal, then let the animal go. If you do not get a response this time, then do not be disheartened – return another time. The Pool of the Beasts is always there, waiting.

8   Return to the Tree. Sit with your back against it. Let the drumming recommence, as you journey back up the World Tree. If you have made contact with your totem, then bring it back to your favourite space.

9   Keeping the totem 'inside', slowly regain consciousness of your actual surroundings. Open your eyes, seeing the world around you through its eyes.

10   Start to move as it would move, on all fours, with wings, etc. Mime its movement. Feel its strength, its agility. Make its sound: bark, screech, roar. Dance your animal. Celebrate! You have found a lifelong friend, one that has always been there, waiting for you to summon it.

11   Ground yourself with a snack and a drink. Write down your experiences immediately in your journal.

12   Feel it always with you. Express its voice through a poem, song, dance or story.

13   Paint it, or collect images of it. Add a symbol of it to your altar or Sacred Space.

14   Visit a sanctuary, or try to see it in the wild (eg: wolf sanctuary, or whale watching trip).

Tarot cards are a good tool for meditation and divination. Some excellent sets are: *Beasts of Albion* by Miranda Grey, *The Druid Animal Oracle* by Phillip Carr-Gom, *Celtic Totem Animals* by John Matthews. Find one with animals of your own country, not another's (ie: don't use Native American animals if you live in Britain) and avoid fantasy ones (ie: Dragons, Unicorns) if you want to connect with something real. Better still, get involved with a wildlife charity, organise a fundraising event, or do practical conservation work to help preserve its habitat.

Nothing replaces actually directly communing with Nature, but there are many great books which help us to understand and value it even more. Apart from all the field guides and ecology books (eco-criticism being a growth area), poetry, fiction and nature writing can help us to imagine the world from an animal's perspective and explore our relationship with the Wild. There's too many to mention here, but some shining examples include: the writings of Thomas Hardy, Richard Jeffries, WH Hudson, *Rural Rides* by William Cobbett, the poetry of John Clare, Wordsworth, Ted Hughes, *Whale Nation* by Heathcote Williams, *Dart* by Alice Oswald, *Watership Down* by Richard Adams, *Ring of Bright Water* by Gavin Maxell, *Tarka the Otter* by Henry Williamson, *The Goshawk* by TH White, *The Snow Goose* by Paul Gallico, *Jonathan Livingstone Seagull* by Richard Bach; and many others. There are some good anthologies out there. Common Ground's excellent trilogy *Trees Be Company, Field Days* and *The River's Voice* is a good place to start. Add your own to the list, or, even better, write your own 'praise song' to Nature.

The Hawk of Achill

This is one of the key Bardic texts that deserves to be studied and meditated upon in full – the current scope of this book does not allow us to print this lengthy **colloquy** here in its splendid entirety. It involves the shamanic conversation between Fintan the Bard and the Hawk of Achill, who discover, by relating their life histories, that they are exactly the same age – an incredible 6515 (close to the Biblical age of the Earth) and furthermore, the Hawk was the one who plucked out Fintan's eye! (like Odin, who lost his eye while languishing on Yggdrasil, the World Ash, for nine days and nights, to return with the Runes, the Elder Futhark). There is another similarity (called 'mythic cross-hatch'): Odin retrieved the Runes from Mimir's Spring at the base of Yggdrasil, while Fintan communes with the Hawk of Achill at a frozen river mouth or waterfall. Within the long colloquy, in the form of gnomic stanzas, there is much lore and revelation including a sequence with a magical branch, which seems uncannily like the **silver branch** wielded by other ambassadors of the Sidhe, and Bards who had travelled there and back again.

Both Fintan and the Hawk have lived for a long time, as super-annuated as Methusaleh, and both expire at the end of the sequence – perhaps suggesting the Hawk is Fintan's totem or soul-bird, sharing a dual destiny. However, the Hawk seems to be more than this – being present at many great battles and delighting in plucking out eyes and snatching limbs of fallen heroes – which suggests he may be Death itself (omnipresent and perennial). Yet there is a fascinating correspondence between Bards and birds in more than name alone. There is the *tuirgin*, the shamanic feathered cloak of the vision-poet. Bards were said to speak the Language of Birds. In the Hawk of Achill Fintan boasts at one point "I am able finely to converse with thee in bird-language". This skill is also possessed by the Bard Gwyrhyr, Interpreter of Languages who, in the Tale of Mabon and the Oldest of Animals, is able to converse with the Blackbird of Cilgwry, the Owl of Cwm Cawlwyd and the Eagle of Gwernabwy, among other totem beasts. The 'Language of Birds' is sometimes another name for the Ogham tree alphabet – said to have been inspired by the legs of a crane in flight. And, of course, the Crane-skin Bag is part of a Bard's sacred regalia. But perhaps this correspondence is not at all surprising when we consider that Bards and birds share the same element (air) and furthermore, are the masters of it. Air, wind, breath and speech are all connected; wind is seen as a cipher for the Holy Spirit, or the Divine itself in several cultures.

The Hawk of Achill preserves a great deal of mythic history, and perhaps was used as a mnemonic for doing so. Spend some time with this poem. It may seem obscure to begin with but with persistence and a poet's intuition it begins to unlock its secrets. As an exercise try writing a dialogue with your own totem. See what wisdom can be channelled in this way.

Fionn and the Salmon

The young Fionn Mac Cumhail went to the hermit Finegas (aka Finn Eces) to learn the Bardic arts. The old man had tried long and hard to catch the fabled Salmon of Wisdom, which fed on the Nuts of Knowledge from the hallowed hazel growing on the banks of the Boyne. With the boy's arrival Finegas finally caught it. Overjoyed, he gave it to the boy to cook, warning him not to eat it. But, while Fionn turned it on the fire, it bubbled, burst and spat at him, scalding his thumb. To soothe it, he placed his burnt digit in his mouth. Immediately, he knew all the wisdom of the ages. Sheepishly, he took the fish to Finegas who could see instantly what had happened. He realised the wisdom had been meant for Fionn all along and bade the boy go in peace, now he had the Bardic skill he had sought. Whenever Fionn wanted to access that wisdom all he had to do was chew his thumb.

In this classic tale of Bardic initiation you have almost identical motifs to the legend of Taliesin: a young accident-prone apprentice is summoned to the grove of the learned one (Finegas the Hermit, or Ceridwen the Crone) where wisdom is being caught/gathered and concocted. The young appren-

Ink drawing from the Gundestrup Cauldron.

tice is instructed in his taboo-defined task – tending the 'cooking' of the wisdom, with strict instructions not to taste the forbidden potion/flesh. Through carelessness (or the action of the subconscious) an accident happens which results in the young apprentice imbibing the distilled wisdom of the world, meant for someone else (Afagddu or Finegas). He has to suffer the consequences (Ceridwen's wrath, Finegas's disappointment) but manages to get away with it in the end (through a series of shape-changes or learning to fulfil his destiny). The wisdom was meant for him all along, but with it comes responsibility (Chief Bard of Arthur's court, or Leader of the Fianna). Throughout his life the Awen/imbas-filled prodigy draws nourishment and guidance from the wisdom he carries.

It is interesting that in the Tale of the Burning of the Thumb we find a triptych of 'Finns': Fintan, the Salmon of Wisdom; Finegas the Druid; and Fionn (or Finn) Mac Cumhail. In the Tale of Taliesin, we have Ceridwen; Gwion Bach and Morvran (the blind man who stokes the fire beneath the cauldron). It's almost as if these triads represent different aspects of the personality: Morvran and the Salmon: Lower Self (or subconscious); Finegas and Ceridwen – Higher Self; Gwion and Fionn – the Ego, or Eternal Child. Both Gwion and Fionn play the Fool in these episodes, the Fool who begins the Tarot journey, the Fool of cleansed perception (like the boy in the Emperor's New Clothes) who 'sees things as they really are'. When methodical logic fails (Finegas's attempts to catch the Salmon) the intuitive leap succeeds (the Salmon is captured when Fionn arrives). Gwion/Fionn the Youth symbolise the power of play, of lateral thinking, of the imagination. Sometimes you have to bypass logic to access wisdom. In the Taliesin story two salmon 'incidents' crop up – at one point Gwion becomes a salmon, while being chased by Ceridwen in the form of an otter-bitch; and later on, when he is cast adrift in a leather bag, inside a coracle, he is caught by Elphin, son of Gwyddno, in the salmon weir on May Eve. It seems the fate of Bards and salmon are interwoven. Why? Because the poet was said to receive his inspiration directly from the Salmon of Wisdom, which ate the hazel nuts from the nine hazels that grow around the Well of Segais, or Connla's; nine being the number of the goddess, of the Muses.

Nuts of Wisdom

Sinend daughter of Lodan Lucharglan…went to Connla's Well, which is under the sea, to behold it. That is the well at which are the hazels and inspirations of wisdom, that is the hazels of science and poetry, and in the same hour their fruit and their blossoms and their foliage break forth, and these fall on the well in the same shower, which raises on the water a royal surge of purple. Then the salmon drew the fruit, and the juice of the nuts is in their bellies. And seven streams of wisdom spring forth and turn there again…

From the *Dindsenchas*

A well at the bottom of the sea… A strange dream-like image, in the same category and of the same calibre as 'the tree half in leaf, half in flame' from the *Mabinogion*. Like the Buddhist koans designed to send the pupil's mind into a state of zen-like contemplation, these visual paradoxes achieve the same – sending us into a state of mind between the literal and the lateral, between the left and right side of the brain, between worlds. So, the Salmon of Wisdom draws its knowledge from the hazel grove that grows around the well at the 'bottom of the sea'. This not only symbolises the subconscious, it also echoes the Nordic notion of the World Tree, Ygdrassil, which grows between the worlds – at the base of which is Mimir's Spring, home of the Three Norns (Norse Fates) where Odin received his blinding flash of inspiration about the Runes, losing an eye in the process. In the Taliesin legend it is the old man who stokes the fire beneath Ceridwen's cauldron, Morda, who loses an eye, paying the price for Gwion Bach's appropriation of the Potion of Inspiration meant for Afaggdu. It is said that 'in the kingdom of the blind the one eyed man is King', but such insight comes at a price, and with responsibility.

EXERCISE: Cut and Peel a Hazel Wand

Druid rods made of hazel were found on Mona, the lost stronghold of the Celtic priesthood (Anglesey). Hazel is traditionally used for dowsing water. It is an excellent wood for tapping into the subconscious and divining answers. Following the example of Yeats' Wandering Aengus, "cut and peel a hazel wand". There's no need to "hook a berry to a thread" because we are going metaphorical fishing. At twilight, "when white moths were on the wing, and moth-like stars were flickering out", sit by a body of water (a spring, well, pool, lake, inlet or river), holding your hazel wand, and wait to see what happens… Fishing is a popular past-time probably just as much for its contemplative aspect as its competitive side. You can sense all those hermit-like fishermen along the waterways of Britain being reflective, searching the waters for answers, or just for some peace – in such a passive state wisdom surfaces, as in meditative practice. I am not suggesting you try to catch a fish – this exercise is about 'fishing' for answers. Perhaps you don't even know what the question is to begin with, but, given time, all sorts of interesting things may surface. Elphin was not expecting to discover the coracle containing Taliesin when he went fishing that May Eve at Gwyddno's Weir. Who knows what you may stumble across? Write down your experiences and thoughts in your journal as soon as you get back.

The Weir of the Twice-Born

The weir represents, in a mythopoeic sense, a shift of levels, of layers of consciousness. According to the Welsh legend, the reborn Taliesin was first discovered by Elphin, son of Gwyddno, at his father's salmon-weir on May Eve – thus dramatically changing their fortunes (if you recall Gwyddno had all of his horses poisoned when Ceridwen's Cauldron of Inspiration burst asunder and polluted the river adjoining their lands). Elphin becomes Taliesin's 'lord' during his early years, but one could argue Elphin himself, an empty character until activated by this incident, by fishing at the weir for salmon (wisdom) awakens his own Bard within.

At any of the eight festivals it is a good time to assess one's progress, and reflect upon what being a Bard means. Each year one experiences a symbolic death and rebirth around one's birthday, but if one synchronises with the seasonal cycles, this cycle becomes more meaningful. Let us imagine it is Maytide: the period of Winter hibernation and deep dreaming is over; one should have been busy seed-sowing and preparing for the busy months ahead. Those inklings of Spring are fully manifest, bursting forth with all the passion of Beltane, seemingly from nowhere, like those 'overnight successes' that are usually the fruit of years of dedication. Now we shift to the extrovert time of the year, when we begin the season of festivals and performances, when we show off our 'wares' and all that dreaming and hard work over the long Winter months hopefully pays off. Yet, before the storm the blessed calm. Now, briefly, is the moment to savour the stillness and silence, like Elphin at Gwyddno's weir. You may be down on your luck; it may have been a tough year, thus far. But take heart: things can only improve. Such times teach us a powerful and necessary lesson – making us appreciate good fortune when we are blessed with it, rather than taking it for granted. So savour the nadir and you will enjoy the zenith even more. At the first stroke of luck you will feel reborn and all your fears will be forgotten – like Saint George's annual death and resurrection, performed by the Mummers Players at midwinter. We must not let the 'dragon' win, although we must let it 'devour' us to be reborn – this Belly of the Whale experience is actually a symbolic return to the womb, to an embryonic state, within the Great Mother. The proverbial 'dark night of the soul', the Cloud of Unknowing, has descended and we must trust that the Goddess will provide. We drop our line in the pool – like our Silver Cord, connecting us to the Earth, to our mortal frame. We need something to bite, or we'll slip off. But we must be patient and let the subconscious do its work. Like all forms of meditation, it is not about effort, but opening and release – passivity and patience, not action – trust, not tension… Gaze deeply into those deep dark still waters – what do you see? What is reflected from your heart? What do you wish to manifest? Before we speak we must listen: what does the universe want you to say? Ask for Awen. Let it speak through you. Like Elphin we are fishing for salmon, for wisdom. And what does he find? A twice-born babe of ancient wisdom: the fledgling Bard himself. You must give 'birth' to it. Call it to you. Let it in, let it manifest in you, give it a voice; give yourself permission to speak up, to sing. You will shine, once you 'behold the Radiant Brow'. **Taliesin** is not only a name, it is an energy and an office, a mantle we can aspire to, we can honour. Open yourself up and let the Taliesinic energy be channelled through you. Let the brow shine!

EXERCISE: Changing Your Wyrd

Go to a weir or a waterfall on May Eve (or another threshold time: dawn/dusk/full moon/festival). Time to dream what you dream to be! What do you want to become? Tap into your hidden potential. Picture a salmon-rich stream, the great ocean-spanning fish trying to return to their spawning grounds, to the Source, overcoming obstacles in bold leaps. You can take that leap of faith also. Imagine the two levels of the weir symbolising where you are now and where you want to be. See this as an exercise in positive visualisation, in imagineering. Change your fortune by giving yourself permission to change. Often we hold ourselves back, through lack of confidence and a myriad of other reasons. Let the noise of the white water drown out those nagging doubts and just do it! Make a vow to yourself to make it happen and work out a series of steps to get you there.

Voice of the Sea

I sailed the ice-cold sea all winter,
The road of the wretched bereft of kinsmen,
Hung with icicles. Hail flew in showers.
There I heard only the ice-cold wave,
The sea, make song; the swan at times.
I took my glee in the gannet's voice,
Had lay of whilp for for laughter of men,
And mew music for mead-drinking.

The Seafarer, Anglo Saxon, Anon.

Britain is a seafaring nation, and for centuries we have 'ruled the waves' as an island race; from the mythic god of the sea, Manannan Mac Lir, who gave his name to the Isle of Man, Celtic saints in tiny curragh spreading the light of Christianity, Norse and Saxon raiders going native, bringing their sea skills and verse, Drake taking on the Armada, Nelson's victory at Trafalgar, the brave souls who fought and died in the Battle of the Atlantic – to record-breaking yachtswoman, Ellen MacArthur. It is the source of our great wealth, bringing trade to our well-positioned ports, and shame, with the legacy of the slave trade and the deportation of convicts to Australia and exiled Celts to the Americas. Without the tempering effects of the Gulf Stream we would be suffering the climate of Newfoundland. And the once full nets of the deep sea trawlers prove what happens when we exploit this seemingly endless resource. We are at its mercy and it is at ours – as the devastation of oil slicks and other pollution proves. It seems every other day there is a sea-related disaster. It supports so much life, yet it can take it without mercy. The legends of sunken kingdoms that frequent our shores, such as Dunwich, Cantre'd Gwaelod, the Fortunate Isles of Scilly, or Kêr-Ys, warn us not to be complacent or arrogant. And the many tales of selkies and other people of the sea illustrate again and again what happens when taboos are broken.

What is it to have the voice of the sea? It is to speak from the heart. It is to listen to your soul, to give voice to your subconscious. It is to move people and be moved, to be swept along by the power of your words, to be filled with passion and to pass it on. Oriah Mountain Dreamer, in *The Invitation*, advises: "tell the tales of your heart, offer them up like perfect pearls coming up from the depths of the sea to be strung together, each gently clicking against the other, luminous and iridescent as they roll out of the moistness."

Our internal seas need expressing, but it is also about connecting with something bigger than ourselves. The sea puts us in our place, reminds us who's really in charge. With Climate Change ever more apparent the sea will play an increasingly more dramatic role in our lives. Global Warming, which now has wide scientific consensus as an established fact, will make the sea levels rise, resulting in inundations, devastation, population shifts and pressure on land-based resources. Study its moods, its tides, its currents, carefully, but without losing sight of its diversity, its vast mystery.

As if we were setting sail, whenever we perform we should do so humbly, and with care – aware of the immensity of life's ocean. All we have to preserve us is our craft, so we must tend it well. A careless skipper will come a-cropper: blasé hubris brings downfall. We must be prepared to give our all, or She will take. No falsehoods will survive here. The Goddess can be a cruel mistress. She will have no truck with fools or charlatans. And so in a spirit of awe and humility, we enter Her embrace, as though cast beyond the Ninth Wave in a tiny coracle – wrapped in a leather bag, like the infant Taliesin. In a similar state we begin our voyage as Bards – vulnerable, but with the knowledge of the cauldron to guide us.

EXERCISES:

1 **Spend some time by the sea.**
   Walk along the beach or shore. Gaze out from the cliffs. Visit an island. Go dolphin-watching (but avoid swimming with them: respect their wild state). Try snorkelling or scuba-diving. Explore coral reefs and be reminded of the ocean's fragile ecosystem.

2 **Compose a poem to the sea.**
   Make notes while visiting the sea. Write a poem about your experiences and sensory impressions. Make it as vivid as possible. Now go down to the beach with your poem. Listen to the waves. Mirror their sound. Now express your feelings through sound – whatever rises to the surface. Don't filter or be inhibited. Shout it or sing it to the sea. Afterwards record how you felt in your journal – what did it stir up? – but finish by reciting your poem to the sea, offering it back to its source.

3 **Salty Tales.**
   Research sea stories, shanties, lore (eg: it's bad luck to whistle on a boat). There's a plethora of great sea literature: from the Anglo-Saxon poem, *The Seafarer*, onwards – Samuel Taylor Coleridge, Herman Melville, Ernest Hemingway, William Golding, Patrick O'Brian, E Annie Proulx, Yann Martel, Joseph O'Connor, and others. Yet the best tales are one's you hear directly from 'ancient mariners', if you are fortunate enough to meet one. Talk to deep sea fishermen, lifeboat men and women, crew of passenger ferries, lighthouse keepers, Naval officers, yachters and divers.

The Crane Bag: Tipping the Cauldron
RECHARGING ENERGY CENTRES

Cauldron of Knowledge, Cauldron of Vocation, Cauldron of Warming.

As a practising Bard, it is essential to 'replenish the well'; otherwise you'll dry up, or burn out! Using the Tipping the Cauldron technique will help, as will decent R&R and occasional **retreats**. Energy is fundamental to a Bard – it is not just stating the obvious to say you need it to be able to perform well. Performance-wise, energy is everything. I believe audiences respond first and foremost to energy: to a performer's 'charisma', or aura. It is essential to husband one's energy wisely, especially in festival situations, which can be tiring enough. But if you have more than one performance on, workshops, or a late slot, you really need to 'pace yourself' and save reserves of energy for second halves, repeat sets or encores. You don't want to be flagging half-way through a show. A one or two hour extravaganza, even in a group, can be incredibly demanding for the performers and audience. The Bard needs to keep not only themselves going but the listeners as well, especially towards the end of a longer show, when attention span wanes. On such occasions it is only the act of will of the showman/shaman that keeps the audience focussed and able to complete the journey. Of course, the audience's good will and reciprocation of the performer's efforts help – in their expressions, body language, applause and participation – but one cannot always rely on this. Apart from the obvious, such as good food, plenty of fluids, a good night's sleep, comfortable clothing (ie: warm or cool enough) and relaxation, it is possible to store and use Chi, or energy as and when it is needed. Through breathing techniques you have already seen how you can build up your Chi, and **Raising the Awen**, it is possible to summon inspiration and eloquence. The Three Cauldrons system offers a combination of both and is a rare example of Western 'body wisdom', so prevalent in the East. The purpose and placing of the Three Cauldrons (knowledge, vocation and warming) seems to echo the function and spinal alignment of the seven Chakras (wheels): Root, Spleen, Solar Plexus, Heart, Throat, Brow and Crown. The Cauldrons also relate to different parts of the body, (belly/womb, heart, head) and depending upon their position, they can effect changes of perception, as Caitlin Matthews explains: "The alignment of the three cauldrons is obviously critical to the reception and dispensation of inspiration…In poets and other inspired people, the second cauldron is turned on its side, as a kind of receiver of experience". This 'tipping the cauldron' can be caused by either joy or sorrow, by extremes of emotion or circumstances, which force us to reconsider who we are and what we do. Accidents, break-ups, breakdowns, mid-life crises, menopause, bereavement – all of these dramatic events will threaten our equilibrium and will either reaffirm or realign our cauldrons. Yet it is wiser to monitor the condition of them, and to recalibrate accordingly as life dictates, so that we are well-adjusted and 'firing on all cylinders'. Of course, we are talking about our physical-emotional-spiritual centres, not components of a machine. If anything, the Cauldron-system reinforces that we holistic beings require all these essential needs met, otherwise we do not live fully, we do not live well.

A Celtic treatise on poetry, transcribed in the 15th or 16th Century and found in an Irish legal codex, quoted in the *Encyclopaedia of Celtic Wisdom* (Matthews, Element 1994) talks of the Three Cauldrons, and gives them their names:

1. *CO IRE GOIRIATH* – THE CAULDRON OF WARMING
The Powerhouse of Chi

"This vessel is born and operative in every person; it is the foundation vessel which maintains vital energy and power, as well as preserving the cultural nourishment which each person receives in their upbringing. It provides the essential nurture which all human being require. It is upright in all people." Caitlin Matthews calls it "the vessel of physical health", and locates it in the belly/womb. It is connected etymologically to Goirias, the place of warming, where the Spear of Lugh is guarded by Esrus the Kindler. It is our Chi, our vital spark, which can be increased by breath. I don't think it is a coincidence that this upright cauldron resembles a container of food – and, of course, there are Cauldrons of Plenty galore in the Celtic Tradition. One can imagine a bowl of steaming broth, warming one on a winter's day. It is also similar to the alms bowl of the Buddhist monk, as well as the chalice of the Last Supper, a personal grail, nourishing from within.

2. *COIRE ERNMAE* – THE CAULDRON OF VOCATION
Our Heart's Calling

"This vessel is inverted in some people who have no apparent gifts or skills. In those who are aware of their gifts it is positioned on its side, like a receiver or satellite dish. In those who are fully enlightened it is in the upright position. It can, however, be turned from its inverted position by either joy or sorrow. It gives a rich selection of gifts to those in whom it is operative, helping them interface with ordinary and non-ordinary reality." Healers and seers must share a similar, if not identical faculty, an overlap in roles with that of Bard explored in the chapter on the **Awenyddion**. Caitlin Matthews calls this a "vessel of psychic health" and locates it in the heart or Solar Plexus, relating it to emotional or psychic health. If you are not fulfilling your vocation, you may feel dis-eased, and be experiencing soul-sickness. The correct application of the Cauldron of Vocation is critical to our well-being. For me this poem, from the same ancient text, sums up my vocation as a Bard:

The Nine Gifts of the Cauldron

> The Cauldron of Vocation
> Gives and is replenished,
> Promotes and is enlarged,
> Nourishes and is given life,
> Ennobles and is exalted,
> Requests and is filled with answers,
> Sings and is filled with song,

Preserves and is made strong,
Arranges and receives arrangements,
Maintains and is maintained.
Good is the well of measure,
Good is the abode of speech,
Good is the confluence of power:
It builds up strength.
It is greater than any domain,
It is better than any inheritance.
It numbers us among the wise,
And we depart from the ignorant.

3. *COIRE SOIS* – THE CAULDRON OF KNOWLEDGE
The Shining Brow

"This vessel is originally in an inverted manner. Like the *Coire Ernmae*, it can be turned by joy or sorrow, and there is some suggestion that the *Coire Ernmae* may actually need to be fully operative before the *Coire Sois* turns. In those who are spiritually operative or enlightened, it is upright and has the greatest capacity for spiritual and artistic gifts." Caitlin locates this in the head and calls it 'a vessel of spiritual health'. Is this identical to the Brow Chakra, the Third Eye, whose colour is indigo and is associated with vision and insight? If so, this would explain why Taliesin is so-named (the Radiant or Shining Brow). He has imbibed the potion of inspiration from Ceridwen's Cauldron of Wisdom, all his 'lights are switched on' and his Cauldron of Knowledge has been activated and filled.

EXERCISE: Awen and the Art of Cauldron Maintenance

Visualise the Three Cauldrons within yourself. How do they look? In good condition? Empty or full? Tilted, inverted or upright? Tip them if they need realigning (like Chakra balancing, or Reiki re-attunement). Periodically, at every festival for instance, fill them with Awen (one at a time, starting from the top, like a pyramid of champagne glasses) by channelling your breath and energy into them. Visualising them filling with light. You can never have enough Awen, so don't worry if they 'overflow' – there's more to share around! When you are feeling depleted, (ie: after a show) visualise your Cauldron of Vocation tilting back to an upright position, and let it fill with Awen for a few days, before actively tilting it sideways again before your next performance. Fully-functioning Cauldrons are essential to your well-being, to be a well-balanced Bard. Rather like Maslow's Need Hierachy, you need to take care of the fundamentals before you can rise up to more ethereal things (essential in other ways). A starving man can only think of food; similarly, if you are cold, wet, scared, annoyed, or depressed, you are not going to be able to think of 'higher things', or transmit them to an audience. The Cauldron of Warming must be filled (with good food, exercise, rest, TLC and so on) before you can easily access the Cauldron of Vocation or Knowledge. Having fed your body you need to feed your mind (The Cauldron of Knowledge) with study, research, training, meditation. Then your Cauldron of Vocation will activate fully – it will be filled and ready to tilt, sharing its 'goodness' with the world, all the Awen you have accrued, both physically and spiritually.

Month 8: Calling the Inner Bard

We all need guidance now and again – someone we can turn to for support, advice or sound judgement. A good role model is invaluable. Think back to inspiring teachers, relatives and friends who have been there in your hour of need: friendships that have endured fair weather and foul. So, if it is agreed that such figures are important, then where do we turn to for Bardic advice as you walk the Way of Awen?

Your first port of call should be this handbook, as a quick-reference guide and baseline. Secondly, I have established the Silver Branch Bardic Network to provide peer support and foster a sense of community with fellow Bards (see inside back page for details). Thirdly, you can give yourself advice, indirectly, via an Inner Guide or Teacher. This figure could be seen as your Higher Self, psychologically speaking, but they are more than that. These are the Elders, Ancestors and Inner World Guardians waiting to share their wisdom with you – if you approach them respectfully. The right 'frame of mind' is essential, because it provides a gateway for their archetypal wisdom to be channelled – but also these beings should be considered to be autonomous (as AE suggests in *The Candle of Vision*) and not obliged to you in any way. Their guidance can only be asked for, politely – never demanded. And you must accept what they offer you, however obscure, or seemingly unsatisfactory.

The Bardic Teachers always used questions and riddles to trigger the students' own wisdom – for a truth gained by personal insight and experience is far more powerful than a truth handed to you on a plate. The Bards use metaphors and symbolism, as well as music and other enchantments, to weave their spell and deliver their 'message' – which is often what your subconscious wishes to tell you, as the story, song or poem stirs up thoughts and feelings and makes you reflect upon your own attitude and situation. Bards empower by engaging the imagination of the audience – that greatest gift of humanity. Author of the imaginary, Ursula K Le Guin, said: "It is above all by the imagination that we achieve perception, compassion and hope". With imagination, anything is

Bladud Oak Dragon. Oil painting.

possible. Stories helps us to see the other side of things, to empathise with other lives, consider alternative narratives to our own, and by doing so they provide us with quantum possibilities.

The ambiguity inherent within Tarot card imagery acts in a similar way, drawing up the dormant wisdom of the reader. We already know the answer – it's just that we don't know we know it. Often we need someone to point it out. Yet our Inner Bard is not there to state the obvious, to tell us what we already know – if anything they are there to remind us how little we do know, not in a sanctimonious and patronising way (although some may come across like this!) but because as soon as you think you know it all, you have serious problems – of humility as well as understanding. If you stop asking questions, then you resort to knee-jerk responses, preconceived notions and even prejudices. You have already made up your mind. By doing so you are not only in danger of being arrogant (to think yourself superior is the reason why you are not), but of losing the 'awe' which is an essential part of the Awen. John Keats called this 'negative capability': the ability to dwell in mystery, uncertainty and wonder. When we stop wondering about the Universe, something dies – our own Inner Child, constantly asking questions. The innocent curiosity and cleansed perception of the Holy Fool can reveal the Emperor in his nakedness and even heal the Fisher King (See Cecil Collins, *The Vision of the Fool.* Golgonooza 1994). The Fool-Knight Parsifal 'pierces the veil' and wins the Grail, healing the Wounded King and the Wasteland, as he frees its waters.

The humbling thing about walking the Way of Awen is that the further along it you go the more you realise there is to know, to learn: as epitomised in the paradoxical truism 'the older I get, the less I know'. As you become aware of the Bards on the circuit out there, you realise there is always someone who is more proficient than you, and someone who is just starting out. This should keep you on your toes and stop you from becoming complacent. Hopefully it will make you appreciate what ability you do have, but also realise there is more to learn.

Apprenticeship with a Professional Bard is one very good way of improving your learning curve. Bardic courses are starting to crop up, and the Silver Branch is working to re-establish a Bardic College in Britain. In the meantime you can seek guidance from your own Inner Bard following the exercise below. I can verify the efficacy of this – because my Bardic path really took off when I started working with Taliesin. Acknowledging a master Bard gives you something to aspire towards. There are living and breathing role models I draw inspiration from as well – by attending their performances and workshops you can receive the best tuition – but having an Inner Bard infuses your life and permeates your own practice. It can change your life, in the same way that having a mentor on a 12 Steps recovery programme facilitates the road back to health and keeps you on the straight and narrow – a stabilising influence, who becomes 'hard-wired' into your system as their teaching or guidance becomes second nature.

The Mentor figure is very important in the Hero's Journey, as illustrated time and time again in classics of myth, literature and cinema: Odysseus and Nestor, Finn and Finegas, Lleu and Gwydion, Frodo and Gandalf, Luke Skywalker and Obi Wan Kenobi, Harry Potter and Professor Dumbledore… The list will never end, because the Mentor is an eternal archetype, a figure humanity will always be in need of.

Time to find your own mentor.

EXERCISE: Calling your Inner Bard

In a quiet space sit upright and close your eyes. Relax your body, but keep your spine erect. Slow your breathing. Ask for Awen. Then visualise a doorway. It could be ornate or plain, magical or mundane. Imagine a figure silhouetted there. This is your Inner Bard. Call them forward by saying something like: "My Inner Bard, step forward and show yourself to me. I wish to know your wisdom, if you are willing to share it. I am ready to meet you". Allow them to come forward into the light, if they are obliging. Don't force them. Wait in silence and stillness. Let them introduce themselves. Greet them respectfully. Listen to anything they say. Observe their appearance in detail. This is what you will aspire to be: not directly, but in your own way, with your own voice. Metaphorically, let them 'enter' you. Now you have made contact they will always be with you. Ask them for guidance whenever you need it. Thank them. Promise to make them an offering: a poem, painting, song to honour them. When you feel the encounter is over, say farewell and let the scene fade. Slowly return to consciousness. Make yourself a snack and drink. Write up in your journal and draw them, however crudely. Try to recall all the details of the meeting: what they said, how they looked and acted, how you felt and reacted. If you failed to make contact the first time, do not be disheartened – try again in a couple of weeks and don't give up. There's an Inner Guide waiting for you.

INNER BARDS

There are many mentors from myth and history we can draw upon for inspiration. One of them could be the Inner Bard you are waiting for. Try to contact them and see if they are willing to 'speak' to you. Try to channel their wisdom by writing in their voice, in First Person. I wrote a poem about Taliesin in this way and every time I perform it, his energy is raised within me – it is a form of invocation. Create a performance to honour your Inner Bard, incorporating story, song, poetry, movement, music, artwork – whatever he or she inspires you to do. This is a way of honouring them and tapping into their wisdom and talent in yourself.

You may come across references to master Bards in the archives, eg: Nennius, in his *Historia Brittonum* c796 CE, writes that between 547-559 (reign of Ida of Northumbria): "…Talhearn Tad Awen [ie: Father of the Muses] won renown in poetry: and Anerin and Taliesin and Blwchfardd and Cian who is called Wheat of Song won renown at one and the same time in British poetry". These tantalising fragments not only mention Taliesin, but suggest other such accomplished Bards. We know little more about them, but you may be able to contact them through meditation, arcane retrieval methods (**Retrieving Lost Knowledge**) and Underworld Journeying.

Below are examples of great Bards, historical, legendary and fictional you could possibly contact or draw inspiration from. One of them may appeal to you, otherwise find your own from whatever culture, era or idiom you are inspired by. This list is not meant to be prescriptive in any way – it is merely limited by my own preferences and paradigm – but I hope it suggests that Bards can be of any particular gender, race or milieu. The history of humanity has countless sung, and unsung, Bards. If one has been neglected, then perhaps you should help raise their profile – with a conference, society, journal or celebration – honouring their spirit and keeping their name alive.

Names of potential Inner Bards:

Plato	Geoffrey Chaucer	AE (George Russell)
Homer	Thomas of Ercildoune	Fiona Macloed (William
Orpheus	Robert Burns	Sharp)
Sappho	Dafydd ap Gwilum	Khalil Gibran
Dante	Turlough O'Carolan	Dylan Thomas
Basho	Christopher Marlowe	Jimi Hendrix
Lao Tsu	Shakespeare	Janis Joplin
Omar Khayam	Blake	Jim Morrison
Taliesin	Keats	John Lennon
Amergin	Shelley	George Harrison
Ossian	Byron	Nick Drake
Anuerin	John Clare	Tim or Jeff Buckley
Hervé – Breton Saint of Bards	Milton	
Ganeida, Merlin's sister	Tennyson	Find your own…
Hildegard of Bingen	WB Yeats	

Brown's Folly, Bathford.

The Crane Bag: The Inward Spiral – The Joy of Solitude

> I will arise and go now, and go to Innisfree,
> And a small cabin build there, of clay and wattles made:
> Nine bean-rows will I have there, and a hive for the honey-bee,
> And live alone in the bee-loud glade.

The Lake Isle of Innisfree, WB Yeats

The Bardic life is, by its very nature, a sociable one. As has been stated before, a Bard cannot truly exist without a community and certainly cannot perform without an audience. Bards have to go to places of gathering, the great multi-tribal festivals (these days largely replaced by the likes of Glastonbury Festival, Big Green Gathering, etc.) or more specifically, the 'clan' camps such as Wessex Gathering, the Druid Network Camps, Lammas Games or the Mercian Gathering. Wherever there is a Gorsedd (eg: Avebury, Stonehenge) or Eisteddfod (Bath), Bards should congregate; and more locally and frequently, any 'open mic' night or Bardic circle – basically, any opportunity to perform, to share material and Bardic wisdom.

Bardsey Island (*Ynys Enlli*), a place to retreat from the world.

Thus, it may seem that the Bard is always in the public eye. However, the reality is far different. Like the old maxim about writing (or anything else creative for that matter) being 10% inspiration and 90% perspiration, in a similar way the Bardic life is divided between public and private, the extrovert and the introvert. Perhaps a tenth of the time the Bard is performing, if he or she is lucky. The other nine-tenths they are researching and working on new material, reading, journeying, marketing, recharging 'Bardic batteries', and so on. This is healthy and essential – for one's practise and one's wellbeing. As explored in the **Tipping the Cauldron** it is imperative to 'replenish the well'. If we are pouring out Awen all the time, then we will just become depleted.

In Gestalt practice, time is divided between connecting and withdrawing. This rhythm of expansiveness and decay or contraction is the dance of life, of the seasons, of plant and animal life, mirrored in the cycle of the year. We observe and learn from the wisdom of Nature. The deep dreaming and hard work of Winter and Spring is rewarded by the exuberance and abundance of Summer and Autumn. Yet come harvest-time it is time to gather in what one has gained and reflect upon what one has learnt (and this cycle can be mirrored in a microcosmic way with each project). As in the learning cycle of Theory-Practise-Review this final stage is essential. You should do this after every performance. What lessons have been learnt? What went well? What could be done better next time? What could be added or removed? Celebrate – just to perform is an achievement, however well it goes. Without some sense of acknowledgment of one's efforts, it just becomes a relentless slog and morale quickly drops. Reward yourself with a favourite meal, new book, album or item of clothing. If you are at a festival, treat yourself to something: a massage, or something more long-lasting – it is good to have a souvenir of each gig as a mnemonic about it, its lesson encapsulated: an amulet, a CD of an inspiring performer, or book of a good speaker. Traditionally, a Bard may have been rewarded by his host for a good performance with a trinket of some kind, a ring, brooch or necklace. At the 'Coming Together' Maori-Druid Camp near Bath in 2004, well-crafted wrist torcs were handed out to the best performers in the Eisteddfod. You have shone in the public eye, and now like the moon, you can enter a more reclusive phase.

Over the centuries there have always been those who wish to be alone, who wish to withdraw from the social hub, to be 'far from the madding crowd': mystics and hermits, who seek to gain a perspective on life, who wish to journey deep into their mysteries without the distractions of everyday life. This may be achieved within an intentional community, such as a monastery, which may still be within the larger community, ie: a city, but separated by its walls and ways (spiritual retreat) or by actually dwelling in a remote place (physical retreat), such as the Celtic monks did in their tiny beehive cells on wind-swept islands, or the ascetic Buddhist saints and Indian holy men who dwell in caves or holes, subsisting on little more than thin air. You need not go to these extremes – a Bard should be engaged with life, after all, not completely cut off from it – but it is recommend-ed to have somewhere you can be on your own (a study, a shed, a gazebo or summer house, hillside, or grove – your **Bardic Space**) on a semi-regular basis.

It is important to be able to reconnect with the Awen as often as possible – in the next Month we will be looking at ways to do this on a daily basis. But it is also essential to spend times in Retreat reflecting, refilling the cauldron and journeying deep to find new inspiration and clarification of one's path and practice. The Tarot card of the Hermit sums this up best of all, and the hermit, as an archetype, crops up throughout myth and history as a touchstone of wisdom. At one point in his career, Merlin the magician becomes Myrddin Wyllt, or Wild Merlin when, traumatised by a terrible battle, he retreats to the Caledonian wildwood to live as a wild man with the animals. At such times it is the wisdom of totems and companions that guide us through the lost forest. On occasion we ourselves are like the wounded bird or animal that needs healing. Time (and Nature) heals all wounds, it is said. But sometimes we go on retreat for proactive, not reactive reasons – to find a solution to life. This is a direct echo of the Native American Indians, who would go to a holy mountain on a vision quest, for the good of the tribe (see **Sitting Out**). Henry David Thoreau's *Walden, or Life in the Woods*, is the practical hermit's classic. It describes how he set out to live simply and well off his own resources:

> I went to the woods because I wished to live deliberately, to front only the essential facts of life, and see if I could not learn what it had to teach, and not, when I came to die, discover that I had not lived. I did not wish to live what was not life, living is so dear, nor did I wish to practise resignation, unless it was quite necessary. I wanted to live deep and suck out all the marrow of life, to live so sturdily and Spartan-like as to put to rout all that was not life, to cut a broad swath and shave close, to drive life into a corner, and reduce it to its lowest terms, and, if it proved to be mean, why then to get the whole and genuine meanness of it, and publish its meanness to the world; or if it were sublime, to know it by experience, and be able to give a true account of it in my next excursion.

Thoreau's mantra was simplicity, simplicity, simplicity! We should all aspire to live so lightly.

Once, I spent a winter on a narrow boat, moored along a frozen canal – and there, in the solitude and peace, I journeyed deep and did a lot of work on myself. It was a kind of chrysalis phase for me, at a critical time of my life (my Saturn Return) and I emerged from my 'metal cocoon' stronger and surer, with a collection of poems to preserve what I had learned (called *Immrama* – wonder voyages*),* ready to re-enter the community and the next phase of my life.

EXERCISE: Retreat

Spend this month reflecting upon your Bardic year so far. Read through your journal. Take stock of what you have learned. If possible, arrange for a week's (or long weekends) retreat. Find a quiet B&B, self-catering cottage or centre (*Places To Be*, published

by Edge of Time, is an excellent guide for holistic centres around the UK and Europe offering accommodation, workshops, and volunteering opportunities). Be careful not to let it become an 'activity' holiday. Don't be talked into going with a well-meaning partner or friend (arrange 'quality time' with them to compensate on your return). This retreat is for you. If you can't bear going by yourself, then arrange a retreat with kindred spirits also wishing for a retreat – clearly establishing guidelines beforehand (ie: no loud music, no alcohol, no talking even – whatever you need). Take plenty of writing and reading materials. If it's a particularly inspiring area you may want to bring walking gear – a peaceful quiet walk every day will provide inspiration and exercise. The main thing is not to have an agenda or a set itinerary – just give yourself time to reflect, to think, to explore your feelings, to dream and, perhaps, to write. Take your journal for self-reflection, but don't set yourself a burdensome goal (ie: I must write 1000 words every day, a series of poems, songs, or a novel – although if these things happen, all well and good, but don't force them). Remember you are going on retreat to replenish the well. Savour this quality time with yourself and reap the benefits afterwards, as you return re-energised, inspired and ready to join the circle of the community once again.

Bard and Community

> The poet is accountable to society, and is its spokesman.
> He is recorder, instructor, and celebrant.
>
> *Gwyn Jones*

A Bard cannot truly fulfil their role without a community to serve. It may be a family, a group of friends, neighbourhood, school or college, workplace, church, mosque, temple, grove, village, town, city, region, country or nation. Large or small, it has to be a community of some kind – a Bard cannot exist in isolation. There are no 'hedge-Bards' – an untenable notion, in truth – although that does not exclude the value of solitude, retreats and the long-term solitary commitment required, ie: no one else will make you a Bard – *you* have to put the hours in. It may seem like a very public life, being a Bard, but in fact the public side of things (the performances, Gorseddau, etc.) are only a fraction of the Bardic life. For the rest of the time you are working mainly on your own (meditating, writing, practising, seeking Awen) or perhaps in a small group: this is the 'moon' side of the more extrovert 'sun' life, when you are up there shining. That is why the value of a peer support network is essential, to compensate for an otherwise predominantly lonely path, to share the woes and joys of the Bardic life with, good times, good news and bad.

I believe a Bard is not defined by what she or he is (ie: a Celt of blood descent) but by what he or she *does*. And I do not think 'Bard' is something that it is easy to call oneself. It is something one is called, as a mark of respect – in the same way it is difficult to swallow it if someone calls themselves a 'poet' (you may write poetry, but that doesn't necessarily make you a bona fide poet: that is only apparent in the quality of the poetry. This is not an elitist thing, but just the fact that 'quality will out'. Someone who is tone deaf in all honesty can't call themselves a singer – although training and commitment may remove most obstacles and handicaps). I did not start calling myself a Bard until I won the Bardic Chair of Caer Badon: *then* I felt authorised to do so. I was given the modus operandi to be the Bard for the City of Bath for a year: I had my mandate and I had to fulfil it.

Coming Together, Maori:
Druid Camp, Rocks East Woodland 2005.

So, the community's acknowledgment and receptivity of your role is essential. It does not have to be a physical community – it could be a community of intent, a society, organisation, or network. Being a Bard is a public act, and has been from its very beginnings, around those first primal fires with the first audiences, to the courts of medieval nobility, the rigours of the Welsh Eisteddfod, the public ceremonies of the Druids, and the gatherings at Stonehenge and Avebury today. When Bards gather, a Gorsedd is held, eg: the Gorsedd of the Bards of Caer Abiri. The Chaired Bard is at the centre of the circle, in a metaphorical and sometimes literal sense. The Gorsedd surrounds and supports him or her. And the Eisteddfod is the wider public festival around the spiritual heart of the Gorsedd (see diagram overleaf). Each one of these circle clusters is like an apple on the silver branch. **The Silver Branch Bardic Network** has been set up to link and honour these 'fruits' from the same tree of tradition. A very active Bard may be at the centre of one of these circles – running Bardic circles, the local Eisteddfod, regular Gorseddau, and other events – or they may be just part of it, a 'planet' orbiting a main 'sun' (Arch-Druid). But whatever the context, Bards have an interdependent existence within their community. No Bard is an island. The image of Ogma, Celtic God of Eloquence, chaining men to him with his spellbinding words (from tongue to ear) is a mutual linkage – the Bard is just as bound to his or her audience. They have an obligation: with the role comes responsibility. To paraphrase a famous saying: ask not what your community can do for you; ask what you can do for your community. The bard's role is one of service – not in a submissive way, but in a very self-motivated, pro-active sense. Your role in the community is what you make it. This is not to kowtow to anyone, or compromise the integrity of the Tradition, but to maintain its relevance in the modern world and to remind people of the wisdom of the past.

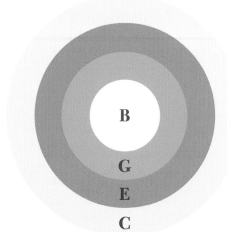

B = Bard
G = Gorsedd
E = Eisteddfod
C = Community

The Circles of the Bard.

WAYS BARDS CAN SERVE THEIR COMMUNITY:

- ❖ Tell the story of a place, its people.
- ❖ Empower others to do so (ie: local voices).
- ❖ Celebrate local identity, heritage, attractions, and achievements.
- ❖ Mark events with performance, special poems, songs, or stories.
- ❖ Act as MC for events.
- ❖ Judge poetry, storytelling or song-writing competitions (see **Setting up and Running a Bardic Chair** in Appendices)
- ❖ 'Bless' new births, unions, businesses, initiatives, etc., with words.
- ❖ Create **Bardic Circles** and other showcases.

Respected members of the community collect their honorary Bardic awards, as elected by the Gorsedd of the Bards of Caer Badon, The Circus, Bath, Midsummer 2005.

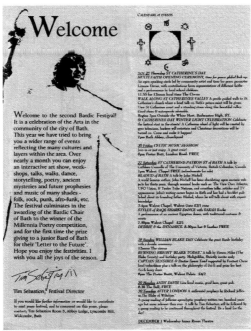

Programme for Second Bardic Festival of Bath, 1999.

Marking Rites of Passage

Rites of Passage are ceremonies conducted to facilitate a shift of consciousness and/or a change of status in the recipient. They are empowering for the initiate and the initiator. The secret knowledge is passed on, honouring the dual notion that **1:** it is worth having and **2:** the initiator is wise enough to have it.

As has been stated, the Bard, first and foremost, should serve his community. This means being there, being available and providing suitable words for different occasions, as and when required, such as namings, handfastings, funerals – in the same way the nation's Poet Laureate is expected to pen an ode for certain state events, birthdays and anniversaries. I have been asked to compose and perform poems for friends, and sometimes I have done so voluntarily – to express my feelings for them (ie: a birthday poem for a good friend). There are few greater honours I think than performing for friends, on a day special to them, in front of all their friends and family. I have done this in a Scottish castle for a Highland wedding, reciting a poem about love I was asked to compose especially for the occasion. Similarly, I have recited a poem about a friend at a celebration of his life – one of the most moving and difficult things I've ever had to do, but it is a real validation of one's role as Bard, and we are ideally expressing sentiments that many share at such times, but find difficult to express. That's why we still need Bards.

At times of private or national tragedy or disaster we seek recourse in poetry and music, whether secular or sacred, for consolation and celebration, to express how we feel when words fail us. Who could forget that powerful scene in Richard Curtis' film, *Four Weddings and a Funeral*, when the John Hannah character recites the famous WH Auden poem *Stop all the Clocks*, for his lover played by Simon Callow. There are many real examples of this, of the power of speech, in the public arena, eg: the angry elegy by Earl

Spencer, Princess Diana's brother, at her state funeral. People respond to real emotion – rare in the spin-doctored realm of politics – when people say what they mean and mean what they say in a direct heartfelt way. Sincerity shines through. Words for rites of passage should be simple, appropriate and cut to the core emotion.

These days we can send cards for every imaginable occasion and anniversary, often with anodyne or tacky messages. However commercial the reasons, such ephemera of modern life also serve an ancient function: expressing something for people who are unable, or rather, too busy or unwilling, to express themselves. Saying something in your own words is far better, however basic – because it is from the heart. Failing one's own efforts, a Bard should be able to provide this service – offering meaningful and beautiful words for a loved one, or for an occasion of wider significance (ie: a recent tragedy, or regional disaster). Bards should be able to contribute to a celebration, a memorial service, an opening, an anniversary, a national holiday or a global 'focus' day, eg: Peace One Day. This is a real mark of one's ability and acceptance as a Bard. Do people consider you when such opportunities arise? Do they even know if you are willing to provide such a service? And are you going to be able to rise to the occasion?

EXERCISES: Writes of Passage

1. Write a poem or song for a loved one's birthday. Give it to them as a present. Perhaps recite it for them if there's a party, or after a special dinner, then hand them it on a scroll, on a disc (if it's a song) or in a nice card.

2. Are there any naming ceremonies, weddings, etc. coming up in your calendar? Ask those involved if they would like a poem, song or story. Consult them as to what would be appropriate, the context of the performance (ie: at the Reception), length, tone, and so on.

3. Make it known locally/in your community that you are available for 'rites of passage' (ie: poet for hire). Is there a new shop opening? A small business launch? A village fête? A Spring Dressing? An anniversary? Contact the organisers and ask if they would like some special words for their special occasion. This could lead to your first commission...

Voice of the Trees

> Hear the voice of the Bard!
> Who present, past, and future, sees;
> Whose ears have heard
> The Holy Word
> That walk'd among the ancient trees.
>
> *Songs of Experience* – 'Introduction'
> William Blake

What is it to speak with the voice of the trees? It is to first listen to the forest – to go for a walk in the woods and soak up the atmosphere, as the trees soak up our carbon dioxide and give us fresh oxygen in exchange. Our brains receive this oxygen from our bloodstream and we feel more awake, relaxed and refreshed. The bronchial passages of the lungs mirror the filigree of branches, form and function encapsulated by the isness of the tree. The tree is a pure expression of itself, yearning for light, shaped by the wind, by its surroundings, by the soil and by what lives on it. Each tree has its own special energy, its own character and quality. Look at each tree as an individual, not a type. What makes it unique? And what does it have in common with its own species? The elegant grace of an ash sapling, the majesty of a beech, the deep mystery of a yew tree, the ethereal light of a silver birch… Each tree speaks to us in a different way. What does it say to you?

It is about getting in touch with one's own intuition. Away from the white noise of the madding crowd profound thoughts bubble up. We can hear ourselves think. Thoughts mushroom. Walking through a forest reminds us how everything is connected – as we see the matrix of the forest, the network of mycelium beneath the mulch, we remember that we are part of Nature, not apart from it. Nature helps us to find our centre again.

As a child I would walk every day over Delapre Abbey. I would sit against my favourite oak tree in the central glade, and find myself again – it was my *axis mundi*. It taught me patience and endurance. From it little acorns of wisdom fell into my lap, which have grown ever since.

Observing the seasons – no more visibly than in trees, those great barometers of the year – helped me to understand the cycle of life. Trees show us how to share and shelter, protect and

Oak growing out of rock   Alltwen, Wales   KM 10/9/97

provide. A tree is selfless without compromising itself. It follows its destiny, the destiny locked in the seed that spawned it, inevitably, with endless vigour, and invention. It finds nooks and crannies of rock to grow in, splitting and holding them; it seeks light upwards and water downwards. It knows what nourishes it and what does not. Even in its demise it provides nourishment for others, offering a home for fungi and insects as it rots away. As fire, its stored time is released. Its many years of growth are consumed quickly, its slow life suddenly burning with brightness as we revel in its quickening death.

Trees bear fruit after much hard work – we can take lessons from this. We reap what we have sown in the dream-loam of Winter, planning a show that finally comes to fruition in the brighter months. We scatter our fruit, hoping some will find fertile soil. Then cold-breathed Autumn comes to cut the wheat from the chaff, to strip the leaves from the trees, and from our cloak of bright feathers – paring us down, preparing us for the harder, leaner months ahead. But the austerity of Midwinter allows us to reimagine our strategies as we see the skeleton of our lives stripped of its Summer excess. We 'downsize', withdrawing from the public gaze to tend the hearth, to take stock and reflect, assessing what has succeeded, what may have failed, learning the lessons of the year.

The voice of the trees is about finding your own unique voice, about standing up 'to be counted' for what you believe in. It is about forging your own unique path through life, about being self-defining. And being rooted, down-to-earth, but at the same time aspiring – balancing the qualities of Heaven and Earth, and of all the

Shining Word workshop participants in the Mistletoe Grove at the Druid Network Bardic Camp 2005.

elements that sustain us. The famous dictum 'As Above, So Below' could have been said about trees – they are a perfect symbol of that Divine Symmetry: they transform sunlight into food through photosynthesis – the baseline of the world's food chain, and they inhale what we exhale – in return offering us the breath of life itself.

EXERCISES:

1. Planting Trees

This is something you can't ever do enough of. Plant as much as possible: for friends, for charity, for the Earth. Establish groves for future generations. Collect nuts, pot them, tend them until saplings, then plant in a suitable place with a stake and protective tube. Participate in tree-planting projects like Trees for Life. Read *The Man Who Planted Trees*, the inspiring environmental classic by Jean Giono (Peter Owen 2000).

2. Favourite Tree

Which tree do you most relate to? Is there one from your childhood? A lifetime favourite? Which ones leave you cold or unimpressed? Why? Explore your relationship with trees – spend time with different species and try to sensitise yourself to their energy and character.

Tree planting at the Millennium Grove, Rocks East Woodland.

3. What's your Taproot?

What sustains you? What are your 'fruits'? What do you support and what supports you? Draw a tree diagram of yourself – listing the key factors in your life. Is there a reciprocal cycle here? Are you getting back as much as you give out? More? Less? Seek to attain a healthy balance. Work with your own seasons of growth and withdrawal.

The Silver Branch

The silver branch is a symbol with mythic resonance, with allusions to Celtic and Classical traditions, as well as echoes in other cultures. It is said to transport the wielder to the Otherworld. Perhaps this is possible, but it also transports in other ways: by acting as a key to the imagination – that doorway to other worlds we all possess. Yet often we need triggers, clues and symbols and the silver branch acts as one. It is most potent in its ambiguity, in its mystery, but it will be productive to explore its roots.

In his book on Taliesin John Matthews describes the Silver Branch as: "…an emblem of the Poet's Craft…a symbol of entry to the Otherworld". In the Celtic Tradition the Poet's Branch is called *craebh ciuil*. "It could cause hostilities to cease or promise an Otherworldly experience through the eloquence of the Bard, which enable his audience to share in his knowledge of the inner realms", Matthews explains.

Magical branches of silver, gold or bronze crop up throughout Celtic literature, as though poking through from another dimension, and in a way they are: for in some senses these branches grow from the World Tree that connects the worlds and is common in many religions and traditions (eg: Yggdrasil, the World Ash in Norse mythology, the Tree of the Qabala, the Cross of Christ connecting man to God, etc.). A magical branch makes an appearance in *The Voyage of Bran mac Fabel to the Land of Faery*, wielded by a mysterious woman, who tempts Bran to the Otherworld with it:

> A branch of apple tree from Emhain
> I bring, like those we know;
> Twigs of white are on it
> Crystal grows with blossoms

This is a common motif in Celtic literature. In the Scottish ballad, *Tam Lin*, it is a woman, Janet, who encounters Faerie when she 'pulls a rose' at Carterhaugh – another kind of blossoming branch – making its guardian, the spellbound Tam Lin appear. Normally it is the Goddess who appears, initiating men into the deeper levels of being, as the Queen of Elfland does to Thomas of Ercildoune. Her Faerie steed has a rein hung with silver bells, echoing the Silver Branch: "And upon the bridle of her rein hung fifty silver bells and nine". With it she transports Thomas to Elfland: "And then her bridle she did ring and they flew swifter than the wind". Perhaps there is a connection here with the rattling, shaking, jangling, drumming shaman or shamanka, who may dance or sing themselves into a trance, or use other methods, such as drinking the Fly Agaric-saturated urine of reindeer: not recommended! Could this tradition have given birth to Odin's eight-legged horse, Sleipnir, and to his modern manifestation, Santa Claus's flying reindeer? And Odin, in the guise of **Bolwerk** the trickster walks the land with staff in hand.

Looming over the Downs of Southern England, the chalk giants of the Long Man of Wilmington and the Cerne Abbas giant both wield staves or clubs. They both straddle the line between myth and history, and the Long Man himself seems to walk both into and out of the hillside at the same time, between the worlds. In *The Aeneid*, Trojan exile Aeneas wielded the 'golden bough' of mistletoe to allow him safe passage into Hades' realm, so he could converse with the shade of his father. Similarly, Orpheus wielded his lyre to gain access to Hades' realm, while Dionysus uses his thrisos – a pine-cone stave. Perhaps these are linked with other 'special branches'. The Mayoral mace, the Royal Sceptre, the Poet's Wand, the conductor's baton, the judge's hammer, the Druid's staff, the shepherd's crook and the bishop's mitre are all symbols of office, bestowing power and status upon the wielder. Perhaps all of these emblems are descended, in spirit, from the Caduceus, the rod of Hermes, god of communication? If so, it is fitting the Bard should carry on the baton with his silver branch.

By wielding the silver branch, the Bard announces his intent to perform. It should afford him 'safe passage' through the treacherous world of the court, like waving a white flag; it should grant him peace to speak, and create peace in the gathering, like an olive branch. A Bard does not wield a sword; he (or she) wields words. The silver branch is the Bard's 'talking stick', which passed around in gatherings to allow everyone to have their turn (only those who wield it have the right to speak). Perhaps the silver branch is akin to the wizard's staff, which relates back to the shaman's rattle or medicine stick, with feathers, bells, skulls attached? Wielding the branch shows connection to the World Tree, to other worlds. And in a more mundane but equally important way it should remind the Bard to remain connected to all those around him, to his audience, to his community – because without those he ceases to serve a function. The silver branch affords certain privileges: access to the public forum, to the Royal Hall, but with those privileges come responsibility: to speak in truth and beauty, to speak for those without a voice, to speak for the silent ones – the ancestors, the spirits – to speak for all.

The silver branch can be wielded by any. One does not need to physically hold one to be transported to, or transport others to, other worlds, but it is a good mnemonic to remind us of what we are trying to achieve through our words: enchantment and transformation. We want our words to bear fruit, to bring healing and wisdom. This is a lot to bear by oneself, a tall order for some, but with the silver branch we are reminded that we are not alone, that we are connected to the world and worlds, and that we can be a channel for that otherworldly wisdom, for the Awen, so that we can sing, like Nick Drake in his haunting ballad *Magic* of, "the frost on the broken tree…" We all hold part of the branch – and can be connected to everyone else who does so also. The silver branch is a real 'world wide web', like the lattice work of a forest canopy. We can be connected in spirit, or by intent (see **The Silver Branch Bardic Network**).

The silver branch has many facets, and can be seen as an Otherworldly key, a sign of office, a shaman's tool and a metaphor for connection. It summons us to ourselves – with a shake of its bells our Bard awakens and the enchantment begins.

EXERCISE: Make a Silver Branch

The Silver Branch can be used practically in performance (I first wielded mine at a medieval banquet, holding it above the heads of the crowds to show them my purpose). The bells can create a hypnotic sound, similar to the shaman's rattle or drum. At an auspicious time, such as new or full moon, cut a branch from a tree you feel connected with (asking permission first), strip the bark, smooth it with sandpaper and spray it silver. Attach silver or gold bells. Use in performance. Alternatively, make a silver branch amulet, cloak or banner.

The Crane Bag: The Three Illuminations

Dichetal do Chennaib

DEFINITION:

1. Extempore or inspired incantation.
2. Cracking open nuts of wisdom.
3. Incantation on the bones (or ends) of the fingers.

This is what I call the Illumination of the Hand, to differentiate it from **Imbas Forosnai** (eye) and **Teinm Laida** (mouth). There is some obscurity over this last technique but John Matthews suggests it means basically 'inspired spells' and probably involved 'a kind of hypnotic mantra of power', either used with hand gestures, or spelled out by the use of Ogham sign language. It seems inspiration was gleaned in this way: instead of 'on the tip of the tongue', **Dichetal do Chennaib** suggests the answer is 'on the tips of one's fingers'.

The second and third interpretations could be related in a mythopoetic way and may give us a clue: the former refers to the nine hazels of wisdom that grow by the side of the Well of Segais at the bottom of the sea. John Matthews offers a comprehensive but unwieldy definition: "the gaining of wisdom through the cracking open and eating of the fruit of the sacred Wisdom-Nuts, the hazels from the Otherworldly Well of Segais, which rises in the inner realms but sends forth its messages to the poets who seek to know". The third definition must refer to the Ogham tree alphabet, which was signalled using subtle hand gestures, each knuckle and joint of the hand referring to a particular letter, thus enabling coded conversations across a crowded hall, making it be known as 'the Dark Speech' of the Druids, for only they understood it.

Interestingly, it was only this Illumination of all the three that was *not* banned by St Patrick as a 'denial of baptism', as it states in *Cormac's Glossary*: "**Dichetal do Chennaib**, 'extempore incantation', however, *that* was left, in right of art, for it is science that causes it, and no offering to devils is necessary, but a declaration from the ends of his bones at once". Perhaps then, it was purely a sign language for initiates. Harmless, or was it? Maybe that was how it appeared to observers, or how it was interpreted by the Church.

Clearly, further research needs to be done on The Three Illuminations, both academically and bardically, perhaps through lost knowledge retrieval techniques and practical experimentation. It is up to us to unlock their secrets and make them applicable today.

EXERCISE: Hand Ogham

Draw the Ogham alphabet on your left hand (see diagram below) and use your right hand to spell out words with it. Practise in a mirror to begin with. Then get a friend or fellow Anruth to join you for practice, with the Ogham inscribed on their hands and an alphabet key (see next chapter) close by. Try spelling out words to one another to begin with. Don't be tempted to mouth the letters or give any clues. Imagine you are struck dumb or have taken a vow of silence and this is your only form of communication. When you feel confident, try in a larger circle with other willing participants. See how many conversations you can hold. Finally, try in a noisy public space (ie: train station or football stadium), and a quiet space (a woodland or bird hide) where silence is important. This exercise will help you to familiarise yourself with the Ogham and use it in day-to-day life. It is a code with all kinds of applications, but don't misuse it or annoy your friends with it. Keep it as a special language you can share with fellow initiates. One may even be able to identify a fellow Anruth by a certain hand-signal, but we don't want to get too Masonic! Keep it sacred. By using the Ogham in this way, we are talking in the same tongue as our ancestors – a silent language reaching across the centuries. You may even be able to communicate with your Inner Bard in this way, when you become fluent.

HAND OGHAM DIAGRAM

Although this is based upon traditional interpretations from ancient sources I have added the missing letters (**J, K, P, V, W, X, Y, Z**) to make it possible to communicate in modern English. The correspondences I have given these new letters are purely arbitrary – they serve as mnemonic-tags in the same way the Radio code does (eg: Alpha, Bravo, Charlie, etc.). To begin with, you may want to draw the letters onto your left hand. Display palm towards recipient (or mirror, if practising). Point with the right thumb or index finger. Try remembering the letters without writing on your hand (pressing the actual position as you speak it helps to reinforce it). You may want to add other useful signals, for 'repeat', 'explain', 'understood', 'over and out'. Have fun communicating with a friend.

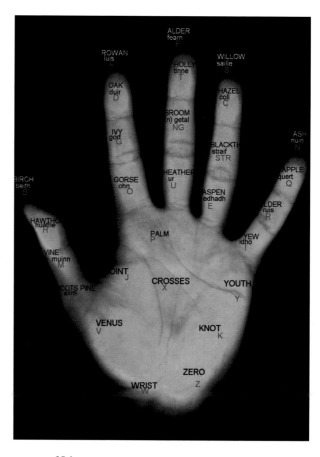

Ogham – The Celtic Tree Alphabet

The Ogham was known as 'the secret language of the poets'. It was a secret system of signs and correspondences used by the Druids, and was known as the 'Dark Speech' – which only initiates understood. Traditionally a set of twenty five tree-letters (as you can see, there are more than 25, because there are variations on the actual trees included, perhaps indicating regional variation), they were divided into four categories or ranks:

I   Chieftain (oak, hazel, holly, yew, ash, pine, apple)
II Peasant (alder, willow, hawthorn, rowan, birch, elm, beech)
III Shrub (blackthorn, elder, aspen, juniper, box, reed)
IV Bramble (dog-rose, bramble, broom, heather, ivy, vine, honeysuckle, fern, spindle)

This hierarchy is brilliantly illustrated in the ancient Celtic poem, *Câd Goddeu*: the Battle of the Trees (see Robert Graves' *The White Goddess*). An even more practical categorisation was into five groups of five, in their traditional order. These seem to fall into categories of phonemes (the word-sounds which language consists of) corresponding to soft and hard consonants, consonant-based diphthongs, vowels and vowel-based diphthongs:

1. B, L, F, S, N;   2. H, D, T, C, Q;   3. M, G, NG, STR, R;   4. A, O, U, E, I;
5. EA, OI, UI, IO, AE.

This gives us the strongest evidence that it was used in the oral tradition, originating out of a spoken rather than written language.

As discussed in **Dichetal do Chennaib** it was also a means of non-verbal communication through the use of hand-signals illustrating the different Ogham (the secret language) ideal for sending surreptitious messages across a court or mead-hall. It could also be used for leaving messages in the wild (famously in *The Tain*, where Cuchullain leaves Ogham in the trees). And less transiently, the Ogham has been used for inscriptions upon stones, (hundreds have been found across the British Isles) thus paving the way for actual writing.

Perhaps the Ogham exists not to follow religiously, but to act as an approach to developing an intimate familiarity and harmony with Nature, for the important thing is not to impose a system upon Nature, but to develop a close and sustainable relationship with it, one in which we are sensitised to its energies and the lessons it can teach us. I suggest one finds one's own correspondences by observing and working with the trees over the seasons.

There are a couple of extant 'glossaries' that provide clues in interpretating the Ogham. John Matthews has translated the list of Morann mac Main in *Taliesin – the last Celtic shaman*. The following chart includes my interpretation based upon the Mac ind Oic word oghams.

If nothing else, Ogham helps us to relate to trees more, which has got to be a good thing. The more we can live in harmony with nature, the better for us, the animal kingdom and the planet. Of course, Ogham has deep and complex levels that probably require years, if not a lifetime of study to fully explore. It is not called the Dark Speech for nothing! It will not yield up its secrets easily. Yet, with dedication and intuition I feel it will give the serious student the equivalent of birdsong identification for ornithologists – it will make the woods come alive; you will be able to understand the parliament of trees.

Further reading: *The Celtic Tree Oracle*: Colin & Liz Murray. Rider, 1988;
Ogham, Koelbren and Runic: Kaledon Naddair. Keltia, 1986/7

OGHAM	LETTER	TREE	WORD-OGHAMS	KENNING	MEANING
Beithe	b	Birch	Glaisium cnis	Most silvery skin	Salmon wisdom
Luis	l	Rowan	Cara ceathra	Friend of cattle	Gentleness
Fearn	f	Alder	Comet lachta	Guarding of milk	Protection
Saile	s	Willow	Luth bech	Activity of bees	Business
Nuin	n	Ash	Bag Ban	Flight of women	Speed
(H)uathe	h	Hawthorn	Banadh Gnuisi	Blanching of face	Terror
Duir	d	Oak	Gres Sair	Carpenter's work	Construction/joining
Tinne	t	Holly	Smir guaili	Fires of coal	Constant heat/stamina
Coll	c	Hazel	Cara bloisc	Friend of cracking	Inspiration
Quert	q or kw	Apple	Brigh annum	Force of the men	Strength
Muinn	m	Vine	Aruusc n-arrligh	Condition of slaughter	Battle frenzy
Gort	g	Ivy	Mednercc	Knot of intention	Entanglement
Negetal	ng	Broom/fern	Etiud midach	Robe of physicians	Healing touch
Straif	str	Blackthorn	Moridrun	Increasing of secrets	Concealment
Ruis	r	Elder	Ruamna dreach	Redness of faces	Embarrassment/satire
Ailm	a	Fir/pine	Tosach fregra	Beginning of an answer	Clue
Ohn	o	Gorse/furze	Feithim saire	Smoothest of work	Ease/effortlessness
Ur	u	Thorn/heather	Siladh clann	Growing of plants	Expansion/profusion
Edhadh	e	Aspen	Comainm carat	Synonym for a friend	Trust
Ido/Ioho	i	Yew	Crinem feada	Most withered of wood	Decay
Ebadh	eba	Aspen	Cosc lobair	Corrective of a sick man	Health
Oir	oi	Spindle tree	Li crotha	Beauty of form	Attraction
Uilleand	ui	Ivy/honeysuckle	Cubat n-oll	Great equal length	Balance
Iphin	io	Pine	Amram blais	Most wonderful of taste	Love/nourishment
Phagos	ae	Beech	unknown	unknown	Teaching

EXERCISE: Composing an Ogham Englyn

The Welsh verse form *englyn* is an appropriate form in which to capture the wisdom of Ogham. In the *Mabinogion* Gwydion calls down from an oak tree a Lleu Llaw Gyffes transformed into an eagle by Blodeuwedd's treachery with a trio of englyns, an excellent example of Bardic healing – shamanic in the way Gywdion 'sings the soul back home' (see Caitlin Matthews' book of the same name), from an analogue of the World Tree:

> …he looked up into the top of the tree and there was an eagle; when the eagle shook, worms and rotten flesh fell away and the sow would eat, Gwydyon thought that the eagle was Lleu, so he sang this englyn:

> An oak grows between two lakes,
> Dark sky and glen.
> If I speak truly
> This comes from Lleu's feather.

At that the eagle dropped into the middle of the tree. Gwydyon (sic) then sang another englyn:

> An oak grows on a high plain;
> Rain soaks it no more than does putrefaction.
> It has supported twenty crafts;
> In its branches is Lleu Skilful Hand.

At that the eagle dropped down into the lowest branch of the tree, and Gywdyon sang still another englyn:

> An oak grows on a slope,
> The refuge of a handsome prince.
> If I speak truly
> Lleu will come to my lap.

At that the eagle dropped down onto Gwydyon's knee, and Gwydyon struck him with his magic wand so that he regained human form.

The Mabinogion, trans. J Gantz

So, you can see the englyn is a powerful form associated, in this instance, with Bards and trees. It is the commonest form used in the Welsh Eisteddfod competition, so it is a good one to master. It traditionally consists of four lines: of ten, six, seven and seven syllables. By writing to this form it teaches you discipline, but also encourages genius of invention – a poetic form, such as an englyn or sonnet is like a wine bottle into which you pour the wine of your words. Poetic 'beauty' comes from a synergy of form and content – if you choose to write in a traditional poetic form, rather than, say, free verse, then select one appropriate to your subject. For a poem about the Autumn Equinox (which for me symbolises balance among other things) I chose to use rhyming couplets to echo the relationships explored in the verse. I have already explained why I think the englyn is a good verse form for Ogham incantations, so here is a selection from my Ogham cycle, penned while sitting under an example of the species concerned:

Birch (beith) First in the forest, white bark curled like scrolls –
Pale maiden of winter,
Frozen, silver leaves shiver,
Shriving, the new life begins.

Rowan (luis) Mountain mother, cast your runes upon high,
Leaves like letters, wise staves,
Star in the berry, ward eye,
Protect us on the threshold.

Ash (nuin) Swift spear in battle, deadly in the fight –
Fierce in warrior's hand.
Tall and straight, linking the worlds.
Sky keys, givers of insight.

In composing these Ogham englyns I have drawn upon tree lore, direct observation and poetic inspiration. I sat underneath or near the tree in question and tuned into its 'energy', trying to 'seize its inmost form', its dryad if you like. This is what I suggest you try in this exercise. Go for a walk in some woods and find a good example of tree from the native tradition (native hardwoods such as oak, ash or thorn – use a Tree Identification book if necessary). If you are lucky, you may have a garden with specimens in. Spend some time with the tree. It is important to be within its auric field – normally the size of its canopy downwards, although some trees exude larger energy footprints if they are especially old or powerful. Soak up its atmosphere, literally, as you breathe in the oxygen that it gives you, in exchange for your carbon dioxide. Let it recycle your air. Listen and observe. Feel its spine against your back, its leaves, catkins or flowers between your fingers. Hold a nut or fallen twig in your hand. Call the Awen and pick up your pen and begin to write whatever comes to mind. Do not try to write in metric form to begin with – just brainstorm. Start with single words – feelings, images, sounds, anything. Then perhaps try to craft the odd phrase, without forcing it into 'poetry'. Don't try to write poetry – write with your voice. Be authentic and precise to the experience and emotions it conjures. Now you have a word-hoard try to shape into the syllabic lines. This may take two or three attempts. That's okay – just try variations until the right line falls into place. Then finally, recite your poem back to the tree as a way of saying thank you for its inspiration.

The Crane Bag: Walking

I will clamber through the clouds
and exist

John Keats

One of the simplest but most effective techniques available for the Bard seeking inspiration is simply to go for a walk. This sounds almost too obvious to mention, but how many of us walk with full awareness? All too often our thoughts are cluttered with mundane preoccupations, or the distractions around us, ie: in a busy municipal park. We may take headphones, sunglasses, thick coats – anything to block out our surroundings and desensitize us even further.

Most people have walked barefoot on the beach at some point – and what a wonderful feeling it is, but have you ever

Steps, Beechen Cliff, Bath.

walked barefoot through a field? Or a forest – feeling the mud, moss, twigs and leaves between your toes? This is how many hunter gatherers 'forest peoples' still traverse rainforest – it really sharpens your senses and stops you clomping along, crushing everything in your path with big boots and making a hell of a racket.

To go for a ramble, a meander, a tramp in the woods, when you get lost in your thoughts, is to access one's subconscious. It is a form of moving meditation – which is exactly what Buddhist monks use it for in the practise of the *jongrom*, when they walk barefoot very slowly and purposefully, with their full attention on the sensation of their soles (and souls), feeling the 'filling' and 'emptying' of weight in each leg, as in the art of Tai Chi. Try this, spending fifteen minutes walking from one end of your garden or house to the other barefoot. If you are brave, or foolish, you may even want to try walking barefoot through a city – but beware glass, chewing gum, faeces and mockery! A couple of friends of mine decided to walk backwards for a whole day on April Fool's Day – saying 'goodbye' to people as they approached. Such foolish behaviour can change perceptions.

How many times do we pass by people in our neighbourhood without proper greeting: those familiar faces who we see every day but do not acknowledge, or if we do it is with a desultory 'morning', as if we ourselves are mourning, voices low, heads down, shoulders hunched, unwilling to meet one another's eye? It is good to 'wake up' to what is around us, what we become blind to on our daily peregrinations to the shops, school, pub, or friend's house. Notice any wildlife, any natural thing, even the 'weeds' in the pavement cracks. Do you ever look up above the level of the ground floor? Notice the rooftops, the trees, the birds, the clouds, and the whole world above – but still take care crossing roads. Don't bump into people! You may find if you stand and stare at something, others will automatically do so. You may strike up some interesting conversations doing this, or attract other 'weirdos'!

Personally, a walk in Nature is my preference, although some find meandering in an urban landscape inspiring. Wordsworth famously went on inspiring walks when composing, as did his fellow Romantic, Coleridge, on the Quantocks. There is a plethora of great nature poetry inspired by walks and an intimate familiarity with the natural world: the so-called Peasant Poet, John Clare, who witnessed the Enclosures Act firsthand, had a close relationship with the land, for he worked it as a labourer, rather than just waxing lyrical about it. He had an eye for the minutiae of Nature, the quieter, humbler things that the Lord Byrons of the poetry world would not register, galloping by on their high horses. Some would call this myopic and provincial, but in fact it is about detailed observation, about being able to "see a world in a grain of sand, and heaven in a wild flower", as Blake did. God, and poetry itself, is in the details – not generalisms and abstractions. Peter Alfred Please, storyteller and author of the *Holine Quartet*, calls this eye for the mundane 'wayside inspiration'. It is about seeing what's actually in front of you, or at your feet – not what you expect to be there. It is best to walk with no expectations, or projections – as the saying goes: it is the journey, not the destination.

It is good to be prepared, even for a short walk, but don't get obsessed about kit. The less you can carry the better and no one is going to be worrying about designer labels in the wild. Functionality is most important, along with weight and durability. So, a basic checklist would be: strong footwear, appropriate clothing (according to climate), packed lunch, sun lotion or hat, gloves, and scarf, plenty of water, and emergency equipment if wandering somewhere rugged, such as first aid kit, whistle, emergency blanket, torch, energy sweets. Take a good OS map and compass, even a GPS gadget, and certainly a mobile phone (but turn it off while you're walking). Always let someone know where you are, but don't have too much of an itinerary, otherwise you become set on your goals, checking off the landmarks, rather than seeing what's around you.

It is often when you become lost that you find something of interest. In traditional stories it is always when a character 'strays from the path' that something dramatic happens

– but be wary! It is at such times that we can perhaps rely upon our totem animals to guide us (but common sense and orienteering skills should be the default safety option). Record what you experience in your journal – take back mementoes, such as feathers, stones, nuts, shells, and so on, but nothing rare (ie: wild flowers). Be respectful of all animal and plant life, and bide by the Countryside Code. You may want to take a carrier bag in case you see any litter – but be careful not to pick up any broken glass or needles. As always, be careful where you walk.

Glastonbury Tor

As a child 'I longed to walk where man had never trod', like John Clare, but the chances are that if you are walking anywhere in Britain someone would have been there before, and not everyone is as respectful. There is the paradox of seeking an unspoilt utopia – because by our very presence we are contributing to its denigration, unless we tread very lightly. Wearing bright colours can alarm animals and warn them off, as will our scent and the noise we make even without realising it. And however pleasant it is to share a walk in company, it keeps us within a human bubble. Our interface with Nature is significantly different if we are by ourselves: we may still be the 'intruder' but at least we can possibly eavesdrop upon nature (if we are very quiet) rather than continue a conversation. Listen to what the natural world has to say. It is the best teacher, and the best medicine. A good walk can replenish oxygen in our bloodcells, wake the brain, exorcise toxins, give us a Vitamin D boost from sunlight on skin and blow away the cobwebs. We return refreshed, with a clearer perspective on things. G M Trevelyan once said: "I have two doctors, my left leg and my right". John Cowper Powys in *Wolf Solent* writes: "Walking is my cure…As long as I can walk I can get my soul into shape! It must have been an instinct of self-preservation that has always driven me to walk". In Japan walking through woodland is prescribed as a therapy. And a Celtic valediction offers a traveller's blessing, although it suggests that travel itself is healing in the way it attunes us with the elements and with the immanent Divine:

> May the road rise to meet you,
> May the wind be always at your back,
> May the sun shine warm upon your face,
> May the rains fall softly upon your fields.
> Until we meet again,
> May God hold you in the hollow of His hand.

So walk with awareness and walk in beauty.

Visit ancient sites or natural wonders for inspiration. Take your journal or a notebook. Try these different length walks in order, building up your stamina and experience each time:

❖ Short walk: (1-2 hrs) Ideal for a reverie. Wander in the local park, riverside or bay.
❖ Half-day walk: (2-6 hrs) Great way of exploring an area. Even better with a pub.
❖ Day walk: (dawn until dusk) Make this a pilgrimage to a holy place, or plan a circular route for a good cause and get support and sponsorship, eg: Walk for Peace.
❖ Night walk: Try at full moon with a friend. Start at midnight. Aim to reach a good place to see the sunrise. Make sure the route is well-marked, ie: a National Trail. Even a small familiar area can be transformed by moonlight.
❖ Long walk: Book some time off. Follow a Long Distance Footpath, such as the Ridgeway. There are plenty of guides for these. Check accommodation availability. Pace yourself, ie: ten miles a day, especially if you're carrying all of your gear. Make sure you have good broken-in boots and plenty of blister cream and plasters!

Further reading: *Wanderlust: a history of walking* by Rebecca Solnit. (Viking, Penguin 2000)

Month 9: Awenyddion

Becoming an Inspired One

You have nearly reached the end of the third quarter of your Bardic year and by now you should be familiar with Awen: able to raise it and use it (or rather let it use you). Yet, as a Bard, it is not enough to tap into this source now and again – as Bards we have to live it. We should use the wisdom and inspiration we gain in all aspects of our lives. We should lead by example and aspire to be ambassadors for the Bardic Tradition through how we speak, carry ourselves, consume and contribute. We should live the Awen. I call this the Way of Awen (see **A Bardic Life**).

Try to infuse your life with Awen. Live lightly, live rightly, live well.

In Wales there was a class of Bards called the Awenyddion ('inspired ones'), who were able to channel spirit at will. These are akin to the Vatic or Filidh aspect of Druidry. The Awenyddion were vision-poets, seers, who could speak-in-tongues and utter oracular prophecies in verse, in extempore style. They were filled with Spirit and, to some, they must have seemed mad.

How can we be Awenyddion today? By opening up to Spirit, speaking with Spirit, acting with Spirit. Yet it is a precarious path to follow: one has to take measures to protect oneself, to filter out the voices of Spirit, or dampen them down at least; otherwise it could drive one insane if they were audible all of the time. Perhaps what we know as schizophrenia is a manifestation of this: the many personalities vying for dominion being actual spirits wanting to be heard, wanting to get through. If one opens up to such forces there is a real danger of becoming possessed. Yet this is an extreme and unlikely example. After all, the Way of Awen is about balance, about harmony. It is about keeping one foot on the ground at least! Walking between the worlds of the magical and mundane, and bringing the vision back for the tribe. Awen, as you know by now, means 'flowing spirit' – it is about working with the flow of things, in harmony with the spirits of place, the lunar, solar and cosmic tides. It is about being aware of the ripples one makes and taking responsibility for them, for one's words and actions. The Way of Awen is about being ever-mindful of the Web of Life and having 'joined-up thinking': seeing the connections and pointing them out.

There are multi-cultural equivalents of the Awenyddion in the spirit-doctors and medicine men and women of other traditions:

> Here in Brazil there is a certain class of inter-tribal priests called 'Caraís' who gain their knowledge through induced trances. This knowledge is the blueprint for several types of 'healing' - physical, mental and spiritual, individual or collective and so on. The most interesting thing is that they receive this knowledge in the form of songs, whispered in their ears by the ancient spirits of the forest. This is very similar to the Welsh Awenyddion as described by Giraldus Cambrensis in the 12th Century - those who gain knowledge and wisdom through songs.
>
> Email discussion, The Druid Network website

This fascinating correspondence to the Bardic Tradition seems to echo one of The Three Illuminations, **Teinm Laida**: Illumination by Song. Taliesin himself perhaps alludes to this in *The Hostile Confederacy*: "…by the end of his song he will know the starry wisdom".

THE SONG OF THE AWENYDD

Perhaps the finest and most famous example of such extempore composition is the immortal Song of Amairgen, said to have been uttered by the eponymous Bard of the Milesians when he set his right foot upon the shore of Erin (Ireland) for the first time in 1268 BCE. This is a version by Robert Graves:

The Song of Amergin

I am a stag: *of seven tines,*
I am a flood: *across a plain,*
I am a wind: *on a deep lake,*
I am a tear: *the Sun lets fall,*
I am a hawk: *above the cliff,*
I am a thorn: *beneath the nail,*
I am a wonder: *among the flowers,*
I am a wizard: *who but I*
Sets the cool head aflame with smoke?

I am a spear: *that roars for blood,*
I am a salmon: *in a pool,*
I am a lure: *from paradise,*
I am a hill: *where poets walk,*
I am a boar: *ruthless and red,*
I am a breaker: *threatening doom,*
I am a tide: *that drags to death,*
I am an infant: *who but I*
Peeps from the unhewn dolmen arch?

I am a womb: *of every holt,*
I am the blaze: *on every hill,*
I am the queen: *of every hive,*
I am the shield: *for every head,*
I am the tomb: *of every hope.*

This poem deserves to be meditated upon and visualised. It foreshadows the songs of Taliesin and is a style of transcendental poetry in which the poet identifies with all life, in a kind of global consciousness. In her notes on the Milesian Invasion of Ireland, in the *Encyclopaedia of Celtic Wisdom,* Caitlin Matthews says: "In Amairgen's mystical identification with all things, he becomes one of the physicians of the soul, reweaving the scattered elements of life into a new wholeness. This is the task of the Celtic poets, whose skill is to bring the soul to the point of vision, rest and stillness".

Nineteenth Century American Bard Walt Whitman updates this form brilliantly in his *Leaves of Grass* epic of 1850. In his egalitarian classic *Song of Myself* he seeks to identify with every one of his fellow countrymen and the land itself – seeing all connected, being connected to all: "for every atom belonging to me as good belongs to you".

In a similar way Amairgen sings the song of the land, thus immediately synchronising with the spirit of place. Joseph of Arimathea was said to have plunged his staff into Wearyall Hill as he stepped ashore – his staff took root and became the famous Glastonbury Thorn, which is still there to this day, budding at midwinter when a sprig is sent to the Queen (cuttings were also planted in the Glastonbury Abbey and in front of the Church of St John the Baptist on the High Street). The moral of this digression is: flourish wherever life puts you. Make you mark. A contemporary equivalent is Sir Paul McCartney's Celtic eulogy *Standing Stone,* a tale told in music, but with an accompanying poem in the sleeve notes. The story tells of the dawn of the Celtic lands, when a displaced seafarer makes land on a distant shore, and raises a monolith in honour of his safe arrival.

Celtic people are renowned for having the 'Second Sight', *dha shealladh,* literally 'the two seeings'. The Awenyddion would be able to find a solution without needing a ritual – able to slip into this state of consciousness at will. "We use both the physical and subtle sight to read the universe around us", says Caitlin Matthews. The answers don't come in obvious, verbal ways. Caitlin explains further in her foreword to the *Celtic Seers Source Book*: "We may receive impressions, remembrances, tautly drawn connections of information that fire our synapses, strong physiological surgings in our body, tears, laughter, songs…" These are what I call 'Matrix Moments', when we 'see the world as it really is' – when the surface of things is stripped away, the Web of Life is revealed, and we sense the connections between all things, experiencing a kind of revelation. Such epiphanies are what poets search for and savour and try to 'recollect in tranquillity.' Yet the Awenyddion can sense this all of the time, with the two-seeings of his or her vision, a layering of reality William Stafford expresses in his poem *Bifocal*:

The world happens twice.
Once, the way we see it, and
Then it legends itself
Deep, the way it really is.

Over the centuries, visionaries and poets have the ability to see the world this way. AE (Irish mystic George Russel) explores this in his seminal *The Candle of Vision,* in which he describes the Celtic seer's perception of things. In *The Crystal Cabinet,* Bard of the imagination William Blake describes how he saw things with his 'doors of perception' open:

> Another England there I saw,
> Another London with its Tower,
> Another Thames and other hills,
> Another pleasant Surrey bower,
>
> Another Maiden like herself,
> Translucent, lovely, shining clear,
> Threefold each in the other clos'd –
> O, what a pleasant trembling fear!

Yet one must be careful not to grasp this otherworldly vision – it cannot be possessed.

> I strove to seize the inmost form
> With ardour fierce and hands of flame,
> But burst the Crystal Cabinet,
> And like a weeping Babe became –

Like Keats' cast out knight, alone and palely loitering, Blake became "a weeping Babe upon the wild", exiled from the Otherworld and tormented by his taste of paradise. Yet we must take care not to be like the poet in Coleridge's *Kubla Khan*: "with flashing eyes and floating hair", otherwise people will start to be alienated: "Beware! Beware! Weave a circle round him thrice and close your eyes with holy dread, for he on honey dew hath fed and drunk the milk of Paradise". If we claim to have imbibed such ambrosia and nectar, the food of the gods, then we must be careful with whom we share it. Be prepared for mockery, or better still, don't take yourself too seriously in the first place – remember your limitations, your humanity and fallibility at all times. A true vision is a gift; it is not ours to control or to take credit for.

Here are some ways in which you could explore the nature of the Awenyddion over the coming month.

EXERCISES:
1. Inspired Speaking
Practice inspired speaking – try at home first, over a random object, observation or item on the news. Extemporise. Don't worry if it's gibberish to begin with. Just get used to making things up on the spot. If it helps, rhyme, but don't force it. Often one slips into a sing-song voice and the rhythm suggests the next word or phrase. When your confidence has grown, try doing it in conversation.
2. Extempore performance
Try including improvised sections in your performances, perhaps through **Audience Participation**. Watch live 'Impro' by stand-up comedians to see masters of this at work. Fooling workshops will help you develop spontaneity and flexibility, so you are less

precious about the words and more true to the moment and to the power of your imagination (see **Improvisation**, also in **Appendices**).

3. Feel the Awen

Throughout this month try to focus on Awen. Sense it in a room, in a particular place or person. Work with it, raise it every day and 'play' with it in different situations. Send it out into a group of people who are failing to communicate and see what happens (ie: a confrontational meeting or a dysfunctional family). Send it to those who need it, and appreciate it in those who have it (eg: the best singers, storytellers, or speakers).

Quarterly Review

Congratulations! You are nearly at the end of your year's training as an Anruth of the Gwion Grade. How do you feel now – having journeyed three-quarters of the way around the **Wheel of the Year**? You should be able to speak with the Voice of the Sea, the Earth and the Trees. Your range is expanding, your skills improving. Your Crane Bag should be filling with techniques and treasures of Bardic wisdom. You should no longer feel alone, if you managed to connect with your totem and contacted your Inner Bard. The language of trees should be becoming  familiar to you, through Ogham. You should be accruing more poems and tales, relating to the seasons and your journey. By now you should have a healthy **repertoire**, but there is still more to learn. Having tasted some performance in the public eye, you should have gone on a retreat to reflect upon your journey so far along the Way of Awen. So far, you have worked with the Spirits of Air, Fire and Water – now, as we turn to the last quarter of the year, it is time to ground your dream in practical skills and knowledge of the Earth, to look at the bigger picture as you prepare to enter the wider circle of the community. But first use your journal to take stock and reflect upon what you have learnt, what you have liked, and what you need to keep working on.

Tick when you have completed the following:

❖ Spirits of Water
❖ Month 7: Connecting with the Animal Kingdom
❖ Finding your Totem
❖ The Hawk of Achill
❖ Fionn and the Salmon
❖ The Weir of the Twice-Born – Changing your Wyrd
❖ Voice of the Sea
❖ Tipping the Cauldron
❖ Month 8: Calling the Inner Bard

❖ The Inward Spiral: the joy of solitude
❖ Retreat
❖ Bard and Community
❖ Marking Rites of Passage
❖ Voice of the Trees
❖ The Silver Branch
❖ The Three Illuminations: *Dichetal do Chennaib*
❖ Oghams and Englyns
❖ The Crane Bag: Walking
❖ Month 9: Awenyddion

FIVE
EARTH

Spirits of Earth

Turning last but not least to the North, to the quarter of the Earth, of sensation, of knowledge, to Gaia herself, the Earth Mother, Mater Tierra – whose body we live on, which feeds us, nurtures us, sustain us. Consider 'all creatures great and small': the animals with whom we share this world and its resources with. Native Americans consider them their brothers and sisters: the two-legged, the four-legged, the feathered and scaled ones, are all part of the same Creation, of the Creator, *Wakan-tanka*. And always remember that we are part of the Web of Life.

In our **Wheel of the Year,** Earth is associated with the Northern Quarter, with Winter – from Samhain to Imbolc. Think of the harsh, dramatic gods of the Norse: surly and fierce, volatile and earthy. Perhaps their violent tempers symbolise the extremes of Winter weather, how Nature will strip away any excess at this time, and bring us down a peg or two if we don't, unless we batten down the hatches and 'lay low'. Now is the time to be merry: to gather around the hearth with friends and family and share new tales and old to brighten the long dark nights. Storytelling is still at its most popular at this time of year, but these days in the form of blockbuster movies and best-selling books – yet still there is a thirst for these death-and-resurrection myths at this time when perhaps we feel our mortality the most. Does this explain the association of midwinter with the most famous story of all, the Birth and Death and Resurrection of Christ? The proximity of Christmas to the Winter Solstice, when the sun seems to 'die' (at its lowest arc in the Northern hemisphere) on the shortest day of the year and is 'reborn' after the longest night, is no coincidence, I feel. It is the resurrection the earth experiences annually, through the cycle of the seasons, and is emulated in myriad ways throughout World Myths (eg: the slaying of Baldur by mistletoe).

The word 'solstice' comes from 'still point', because the sun seems to pause in its swing South, before beginning its slow return North along the Eastern horizon. Tune into this nadir and work with the energies of ebb and flow, death and rebirth. This is the time for deep dreaming, for seeding ideas for the coming year: what do you wish for? What do you want to come true, to manifest in the coming year?

Yet, at a time when Peace on Earth has been replaced by mass consumerism, now is a good time to consider one's impact upon the planet, upon one's consumption of resources. Rather than think about what you want, think about what you can give back. Can you do more to help the planet? As the Agenda 21 slogan goes: Think Globally, Act Locally. At a time when countless fir trees are being felled to last only until the needles drop, can you plant more trees? Save paper by cutting down on wrapping paper and over-packaging? By fasting rather than feasting? I'm not asking you to become a curmudgeonly eco-Scrooge or killjoy – just to become more aware of your actions and impact. Do you walk lightly on the Earth? We all create an ecological footprint; none of us are completely perfect and we certainly shouldn't feel sanctimonious, but we can always lessen our stress upon the planet's resources. A Bard, if anyone, should be sensitive to the voice of the earth.

The Stone of Fal

The Stone of Fal, one of the four treasures of the Tuatha de Danann was originally located on Tara in County Meath, the Hill of the High Kings of Ireland. It was said to shout out if a true king stood upon it. It was said to have been removed to Scotland to become the famous Stone of Scone, which was itself misappropriated as the power shifted to the English. It was installed under the Royal throne in Westminster Abbey and is still used in the Coronation of British Monarchy. What would happen if the stone was restored? Recently, Tara was under threat by a motorway development. Many people rallied to defend this sacred landscape. Protesters cited the myths, as well as its archaeological sites, to assert its importance to world heritage. When we mythologise a landscape we reinforce its numinosity, and can use the power of story and song to help protect it.

EXERCISES

1: Write a Winter Solstice Poem or Song

Compose a piece to celebrate what this festival and season means to you. Read seasonal classics for ideas, eg: *Gawain and the Green Knight*; *A Christmas Carol* by Charles Dickens; *A Child's Christmas in Wales* by Dylan Thomas; *The Journey of the Magi* by TS Eliot; etc.

2: Write a Mummers Play

Mummers Plays are the layman's cousin of the medieval Mystery Plays: ancient, archetypal, and crude, these rough and ready village skits are performed by local amateurs – masked for anonymity or to save embarrassment, their ritual guise enables them to act outside the social norm, perhaps mocking the status quo while at the same time 'keeping mum'. They are traditionally performed around Yuletide and may be a forerunner of pantomime: there are distinct similarities between the two, in terms of stock characters, stock situations and corny jokes. The formula is unvarying, but that is part of their magic, for they are a kind of unofficial fertility ceremony, the performance of which is 'essential' for another good year – certainly it is seen as a blessing on all who witness it, and on the places where it is performed. Traditionally the players would 'mooch' from house to house, or from one end of the village to the other (or even between villages) in exchange for reward, usually alcoholic (see Wassailing below). The cast of characters consists of the following (with slight regional variation): St George, The Saracen or the Turkish Knight, The Doctor, Fool figure, and others. Nothing can compensate for seeing a Mummers Play live. Although many are Victorian or modern reinventions, there are still some original ones around (ie: the Marshfield 'Paper Boys', who have performed on Boxing Day every year for centuries in costumes of news rags – costumes, so the grandson of one of the players tells me, which would have originally been leaves, thus suggesting how primal it could be. Their cast consists of Old Father Christmas, Little Man John, King William, Doctor Phoenix, Tenpenny Nit, Old Father Beelzebub and Saucy Jack, who declaims in typical Mummers fashion: "In comes I, Saucy Jack, with my family on my back"). These figures have their counterpart in *commedia dell'arte*, an Italian burlesque performed with grotesque half-masks: Pulcinello, Harlequin, Pantagruel, and their like are universal figures of fun, a kind of Continental *Carry On*. I wrote my Mummers Play entitled *The Head of Winter*, based upon the 'Beheading Game' of Gawain and the Green Knight. It was performed in a commedia dell'arte style.

Have a go at writing your own, using seasonal motifs (ie: the battle between Winter and Summer for the hand of Spring). Make costumes and props. Act it out with friends. Then perform for the community. Remember it doesn't have to be polished – in fact, in the tradition of Mummers, it shouldn't be. Use slapstick and plenty of 'business'. Have fun.

3: Hold a Midwinter Celebration

Twelfth Night (January 5th) is often overlooked: it was the Old Christmas in the Julian Calendar, but now it is often just an after-thought – the day after (Epiphany, January 6th) we take down the decorations, otherwise we get 'bad luck for the rest of the year'. Yet it can be much more – for me it is a chance to catch up with friends I have missed over the holiday, and to make merry one last time, before returning to mundane time, to work (Plough Monday soon follows, when farmers would do exactly that). In the West Country, Twelfth Night is traditionally the time for wassailing the apple trees to ensure a good harvest. Wassailing carols are sung, cider poured onto roots, and plenty more down necks. To this day, in the cider orchards of Somerset, shotguns are fired into the trees to scare away the evil spirits and then toast is attached to the branches to literally 'toast' the trees (and give the birds a much-needed winter snack). I know of one place where the youngest child present is given the honour of this task, lifted into the branches almost like an embodiment of Robin Goodfellow himself.

If you have local orchards or a fruit tree in the garden, you can hold your own wassailing with mulled cider, apple poems and songs, a good story or two (ie: The Apple

Wassail!

Tree Man), complete with cider-pouring, toast, and other customs. Improvise and add your own – we use party poppers on the apple tree in my garden instead of shotguns and we always get a good crop! See Common Ground's book on Apple Day Customs.

If you live in an urban area, you could do a 'wassail' instead – gather friends, dress up in your finest bardic apparel, bring instruments, carols, and a wassail bowl and wend your way around town, offering to bless a house, shop or place in exchange for contributions to the bowl: normally some tipple, although one year we did this in a market around the stalls and got given vegetables! With the bowl brimming, toast the host, and all present – peace and plenty for the coming year. This would be an excellent time to try out some of your seasonal songs and poems, although there's some fine wassailing songs out there, as well as the perennial favourites such as *The Holly and the Ivy*.

4. Create an Earth altar

Build a simple shrine in your garden, allotment or even in nature, in a discreet corner of a woodland. Make it out of local natural materials. Use it to connect with the genius loci. Leave biodegradable offerings for the birds and other wildlife. Visit and clean regularly.

Month 10: Your Bardic Debut

Author publicity shot as Bard
of Bath, by Helen Murray.

At the beginning of your year's training your first rite of passage was to dedicate yourself to the Bardic path. As an initiate, or Anruth, you became Twice-Born, like Taliesin, with a new (Bardic) name. You have preserved and followed the Way of Awen throughout the turning of the wheel and now it is time for your second rite of passage – from the private to the public domain. It is time for your first professional performance.

You may have performed during the year, trying out your new skills at 'open mics', storytelling nights, parties and around campfires, but now is the moment of truth: can you 'make it' as a Bard? Will people take you seriously as you step into the spotlight, claiming to be a poet, singer or storyteller? You have to believe in yourself, otherwise no one else will, but the proof, ultimately, is in the pudding: can you entertain an audience with your Bardic skills? Will they pay to come and see you? Well, you could put on a free gig, but unfortunately, it seems that in our money-orientated world, if something is free people generally don't value it (eg: fresh air, clean water, peace and quiet) so it is best to charge a token amount at least – if only to cover the cost of the venue. A couple of quid isn't going to break anyone's bank and most won't mind 'gambling' so little on an unknown act – out of novelty or curiosity value alone (although the audience may largely consist of friends and family).

So, this is the time when you move from the sometimes solitary life of a training Bard into the eye of the community. Remember, you cannot truly be a Bard without a community that acknowledges you. Although your personal self-esteem shouldn't depend upon what other people think (though the opinion of peers is a useful barometer), your value as a Bard does ride on how much your community values you. A community should be able to choose its own Bard, since you are in effect their ambassador, or spokesperson, as well as remembrancer: if they do not wish to have you as their Bard, you must honour their wishes. A Bard, I believe, should be democratically elected by the community (within an **Eisteddfod** judging system).

Since you are possibly a newcomer, and this is your debut, you still have to prove yourself: this is your chance to show your community what you can offer. If they like what you can do, then offers may begin to trickle in for various events and opportunities. Let the people decide. But do not be disheartened if the response is lukewarm or lacklustre: review the performance, get objective feedback if possible (see below), take on board any criticisms and continue to hone your skills.

The checklist below is expanded in the **On Being a Twenty-First Century Bard** section, but this should get you started:

1 Set: By now, you should have quite a healthy repertoire. Select a sample of your best material – ideally an alternating mixture of story, song and poem. A running theme may emerge from this (perhaps all your material is Celtic, for instance – or featuring horses, fairy brides, or magic swords). Select one main motif and focus on it in structuring your set and in publicising it, ie: 'Tales of the Cauldron'. Time your material. A thirty minute set should be sufficient for your first solo performance. You may want to join forces with other performers, eg: musicians, who could complement your act, either by playing before, during, or after the show.

2 Book a Venue: Choose a suitable space, perhaps one that is already being used for similar performances; or you may spot a potential venue. However, this may be more difficult to promote if people aren't used to it being a performance space. Go where the crowds are, eg: your local arts centre, arts café, or open mic pub. Check sound (acoustics and any potential noise pollution), accessibility, facilities (dressing room, toilets, bar), and overall 'feel' – does it feel right? A Working Men's Club will feel very different to a wine bar, and neither may be suitable for a Bardic performance! A dedicated arts performance space will be best, whether it's urban or at a festival. Liaise with the venue manager, get to know them and build up a good rapport – they will be your crucial contact.

3 Rehearsal: Plan a schedule of rehearsals leading up to the performance, at least once a week. Invite friends to sit in and give feedback.

4   PR: Design a poster and a flyer; print as many copies as you can afford, and spread the word – take them around to local shops, libraries, other events and venues – but always ask permission to distribute or display them.

5   Performance: This is your time to shine! Remember to raise the Awen and wear your 'confidence overcoat'. Warm up your voice and body beforehand. Keep calm and have fun. Enjoy yourself and your audience will as well.

6   Sales: You might want to create a booklet of poems, tales, or a CD of songs to sell at the gig. Make sure you have plenty of business cards, or flyers with your details on.

7   Document: Get someone to take photographs of the show, or film it. Keep a copy of the poster, flyer or programme for your Bardic scrapbook.

8   Review: Take stock of the show. How did it go? How did it feel for you? How did the audience respond? What worked and what didn't? Be honest.

9   Feedback: Have a comments book or slips available at the gig. Encourage people to write their comments down – you may have to 'bribe' them with a raffle prize. Start a mailing list to keep people updated about any future gigs or workshops.

The Bladder Stick - Using humour

Humour is an essential part of the Bard's repertoire – everyone likes a good laugh, and it is important not to take oneself too seriously. The lack of a sense of humour is a trademark of fanatics, despots and psychopaths. Bringing humour into your performances is a good way of being down to earth, connecting with the audience and avoiding criticisms of pretension. It also bursts the tension – before someone else does (circumventing any hecklers). Timing is everything, as is timeliness. A good ribald tale to raise the spirits is ideal for long dark nights, and the one below is of interest to Bards, since it mentions a brew of inspiration and the Norse equivalent of the Bard, the Skald:

Bolverk and the Skaldic Mead

Odin donned his broad-rimmed hat and cloudy cloak and travelled down to Jotunheim, the realm of the giants. He was on a quest to win the Skaldic Mead: the mead made from the blood of Kvase the Wise by the dwarves who slew him, the mead that would bestow inspiration to any who drank its three draughts. His keen-eyed ravens, Hugin and Munin, informed him that these were lost to the dwarves because of their cruelty, and kept safe by Gunnlod, the giant Suttung's daughter, inside a hollow mountain.

With his staff in hand Odin strode across the borders of Jotunheim – transforming himself into Bolverk, mischief-maker, in disguise to bamboozle his immortal enemies, the giants. He came to a field where nine ogre-ugly men worked, making hay. Pausing, Bolverk noticed how they sweated because their scythes were so dull. He produced a whetstone and offered to sharpen them – they grunted assent and it was done in a flash. Now the scythes sliced through the grass like it wasn't there. The thralls, for that's what they were, asked for that marvellous stone if Bolverk had no need of it. He gladly obliged, throwing it up into the air – the thralls all lunged for it at once and succeeded in chopping each other's heads off!

Bolverk picked up the stone and, whistling, carried on his way.

The mischief-maker came to the hall of Baugi, who was the brother of Suttung (whose daughter, you may remember, guarded the skaldic mead). The giant was lamenting his lot – he had lost all of his farm-workers in one calamitous agricultural accident. Somehow they had all been beheaded with their own scythes…Now there was no one to bring in the harvest. What was he to do?

Bolverk offered to help. He would do the work of nine and all he would ask for in return was a draught of the finest mead the giant's family had at the end of the summer. A draught of mead, was that all? Without thinking (not a strong point for his kind), Baugi agreed – unable to believe his luck. Then he remembered the skaldic mead, the best his family possessed. He was sure he could persuade his brother, Suttung, for a drop…

So, Bolverk set to work with a zest, working as well as a gang of ogres. By the end of the summer the harvest was home and Bolverk asked for his dues. Baugi looked awkward. He had put off and put off going to see his brother. When he finally did, Suttung could not believe his audacity or stupidity – and bluntly refused. So, Baugi explained, we are going to have to get this draught of mead by guile.

Bolverk did not have much, indeed any faith in the giant's wit, so he got him to explain what he had in mind as they set off for the hollow mountain. The plan was to drill a hole inside and for Bolverk, in the form of a snake, to wriggle in and steal a draught of mead from under the sizeable nose of Gunnlod, the giant's daughter.

They arrived at the hollow mountain. Bolverk produced an auger and Baugi set to work. When he claimed to have finished, Bolverk tested by blowing into the hole – dust and chips flew into his face. It wasn't finished yet. He suspected something but let Baugi continue, then when the hole was finally complete, he changed himself into a snake and slipped in. He had to wriggle fast, because no sooner had he done so, than that treacherous Baugi plunged the auger in after him. But Bolverk popped out the other side just in time.

Near Gunnlod's chamber Bolverk transformed himself into his divine form. Looking magnificently godly, he appeared before the giant's daughter. Despite the genetic ugliness of her kin, Gunnlod herself was surprisingly beautiful – tall, statuesque and blonde. Odin introduced himself and she was impressed. She didn't get out much. Without further ado she grabbed him and they didn't beat about the bush. Odin and Gunnlod made love for three days and nights – on the last night the god stopped for breath. He was exhausted and wondered if he could have a little mead?

Giddily, Gunnlod fetched him the three vats of skaldic mead – expecting him to take a sip. But Odin swigged down the whole lot before she could do anything about it – then turned himself into an eagle and flew out the top of the hollow mountain, leaving a furious Gunnlod. Men! She was enraged, but not empty-handed. Odin had left her with child and she was to give birth to the greatest skald of all, Bragi – who was himself to give birth, in a way, to the noble and exalted art of bragging… but that is another story for another time.

However, Gunnlod and child considered, Suttung was not going to let the thief – god or otherwise – get away with stealing his hard-won mead. Transforming himself into an eagle he gave chase. Odin's belly was full of skaldic mead and flew slowly and drunkenly – rather like a fat bumblebee – so Suttung soon began to catch up.

Yet Odin had help. In sight of the fabled halls of Valhalla, he called out and the Aesir came to his aid – lighting a great pyre at the walls of Asgard. Odin managed to fly over without getting singed –as he did so, spitting out the skaldic mead into vats made ready – but Suttung wasn't so lucky. His feathers caught fire and he plunged to his death into the pyre – well and truly scalded.

Odin had won the skaldic mead for the Aesir, and they made divine song with its wisdom. Yet some of the drops of the inspiring brew had fallen from Odin's lips as he spat it out, falling to Earth – and it is those drops that gave the gift of poetry to some. Rarely a skald is granted a purer draught and his songs become renowned around the world, lasting for all time. Other, less pure drops fell onto the lips of journalists and politicians: they came from Odin's bladder, as he relieved himself over the walls of Valhalla.

Yet the maker of this story must have drunk from the good stuff, and I have tasted it in telling it, and I hope it has been honey to your ears…

Adapted by the author from *Of Gods and Giants: Norse Mythology*
by Harald Hveberg (Tokens of Norway, 1976)

Interesting that this seemingly ribald tale has echoes of Taliesin's Bardic initiation, with a potion of inspiration (skaldic mead) and a shape-changing chase sequence. The fact there are three drops as well is also resonant: akin to the three splashes on Fionn's hand and the Three Rays of the Awen… Are they from the same source, or a case of simultaneous invention and the universality of myth?

Perhaps I'm being too serious. The main thing to bear in mind is to spice your sets with dashes of humour, either during or between numbers. A joke or witty aside acts as a safety valve for the tension and delivery of material. The classic ice-breaker is a gag thrown in at the beginning. Make the audience laugh and you make them feel at ease. Laugh and the world laughs with you, they say, but don't force humour and don't feel obliged to shoe-horn in jokes, especially not if you are trying to create a certain mystical or melancholy mood. Break the spell, by all means, but do it consciously, when the enchantment is complete.

Interruptions, gaffes, Freudian slips and trips are all opportunities for comedy (see **Improvisation**). The universe has ways of making us laugh, or be laughed at. It is said if you want to make the gods laugh, tell them your plans. Well, perhaps you can tell them your stories as well and join in the Cosmic Joke. The Trickster, in the form of Loki, Hanuman, Coyote, Anansi and crew, has a way of cocking a snook at all that become po-faced. Although extreme at times and distasteful to some – especially those on the receiving end of his japes – the Trickster is providing an essential catabolic function: breaking down that which needs to be broken down. Laughter is a great leveller and offers a healthy catharsis. It's better out than in.

EXERCISE: Start a joke-book

Every Bard should have a few jokes up their sleeve: as icebreakers, when things go wrong, the PA packs up or you go blank. You probably know a couple of jokes already. Start collecting any you hear in a jokebook, or on a Dictaphone – because it's all in the delivery. Watch famous comedians to see how they work the audience, use timing, expression, tone of voice, etc. They are often masters of improvisation and put-downs (see **Satire**). Go to a Comedy Night. If it's open mic, have a go yourself. Try slipping in the odd gag during a set, to lighten the tone. The harper, singer and storyteller Robin Williamson is very adept at this, blending the mythic and the mundane, enchantment and pure entertainment, with dazzling skill. You don't need to dump in whole jokes for the sake of it: the odd quip or witty aside will suffice to leaven the mood. Often, a situation suggests its own humour, eg: a mobile phone going off at an inopportune moment. Instead of being distracted by it, incorporate it into the tale ('Suddenly, he heard a strange bird...')

The Crane Bag: *Briamech Smetrach* - the Uses and Misuses of Satire

Bards were dreaded for their satire – perhaps the most feared 'weapon' in their arsenal. Lordly hosts despised being lampooned as churlish or thrifty hosts in a time when a man's honour and reputation were everything. This skill was known as *briamech smetrach*, and is mentioned in *Cormac's Glossary*. It is described thus:

Fool, photograph by Julie Manwaring.

...the name of an operation which poets perform on a person who refuses them [aught]. He [the poet] grinds the person's earlobe between his two fingers and the person dies on whom he performs this operation.

Although the 'grinding of earlobe' can be seen as a metaphor for a crushing satire, the consequences can be taken as read: the recipient or victim of the satire can literally die of shame (this has certainly happened with people hounded by the press who commit suicide) so it is a deadly weapon only to be used in extremis, when you are absolutely certain it is justified (ie: on corrupt or misleading politicians). It is better to avoid using altogether, because, like cursing, it is subject to the Threefold Effect – and it is better to be using your Bardic skills to disseminate beauty and enchantment, rather than ugliness and spite.

However, the truth will out, and sometimes it *is* ugly and *has* to be spoken – like lancing a sceptic wound. The truth, mythic or literal, should be sacred to the Bard. We are not in the business of sycophancy any more, like the Court Bards were in the Middle Ages. Our livelihoods (and our lives) do not depend upon Royal Patronage, so we must kowtow to no man, and never compromise our Bardic words. John Matthews says in *Taliesin*: "The role of poet was to uphold the truth and natural laws, almost as a mirror of justice."

Sometimes satire is the only stratagem we have left – think of the scathing slogans and effigies paraded in mass demonstrations. Satire is perhaps the recourse of the disempowered, the voice of the voiceless, the vox populi who feel betrayed and 'out of the loop' of decision-making, yet who are all 'stake-holders' in their country, their planet.

Some Bards were famously able to raise boils on the faces of their enemies. Taliesin memorably caused Maelgwyn's Court Bards to utter 'blerwm, blerwm' like babies, by playing on his lips as they passed – thus casting a spell upon them.

There is mention of the satirising technique of *glam-dichenn* which requires seven poets (including amongst them an *ollamh*) to go to a hilltop placed between the boundaries of their lands at sunrise and perform an intricate series of manoeuvres involving slingstones, thorn trees, 'staves' of verse, and correct wind conditions. This seems to echo the tricky technique of cursing, with one leg raised and one hand over one eye. Such activities can backfire, and the account comes with a caveat: "if it were they that were in the wrong, the earth of the hill would swallow them up". So beware!

Here, I believe the Christian ethic of 'Let he without sin cast the first stone' should apply. Mea Culpa: we are all culpable and all flawed – they say to err is to be human – so who are we to cast judgement on another? Use the sword of words carefully.

EXERCISE: Write a Satire of Yourself

Try this exercise to experience the effect upon yourself. Write a list of all your faults, bad habits, peccadilloes and foibles. Be merciless. This helps to crush any pomposity. We must use the ego as a vehicle to deliver our message – it gives us the confidence to go out there, to stick our necks out – but we can't let it get out of hand. Look at yourself hard in the mirror, beyond the superficial. You really know what you're like deep down. Recall your most humiliating and embarrassing moments – how does it feel to have them read out? Turn it into a poem or song and recite it to yourself every now and again. Bear this in mind if you are ever considering using satire on someone: the mote is often in the eye of the beholder. By remembering our own fallibility we won't be so eager to point out the weaknesses of others.

Voice of the Earth

What is it to speak with the voice of the earth? First and foremost it is to listen: to the spirit of the place (*genius locus*), to the spirit of the land, and to the heart of the planet. Hear the heartbeat of the Great Mother in every living thing, in all flora and fauna – all shrubs, grasses, lichens, fungi and flowers, all insects, birds, mammals, and reptiles. It is to be aware of the Web of Life, the chains, cycles and seasons. Sensitise yourself to your surroundings, to what's under your feet. Walk barefoot: on soft grass, naked rock, the mulch of a forest, and mud. Feel the earth. It is to: "remember, as one must all day/Beneath the pavement the live earth aches", as poet Harold Monro puts it. It is to talk with dragon tongue, giant strength and Gaia wisdom.

It is to speak with feeling, reflecting the sensations we enjoy as incarnate human beings. It is tactile, red, rooty, raw and organic. It is primal, powerful Base Chakra energy we're talking about here – the stuff of sex and deep desires. Yet at the same time the voice of *terra firma* keeps us firmly grounded, with both feet on the ground. But we must be careful not to be 'stuck in the mud.' It is our foundation, but not our destination. With salt of the earth in our hearts, we must rise from this solid beginning and aspire.

Northern poet Basil Bunting, in his epic *Briggflatts*, says: "Words are too light, take a chisel to write". Imagine your poems on tablets of stone. They should be decisive, but not dogmatic. Leave room for ambiguity, but don't be uncertain about your control of the language. On one level, it is about being immensely practical about your words. Think of them as directions of a journey – does it take the reader or listener to where you want them to go (even if that place is one of uncertainty?) Do they perform their function? Focus in on the nuts and bolts, on the nitty gritty stuff of grammar, syntax, spelling and presentation. Consider the raw sound of speech: the earthy quality of language – the glottals of consonants. Try using some harder syllables to make your poetry more muscular, like Anglo Saxon kennings – terse and sparse, with the economy of a haiku, the knottiness of a riddle.

Be tough and unsentimental. Go to deep places. Express the pain of the Earth, her outrage and anguish, like Demeter mourning for her lost daughter, or Boudicca razing cities in vengeance at the rape of hers. Imagine being polluted, defiled, exploited, neglected – your skin pocked by scars, by scabs of cities, running sores of roads, your body desecrated by landfill sites, by opencast mining, by nuclear waste.

It is about the history of what you hold in your hand: the forest of that book, the herd of that leather. Next time you think about buying a crystal, consider where it came from and how it was extracted – was it done with respect, or just ripped from the ground? How much more can Mother Earth take before she is bereft of her riches? How about putting something back? Whether it's picking up litter, tending a garden, or an allotment, or joining a local conservation group or green NGO, we can all make a difference. Get involved at the grassroots. Dig in and make a stand. Use non-violent direct action when necessary, to stop insensitive road or quarry schemes, pollution, exploitation, or the destruction of the land's resources and beauty. The inheritance of tomorrow's children – Planet Earth – we steward, but do not possess. We look after the land, and it looks after us – simple. Our words can help remind people of that sacred trust, and encourage care of the land by celebrating its beauty and diversity, its fecundity and fragility.

Finally, to speak with the voice of the earth is to be in your body, to be aware of your body, your posture, your body language, and your **movement**. It is about **Using the Space**: the physicality of your performance environment, the floor, walls, ceiling, any furniture, the architecture, and most importantly, your audience. It is to be fully present, and to encourage your audience to be the same – to look around them, to leave with a greater awareness of their location and the time of year.

By sharing regional folk tales and celebrating local customs, we honour the spirits of place. Through learning the stories of a place we get under the skin of the land, and have a direct insight into the psyche of its people. As the Native American saying goes: "Never judge a man until you have walked two moons in his moccasins". The voice of the earth enables us to walk in the footsteps of our ancestors and to walk lightly.

The 'giant's chair' of Cader Idris, Wales. A place of poetic inspiration.

Sitting Out: A Night on Bard Mountain

> Great things occur when men and mountains meet.
> It is not done by jostling in the street.
>
> *William Blake*

As part of our focussing and attunement with the element of Earth it is important to go out into the land and experience it directly. No amount of inner work will compensate for this. Apart from the daily and practical things you can do such as taking your dog for a walk, gardening or running an allotment, I suggest you need to interface with a wilder Nature, with wilderness. Very little genuine wilderness remains in Britain, but it is still possible to get a taste of the wild in some out of the way places (see *Wild Britain* by Douglas Blotting, Ebury Press 1988): the Moors, the rugged coastlines, lonely islands, remnants of ancient woodland and mountains are such places. On a wet and windy day, walking by oneself in the middle of nowhere, it would be difficult not to describe it as 'wilderness'. Technically, this implies a self-willed landscape, where nature is in charge and you are the interloper. Of course, the majority of the British landscape has been altered by man over the millennia; even the treeless 'wet deserts' of Dartmoor and the Scottish Highlands, which seem very wild at times.

The main thing is to approach these places respectfully. I believe you do not conquer a mountain – a mountain conquers you. Any kind of hubris will be dealt with severely (ie: as depicted in the harrowing book and docu-drama *Touching the Void*). If one doesn't take the necessary precautions one risks serious injury or death. Yet in our molly-coddled Nanny State I think a little bit of risk is a healthy thing. If we have a close call, it chastens us – and we learn a powerful lesson that we'll never forget – not that I advocate taking any unnecessary risks! All who enter the Wild do so at their own risk, but you can be prepared. Have the right gear, the right information and the right skills. If you have no experience orienteering or hill-walking, then go on a course or join a Ramblers Group – there's safety in numbers, but ultimately you will have to face this test alone.

The Native Americans use the technique of the Vision Quest to gain a healing vision for the tribe: it is not to be undertaken lightly, or without preparation. The excellent book-let *The Wilderness Quest for Vision and Self-Healing* (adapted from *The Sacred Mountain* by Steven Foster and Meredith Little, by Jeremy Thres and Caroline Wood) tells you all you need to know and it is possible to undertake such an endeavour under supervision – there's a few modern practitioners who offer 'vision quest' experiences. The Vision Quest is based upon the classic rites of passage structure of Separation, Initiation and Return –the same as in many Quest myths and legends. But in this one, you're 'starring'! (Though don't embark upon such a venture with any illusion that your success or safe return is guaranteed – unless you act sensibly and take the necessary precautions: see below).

There are numerous locations where you could undertake such a Vision Quest – virtually any of the National Parks, but abide by any byelaws about camping, lighting fires, wild-life, and so on.

In Wales there are two sites in close proximity that are both associated with the same legend, interestingly enough: it is said if you spend a night on Bedd Taliesin *or* Cader Idris you'll end up either dead, mad or poet – or a possible combination. Sometimes it's hard to tell the difference between madness and genius: you may come down a dead mad poet! Or you may get hypothermia, so keep a close eye on the weather – don't go up if there's mist covering the top, rain or high winds. The weather changes rapidly in such places to catch the unwary.

Why should we do such foolish things? Well, it is a form of self-initiation – one that you will never forget. You will have a powerful experience and possibly gain wisdom, like Conaire who slept on Tara, the hill of the Ard-Ri, and received the Crane Bag. Other stories tell of similar initiatory experiences: Pwyll, Lord of Dyfed, sat on Gorsedd Arbeth, by his castle at Narbeth – whoever stood upon it was said to receive a wound or a wonder, and in a way, he received both, in the form of the lovely Rhiannon, who stole his heart. Thomas of Ercildoune famously lay on the Eildon Hills, met the Queen of Elfland, and was whisked away by her for 'seven mortal years' in which time he received the Tongue That Cannot Lie, the gift of prophecy. But be warned: encounters with the Otherworld can be notoriously treacherous – the Seventeenth Century Scottish Minister Robert Kirk went walking on the hills near Aberfoyle and stepped into a Faerie Ring, to be whisked away into the Otherworld, so the legend goes, exchanged for a changeling!

Return safely and write down your experiences as vividly and as accurately as possible.

You may have come back with 'fire in the head', to write a poem, song or story. Perhaps you had strange dreams or experiences – you could have 'heard' the dreaming of the place.

There are several legends of lost lords and kings sleeping 'under the hills', most famously King Arthur, Fionn Mac Cumhail and Charlemagne: to be awoken in the hour of the land's greatest need, either by horn or bell. An intruder stumbles upon their cave and disturbs them from their slumber too early – and receives a good ticking off!

Janet and Colin Bord, in *The Secret Country*, relate the tale of a young boy who finds a stone portal, enters an Otherworldly realm, finds a faerie wife and has a son by her called Taliesin:

> …a shepherd boy, lost in the mountains…was led to a certain menhir by a merry blue-eyed old man. The old man tapped three times on the stone and lifted it up, revealing steps lit by a blue-white light. Down they went, and came to a wooded, fertile country with a beautiful palace. The shepherd boy began a marvellous life among the 'fair-folk', and eventually married one of them. Later, he decided to return to the upper world and took his wife with him. They lived well; for they were rich, and had a son they called Taliesin, who became a famous Bard. This story may have been a remnant of an ancient Bardic tale…

This particular tale could be the fragment of an initiation rite, possibly replicated since the dawn of humankind in sacred 'illuminated' caves such as Les Trois Frères in France, made famous by the Palaeolithic icon of the horned sorcerer, places where initiates were possibly taken either blindfolded or by torchlight to the deepest, most sacred part of the cave to be shown the magical images of sympathetic magic (see Mircea Eliade's *Shamanism: techniques of ecstasy*, Arkana) and to return to the upper world with the secret knowledge.

Yet in general these tales of sleeping heroes in hills and mountain seem to me to be allegories for the dormant potential within all of us: we can all 'awaken our king', or queen for that matter. In some ways they are our Higher Selves, but the *actual* heroes within are the Innerworld Guardians – they are real and deserve to be treated with the caution and respect due to them. Many people work with the energies of Arthur, Merlin, Morgana, and the like. Perhaps these heroes do stir in their sleep each time we tell their stories and sing their songs…

In a late tale of Fionn, told by harper Fiona Davidson, a man discovers the sleeping legend. He blows a magical horn, much to the annoyance of the Captain and his Fianna, for their time to return is not yet, but in doing so the intruder stirs the heart of "every true Celt to touch the Earth".

Such stories remind us that we are part of the land: our ancestors fought for it and left us its riches, its wisdom, its amazing legacy.

It is said of mighty Fionn that if his name is not mentioned every day, the world will come to an end. If we forget their tales, then these heroes will slumber still and who will defend the land in their place?

On the mountain will you rise to the challenge and find your higher calling? What vision will you return with? What songs will you carry back in your heart?

Bedd Taliesin, Ceridigion, with views of South Snowdonia.

SITTING OUT ESSENTIALS:

- ❖ Inform a close friend or loved one of your plans. Take a mobile phone and turn it off to save batteries. Only use in emergencies – not to chat to mates on the summit! The idea is to experience and enjoy solitude. Step out of the human bubble for a while.
- ❖ Wear appropriate clothing: warm, breathable gear, waterproofs, strong footwear. Layers are best, which you can strip off or add according to temperature/activity, ie: climbing/sitting.
- ❖ Take food and plenty of water (amount dependent upon climate and altitude). Bring a stove to make hot food and drinks, even if you plan to fast. You may need extra energy to get down.
- ❖ A 1:25,000 scale OS map (laminated or in a map pocket), compass, NB: a GPS system does not replace these. Remember to delineate between Map, True and magnetic North.
- ❖ Emergency bag containing: whistle, rescue blanket, energy snacks, torch with spare batteries, lighter or waterproof matches, penknife, spare socks, small mirror for signalling and testing for breath, First Aid kit, inhaler or other essential medicine, ID, contact details of next of kin and any medical information. Keep on person at all times, along with filled water bottle.
- ❖ Check weather conditions. Heed local advice and signs.
- ❖ Do not trespass. Follow Country Code and National Park bylaws.
- ❖ Take a good torch. Don't attempt to ascend or descend in bad weather/poor visibility.
- ❖ Be sensible. Monitor well-being: if you are freezing or on the verge of losing it, then don't feel bad about aborting. Get home safe and soon.

The Crane Bag: *Dindsenchas* - Stories of Place

Within the Bardic cannon there is a genre of tales called **Dindsenchas**, or 'place-name stories'. They are first mentioned in the Irish *Book of Invasions* (*Lebor Gabala Erenn*) and are found in *The Book of Leinster* and in a Breton manuscript also. They celebrate the genius loci of springs, rivers, pools, hills, woods, settlements, and nations. In a time before travel guidebooks and travel agents, these stories were the first authoritative means of finding out about an area, and not just the surface details – although **Dindsenchas** often include detailed descriptions of a locality or feature – but also the residing spirit. This knowledge is important if you are not to offend any. The stories created, in effect, taboos preventing the desecration of a place. Basically, if you were to do anything to it you would have the ancestors and Sidhe to answer to!

This is illustrated time and time again in tales about the consequences of breaking some kind of Faerie taboo – pulling a flower, stepping into a Faerie ring, striking a Faerie bride, eating a certain fruit, cutting down a particular tree, and so on. The folk tale of *The Faeries Revenge'* is an extreme example of this (as recorded by Antony Roberts in the pamphlet of the same name, which is subtitled 'a fable on the nature of geomantic and ecological justice', Apocalypse Archives #1, Zodiac House Publications). The Cochion, or Red Ones, of Merionethshire were said to haunt an area called Coed y Dugoed Mawr (the Great Dark Wood). It is recounted that on Christmas night 1534 there massacre prompted revenge, when: "a man known as John Wynn ap Meredydd recruited the help of a local landowner and magistrate, Baron Owen and with the Baron's retainers, fell upon the Cochion in the dark, killing many and later hanging a hundred more. The few survivors swore a deadly revenge, cursing the Baron and his family and they exacted part of that revenge on the Baron himself. It is written that some time after the massacre a band of Cochion waited in ambush upon their

Stanton Drew, aka the Wedding Stones, associated with the common legend of revellers being all turned to stone for dancing on the Sabbath.

tormentor while he was proceeding to the Montgomery Sessions to preside over court hearings. In the ensuing battle Baron Owen and his men were wiped out, the Cochion warriors escaping into the woods around Llangurig where their descendants long maintained a dwindling enclave". This vivid fragment suggests not only ecological justice (if we take the Cochion to be the spirit of the land) but, if literally true, the last struggle of an aboriginal breed, offering guerrilla-style resistance in the face of genocide.

The same fate hangs over the head of many indigenous peoples, either forced from their nomadic lifestyles by habitat destruction or exploitation (oil companies, cattle barons, logging industry) or 'ethnically-cleansed' from an area by the avarice of an aggressive regime. Survival International does exemplary work in highlighting the plight of such peoples, but we can also 'protect' such tribes from extinction by telling their stories and celebrating their culture. Adrian Beckingham's book *Stories That Crafted the Earth* offers one such excellent resource for this, anthologising Creation Myths from native peoples across the globe.

Stories preserve the collective wisdom of a people, and are often tied intimately to the landscape, thus wedding people's sense of identity directly to the place they live. Everyone can relate to this: we all have a personal geography populated with memories, with associations, from the landscape of our childhoods to the towns and cities we become so attached to (mass pastimes like local festivals or sports fostering a sense of tribe and fierce loyalty). If a favourite tree from our childhood is cut down we feel devastated. Imagine how much more so if your very soul is tied to the land and you are removed from it. No wonder so many native peoples seem to suffer from 'soul-loss', and spiral into alcoholism and depression in reservations and trailer parks. This is not the case for all native people; not all are disempowered. Some manage to maintain their cultural identity, the customs and the lore – often through a lucrative tourist industry. Native rights are being fought for and won back by pro-active campaigners. In Canada, land has been reclaimed back by descendants of the original tribes, and in North America heritage such as the famous Ghost-Shirt has been returned (in that instance from the Glasgow City Museum). In the wonderful storytelling epic *Dreamkeeper* (originally a TV series made by Native Americans) the grandson of a tribal elder who is going down the slippery slope of drugs and crime is persuaded to take a journey with his grandfather to a Pow-wow – in doing so many tales are related in true Canterbury Tales style, and by the time they reach their destination the grandson is persuaded to stay on the 'good Red Road'.

This notion of a healing pilgrimage realigning the traveller with the tribal tales is no better illustrated than in Australia, where the land itself is The Story. In the Aboriginal Dreamtime Creation Myth, the windings of the Rainbow Serpent across what was to become Australia, left a trail of tales belonging to respective tribes. Each had 'exclusive rights' to that part of the story. By walking these Songlines the Aborigines maintained them and themselves synchronised with the primal energies, in a seasonal act of remembrance.

Yet even in over-developed countries like Britain it is still possible to connect with ancestral songlines. English storyteller Hugh Lupton explores the concept of stories of place and place memory in his Oracle booklet *The Dreaming of Place*:

> The ground holds the memory of all that has happened to it. The landscape is rich in story. The lives of our ancestors and our remote ancestors have contributed to the shape and form of the land we know today – whether we are treading the cracked cement of a deserted runway, the outline of a Roman road or the grassy tump of bronze-age tumulus. And beyond the human interactions are the huge, slow geological shapings that have made the land itself. Every bump and fold is part of a narrative both human and pre-human. And for as long as men and women have moved over the land these narratives have been spoken. Language and place have become inseparable, indivisible.
>
> (Lupton, Society for Storytelling, 2001)

In the Arthurian epic, rightly called the *Matter of Britain*, the adventures of King Arthur, Merlin, Morgan le Fay and the Knights of the Round Table populate the land with Romance, thus mythologizing and consequently protecting the features attributed to the tales, in a similar way that literary or cultural heritage does today (eg: Hardy's Wessex, D H Lawrence's Black Country, Brontës' Yorkshire, Housman's Shropshire, Laurie Lee's Gloucestershire, Dylan Thomas's Swansea and Laugharne).

The stardust touch of celebrity is made great capital of by the tourist industry, especially in North America, where film stars are the new pantheon. The peregrinations of their folk-King, Elvis, echo that of Arthur – immortalising the landscape through which he passed.

Blake invokes the Son of God himself as a tutelary guardian in his hymn to Albion: *Jerusalem*, when he asks: "And did those feet in ancient time walk upon England's mountains green?" This notion that even Hyperborea, the Land Beyond the North Wind as the Greeks called it, was 'touched by the divine' makes it feel not such a backwater, and also serves to imbue the mundane with the numinous – which is of course always there if we have but the eyes to see it. The land remembers, even if we do not.

Yet we can salvage the fragments and create new narratives celebrating what Common Ground calls 'local distinctiveness', the cultural DNA of an area. In his 'Norfolk Songline' story tour Lupton endeavoured to create a 'new' songline for his neck of the woods, based upon the Peddars Way:

> A storyteller's job is to enter the Dreaming, that invisible parallel world, and salvage the stories. To re-charge the landscape with its forgotten narratives. So that place-names regain their power – so that they become something akin to the titles of songs or stories.

In my month-long tour for my novel *The Long Woman* I read chapters set in all the places featured in the book, as a way of saying thanks to the place for its inspiration, as a way of giving something back (books were left in libraries along the way) as I followed my English songline, in what I called the 'LandSong Tour'. After each reading I encouraged people to share what they knew of the area – I expected to meet people who knew more than I did about a place, inevitable if someone had lived there all or most of their life, but sometimes my stories highlighted features that newer residents weren't aware of. It encouraged some to go out and explore and even long-term inhabitants to look afresh at their locality.

It is important to make the most of where we live: unearthing old neglected stories, dusting them down and polishing them up, to tell them anew – making them shine once more. It is not about if where you live is interesting, it's whether you are interested in it. This is part of the Great Work: the Re-Enchantment of the Wasteland, the 'wasteland' being places where people have become disconnected to Spirit, to Nature and to each other.

There are many examples of **Dindsenchas** too numerous to mention, yet here's some to whet your appetite: Bladud (Bath), Sabrina (Severn), Herne the Hunter (the Royal Forest of Great Windsor), Robin Hood (Sherwood, and the North Country), Giants Causeway (Ireland). There's many more out there. Find them, dust them off and make them shine once again, reminding people of the amazing land we live in.

Where to find such stories? In regional folk tale collections, Local Studies sections of the library, in museums, records offices, on plaques and maps, from locals, and historians.

Geoffrey of Monmouth's *Histories of the Kings of Britain* is, in effect, a series of **Dindsenchas** of the whole of the kingdom and so, for Bardic purposes, is useful, whatever you think of its authenticity. In this sequence we discover how, in a mythopoeic way, several parts of Great Britain acquired the names we know them by:

> Brutus built his capital city, and called it Trojanova (New Troy), changed in time to Trinovantum, now London; and, having governed the isle twenty-four years, died, leaving three sons, Locrine, Albanact, and Camber. Locrine had the middle part, Camber the west, called Cambria from him, and Albanact Albania, now Scotland. Locrine was married to Guendolen, the daughter of Corineus; but, having seen a fair maid named Estrildis, who had been brought captive from Germany, he became enamored of her, and had by her a daughter, whose name was Sabra. This matter was kept secret while Corineus lived; but after his death, Locrine divorced Guendolen, and made Estrildis his queen. Guendolen, all in rage, departed to Cornwall, where Madan, her son, lived, who had been brought up by Corineus, his grandfather. Gathering an army of her father's friends and subjects, she gave battle to her husband's forces, and Locrine was slain. Guendolen caused her rival, Estrildis, with her daughter Sabra, to be thrown into the river, from which cause the river thenceforth bore the maiden's name, which by length of time is now changed into Sabrina or Severn.

EXERCISE: Local Folk Tale

Find a local folk tale of your area, learn it and share it with the community – perhaps even get them involved in the telling of it. I was involved with writing scenes for a community play called the Story of Solsbury Hill, a millennium project tracking the narrative of place of the famous hill near Bath, from Iron Age occupation to the bypass protest of the late Twentieth Century. Ideally, perform the story in situ – make it a public event, with permission and required health, safety and insurance. Tell the story back to its community – some people may have only just moved to the area and will be all too glad to find out about their area more. Long-term residents may see their neighbourhood with new eyes. Such endeavours can really help to lift the morale of an area, especially if it is run down for various reasons. With story we can re-enchant the land and people's lives.

Kelston Round Hill   Kevan Manwaring '99

Month 11: The Tongue That Cannot Lie

Syne they came on to garden green,
And she pu'd an apple frae a tree:
'Take this for thy wages, True Thomas,
It will give the tongue that can never lie.'

Thomas the Rhymer, trad.

Now you are nearing the end of your year-long training programme, it is time to look ahead. This is an essential skill as a Bard: you need to have a certain degree of foresight in terms of planning and preparation on a practical level, but also far-sightedness about the way of the world (these are separate 'modes of consciousness' as RJ Stewart calls them in his *Merlin Tarot,* making the distinction between Divination, Farsight and Insight). It is healthy to keep one foot firmly on the ground whilst tapping into other realms; and one eye on trends and patterns – not in the sense of fads or fashion, but in the larger sense, especially environmentally, eg: Global Warming, the water crisis, escalating conflicts and flashpoints.

Nostradamus was on one level, whatever you think of the accuracies of his prophecies, a poet – and in the way he used symbolism and ambiguity, he set up his work to be interpreted in myriad ways: possibly to 'hedge his bets' over the accuracy of his utterances – the more gnomic, the more likely they could be interpreted in numerous ways, depending on the projection and expectation of the reader. Augurers have been doing this for millennia – that's not to say that some are genuine and some have actual divinatory gifts. Penbeirdd Taliesin himself left prophecies, most famously:

Their God they shall praise.
Their language they shall keep.
Their land they shall lose,
Except Wild Wales.

Such utterances seem part and parcel of being a truly inspired one, an **Awenyddion**, through whom the Awen speaks. Once the 'gateway' is open, it is difficult to stop the flow of Awen – a gift that can be a blessing or a curse, as True Thomas found out, protesting:

'My tongue is mine ain,' True Thomas said,
'A gudely gift ye wad gie to me!'

Despite his resistance True Thomas is still given the Tongue That Cannot Lie by the Goddess in the guise of the Queen of Elfland: "For as I say, so must it be". Does this suggest the faculty of prophecy is an inevitability in those so chosen, in the same manner as the shaman who as a child is stricken with a life-threatening illness? Are such people marked out by the gods from birth? Certainly, those with a true gift seem rare and almost legendary.

Further North of the Scottish Borders and we find the Prophecies of Merlin, which RJ Stewart has explored in depth in his book of the same name. Perhaps Taliesin, Thomas of Ercildoune and Merlin were part of the same oracular tradition, akin, if not identical, to the Vatic role of Seer. The Irish *fili*, the vision-poet, seems part of this tradition common amongst the Celts. It appears to be a genetic trait, passed down through the generations (as in the 'seventh son of the seventh son') although I believe a certain degree of prescience can be fostered in anyone who taps into the Great Web, or the aether, and sensitises themselves to what is 'coming through' and what is causing ripples. This is about tapping into the zeitgeist, the spirit of the age – and expressing it through cutting edge, avant garde Bardic composition, which at the same time echoes the past and has a quality of timelessness about it. The more topical a piece is, the quicker it will lose its relevance. It is wiser to deal with the wider scheme of things, although we can only make the universal speak to us through the particular, Blake's 'grain of sand'.

EXERCISE:
1. Self-fulfilling Prophecies

We often make something come true by our attitude. How we speak can affect how we act and the quality of life we lead. This concept is explored fully in NLP (Neuro-Linguistic Programming). What is the script you have given yourself? Someone who has a tendency to say 'oh, that always happens to me' is reinforcing their victim status, whereas someone who claims to have been 'born lucky' is more likely to be, just by their positive attitude. We can change our scripts and make our own luck. For this exercise be mindful of what you say and how you say it: tone of voice is important. Don't just say to yourself "I will get that interview", really mean it. And don't give out negativity – unless you want to get it back. We can create our reality with the language we use on a daily basis.

2. Personal Prophecy

Spend this month thinking about your future. Make one, five, ten, and twenty year plans. Where do you want to be in these times? How do you intend to get there? Try to visualise yourself in a decade's time. Write a description of each ten yearly 'snapshot'. Keep it safe and refer to it over the years to see how accurate it proves to be.

Voice of the Ancestors

And when, on the still cold nights, he pointed his nose at a star and howled long and wolf-like, it was his ancestors, dead and dust, pointing nose at star and howling down through the centuries and through him.

Call of the Wild, Jack London

At the time of Samhain, when the veil is thinnest, as the old year dies and is reborn, we need to honour those who have gone before, for they are always with us. We walk in their bones, their skin, see with their eyes, think with their minds, and feel with their hearts. Not only are we our living ancestors through familial inherited genes, but through racial inheritance and memory do they also live on.

In Cheddar Gorge the oldest intact human skeleton in the British Isles was found – 8000 years old, dating back to the end of the last Ice Age. When DNA tests were taken in local schools, a history teacher was discovered to share the same (mitochondrial) DNA – passed down the female line for many generations. The voice of the ancestors spoke through him as he taught the past to his pupils: a bona fide 'history man'.

We can speak with the voice of the ancestors in several ways — most directly by getting in touch with our own: by honouring the stories of our families, their homelands, their heritage. What folk tales can be found on your doorstep? Talk to your living relatives – what do they remember? If your grandparents still survive, what stories do they know? Did they experience World War Two? What about before the war? Research family archives: photograph albums, birth certificates, papers, diaries, clippings, certificates – anything you can find. What stories do certain mementos tell? Do you possess any souvenirs or heirlooms – rings, brooches, medals, watches and other items of great 'senti-mental value'? You may even be lucky enough to have an antique, although our name is often the oldest thing we possess. We can contact the past through it. Research its history: was it an old profession, eg: tanner, archer, fletcher, cooper? Or does it relate to a place, ie: Oxley (meaning 'cattle pasture', suggesting ancestors of yeoman stock); or different status, ie: Manwaring (Norman: *Mesnil Warin* – the Manor of Warin). Trace back your family tree. How far does it go? Do you have a heraldic shield? It could depict a clan totem. In *The Seven Daughters of Eve* Bryan Sykes explains his ground-breaking method of tracing people's genetic ancestors. Those of European descent originate from seven continental 'clan mothers' in the distant past. It is possible to find out which one (through a paid search using one's own genetic material) whose lives he recreates through evocative anthropological stories.

Another way of contacting the ancestors is in a more general way — at a historic, or prehistoric, place. Visit a castle, stone circle or ancient tree (yew trees especially, which can live for thousands of years) and spend some time there, silent and still, in meditation. Listen — and see what emerges. You may hear whispers of the past. A song may sudden-ly rise up, or a poem. You may feel a strong link with that place and wish to write a story about it. Take a photograph, or better still, paint a picture, and later reflect upon it. Something may come up, a fragment of Place Memory perhaps.

Such places are liminal, physically, and in time. They can act as thresholds — gateways into our past and ways of accessing the Collective Unconscious, that vast reservoir of human experience and wisdom. A flash of a 'past life' may well be simply part of this collective past. Or you may have stronger evidence, or convictions, that you *were* there – especially if you are fascinated about a particular period, and have recurring vivid dreams about it.

Perhaps the entire past is there, waiting for people to tune into and become channels for. When an event has happened it resonates in space and time — never completely going away. Particular strong experiences, tragedies, crimes, etc. linger longer, or at least effect people more who 'pick up' the violent emotions discharged. Battlefields have certain atmospheres, and are often haunted – there are countless examples of Place Memory in such sites, and at minor ghost spots. One only needs to go on a ghost walk to have a taste of this.

Channel these voices of the past, but be careful to protect yourself. Don't let anything in lightly – make sure to banish anything raised, or, better still, don't dabble at all. All that is required of us, our obligation to the past if you like, is to merely honour those who have gone before – with our words, with our deeds, with our intent. The greatest insult is to forget them, their sacrifices, their efforts, their innovations, their love. Remember them, and perhaps one day you will be remembered too.

EXERCISE: Personal Ancestors

Try **lost knowledge retrieval** methods to try and talk with your ancestors. Either go on a shamanic journey into the Underworld to meet them (this is not the Christian Hell, but the collective place of the ancestors) or simply imagine having a conversation with them. Often they want their story told. Channel their voice onto paper – let them 'speak' through you, via the planchette of the pen. You could try Past Life Regression if you feel a deep need. Sometimes there are things in the past that need reconciling. We may need forgiveness or to forgive. Some act of appeasement or atonement may be required before we can be 'cleansed' and start afresh: a kind of karmic irrigation.

The Crane Bag: Stone upon the Belly

A bard recites with the breast of a magician:
When he recites his store of Awen flows
In midnight's stony-dark

The Chair of Taliesin, Taliesin

One of the techniques at the disposal of the Bardic student is that of sensory deprivation. These days sensory deprivation tanks are available (though not recommended for the claustrophobic!) but traditionally the technique was a lot simpler and low-tech. Basically, the Bardic student would lie in a darkened room and meditate upon the given theme or subject set by the Chief Bard, sometimes with the aid of a cloth covering their eyes, or a stone upon the belly, as described below in two accounts of Bardic Colleges, still in operation as late as the Eighteenth Century. The Marquis of Clanricarde, 1722, writing of a

Bardic School in Ireland, describes in detail the Bardic Cells used:

> It was ... necessary that the place should be in the solitary recess of a garden or within a sept or enclosure far out of the reach of any noise, which an intercourse of people might otherwise occasion. The structure was a snug, low hut, and beds in it at convenient distances, each within a small apartment without much furniture of any kind, save only a table, some seats, and a conveniency for clothes to hang upon. No windows to let in the day, nor any light at all used but that of candles, and these brought in at a proper season only ... The professors ... gave a subject suitable to the capacity of each class ... The said subject ... having been given over night, they worked it apart each by himself upon his own bed, the whole next day in the dark, till at a certain hour in the night, lights being brought in, they committed it to writing... The reason of laying the study aforesaid in the dark was doubtless to avoid the distraction which light and the variety of objects represented thereby... This being prevented, the faculties of the soul occupied themselves solely upon the subject in hand.

This focussing on a theme overnight is perhaps where the notion of 'sleeping on it' came from: letting the subconscious do its work when more direct, logical methods would fail (and there are many accounts of solutions coming to people preoccupied with a problem in the dead of night, most famously the anecdote about the scientist Kerkule, as cited by Arthur Koestler in *The Act of Creation*, who had a dream of a snake biting its own tail – the Ourobouros of mythology – thus suggesting to him the formula for penicillin) although the second extract below, from M Martin's *Description of the Western Islands of Scotland* (1695) may suggest that this being 'weighed down by a problem' was even more literal:

The Three-Shires Stone

> They (the poets) shut their doors and windows for a day's time, and lie on their backs with a stone upon their belly, and plaids about their heads, and their eyes being covered they pump their brains for rhetorical enconium or panegyric; and indeed they furnish such a style from this dark cell as is understood by very few...

This last remark perhaps explains why the language of Bards was sometimes known as the Dark Speech, but it is also interesting to consider that such Bardic compositions came out of the dark, often the place of the subconscious and maybe a doorway beyond the Self.

The Bard's attempt to express the spirit of the place and the ancestors is perhaps best channelled through this voice of the darkness. If we sit in stillness and silence in, for instance, a long barrow or fogou (subterranean burial chamber), then we can sometimes hear it. There is a possibility that fogous were designed especially for such experiences – certainly crawling into and out of one on one's belly facilitates a sense of death and rebirth, as one literally sees the proverbial 'light at the end of the tunnel'. Once in Cornwall I entered a fogou with an Australian couple. The man played his didgeridoo to amazing effect: in the smothering darkness it sounded like the voice of the stones speaking.

Returning to the method of composition by darkness, or night, the modern Welsh Bard Dylan Thomas captures this process memorably in his poem *In My Craft or Sullen Art*:

> In my craft or sullen art
> Exercised in the still night
> When the moon rages
> And the lovers lie abed
> With all their griefs in their arms,
> I labour by singing light.

So many writers find they can write best at night (although others, like myself, are 'morning people'). There is a kind of illicit thrill at being awake when the majority of people are asleep, of being the only conscious soul in a town full of sleepers. Part of its conduciveness though is purely practical: it is usually the most peaceful time (unless you live in the middle of a city). Certainly there are fewer distractions from family, partners, friends, neighbours, work, random phonecalls and mundane chores.

It is essential to keep a notebook, or your journal, by your bedside in case inspiration does strike in the middle of the night. I have awoken several times with a 'fire in the head', forced to write it down if I am to get back to sleep. Sometimes an idea or solution comes to me in the quietus before dawn, when I wasn't even aware I was contemplating it: it must have buried deep in my subconscious, and only after being sufficiently still for long enough does it rise up – after dreams had 'downloaded' the concerns of the day – in an elliptical form. When the white noise of life is turned down, we can hear the voice of the darkness.

The Bardic sense-deprivation technique directly relates to Northern Irish writer Brian Keenan's experience as a hostage in Beirut with John McCarthy in the 1986. They were held captive for four and a half years by Shi'ite Fundamentalist militiamen. Turlough O' Carolan, a blind Irish Bard-harper came to Keenan in his dark cell. He swore if he ever escaped he would write about him, which he did in the 2000 novel *Turlough* – "a personal debt repaid", as he put it.

This is an amazing example of ancestral memory, triggered by extreme conditions. An ancestor gives the victim strength to endure. Turlough's blindness mirrors Keenan's own, imposed by solitary confinement in a dark cell: "another life imprisoned, shaped by the dark'. Yet like the Bardic students, such conditions – extreme in this case – produced inspiration. As Shakespeare's *Hamlet* claims: "I can be bound within a nutshell and be king of infinite space". Such claims can be no consolation to those who have had to endure enforced imprisonment like Keenan, but his harrowing experience yielded much treasure. He crossed over and returned.

Taliesin echoes this, referring to his confinement in Caer Sidi, Arianrhod's glass tower of Bardic initiation:

> While I was held prisoner, sweet inspiration educated me
> and laws were imparted me in a speech which had no words

In Arthur Miller's parable of McCarthyism, *The Crucible*, based upon the Salem witch trials, there is a scene where a man accused wrongly of witchcraft has a stone placed upon his chest to extract the 'truth' from him. Yet the laying on of a stone weight need not be a crude torture method, it might simply be a way of making the Bardic student not fall asleep as he or she meditates upon the set subject. The druidic bird, the heron or crane, was said to sleep with a stone in its claw – so that if it nodded off completely the stone would drop and wake it up.

The dark cells of the Bards are similar to the *abatons*: incubatory sleeping cells used for healing at the Temple of Nodons, Lydney, Gloucestershire. These are identical in purpose to those at the Temple of Asklepios in Epidauros, Greece, where patients in need of healing would lie down in chambers surrounded by snakes (perhaps suggesting why the Caduceus, Asklepois/Aesculapius' serpent entwined staff, is still associated with healing)! These darkened cells are found all over the world, from the austere beehive cells of the Irish saints to the caves of the yogis in India – and the method of **retreat** is a protracted version of a period of sensory deprivation, shutting oneself off from life to reflect upon it – the technique seems universal.

A method of sleep-prophecy is also used in the *Tarbh-Feis*, the Bull Feast, a King-divination method of ancient Ireland in which a bull was slain and a broth made from its bones that the Bard or Druid glutted himself upon until he fell down in a feverish slumber. He was covered in the bloody hide of the slaughtered bull and sung over by four Druids. In a trance, the Bull Feaster was meant to journey in search of the name of the next king and recite it upon waking. This strange and disturbing practice is echoed in 'The Dream of Rhonabwy' in *The Mabinogion*, where Rhonabwy sleeps on a yellow ox-hide and receives a bizarre prophetic dream (see **The Stone on the Emperor's Hand**). Fortunately, modern Bards do not have to resort to such extreme methods (a relief to the vegetarians amongst us!) Below I propose a contemporary equivalent of 'the stone upon the belly'.

EXERCISE: Sleeping on it

When you are confronted by a difficult tract or complicated story, which you cannot find a 'way into', read it through just before going to bed. Make sure you have pen and paper by your bedside. Try to run through it in your mind as you nod off, but don't force yourself to think about it too much – otherwise your mind won't settle down and you won't be able to sleep. Your rational brain has had a chance to solve it and failed, so now's the chance of your subconscious, or the Awen, to do its work. In a hypnagogic state the mind's theta waves work best, the synapses fire across the hemispheres of your brain, allowing you to make greater connections and leaps of logic. You may wake up in the small hours of the night with a solution, or a breakthrough, but if not, don't worry – try tackling it in the morning with a fresh mind, and if that doesn't crack it, then repeat the process each night until you do.

Night Camp. Pastels.

Voice of the Stars

What is it to speak with the voice of the stars? It is a question Penbeirdd Taliesin could have answered:

> I know the name of the stars
> From the North to the South…
> I was in the Hall of Don,
> Before Gwydion was born…
> I have been three times resident
> In the Castle of Arianrhod.
>
> *Hanes Taliesin*

Not only does he claim knowledge of the constellations, he is said to have resided at Caer Arianrhod – associated with the Corona Borealis. The Welsh goddess Arianrhod is also equated with the moon (which is sometimes referred to as Arianrhod's Wheel) and so is very much a Celtic *Stella Maris*: Mother of Stars, Queen of Heaven. When her castle is described as being made of glass and revolving, then this makes more sense if one realises it refers to a constellation. In his book on *Taliesin*, John Matthews calls Caer Sidi, "the initiatory place of poets where Taliesin has several times journeyed, and where Manawyddan has also been". King Arthur himself journeys there on his Underworld raid for the Cauldron of Plenty (as featured in the poem *Preiddu Annwn*). As his Royal Bard, Taliesin accompanied Pendragon on that proto-Grail quest to the source of inspiration, so we shall let him describe it:

> My chair is in Caer Sidi,
> where no one is afflicted with age or illness.
> Manawyd and Pryderi have known it well.
> It is surrounded by three circles of fire.
> To the borders of the city come the ocean's flood,
> a fruitful fountain flows before it,
> whose liquor is sweeter than the finest wine.
>
> *Defence of the Chair*

So what does this mean to budding Bards? Well, to speak with the voice of the stars is to have knowledge of the stars – to have an awareness of not only their names, but the patterns we impose on them, their cycles, and the influences they have on our lives. It is not necessary to be an astrologer – though some knowledge of the zodiac's underlying archetypes in interpersonal relationships is always beneficial – but to be aware of the greater pattern of things and our place within it.

Gazing at the stars fills us with wonder but also reminds us of our insignificance in the grand scheme of things – yet also the miracle that brought us and our life-sustaining planet into existence. It is humbling and awe-inspiring. We would do well to remember the vastness of the universe and the awesome silence of Space in our Bardic endeavours.

Before you begin a new piece, ask the universe – what does it want you to say? Meditate: in deep peace you will find truth and your true voice. After the white noise of the world has faded from your consciousness you will no longer act as a mirror to reality, but a window to another. Open yourself up and be a portal to cosmic wisdom. But with one's head in the stars, it is essential to keep one's feet on the ground at all times. Otherwise, one runs the risk of being 'spaced out'. This is not how you should come across – if you want to be taken seriously and not to be seen as just another 'space cadet'.

Knowledge of the stars should give you a greater perspective on things if interpreted correctly – but don't let it give you a cold inhuman distance. Earth yourself with body work and working in the land. We are here on Earth for good reason – it is our sphere of learning, one that we must steward wisely if we are not to squander its gifts. So husband your resources. Learn new skills or hone old ones. You need to be practical and motivated to manifest your vision. And with your vision you are going to shine, but you first need to learn how to release it, do justice to it, so it pours forth in purity and people can 'behold the radiant brow'.

It is said wisely: 'he who gives no light will never be a star'. If you want to be a Bard and enchant people with your words then you need to give the best of yourself. Above all audiences respond to energy – they are soaking up the charisma of the performer in the same way the tribe would imbibe the medicine of the shaman's healing dance. That is why some performers can get away with saying almost anything, and the littlest phrase or gesture will have them weeping or rolling in the aisles – they have them 'in the palm of their hand'. As Blake said: "To hold infinity in the palm of your hand, and eternity in an hour", is to have heightened awareness of the microcosmic and macrocosmic. Be in the moment, but be also aware of the greater picture. You have an obligation to not only your audience, but your ancestors and the spirits of the place. Be mindful of all those who have spoken the words that you now share (if it is traditional material). And be sensitive and responsive to the people present. Honour them and they will honour you.

Charge up your Chi and give out good energy. Speak your 'peace' with sincerity and enthusiasm and people will respond to it. Folk are prepared to listen when someone is 'saying what they mean and meaning what they say'. Such a person is standing up to be counted – saying it loud and proud – and by doing so is giving the audience permission to do the same.

When one performs it is like saying: "Hello Universe, here I am!" It is a celebration of existence and of one's humanness – of being human. So, don't worry about failing – just do it with courage and integrity. Better to be a brilliant failure than a mediocre success.

Every time one performs it, like being the Fool stepping off into the abyss – it is a leap of faith, but if you believe in what you are saying and doing, then it will carry you across. If it is 'in the stars' then all will go your way – but you can also make your luck by being positive and working with the greater pattern. Gauge the conditions conducive to what you want to bring through. Everything has its season, so if you encounter blockages it is wisest to wait for the right time, when things just 'fall into place'. That is when the stars are working for you, and you with the stars. Work in harmony with the lunar, solar and stellar cycles, as well as your own natal chart, and dance to the music of the spheres. By doing so you will feel at home on stage, or wherever you perform, for you will be fully yourself and in your power. Like Taliesin, whose native country was in the Summer Stars, you would have come home to your own 'stardom'.

EXERCISES:

1. Star-singing

Go out on a clear night – wrap up, take a flask of hot drink, a torch and a mobile or companion. Stand on a hillside or somewhere away from people and gaze at the heavens.

Try to hear the music of the spheres, and give voice to it. Don't feel ridiculous or self-conscious – the night will hide you. Reflect on how incredibly ancient the light is you are finally receiving – the star it is coming from is probably long dead. It has travelled vast distances to reach you. And consider how we are made from the dust of dead stars…Express this through toning, chanting, see what words come to you. Raise the Awen and feel the inspiration of the stars pouring through you…Take a constellation guide or an astronomer friend and identify the various constellations – many are based upon characters from myth and legend. Tell their stories or make up new ones. Create your own constellations by joining up the stars: name and invent tales for them. Find patterns in your repertoire. Make links between different songs, stories and poems. Finally, see the constellations in your own life – the connections and correspondences, the zodiac of relationships that populate our personal firmament.

2. Star Quality

Study celebrities who are widely regarded as having 'star quality'. What is it about them? Is it their charisma, their bearing, their style, or their talent? Read biographies of famous 'Bardic' stars, eg: actors and singers, and try to understand what motivated them and how they achieved what they did. Many were very driven, and some were deeply flawed. I am not suggesting emulating their arcs – often very self-destructive – just to learn from them. For fun, try acting like a star yourself. Not to be a prima donna, but just to feel the confidence and to use it in your performance. Why not organise a fancy dress party with friends based on film or pop stars? Put on the glitter, the old razzle-dazzle, and have a taste of showbiz! This is a way of raising some pizzazz. Create a costume and adopt a **persona**. Use it as a 'vehicle' to deliver your message, but don't forget who you are – and remember to drop the act with friends and loved ones – otherwise you'll soon alienate them, if they stand for it!

On Being a Twenty-First Century Bard

What is it to be a Twenty-First Century Bard? By now you should be able to reply 'not hard to answer': an ambassador for the wisdom of our ancestors, a chronicler of his community, and a prophet of the future. By not attempting to recreate the archaic ideal of a Bard, but to reinvent what it means to be a Bard today, you can be ever-relevant and vital.

The Twenty-First Century Bard walks between the worlds of the past and the future, straddling the present: he is part of a long and venerable tradition, yet is not bound or blinkered by it. He knows when it is necessary to innovate, when it is essential to preserve. He takes the best of the past and blends it with the best contemporary insights, with an ear to his peers and an eye on his audience. He does not work in isolation, but at the same time he isn't at the behest of nobility. His job is no longer to sing the praises of lords, the vanities of ladies, or the glories and follies of

Photo: James Bloom

battle. Yet many of his stock-in-trade specialities are as relevant as ever: the Three Strains of Joy, Sorrow and Sleep, satire, the power to bless and honour, and the tales, songs and poems relevant to the cycle of life: births, wooings, weddings and deaths. The ancient tales are timeless and will continue to reflect and comment upon the human condition and our relationship to Nature in wise and witty ways. Yet coupled with this is a need to create new narratives and tell the stories of modern day struggles and fables, to honour the lives and sacrifices, achievements and disasters of the people of the present.

The Twenty-First Century Bard should be able to draw upon personal anecdote, topical reference and ancient motif and weave them all together with dazzling skill. He or she has a duty to be well-informed about current affairs, environmental and social issues, innovations of craft, cutting-edge ideas in their respective field or tradition, so that they stand before the audience, Janus-like, and act as a channel for the past, present and future, expressing, even embodying the zeitgeist, without being subject to the whims of fashion – by being rooted in tradition, in connection with the Earth and the Cosmos, with the timeless and universal. In essence then, the Twenty-First Century Bard is no different in modus operandi than his venerable ancestors, but what does distinguish him or her are the range of techniques at their disposal today, as shall be explored in the **Checklist**. But first, let's look at relevance and motivation.

VOICE OF THE WORLD – RELEVANCE AND MOTIVATION

Is the very notion of a Bard in the Twenty-First Century anachronistic and outmoded? Well, some would undoubtedly say yes, but it really depends upon two things: **1.** one's notion of a Bard; and **2.** one's notion of time. A Bard does not have to be archaic in his or her approach (as I have shown in this book, a balance between ancient and modern techniques is best). And time is not as linear as most people think – as Einstein suggested, it is relative. Our activities ('time flies when you're having fun') and the comings and goings of memory (day-dreaming, reverie, reminiscence, flashback) affect our experience of it constantly. We spiral around ourselves, going through twenty year cycles of fashion and music (trivial manifestations of the 19-year Meton cycle perhaps). Stories, and the Otherworld from whence they came, exist outside time – and are always there to tap into. Our ancestors never 'go away' – it is only us who become more distant, 'moving on', or drifting apart. People often see the past as far away – along a long timeline, when in fact we often inhabit the same space as our ancestors, in terms of the landscape, the neighbourhood and even the same house or karmic patterns.

So if the notion of a Bard *is* relevant, what is their role? In a nutshell: expressing what needs to be expressed and remembering what needs to be remembered. Humanity is always in a process of forgetting – civilisations seem to suffer from collective amnesia as they make the same mistakes as previous ones, and so they need to be reminded time and time again of the lessons of the past. Yet the joys of existence need to be celebrated too: those little epiphanies that make life worth living – seeing an animal in the wild, beholding a stunning sunset, a sublime moonrise, shooting stars, the kindness of a stranger, small mercies in unexpected places, and all the miracles of life.

As well as celebrating, it is essential to Speak Up, either for oneself, or for the underdog. "Poets sing for all the world," says Ben Okri in *A Way of Being Free*. They have a duty to express the voice of the world – of humanity and Nature and our place within it – but also other worlds, of the ancestors and spirits, gods and guardians. Not so much *vox populi* as *vox mundi*. Yet they may: "…choose to align themselves with the wretched and the voiceless of this planet," in the words of Okri. The disenfranchised need our Bardic skills most of all, either directly – if we can teach them – or indirectly, by telling their story for them (with permission, if possible). Sometimes it is up to us to sing the song of the dispossessed, to make people listen. There is an ancient Celtic saying, surprising in its reference to a lion, but mountain lions did exist in the mountains of Central Europe at one time:

Until the lion learns to write, the hunter will always tell the story of the hunt.

By singing the unsung, praising the unpraised, eulogising the neglected corners of Creation, we re-enchant the land and mundane or damaged lives, helping others to appreciate and protect it and each other, and preserve from extinction the rich experiences life offers us. It is drawing the pith out of life, and living life twice, more richly, more deeply.

What motivated me to begin performing was a desire to share with people the wonder of the world, its magic and majesty: how magnanimous of me! Yet I felt such things deserved drawing attention to – every poem tells us to Pay Attention, to this microcosmic detail, to that – but even if some of the audience were aware of such things, I felt obliged to offer my praise anyway, as a form of informal worship. It is perhaps enough sometimes just to 'sing' one's praise, without expectation of appreciation. Yet it is better if we can convey to people the nascent sacredness we intuit, the beauty and the wisdom we behold, by the power of our Bardic words and voice. It sometimes feels like it is the Bard's role to honour the complexity of Creation, the patterns of life, the vast weave of the world, singing the songlines that run through the land and through our hearts.

Yet, at other times, our job is to run counter to the way of the world if it is going 'astray', as WB Yeats ominously captured in his poem, *The Second Coming*:

Turning and turning in the widening gyre
The falcon cannot hear the falconer;
Things fall apart; the centre cannot hold;
Mere anarchy is loosed upon the world,
The blood-dimmed tide is loosed, and everywhere
The ceremony of innocence is drowned;
The best lack all conviction, while the worst
Are full of passionate intensity.

At such times the Bardic Dictum 'Beirdd byd barnant wyr o gallon' (Truth Against the World!) seems to ring out with poignancy. In this context 'the World' means shallow and corrupt civilisation: gameshows, not Gaia, hypocritical politicians, greedy multinationals, a trivial celebrity-obsessed Media, ad nauseam. Truth – that is mythic truth, which may seem like a contradiction in terms to some, but for me is the quintessence of a situation, not the superficiality of it – is fundamental to a Bard. He or she should be guardian of it, although we should always bear in mind our fallibility and that Truth is notoriously hard to get a complete grip of (as in the Greek myth of shapechanging Proteus, who was doomed to see into the future and speak the truth – The Tongue That Cannot Lie – but always changed shape to avoid giving a straight answer). We all have grains of the truth, we should always honour other people's perspectives, but at the same time we should endeavour to reach the heart of the matter, however unattainable, for Truth is sacred:

The virtue of truth…was the highest royal virtue in Ancient Ireland…Truth is a quality which makes magic work and which enables a person to live up to his archetypes and ancestors.

Professors Bloomfield and Dunn, quoted in *Taliesin*, J Matthews

Here, truth is perhaps being equated with what Blake referred to as 'the inmost form', the *is*ness of a thing. Truth is our touchstone, or quality mark, that we must always aspire to. It is the acid test which we can survive only if we are not only speaking the (mythopoetic) truth but by being true to ourselves, by being authentic, in our performance, in our presence. This may seem paradoxical when dealing with myths, legends and fables, but such tales are lies that tell a greater truth, as opposed to a literal, trivial one. Tolkien, that master fabulist and linguist, was accused of purveying stories that were "lies breathed through silver". JRR thought this was a rather good way of describing his art, which he called Sub-Creation, and expressed it beautifully in his poem *Mythopoeia*. He believed that 'we make by the laws by which we're made' – basically, by being creative we are taking part in Creation, and working in harmony with the laws of the Universe, the greatest story of all.

Our art, like our path, is an act of faith, in ourselves as well as in what we are saying. We have to believe in ourselves as Bards: if we don't, no one else will. Yet coupled with that is perhaps a dogged belief in the unbelievable, the fantastic, the otherworldly. We have to believe in these worlds and wonders we talk about – if we don't, our audience won't. It is summed up in the phrase: *Credo Quia Impossible* – I believe, because it *is* impossible. It is that faculty Keats' called Negative Capability, which we have mentioned before – the ability to dwell in mystery. Another phrase, from an unknown Greek philosopher, epitomises this belief in 'make believe': "These things never happened, but are, always."

The Bardic Arts can fire the imagination – for a public performance is a co-creative act, the stories, songs and poems coming alive in the audience's imagination and hearts. Imagination is a spiritual vitamin and a tool of emancipation: it can help us to re-imagine the world, or teach us that another world is possible, that the only limits on our lives are the ones we impose, that anything is possible with enough imagination, coupled with empathy.

Another important motivating factor in storytelling is Being Connected: to ourselves, our communities, our fellow human beings, to Nature, and to the World. Stories help us to understand different cultures, other lives, as the narrator of Mario Vargos Llosa's book discovered in *The Storyteller*:

Becoming a storyteller was adding what appeared impossible to what was merely improbable. Going back in time from trousers and tie to a loincloth and tattoos, from Spanish to the agglutinative crackling of Machiguenga, from reason to magic and from a monotheistic religion or Western agnosticism to pagan animism, is a feat hard to swallow, though still possible, with a certain effort of imagination…

Talking the way a storyteller talks means being able to feel and live in the very heart of that culture, means having penetrated its essence, reached the marrow of its history and mythology, given body to its taboos, images, ancestral desires, and terrors. It means being, in the most profound way possible, a rooted Machiguenga, one of that ancient lineage who—in the period in which this Firenze, where I am writing, produced its dazzling effervescence of ideas, paintings, buildings, crimes, and intrigues—roamed the forests of my country, bringing and bearing away those tales, lies, fictions, gossip, and jokes that make a community of that people of scattered beings, keeping alive among them the feeling of oneness, of constituting something fraternal and solid. That my friend Saul gave up being all that he was and might have become so as to roam through the Amazonian jungle, for more than twenty years now, perpetuating against wind and tide—and, above all, against the very concepts of modernity and progress—the tradition of that invisible line of wandering storytellers, is something that memory now and again brings back to me, and, as on that day when I first heard of it, in the starlit darkness of the village of New Light, it opens my heart more forcefully than fear or love has ever done.

The Storyteller, Mario Vargas Llosa, trans. by Helen Lane. (Faber & Faber, 1991)

Aboriginal storyteller and Elder Francis Firebrace, quoted in Adrian Beckingham's *Stories That Crafted the Earth,* echoes these sentiments, saying: "The natural way of storytelling is the most powerful spiritual way to reach people, open their hearts, and sow the seeds of truth". What better motivation could there be?

Checklist ✓

Throughout this book we have explored different techniques, both ancient and modern, and have reflected on the Way of Awen throughout a Wheel of the Year. Your Crane Bag should be bulging with the tricks and tools of your trade, yet there is always room for more within it, for it is as vast as the sea, and you should never stop learning. Below is a checklist and almanac of essential techniques for the modern-day Bard. Use it as guide for the creative process and the arc of composition, rehearsal, performance and reflection mirrored by the seasons of the year (Quickening, Shining, Gathering, Dreaming) and the cycles of life.

A	Finding Material	O	Selecting your Set and Pitching it Right
B	Brainstorming/Mindmapping	P	Working with the Space
C	Breaking Down the Bones	Q	Working Solo
D	Visualisation	R	Working in a Group
E	Inhabiting the Story	S	Timing
F	Structuring	T	The Warm-Up
G	Rehearsal	U	The Walk Through and Warming
H	Direction		up the Space
I	Using Music and Sound Effects	V	Audience Participation
J	Using Movement	W	Working with Interruptions
K	Improvisation	X	Multi-Media
L	Persona	Y	Reciprocation and Remuneration
M	Repertoire	Z	Documentation
N	Promotion/Marketing	aa	Closure and Follow-up

Checklist ✓A
FINDING MATERIAL

As a Bard you are practically naked if you do not have 'material': the stories, songs and poems of your repertoire. So where do you find them? Well, first off, it is important to remember that stories are all around us. We make sense of the world through stories: we are *all* habitual storytellers and are always telling stories – whether it be a joke, an anecdote, a traveller's tale, a shaggy dog story, involvement in a recent tragedy, a personal triumph, an urban myth, a white lie or a home truth.

As with all Bardic endeavours the first thing we should do is *listen*, and we shall find material everywhere: in our homes, from our families, our circles of friends, our communities. In *The Celtic Twilight* WB Yeats says: "The things a man has heard and seen are threads of life, and if he pulls them carefully from the confused distaff of memory, and who will can weave them into whatever garments of belief please them best". That is not to say you should use people's experiences without permission (wherever possible, if not, then do so in a respectful way). We would soon start losing friends if we exploit their lives as 'material'. If you tell someone's story, ask their permission whenever possible. If not, then cite them as the source (ie: "my grandmother once told me…")

Beyond these immediate circles, there are the traditional sources of material: from the written or spoken word, the collections and the performers. In keeping with the oral tradition, it is best if you hear a story or song being performed live, and then be inspired to have a try yourself – this was how the corpus was passed down, from mouth to ear, linking the past to the present like Ogma's chain of eloquence. Failing that, we can find stories and songs in the numerous collections of myths, legends, folk tales, fairy stories, and ballads. It is wise to read two or three different versions before deciding on the one you wish to learn (because there are always variations), or better still, triangulate between the different versions and create your own. This is not to corrupt the integrity of the original (it will always be there), but to dust off sometimes archaic, obscure and un-PC material and make it shine once more – keeping its essence, whilst altering cosmetic or structural details to bring in topical references and to make more palatable and appealing to a modern audience. This is what storytellers have been doing throughout history, retelling the old tales anew.

We'll be looking into the way to turn a printed story into a performed one in this **Checklist**. The main thing is to find a story that you really love, one that calls to you in some way and resonates deep in your heart. It may have been picked at random from a collection, but there is often serendipity in such actions… If at first you don't know why it has presented itself to you, don't worry about it yet. Even if the story doesn't grip you at first, it often will with a bit of work. Such stories (and songs) are lessons that the universe presents to us. It is wise to take heed of what they are trying to tell us, even if it isn't apparent at first. A story's secrets unlock themselves with persistence, like the object of quest attained by the hero or heroine. RJ Stewart in *Magical Tales* suggests that such stories contain keys of transformation and have an outer and inner meaning, hiding in plain sight, as it were.

You should never run out of material: you are truly spoilt for choice. This world – and even others – is up for grabs, as WB Yeats suggests when referring to an Irish seanachie called Paddy Flynn: "He was a great teller of tales, and unlike our common romancers, knew how to empty heaven, hell, purgatory, fairyland and earth, to people his stories."

Here's a list of possible sources for Bardic material:

    i Personal experience
   ii Friends, family and community
  iii Folk tale collections
   iv Storytelling and folk festivals
    v Story circles and 'open mic' nights

It is possibly even easier to find songs than stories. Songs are the *lingua franca* and common currency of the world. We sing while we work, while we play. Songs are the 'soundtrack of our lives', they accompany us throughout the day, help us to mark important rites of passage (birthday parties, weddings, etc.) and send us on into the next world… Music does indeed seem to make the world go around. It certainly is a universal language, perhaps literally when we consider the 'Music of the Spheres'. Yet on a more down to earth level I have 'found' songs most often when I have been walking by myself in Nature. Perhaps it is the rhythm of the walking that summons a melody; maybe it's the spirit of the place we are giving voice to – the atmosphere of a particular brook, glen, grove or hill; or possibly it is the therapeutic benefits of Nature itself, making us feel good, birthing a song in our hearts. Wherever they come from songs and melodies seem to come to us best in solitude, either in our room late at night or inspired by the majesty of nature. For how to weave them into your set see: **Using Music**.

It is perhaps hardest to 'find' original poems – that is, compose one for performance – although so-called Peasant Poet, John Clare, claimed to have found his in the fields and merely wrote them down (which is to say he closely observed nature as a farmworker and amateur naturalist – working and walking the land). I always advise using a powerful personal experience as a starting point for your poem, however metaphysical or universal its theme – this will make it vivid and authentic. But, while at the same time as looking outward, we must also look inwards. First and foremost poems can be found in your heart (see **Fire in the Head** and **Tips on Writing Poetry**), indeed this is where they have to be formed to have any meaning – to attempt a poem in a purely intellectual way results in no more than an academic exercise, however competent: technically proficient, but soulless – and probably songless. For a poem must have 'music', and this music is born in the soul: it is the spark, the core emotion, however intangible, that acted as a catalyst for it. We don't go looking for poems – they come and find us and sweep us off our feet. Not that we can be complacent and expect inspiration to strike – we have to ask for Awen and be prepared with pen and paper, or microphone and guitar (what I call a state of 'creative preparedness'), willing to embark upon a sometimes disturbing journey into the unknown. As Shakespeare tells us, "the readiness is all".

Checklist ✓B
BRAINSTORMING/MINDMAPPING

You have selected a story. Now it is time to start making it your own – that is not to disrespect its maker, its countless tellers, or to impair the integrity of the tale in any way, for the original is always there (or at least various anthologized versions). The truth is that since people have been telling tales, tellers have been retelling them in their own way, adding topical references and stylistic touches. There is nothing wrong with this, in fact it is essential if you are to make a story come alive for a contemporary audience. You run the risk of alienating your audience if you use archaic references and idioms – even from a generation ago. Language, especially slang, shows its age rapidly. It is always changing and assimilating new influences – that's what keeps it alive and so fascinating. Bards should be fascinated by the mysteries of language, and seek to continually re-enchant it.

Bards once spoke in what was known as the Dark Speech; gnomic utterances with obscure allusions only the cognoscenti would be able to decode: this is the same as any group with its slang-like jargon, be they journalists, racing impresarios, hoodies or pagans.

But as a Twenty-First Century Bard we should aspire to communicate with our modern audiences: to fail to do so means you die on stage. A Celtic Bard of Medieval Wales would not speak in the language of Iron Age Britain, although there may well be overlaps and echoes, in terms of the symbolism and techniques. It is painful to the ear to hear mock-Bards performing in cod-Medieval (and even worse to read). You do not need to couch your Bardistry in archaic references to make it seem genuine, because it blatantly won't be. We must always aspire to be authentic. That does not mean there are not timeless motifs and gems from the past that can be reclaimed. To reinvigorate a tale or song we need to explore its symbolism: *this* is what we access when we perform. If we just try to recreate the language, then we are merely dealing with the surface of things – the way it was set down at a particular time, because remember that all genuine material of the folk (Bardic) tradition was originally oral, and only written down later on by collectors and enthusiasts. In his book *Magical Tales* RJ Stewart emphasises the importance of the imagery contained within a tale or ballad: "one of the main keys to the power of magical tales lies in the visualising of emblems or personae within them." (see **Visualisation**)

To make the tale or song your own there are two (initial) methods you can use, familiar to workshop junkies: mindmapping and brainstorming.

Mindmapping: method of deconstructing a situation in a visual way, AKA Thought Diagrams. As the name suggests you can use mindmapping to navigate the treacherous waters of consciousness by charting the different 'islands' of thought. Often we can be overwhelmed by a flood of ideas: mindmapping provides a means of negotiating the chaos. It can provide a clearer perspective and over-view. A similar technique is known as 'clustering', using word association to trigger a chain of connected circles, each containing one word or concept, starting from a central theme, the 'hub' from which the spokes of the word-chains radiate.

Brainstorming: a spontaneous group discussion to produce ideas and ways of solving problems; also 'a sudden clever idea' (North American), akin to the 'fire in the head,' but with everyone sparking off one another. This process is like building a fire, with each swift suggestion as kindling – group members keep adding to the pile with their ideas, energy and breath, until suddenly it 'catches fire' and illumination or break-through occurs. Also known as a 'mind-shower' in PC-SPEAK.

These techniques are similar, but the former is quite focussed, and the latter, open-ended. You use mindmapping to get a perspective on something, by breaking it down into its constituent parts and seeing how they all link together. It is good to use a large sheet of paper and different coloured pens. Mind maps can be creative. Artist-poet David Jones *Portrait of the Artist's Mind* is a brilliant example of a mind-map, one that gives us clues as to his trains of thought and creative process.

Brainstorming is a way of getting the creative juices flowing and the synapses firing. It works best in a group, with everybody throwing in suggestions in rapid succession. This relates to a sister exercise, word association – a good way of getting a poem started. My friends in Fire Springs and I spent a weekend 'brainstorming' a new show about Greek Myths (*Return to Arcadia*) – after a series of intense sessions we had created general content, structure and an action plan for further research and development.

Using an A Board or a large sheet of paper and several different coloured markers try the following:

1. **Mindmapping: getting your bearings**
    *   List imagery
    *   List themes
    *   List any key or memorable phrases

2. **Brainstorming: sparking ideas**
    *   List any thoughts or feelings that the story or song stirs in you. Don't censor, let anything and everything come out: first impressions, lateral connections, and so on.

So, to begin with – in our process of 'deconstructing' the material for reinvention – I suggest you list the main imagery or motifs of the story or song. Some may be apparent, eg: direct references to a certain tree, a horse, castle, etc., while as others may be 'buried' or metaphorical, ie: light and shadow. Next, list the main- and sub-themes inherent in the piece. Now brainstorm any thoughts or feelings you have about the story. Just fire them out, however foolish. Your audience will respond with similar gut reactions and intuitions. What kind of experience do you want them to have, what enchantment do you want to weave?

Join the pages up with sellotape, glue or staples. You should start to see all sorts of connections. Draw lines or arrows between them all. Use Post Its. If it starts to get messy or confusing, then start a new sheet and try to bring it all together, perhaps in a flow diagram, or some kind of symmetry. You may begin to see a structure emerge, ie: journey with a beginning, middle and end, or two mirrored halves, a circle, spiral, or star. Having a strong structure will provide a solid foundation for your endeavour, be it one song, or story, or a whole show or set.

These stages of the creative process are essential so don't skip them, even if the story or song is very familiar to you. It is important to 'think outside the box' and bring fresh insights and interpretations to traditional, sometimes old-fashioned, material. This will make your version original and innovative. This is not innovation for innovation's sake. Stories and songs are precious things: if they have survived for centuries there's a good reason for that – they are obviously doing something right. This process will perhaps help you understand what. If it ain't broke, don't fix it, for sure. But at the same time we can 'bring something new to the party' even if we retain all of the original words, just by our attitude, or intonation. Think of all the classic songs, redone time and time again. Each original performer (as opposed to pub singer or covers bands) gives it a fresh spin, and makes it their own. The timing, the timbre, the key – subtle things can be changed while maintaining the integrity of the song. Folk singers are masters of this.

So by now you should have a clear idea of what you want to tell and what it's about. Now it's time to turn it into a performance.

Checklist ✓ C
BREAKING DOWN THE BONES

Let us focus on storytelling now. You should have a myth, legend, folk or faerie tale, which you have deconstructed into symbolism, themes, phrases, structure and associated thoughts and feelings: this is by no means a finite process – the more you explore a story, the more you will find. Sometimes, stories take years to yield up their secrets. Each time we return to them we find something new, because *we* have changed, matured, had new experiences, and moved on. Now we are going to turn the skeleton of the story into a living thing, one we can remember by heart, but first we must break it down to the bones. This is how, based upon a method taught by British-Jewish storyteller Shonaleigh (expanding the guidelines from **Climbing the Beanstalk**):

- Choose the best version of the story, or cut and paste different versions to make your own.
- Take a clean sheet of A4. Down one side write one to nine, filling the space by spreading the numbers out from top to bottom.
- You are going to condense the essence of your story, however complicated, into nine key points, or 'bones'. If it helps, consider the first three as Act One, four to six as Act Two, and seven to nine as Act Three, or Beginning, Middle and End. It is important to contain the whole arc of the story in nine bones, so be economical – summarise each plot point in a sentence, ie: **1.** Jack and his Mother were very poor. **2.** Jack's mother told him to go to market to sell their cow. **3.** Jack went to market but on the way met a man who bought his cow in exchange for some magic beans. Don't be elaborate in your language: brevity and clarity are best.
- You should now have nine bones summarising the entire story. Now summarise the first three bones ie: Jack sells their only cow for some supposed magic beans. This is Act One.
- Do the same for bones four to six, ie: Jack climbs the beanstalk and finds a golden goose belonging to a giant. This is your second act.
- Do the same for bones seven to nine, ie: Jack escapes with the golden goose and cuts down the beanstalk, killing the giant. This is your Third Act.
- Finally, summarise the whole story in a sentence, perhaps imagining it as the 'strap line' on a movie poster, ie: The tale of a fool who finds his treasure, or a tabloid headline, ie: Jack Gets the Golden Goose: Giant Dead.
- To complete the process, condense each bone into one word, eg: Penniless, Cow, Beans, Beanstalk, Giant, Goose, Chase, Axe, Egg. These will serve as mnemonics when learning the story – the trick to remembering stories is that you only need to know these nine words (or images, next on the **Checklist**) to remember the whole story: they serve as mnemonics that will trigger each section of the tale. Write each of the nine words on small blank cards (cut up a sheet of card, or use

index cards). Use these to practise remembering the story, as you would when revising facts for an exam. These are your Cue Cards. They are like stabilisers when learning to ride a bicycle. But for now keep them for the next item. **Visualisation**.

Checklist ✓D
VISUALISATION

Having broken down the bones of the story, we now can make the story come truly alive in our imaginations by using visualisation. This is the key to remembering stories, for me and many others. There are other mnemonic devices such as word-chains, as mentioned in the previous chapter, music, rhyme, stock phrases, repetition and alliteration, etc., but visualisation is by far the most effective technique of memory. RJ Stewart in *Magical Tales* cites the following example:

A tape recording made by the School of Scottish Studies, interviewing an old Gaelic story-teller, clearly defines his method of memory. He says (in Gaelic) that he remembers the tales because he sees them as pictures upon the wall – in other words as a projected and connected series of images. The images enabled him to regenerate the words associated with each image. Furthermore he had learned the tales by listening to a storyteller when he was young and attuning to the images, the pictures upon the wall. When he knew the pictures, the words came automatically, as if they could not be separated from one another.

So, images can be used to tell a tale, as well as remember it. When I perform it is like I slot a DVD into my head and press play: the 'film' of the story plays itself before me and I simply describe what I am seeing, to a certain extent. There is more to it than that, but the basic principle is: the more vivid it is for the teller, the more vivid it will be for the audience.

How do you make the story live in your mind's eye? Firstly, from each of the nine bones create a corresponding image, eg: House, Cow, Beans, etc. Use the cue cards you made in the previous exercise and draw a simple image on the back, using a felt tip or a dark pencil. It doesn't matter if it is just a stick figure – artistic skill isn't the point. No one has to see these but you, so don't worry. Spend some time trying to visualise each key image as clearly as possible, so it's fixed in your mind.

You have condensed your story into nine words and images – these are all you need to remember your tale. This may seem like a tall order at this stage, but trust me – your tongue will remember what to do. RJ Stewart, talking of the use of Tarot in storytelling, describes how: "Each card or combination acted as a trigger, or sometimes as mnemonic, for portions of a vast oral repertoire already firmly established within the storyteller's memory and imagination."

I believe the images are powerful enough to trigger the story. In some ways they are the most important elements of a story, probably accounting for the success of cinema as the most popular form of storytelling today. Yet there is much we can do with storytelling, with only wits and the audience's goodwill to rely on. Being a storyteller is like being the set designer, the lighting cameraman, the director and the actors all rolled into one. The story has to come alive through you, because that's all the audience has to go on.

Next up, try giving a simple account of your story (easier in a group of friends or fellow students). Don't worry about it being polished – it shouldn't be at this stage. All that's required is a précis. At first, you may need to use your cue cards. Then try doing it without – hey presto! You've told your story from memory!

The next stage of visualisation is to choose a scene from your tale and picture it in your mind's eye in vivid detail, ie: the inside of a cottage, with an old stone fireplace, blackened kettle on grate, herbs hanging to dry in the rafters, light piercing the smoky snug interior through the tiny lozenge windows, copper pans hanging in the open kitchen, a marmalade coloured cat lounging on the fireside armchair with its worn armrests, a pair of hobnail boots drying in front of the merry flames, and so forth. Imagine it in three dimensions, with all the senses, as if you were really there. Move around the room or scene and touch things, breathe in the smells, taste the broth warming on the hob, feel the rough texture of the bark, the sand between your toes, the raindrops on your face, and so on – whatever your scene, inhabit it, make it real. If it helps, relate what you are seeing to a fellow Anruth or friend – describe what you see when you close your eyes and 'explore' your scene.

When you have been successful at this, try it with the other main scenes in your stories – the set pieces, eg: the confrontation in the hall; the dragon's lair, the harbour, the rowdy tavern. You want each one to be as real and vivid as the first.

These scenes are key 'ports of call' along the voyage of your tale. Being familiar with them will help you acclimatise and feel at home in them. They will offer you safe harbour between the choppy waters of improvisation – the segues and asides, which you want to keep flexible, so you can speed up or slow down accordingly. Each scene in your story you can add detail to, as you tell it, or just provide a thumbnail sketch. You don't want to get enamoured by florid literary description, which is not appropriate for oral storytelling. A couple of images or sensation should suffice to set the atmosphere, ie: "Fionn entered the cave; it was dank and dark; water dripped from the walls and an eerie wind whistled through the catacombs beyond…"

The magic of storytelling comes in letting the audience build the action with their own imagination: it is up to them to visualise it and to paint the details. Certain words act as tuning forks, which set off a set of resonances, eg: Castle, Forest, Dungeon, Lake. Allow room for the listener to render these with their own imagination.

Such imagery acts in a similar way to Tarot, which uses archetypal and sometimes ambiguous imagery. The reader projects their own preoccupations or cultural references into the universal icons. RJ Stewart says Tarot can provide a way of accessing these stories again, which come, ultimately, from the same source: "If a traditional cycle of symbols, situations and characters from mythic tale-telling was the source of Tarot, as seems very likely, then Tarot provides one significant route back into that primal creative mode of consciousness."

Tarot can provide ideas for stories, with the Major Arcana and Court Cards providing the cast, and the Minor Arcana the scenes or situations. Many Tarot sets are based around story cycles (Arthurian, Greek, Norse, etc.) so can be used as aide memoires ideal for 'bones', as well as suggesting new narratives created at random.

Storytelling itself, using the same language of symbols as Tarot, can have a similar effect upon the audience, in an identical way to the use of guided imagery in magical path-workings, a powerful technique for accessing the wisdom of the Otherworld. There are many books that explore this, so I won't go into detail here. Suffice to say that when you are telling a story you are planting images directly into the consciousness of the listener, so this has to be done with care and responsibility.

Checklist ✓E
INHABITING THE STORY

You have visualised your story in vivid detail. It should seem so real to you now that you could just step through into it – and that's exactly what you're going to do. It is time to inhabit the story. In *The Art of Storytelling*, Nancy Mellon suggests the theory: "Every detail in a story, its characters, landscape, moods, and the meanderings of plot can be circulated through our own bodies, feelings, and structures of our minds." And in *The Way of the Storyteller*, Ruth Sawyer gives us the practice: by moving through the story via nouns, verbs and emotions. She suggests doing this in a comfortable safe space, where there's nothing to trip over and nothing to distract you. A living room will do, if you pull the chairs back. If there's a group of you doing this exercise then make sure you give each other enough space. You may half-close your eyes if you need to, but be careful of your movements – don't bump into anyone or trip over anything. You may wish to **warm-up** first before beginning this exercise. Firstly, you are going to mime all of the nouns in your story: castle, tree, sword, horse, bridge, village, mountain, and so on. You may feel a little self-conscious at first, but don't worry – no one is staring at you. Everyone is lost in their own story. Stop and catch your breath. Now, move through all the actions in your tale, the verbs: running, swimming, riding, fencing, hiding, etc. Stop and catch your breath. Finally, imagine yourself as one of the main characters and move through the story as them, this time focussing on the emotions. What is the character feeling at different parts of the story? Stop, relax. Get yourself a drink of water, and sit down.

Write up in your journal how you feel, any thoughts, and any insights into the story.

By now it should be feeling very familiar to you, because you have internalised it and have 'body memory'. Try telling the story without the cue cards. See what happens: don't worry about getting it right the first time. Just 'run' the story, and describe what you're seeing. Make it as vivid as it was for you – maybe stand and use some of the movements that you discovered in the 'inhabiting' exercise. Use these to dramatise and punctuate the tale. You are externalising your story and make it easier for the audience to 'see' what is going on. You are also beginning to use non-verbal communication. There are more ways to tell a story than just with speech. We will look at other methods at your disposal as well, including music, props and costume later.

A deeper way of inhabiting your story is to 'sleep on it', as in the **stone upon the belly** technique. Just before going to bed read through your story notes. Perhaps read your source version, or have it read to you (record it onto a tape). Close your eyes and let the words do their magic. Visualise the story, but don't 'tinker' – let the images work upon your subconscious directly. Go to sleep, reflecting upon the story and running its key images past in your mind's eye. If you are lucky you may dream about your story. If not, you haven't 'failed'. If you repeat this process every night for a week, you will truly begin to inhabit the story: as you give it life, it will become more and more of a reality. It will live and breathe in you as you live and breathe it. You may be inspired to paint pictures about it, to write songs or poems. Stories are deep springs – let them nourish you, and they will nourish others as you share them, channelled from this true source. You will no longer be repeating the story 'by rote', but will be describing an inner reality, a place you have journeyed and where you can take your audiences again and again.

Checklist ✓ F
STRUCTURING

You now know the story well. The next step is to decide on the best way to tell it. The version you have, however well written, may not be the most effective way to perform it. As the storyteller you have a right (call it creative license) to tell the story in the way that suits you and expresses what you want it to. This is exactly the same way film directors take an old movie or a book and retell it in their own way, giving it the stamp of their own style – it's the same story, but different (and sometimes better, sometimes worse). Remember not to tinker with the tale for the sake of it. There are essential elements of a story that cannot be removed. For an excellently thorough guide to how stories work I suggest Robert McKee's *Story* (Methuen 1999). Failing that, just watch movies or read books with awareness, noticing how the characters and setting are introduced, the situation developed. As a basic rule of thumb you need three key ingredients for a story: characters, setting and incident. Remove any one of these and you don't have story. Remove the characters and a dramatic incident may happen, but no one there to witness it or be affected by it. Remove the setting, and there is no context for the tale. Remove the incident and nothing happens: no story. Another key ingredient is conflict, internal or external. If there's no conflict, there's no drama, no drama and there's no story. And parallel with that is what is known as the 'character arc'. Basically, this is the cycle the main protagonists go through during the process of the story, changing from how they are at the beginning of the story, to how they are at the end. There needs to be change. If there's no change, there's no story. The change could be subtle, to do with attitude (a grumpy man develops a sense of humour), awareness (a revelation, a religion, a deeper understanding or appreciation of life), it could be physical (a scar, healing), personal (marriage, a new job) or macrocosmic (End of War, a New Age, etc.). Nancy Mellon calls these 'story transformations' and provides an extensive (but by no means exhaustive) list in *The Art of Storytelling*:

> Whatever your purpose for making a story, if you summon patterns that have been stored within you from the story imagination of past aeons and work with these carefully, your story will contain transformative energies.

This relates to the roots of storytelling, in the shaman's art. He or she goes on a healing journey for the 'patient', be it an individual, tribe, or land, returning with the medicine necessary for healing, although the journey is very much part of the process. This is reflected in the universal Quest motif, found in stories around the world. On its simplest level it is depicted as a journey and one could argue that all stories are journeys of one kind or another, journeys that the audience take with the teller.

All stories are based around a journey. Raymond Chandler said there are only two stories: "Stranger walks into town", and "A man goes on a journey". Both are journeys, both involve travelling. However pithy this generalisation, I do not think stories should all be pigeon-holed this way. Along with the idea that there are only six or eight plots, such neat ideas limit the human imagination, which has no limits. There are endless possible variations and inventions. There are, however, common motifs which, once familiarised with, can be used and adapted. The classic one is 'The Hero's Journey' as identified by mythographer Joseph Campbell after an exhaustive study of world mythologies. This is a useful blueprint for a story structure, but it shouldn't be used religiously. True genius lies in how it is reconfigured and reimagined. Hollywood scriptwriters swear by it (see *The Writer's Journey* by Christopher Vogler. Pan 1999) but you can have the right ingredients (the hero, villain, quest, and so on) and still have a lacklustre story, as is all too common in big budget movies. They lack Awen. It is often the small budget independent films that have far more originality, because they haven't gone for the obvious, and they are not beholden to large audiences to pay their way. They're not designed by 'committee' or bowdlerised by test screenings, but usually retain an original voice, an original vision. If references to cinema seem out of place in a book of Bardism, then remember that movies are, and the most successful modern form of storytelling, so it is worth studying them to discover how they work narratively, what an audience 'likes' and what makes them truly great or truly awful.

Tips for Structuring

- Using your cue cards with Blu Tac, or Post Its with the bones on, rearrange the order of the story. Try different variations to work out the best sequence of events. If you wish, include extra cards with 'song', 'poem', 'dance', or other additions: whatever you consider to be the key components of your story.
- Where is the best place to start your story?
- Whose story is this? Focus on them, by telling it from their point of view, ie: select the material relating to that character. Cut out anything which does not have relevance to that character's arc.
- What shape is your story? A line, a circle, a mountain peak? Is it symmetrical, or a loop? Does it begin and end in the same place?
- A rule of thumb is to have 3 climaxes, one at the end of each Act – escalating in size. Make sure you save the biggest until last; otherwise, there is this sense of anticlimax. By following the Hero's Journey to the letter including the 'journey home' section, you risk having a dilated ending after the last climax.
- The classic structure is the simplest: beginning, middle and end (or 'a beginning, a muddle and an end' as poet Philip Larkin once said).
- A golden rule, suggested by storyteller Ben Haggerty is to have something amazing happen every ten minutes, and to 'section' up your story into ten minute mini-stories, with their own arc and energy. This is essential for longer stories, but when beginning, it is best to keep your stories under ten minutes. Short and snappy is better than long and flabby. The better you get, the longer people will want to listen to you, but even then, an audience is only capable of paying attention for so long. It is said our attention spans reach an optimum at 45-50 minutes (hence the length of many lessons and TV shows).
- How do you want to end? This is the point you want to aim for in your story.
- Do you want to go out with a bang, a flourish? Or leave the audience reflective, thoughtful? There are two types of ending: open or closed. The latter is a tidy resolution, where all plot lines are resolved. An open ending leaves it up to the audience to decide what happens next. How do you want to leave the audience? Completely satisfied, or challenged, disturbed even?
- For clues to structure, scrutinise Fairy Tales. Try writing your own. At the heart of all modern stories (in whatever medium they're in: book, film, play, musical) there's a myth, legend, folk tale or fairy story. If you can understand how such primal stories work, then you will have discovered the key to all stories. Fairy stories especially have seemingly simple structures, often involving patterns of

repetition, eg: three brothers, three bears. These ritual patterns have deeper significance, but also serve as mnemonics, for the teller and the audience. It provides a reassuring rhythm. Nancy Mellon suggests sequences of four in stories simulate a heartbeat. Other numbers, such as three, sevens, nines, and twelves, have their own correspondences hardwired into us, because they are fundamental patterns of the universe. We can use such symbolism to act as keys of consciousness and transformation. One way of seeing your story is as a ritual: this may help you in structuring it. Think of the 'story structure' of a Catholic Mass, weddings, funerals, and so on. Stories were often used in rituals, ie: most famously the story of Demeter and Persephone in the Eleusinian Mysteries. Using such symbolism can give your story mythic resonance and perhaps make it a ritual in itself, invoking the gods or heroes you describe and embody. You may want to structure your story like a ceremony, by 'Casting the circle' at the beginning, Invoking the Quarters, going into the Inner Mysteries, before Returning and Banishing.

- Look for organic structures in the patterns of Nature, ie: the four seasons, or the lunar cycle. These will deepen your connection, through the laws of correspondence (Sympathetic Magic) with what you are telling, creating a microcosm of that macrocosm, and a marriage of form and content. Thus, choose the structure most appropriate to the material. Don't make things unnecessarily complex. Beauty arises in saying something in the most elegant, economical but precise way. Let the structure serve the story. Do not shoe-horn your tale into an inappropriate structure – otherwise it will be like the Ugly Sister's foot in the Glass Slipper.

Checklist ✓G
REHEARSAL

Now you have your story ready for rehearsal. This is essential – not to get it 'word perfect' but to become comfortable enough to tell it so that when you perform in front of a live audience, you feel at ease and confident with the material. There is nothing worse than being under-prepared and not doing yourself or your material justice. I believe you can learn a story or a poem in half an hour, but you need a few days to 'sleep on it' and rehearse it properly. While inhabiting the story, you want it to inhabit you, so that it becomes second nature and you tell it with some authority. Basically, you need to aspire to be in command of your material.

Tips for Rehearsal
- Set apart half an hour a day to rehearse the story, going through it a couple of times.
- Practise in front of a full length mirror to check your posture, movement and expression.
- Tape yourself and listen back – you'll be surprised how your own voice sounds. It is not an entirely accurate impression (electronic recordings distort voice) but will give you a general idea whether your voice is clear, loud, varied enough.
- When you feel confident about the tale, invite a few friends around and practise in front of them. You may have to bribe them with a meal or some drink! Ask for honest feedback. If you or they feel awkward doing this, (constructive criticism

should always be welcome) then provide simple feedback forms that they can fill in anonymously. If you are going to recognise their writing, then use multi-choice tick boxes instead, ie: Did you find the story? (tick one):

☐ Enchanting   ☐ Entertaining   ☐ Average   ☐ Dull.

- If you have a video camera (even phones have them these days) then get a friend to record you performing (or use a tripod). However cringe worthy it'll be watching yourself back again, it'll be worth it to spot any nervous 'ticks', blind spots, weak points, or bad habits.
- If it is a rehearsal for a big group show or large set, then plan months in advance and build up to it with regular rehearsals: intensive development stage, followed by a month or two of further research and development, coming together for the first 'run through', further feedback and adjustment, then weekly rehearsals, followed by biweekly rehearsals in the last fortnight.

Checklist ✓H
DIRECTION

If you are planning a large set or an entire show, then it is worth considering getting some direction, ideally from someone with drama experience: someone who will be able to shape your show and see its faults and strengths in an objective way. It is better if it's not a close acquaintance. A well-meaning friend may be more hindrance than help, unless they can be brutally honest with you and you are prepared to take it. Performance is a nervy thing, with people's egos and dreams on the line. If this is a first time show, then you will feel especially vulnerable, and one ill-judged comment may put you off completely, so it is good to workshop in a supportive environment with a professional tutor if possible. Otherwise, try to get together with fellow Anruths, and if there is a fully-fledged Bard in your area, they may be willing to offer guidance and support. Forming a Bardic Grove or circle may be the answer – this would have many benefits, social, spiritual and professional.

Things for a director to consider (many of which are covered by the **Checklist**):

- Entrance and exits
- Structure
- Timing
- Stage presence
- Voice – projection, intonation, variation
- Eye contact with audience
- Audience participation
- Energy
- Content
- Choreography – any movement, dance, use of the space, etc.
- Using props
- Costume changes

It may be worth hiring a director if you have the budget (or advertise for a student director willing to cut their teeth on your show gratis for some experience) even just for one rehearsal. Their perspective and insights will pay dividends.

Checklist ✓I
USING MUSIC AND SOUND EFFECTS

Storytelling has been associated with music since its inception, from the first hunting songs around the first fires, to the Homeric poets reciting the *Iliad* and *Odyssey*, accompanied by a lyre, to the Courtly Bards with their harps and mandolins. There is nothing more spellbinding than hearing a master Bard tell a tale with harp and voice. Yet you do not have to be so adept to make the most of music in your performances. I believe it is possible for anyone to learn an instrument, however rudimentary: possibly the best performance I ever saw was by the master French storyteller Abbi Patrix, who had a marquee of three hundred people in the palm of his hand with only a thumb piano and some reindeer bells.

You don't have to be a virtuoso to use music in your storytelling: there are many musical instruments that require little or no skill to use, but can be very effective, eg: tambourines, rain-sticks, shakers, gourds, bull-roarers. There's a wonderful array of instruments that simulate animal noises, such as crickets, frogs, birds, even sheep! Used discerningly and appropriately, such effects can provide an added dimension to your tale, engaging a different part of the audience's brains (left for words: right for music). That's why they go together so well. Another option is to team up with a musician and alternate your set from story to song – and maybe throw in an odd poem now and again as well, which has a musicality of its own. This alternation keeps the set varied and interesting. A two hour show of 'just' words can be hard on the ears of the audience, however adept the teller. Using music can provide an engaging contrast – it allows the listener to reflect upon what they have heard and also it emphasises the mood. Use song at moments of heightened emotion, as in musicals when the protagonists burst into song at dramatic moments. Poems, which use the musicality of words, can serve the same function as music: it's a shifting of gear, or intensification of mood. It could offer an opportunity to comment upon events, encapsulate the prevailing sentiment, or express the internal dialogue of your characters, their innermost fears and dreams. Poetry can take a story to a deeper esoteric level and conjure real enchantment.

Using Music Tips:
- Playing some appropriate recorded music before the show starts is a good way of creating a mood. And by pausing it you can signal to the audience that the show is about to commence.
- Live music is even better. Team up with a musician or band: ask them to play before, during the break, or after the show.
- Accompany your story (or poem) with music. Use for sound effects or atmosphere. Either play simultaneously (eg: toning or harp) or alternate your story with music or poetry.
- Record your story with music and sell CDs of it after the show; send to venues.
- Get the audience to join in with songs, clapping, stamping, clicking, etc. (see **Audience Participation**).
- Use a song to start or end the show, to make a dramatic entrance, raise energy and to act as a Greek Chorus or Overture.
- Get the audience to help you with sound effects – ask for volunteers/hand out instruments (but make sure you get them back!)
- Use songs to tell stories (ie: ballads).

253

- Use the musicality of speech in the stories themselves (rhythm, rhyme, repetition, cadence, etc.). Use a sing-song voice for certain characters, or even go into a half trance, 'singing' your story in a shamanic chant-like way (ie: The Tibetan epic, *The Gesar of Ling*, which lasts for days, is done in this way, as are many other great epics). Storytellers Lupton and Mordern, in their versions of *The Odyssey* and *The Iliad* use the refrain: "If I could sing, I would sing of…" to evoke the Homeric singers of tales.

Checklist ✓J
USING MOVEMENT

You have already explored how to internalise and bring alive stories through movement in the process of **Inhabiting the Story**. Some of the movements and gestures you stumbled across in that process you may want to incorporate into your story, to illustrate or punctuate certain points. The essential thing is to use any such movement *discerningly*. You want to avoid coming across as being hyperactive, flailing about like a wind-tossed scarecrow! If you are restless, then your audience will be as well. It is better to veer towards a centred stillness and a low voice, than being loud and over-animated. The former reassures the audience and draws them in; the latter alienates them. However, you need to maintain visual interest, especially in a long show or in a large space, by using movement and using non-verbal communication to aid in telling your story. Acting out some key dramatic moments physically will emphasise their importance and 'lift' the whole show. Gain 'body confidence', so you feel at ease in your body on the stage, in front of people. Posture and attitude are primary – carry yourself with the bearing of a Bard and you will be halfway there. It begins in the heart, in the soul – but follow it through in your body. Tell the story with your whole body, but at the same time don't let the story completely take you over – always be in control, ie: don't get too histrionic, unstable, overwhelmed or 'possessed' by the tale. A degree of this is good, but the real master can channel it, and isn't taken over by it.

Tips:
- Be aware of your body language. Watch yourself perform in a full-length mirror. Notice your posture and any 'ticks', such as fiddling or waving with hands, scratching noses, playing with hair, holding head down, hunched shoulders, etc. Theatre director and priest James Roose-Evans says: "our physical posture reveals our inward posture" (*Inner Journey, Outer Journey*, Rider & Co. 1998).
- We can hold blocked energy in different parts of the body by bad posture and stress, ie: in clenched shoulders, hands, stomach. This can constrict the voice. Work to free this energy, ie: with the Alexander Technique, or dance.
- Maintain a neutral position when performing: feet planted firmly on the ground, shoulder width apart, a good centre of balance, arms loose at your sides, chest 'opened' out, head lifted, back straight – poised, but not tense (see **The Warm Up**). Use this as your 'default' posture (when standing) unless you need to use movement, a conscious gesture – precise and controlled, but not too 'symbolic'. Just make it seem a natural part of the act.
- Study mime artistes to see how they 'tell their stories' through body language.
- Study all forms of dance (classical, traditional and contemporary), for the full

range of expression possible for the human body. Draw upon this vocabulary in telling the story. Use elements of dance at heightened moments, in the same way you would music or poetry.

- Go to a dance class, ie: Gabrielle Roth's Five Rhythms, to 'loosen up' and get used to expressing yourself purely through movement.
- Co-ordinate your movement to work with the space and with the audience. In a small performance space (ie: a story circle) use a **Hearth-style** with its small gestures and subtle expressions, while in a large space (ie: theatre) use the more animated gestures, expressions, full body poses and movement of **High Style**.
- Get the audience to copy key movements (**Audience Participation**), especially younger audiences, eg: paddling, swaying, or jumping.
- Remember, less is more: the smallest gestures speak volumes. If you want to move the audience, then be moved yourself – emotionally as well as physically.

Checklist ✓K
IMPROVISATION

There are many qualitative differences between theatre and storytelling – the lack of the Fourth Wall*, the interaction with the audience, the organic structure – but perhaps the main one (for me as writer) is the fact that as a rule (traditionally, at least) plays are script-ed, while storytelling is not. Storytellers do not perform from a rehearsed script verbatim, however often they rehearse and polish their show: at the end of the day it is usually their version of a story, told in their words. And, critically, to be true storytelling, the story should not be told word for word as was originally heard or written, but should be semi-improvised, and be different each time it is told, even if the variations are minor (a gag here, a tweak there) rather than substantive and structural. This is essential, even if the stories are 'sacred': to keep them alive, to give the telling vitality, so it doesn't come across as something learnt by rote and repeated mechanically like the times table ('This happened, so that happened; X went to Y, A became Z…'). No storyteller worth his salt repeated religiously the words of another, but gave it his own 'spin', or style. This is where the creativity comes in and the original voice shines out.

So, it is important to maintain a flexible attitude to one's telling: never let it be completely set in stone, otherwise it may stagnate the story. As soon as you are doing something completely off pat, you stop feeling it and being in the moment: it becomes your shtick. It is essential to remain fully present at all times, and fully conscious of one's actions. The audience will soon see through it otherwise, and the universe may see to it you are taught a lesson. Complacency causes accidents! An interruption, cock-up or heckle will threaten to derail you unless you are able to think on your feet.

And apart from being precautionary, by remaining flexible and fluid in your telling, you keep the tale fresh and the experience different every time. It is also a way of trying stylistic variations each time, to see which one works the best.

Responding to the audience's response is primary in storytelling: that's why it's vital to be able to see them properly (and not be blinded by spotlights or a dark auditorium) and maintain eye contact. There's nothing more disconcerting and draining than perform-ing into the void. A teller needs to gauge the efficacy of his or her performance upon the audience's reaction – sounds obvious, but Bards should be able to recalibrate according-ly and go with the mood of the audience, assimilating their energy and working with it.

Nancy Mellon says, in her advice on storytelling to children and strangers: "One of the most useful guiding principles is to style (their) language and imagery to the prevailing mood of whomever may be listening." As children we always improvised and thought nothing of it, carefreely exploring the land of Make Believe. As adults it becomes increasingly difficult to do this, to let go, to not be goal-driven, but to enjoy something for the sake of it: Sacred Play. To improvise is to dwell in the Awen, in the original creative space in which the story was born, and channel it unfiltered from the source, providing a mainline between the audience and the Otherworld.

*The imagined barrier between the audience and performers that creates the illusion the action is taking place elsewhere and not in the theatre, the other three walls being the set.

Tips:
- Attend a 'Fooling' workshop to learn improvisation skills.
- In a group workshop use 5 words plucked at random and weave them into a story.
- Use the objects immediately around you to improvise a story.
- In a circle of people invent a story, going around with each person adding to it – building upon the previous narrative detail. This can lead to some strange places, like Consequences!
- Respond to any interruptions, accidents, etc. and incorporate them into the story.
- Include topical references (ie: news, locality), setting the action nearby etc.
- Have moveable units within the tale, and 'added extras', which can be used or left.

Checklist ✓L
PERSONA

A stage persona can be seen as a marketing tool, or as manifestation of one's spiritual path: you could adopt a stage name, or use your Bardic name –perhaps the two are one and the same (I use Tallyessin, which is the name of my Bardic persona and small business). Some people may wish to simply use their real name, which is completely fine – and widely accepted in mainstream storytelling circles – but if you want something to make you stand out from the crowd, or to appeal to a certain market, then adopting a stage name/persona would be a useful 'marketing strategy.' There is a long and venerable tradition of this in showbusiness, and it is common in pagan/Bardic circles, eg: Damh the Bard, or Mad Mick, to name two. Such names look good on an event poster, where one is often competing with more famous names and acts. Some would argue that to use an adopted name smacks of artifice and true quality does not need to use such gimmicks. Well, perhaps if you get to the point when people will come and see you by reputation alone, then you won't have to worry about names, but the practise shouldn't be looked down upon – it seems perfectly acceptable for a group of musicians to adopt a band name, why not storytellers? And there have been famous examples of film stars who have adopted a new name and become famous, Marilyn Monroe (Norma Jean) and John Wayne (Marion Michael Morrison) being two classic examples. Change your name and you can change your luck. Destinies can be entwined in a name, so that they become self-fulfilling prophecies, perhaps because people react differently to different names (eg: Norman may be reliable but dull; Jack, 'one of the lads'; Brad, 'one for the ladies'; Damien, slightly sinister, etc.) because names accrue connotations, rightly or wrongly. A perfectly innocent name can be tainted by something in the news, e.g Fred West, Harold Shipman. You may have been fortunate to have been given a poetic or memorable name by your parents, such as Finn, Marion, Robin, Morgan, or Merlin. Otherwise, you may want to use a stage or Bardic name to send out the right 'signals' to a potential audience, something that could depend upon whether you are marketing yourself as a children's entertainer, a medieval minstrel, a punk poet, etc. My advice would be: if it makes you confident, then do it.

The same goes for costume: you may need to don your 'confidence overcoat' to inhabit your Bardic or magical self (in the same way Druids or witches might with their robes). Remember, a suitable costume (ie: period dress) will help the audience to get into the right frame of mind as well. And the more effort you make, the more the audience will feel you are 'putting on a good show' for them and they're getting their monies worth.

At the end of the day, persona is about *attitude*, which is tied in with not only state of mind, but posture. Stage presence is a lot to do with body language, as well as general charisma and audience rapport. Claim the space (see the **Walk Through**). If you have the correct 'attitude', mentally and physically, then you will feel confident and in your power.

Names and costumes are confidence tricks we pull on ourselves to make us feel confident, but with enough conviction you can carry off whatever you want to. For some, the greatest act they put on is themselves. In a way, we are all adopting personas in life, playing roles either allotted to us or chosen. It is the play of life – as Shakespeare once said: "All the world's a stage and we but actors upon it." Yet it is essential to balance this awareness of the masks we wear in the great masque of reality with a need to be genuine. We have to be ever-mindful of our sincerity, our authenticity as Bards: for we are men and women of our word. And without being true to our word, we are nothing, for our whole purpose is to restore meaning to language and to life. It is possible to be genuine, even in the guise of a persona (think of all the great actors who manage this). Use a persona, by all means, but remember: "This above all, to thine own self be true".

Checklist ✓M
REPERTOIRE

> His mind a storehouse of tradition of all kinds, pithy anecdotes, and intricate hero tales, proverbs and rimes (sic) and riddles, and other features of the rich orally preserved lore common to all Ireland three hundred years ago."
>
> Rees Bros., *Celtic Heritage*

The Bard's repertoire is his or her livelihood. Your success as a Bard depends upon it (especially if you want to go professional). The ideal to aspire towards is a story, song or poem for every occasion. Then you'll never be caught 'off-guard' if someone asks for a request out of the blue. Fully-trained Bards were expected to know 350 tales – almost one for every night of the year. Having a new tale to tell every night would be a very useful skill: it kept Scheherazade alive for *One Thousand and One Nights*, and it sustained the plague-besieged denizens in Bocaccio's sequence. Yet it is easy to begin with a more modest repertoire: a favourite tale, a couple of poems, a riddle, maybe a song – and you would be welcome at every hearth, campfire, or 'open mic'. After a year of following the Way of Awen you should have a more substantial range: ideally, something for every season at least, if not, then twelve tales, poems or songs: something for each month. Maybe a common thread has emerged in your repertoire: are they all Celtic or Nordic, all featuring the Otherworld, or the Sidhe, elementals or warriors? Such themes could suggest a show, eg: Tales of the Faerie, or The Deeds of Fionn Mac Cumhail.

The first stories I learnt were from *The Mabinogion*, a classic sequence I recorded onto tape and called 'Tallyessin's Cauldron'. By recording your repertoire it provides a useful way of reminding yourself of a particular set. Essential, especially if you have to revive the show several years later! Stories can be stored in the long-term memory, but may take a little prompting to 'download' or recall. Be reassured that you only need to have your immediate show in your short-term memory – it's not necessary to have everything at your fingertips (although you never know when a particular story may come in handy!).

However, I have found certain poems and tales have become 'hard-wired' into me. The Bard should carry his repertoire with him, not only in his memory, but in his heart and mind: it is the stuff of their soul, illustrative of his or her nature. Every time you perform you lay out your very dreams before people, and as Yeats said in *He Wishes for the Cloths of Heaven*: "Tread softly because you tread on my dreams". (For more on this subject see **Senchus: Bardic Memory** and **The Lore of the Storyteller** for categories of tales)

Tips:

- Keep a folder of material, eg: all bones, story notes, cue cards, ideas, photocopies.
- Track your stories, songs and poems. Create a chart in your Bardic folder with the following headings: Title, Composed, Premiered, Reception, Times Performed, Venues, Versions, Sales (if you have CDs/booklets/or copies to sell). This is a way of monitoring material, gauging what goes down well, what needs working on, and making sure you don't repeat yourself!
- Create a Book of Bardic Tales: in a large blank tome (like a Book of Shadows) write down all songs, poems and stories (the latter *after* you have performed it at least a couple of times – so that you don't get too literary in your telling).
- Try to widen your repertoire with stories from other cultures, stories of varying length, moving or funny, for adult and/or young audiences, different occasions.

Checklist ✓N
PROMOTION AND MARKETING

If you wish to get gigs, or at least get your stories heard, then you need to be pro-active and market yourself: this is not 'selling yourself', merely being professional – and besides which, you are doing what you believe in, and endeavouring to spread wisdom and enchantment, not 'selling your soul to the company role'.

Whether you want to be professional, semi-professional or just want to 'get out there', then you will need to spread the word about yourself, network and make yourself available as Bard. Look out for opportunities to perform and plug what you do. You are your own best calling card, in theory. Making it as a Bard is very much about 'proof of the pudding': if people like what you do, then they'll want to see you again, they even want to book you and give you money! However, opportunities won't just land at your feet – getting established is about hard graft: be prepared to do countless 'open mics' and freebies to get yourself known. If there's a cabaret, a Gorsedd, a showcase, a competition, then go for it. Winning a Poetry Slam, or better still, an Eisteddfod, will immediately raise your profile and help with your marketing. Being able to put an achievement like 'Winner of the Bardic

Chair of Bath' on your literature will immediately boost your chances of bookings. Similarly, any audience/venue quotes or glowing reviews will really emphasise that you know what you're doing and that you are good at it, things promoters like to hear.

All of this may seem tedious and contrary to the Bardic spirit, but Bards have always had to put themselves about and if you want to make a living as a Bard, then you have to tirelessly and shamelessly promote yourself. I sometimes quip in my shows, when I mention my CDs and booklets for sale (always an awkward moment): "Doing this, you have to be a flagrant self-publicist, although sometimes it feels like being a public self-flagellant!"

To mix metaphors, don't beat about the bush in blowing your trumpet! Just remember to always act with humility and grace, sincerity and humour, and you can't go wrong. People respond to someone being fully themselves: it gives them permission to do the same. When we talk about what we're really passionate about, that's when a light comes on in our eyes and we really shine. Give out good energy wherever you are, and the universe will reciprocate it. Energy is never wasted. Even if a gig seemed like a disaster, if one person picks up your card and calls you months down the line with a booking, it would have been worth it. We create ripples with the energy we give out, someone or thing always takes notice, so we should endeavour to always be the best ambassadors for ourselves.

Publicity Tips:

- General leaflet
- Promotional postcard
- Flyer for show
- CD sampler/demo
- Business Card
- Publicity photo
- Copy for programmes
- Press release
- Networking
- Showcases
- Competitions
- Quotes
- Reviews
- Photocopies of clippings
- Publicity stunts
- Know your local correspondents
- Develop other media contacts
- Advertising
- Features in local papers.
- Radio spots
- Interviews

Checklist ✓○
SELECTING YOUR SET AND PITCHING IT RIGHT

Let's imagine you have your first booking. Well done. Your marketing must have paid off. Now the work begins. You have to choose the right material. If you haven't got carte blanche, then you may have been given a theme to work to, otherwise the event may have a theme, ie: Hallowe'en Festival, or the venue itself may suggest one, ie: Environment Centre. Your choice of set will be affected by *who* you are performing it to: adults or children, an informed audience (ie: pagans at a pagan event) or a general audience (without assumed knowledge), festival-goers late at night or the Women's Institute; and so on. This is not about being 'politically correct' (surely a contradiction in terms) but Bardically Correct.

Selecting your set will depend also upon how you would like to shape your show (**Structuring**). As a general rule of thumb, the following applies: start with a bang, with something you are au fait with, that will give you confidence in the nervous early stages of your performance – it could be a poem, a song, a favourite tale, perhaps your 'signature' tale, which could serve as an introduction to yourself and what you do (a kind of setting out of wares, ie: 'I'm a storyteller, and my stories must be told…'). Next you need to add variety, by alternating stories, songs and poems. Look for thematic links, for a sense of journey – going deeper into the mythos, but back out again, into the 'here and now'.

Vary the pace, the mood, the length of the individual pieces, and the different techniques used (eg: riddle, song, story, poem). Remember to add some **audience participation**. Finally, end with a flourish, with a 'set-piece', something you're proud of that will take the audience's breath away, or at least something memorable and uplifting. I like to leave the audience with some hope and perhaps with a 'call to arms', with a sense that the story continues with them, that 'what happens next' is in their hands.

How you begin and end is critical, but people generally only remember these parts of a conversation, if nothing else. They are 'places of power', the entry points between worlds. It's important to captivate your audience: hook them in, perhaps with a riddle or a controversial statement; win them over with your tone of voice and body language, then take them on a healing journey: reassure them they are in safe hands, that you are in control of your material, and that you're not going to bore them!

Not only is your choice of material critical, but how you deliver it as well. This may seem blatantly obvious, but a good set can be murdered by a bad telling, and vice versa: poor material can be redeemed by a Bard who brings it alive in the moment. But by choosing poor material to begin with you are providing yourself an unnecessary handicap. Pitching it is about not patronising your audience, but doing what is appropriate – relating to them, to whatever level they're at. Yet give them the credit of their intelligence (young people have responded well to Fire Springs' adult-pitched shows) and perhaps throw in the odd challenge to 'stretch them'. Author Philip Pullman says: "Children's capacity to listen to a story is not limited by their age or their intelligence, it's limited by the ability of the storyteller to entertain them" (*Venue*, #692). Of course, some material is not suitable for children and you have to be careful and considerate. A Bard should always make sure the audience is 'with them': you are their guide to the Land of Story. Once you have won their trust, you can take them to some strange places, as long as you bring them back safely.

Things to consider in terms of selecting your set and pitching it right:
- Audience: size, age range, ability, attention span/duration, gender mix, ethnicity, faith.
- Theme: relevancy/curriculum links.
- Material: anything inappropriate, controversial, or even offensive?
- Nature of venue/performance space. Atmospheric, informal, public, enclosed, noisy, sacred?
- Have the audience paid, or is it free? What are their expectations and perceptions of you, ie: your appearance and reputation (or lack of, if you are unknown).

Checklist ✓ P
WORKING WITH THE SPACE
The different possible spaces you can perform in are legion. It could be anything from a marquee at a festival, to 'in the round' at a Gorsedd, on a stage, in an amphitheatre, in a pub, on the street, in a house, in a woodland, around the fire, by the hearth, at a

bedside, etc. The performance space, needless to say, is critical and affects the dynamics of the performance. It can make or break a show. The light and noise levels, the temperature, accessibility, the comfort of the audience, toilets, refreshments, etc. An inappropriate venue – perhaps noisy, squalid, soulless, or nonconducive in some way to the enchantment you are attempting to weave – will kill the Awen dead.

So, we have to pick where we perform carefully – rowdy pubs, drug-fuelled festivals, dives, or events at odds with the Bardic ethos are best to be avoided, yet even the most perfect venue can change unexpectedly. I was booked to perform at a medieval banquet in front of a 'sympathetic' crowd, but I was disasterously put on just as they were serving the main course, from the buffet directly behind me. With 300 diners clattering cutlery and chattering, the acoustics of the hall (which I checked beforehand) changed dramatically! Another time, a smaller festival, and I was booked to perform a storytelling show for children in a marquee. Just before I went on, the heavens opened. Everybody crammed inside for shelter so I had a large audience, but they could hardly hear me with the drumming of the torrential rain on the canvas!

Fortunately, such disasters are few and far between. Sometimes everything falls into place: venue, audience, show. A personal highlight was premiering a version of Robin Hood with my friends in Fire Springs – an Eco-Bardic epic called 'Robin of the Wildwood' – on May Day in an open air amphitheatre with the sun setting through the forest backdrop: a perfect setting on the perfect day, providing the ideal atmosphere and a chance for us, as performers, to 'give something back' to the woodland with our words. Sometimes the grandest venues are not the best: a small receptive crowd is better than a large unreceptive one, even in the most prestigious setting. Some of the best audiences have been at story circles, where an ambience of bonhomie and openness often prevails.

The key thing is to pitch the performance (in terms of sound) to the right level for the venue and the audience: you don't want to use your 'Bardic bellows' to an intimate audience of half a dozen, while outdoors, with prevailing winds, you really do need to project. A good auditorium will allow you to 'stage whisper' and still be heard, as in the amazing amphitheatre of Epidauros, with its open-air stone seating for thousands carved into the hillside. It is good to be adaptable and able to perform in any venue.

Some shows are 'site specific', (eg: commissions and residencies based upon local features or heritage) but otherwise it is best to make your material a 'moveable feast'. The essential rule of thumb is to work with the space, rather than against it.

Tips:
- If possible, always visit the venue in advance. How does it feel? Talk with staff.
- Check the acoustics. Do a sound-check and get a friend or colleague to listen in from two or three different parts of the audience space. Remember the acoustics will be dampened by the audience. Will there be any background noises during the show, eg: generators for PAs, or another event close by?
- Check the sight-lines in the audience seating. Any obstructions?
- Check the lighting. Will it change during the show, ie: if outdoors, get dark halfway through?
- Rehearse how you will enter and exit the performance space. Is there an 'off-stage'? A 'green room' or dressing room? Will the audience be seated before you enter, or after? Will they leave in the interval? Where will you go?
- Are there any special features you can incorporate appropriately into the show,

eg: a doorway, a staircase, a tree, a view, etc.? The Minack Theatre in Cornwall is carved out of the cliff, with the sea behind the temple-like stage – ideal for *The Tempest*, its first show.

Checklist ✓ Q
WORKING SOLO

As a Bard, whether you think of yourself primarily as a poet, storyteller or musician, or a combination of all three, you have a choice – whether to collaborate with other performers or to go it alone. There are possible pros and cons to both.

Firstly, let us look at going solo. This is by far the most common path, almost the default setting, but it is important to be conscious in our actions and make informed decisions. The archetypal image is of the lone Bard, journeying from court to court, with harp on back. However romantic this image (in fact a hard life), this need not be the case. Although the path of the Bard is a lonely one – for only he or she can take that road for themselves, only they can make the effort and make it happen – it can be shared by others along the way, either through a 'guild' (ie: **The Silver Branch Bardic Network**), a group show, or the camaraderie and sharing of a festival or Eisteddfod. Yet the dedication and discipline has to be personal or it is meaningless.

There *are* positive aspects of working solo, as listed below. Certainly, there seem to be more solo practitioners out there than (professional) groups. Artistes who really make a name for themselves shine out as masters (or mistresses) of their craft. Taliesin was never 'Taliesin & Co', although he was at the behest of his lord, Urien ap Rheged, and he was part of the fellowship of Bards stretching back through time, so in a sense, no one is alone, or in complete isolation.

We are connected to spirits, to elementals, to ancestors, to gods – although how we connect and 'make our peace with them' is a very personal thing. No one can connect to Spirit for us. If, as Bards, we are to raise and channel the Awen, then we need to have a direct connection with it ourselves. And, ultimately, the quality of our work, the manner of our bearing, the nature of our soul's development, depends on how successful we are at doing that. The truer, deeper, our connection is, the better we will be as Bards, as people.

Benefits:
- Complete creative freedom.
- More payment (rather than a shared fee).
- More opportunities (venues can rarely afford a group fee, but can often pay for a solo slot)
- Flexibility/availability.

Disadvantages:
- No one to share the joys and tears with, the buzz, the woes, etc.
- Less networking/marketing potential (ie: one person spreading the word, instead of a number of you).
- Less variety, voices, pool of resources and skills.
- Missing the gestalt quality of group shows (when the whole is greater than the sum of its parts).

Checklist ✓R
WORKING IN A GROUP

You may want to join forces with other Bards. There are many advantages to this, not the least of which is the camaraderie. Sometimes an experience doesn't seem real unless others witness it or share it with you. The 'laughter and the tears', as they say, the smell of the greasepaint and the roar of the crowds. Even bad experiences can be laughed about afterwards (ie: The Worst Gig Ever). And there is so much more that can be achieved collectively. Ultimately, as Bards, we are aspiring towards connection – if we cannot connect with fellow Bards (because of competitiveness, for instance), our supposed kindred spirits, then who can we connect with? That is why I have set up **The Silver Branch Bardic Network**: to foster a stronger sense of community and facilitate communication, so we can share news, views, triumphs and tribulations. There is no danger of being 'assimilated' and getting lost in the crowd. Bards are, by nature, distinctive individuals. We make great capital of our particularity (some would say eccentricity): we have to – to be authentic we have to draw upon our cultural heritage, our memories, our pains and passions. By being with others, you are not going to be any less yourself, in fact, in my experience, it makes you more so, as you emphasise your 'distinctiveness' in comparison and contrast to your peers. Yet it is heartening to know you are 'not the only one', that you are not a lone voice in the wilderness.

Turning up at an unsympathetic venue may make you seem like that: with a group of you, you have your own quorum – you're not crazy, or 'Billy No Mates'. There's a stigma in our culture about being alone. There's nothing wrong with solitude – which is different from being lonely – in fact I think it is essential to one's well-being and path as a Bard. But, similarly, there are times when we can gain a lot by working and learning from others. We can share the journey, share the joys and lighten the burden when things are tough.

Some of the best nights of my life have been when I have been brainstorming a new show with Fire Springs and we've had amazing conversations, travelling deep into the mysteries. When the Awen flows, creative sparks fly back and forth across the room like synapses firing and something wonderful occurs: something is created that wasn't there before. We have created an original show, one that wouldn't have been so multi-faceted if only one of us devised it. Another person always gives another perspective, and perhaps takes your idea, adds to it, or spins it slightly. The creative process is accelerated. That is why you have teams of writers working on a TV show, or film, in the same way you have a team of scientists researching the same area – they share the load, pool their resources, and make faster leaps and greater discoveries (ie: Crick and Watson, the discoverers of the DNA double-helix).

A Bardic example of ground-breaking collaboration is that of Robin and Bina Williamson, husband and wife performers who, by drawing upon their respective Celtic and Indian heritage, create something unique between them, a fusion of East and West, which sends out a relevant multi-cultural message. By collaborating and performing on stage we are sending out messages of unity.

Benefits:
- Gestalt storytelling, more than the sum of its parts.
- Greater marketing clout. Group effort networking, word of mouth, mailing lists etc.
- More likely to get bigger gigs, ie: theatres.
- Share transport/driving – getting to gigs.

- Share opportunities, ie: if you have a pool of performers and an opportunity arises, if one of you can't do it because of other commitments, someone else in the group might be able to.
- Share interview requests, workshops, and so on.
- Pool resources, experience, skills, contacts.
- Camaraderie.
- More opportunities for a group of professional performers, ie: theatres.
- Shared experience, shared memories.
- Greater variety: an alternating of voices, styles, repertoires, talents.

Disadvantages:
- Possibly less creative freedom or control.
- Less flexibility about bookings, ie: getting a date when everyone is free can be difficult.
- More co-ordination involved, ie: meetings, rehearsals, arriving at venue, etc.
- Less money, as fee is divided up between more performers.
- Clashes of personality, egos, fraught nerves.

Checklist ✓S
TIMING

"What is the secret of comedy?" so the old saying goes, "…timing!" This is another key aspect of performance, which can make the difference between a successful show and a disastrous one. There are different aspects of timing to consider: from the macrocosmic (the topicality or appropriateness of material) to the microcosmic (the subtlest of pauses). The use of timing will flag up the difference between a maestro and a novice. The classic mistake of beginners is to rush, flushed and flustered with nerves. A master carries a sense of having 'all the time in the world' about him, an apparent ability to even suspend time itself in the enchantment of his words or music. He or she can carry the audience 'outside time' and back again. The amateur runs out of time, goes on too long, or finishes too quickly. Yet, timing is also about choosing your moment, gauging when it is a good time to begin a story, and when it isn't. This is something you intuit and pick up over the years. Sometimes it can be very difficult to discern, amidst the merriment of a bonfire party for example, when it is the right time – one may get mixed signals, with someone requesting it, another preventing it. It is about being able to sense the energy and read the nuances of a situation – a complicated thing – for one does not wish to impose or ruin the atmosphere, as I learnt at my peril. Once I was at an 'open mic' in a pub with a poet friend. He had a couple of slots lined up, but at the last moment he kindly offered me one of them. I hadn't planned to perform that night, but I did have a poem on me, one that was 'burning in my breast' about the recent 9/11 tragedy. I felt compelled to do it, but it was completely inappropriate: it was nearly last orders and the crowd were rowdy. My poem killed the atmosphere stone dead and didn't go down too well, to say the least – not very pleasant, but what did I expect? I ruined the party. Sometimes it is necessary to jolt people out of their complacency, their bubble of comfort, but in this case the material was inappropriate and the timing was ill-judged. Other times, everything seems to fall into place: there's a synchronicity of audience, performer and material – the Awen flows and deep enchantments can be encountered.

Tips:

- Rehearse your story and time it accurately.
- Tailor your set to the slot you have been allocated, ie: 10 minutes. Don't over-run or rush! Act as if you have all the time in the world, but keep an eye on the clock.
- Be mindful throughout the performance of the time. Have a clock or watch in view, but glance at it subtly or you will make the audience 'clock watch' as well.
- Play with the timing of your delivery: speed up or slow down, pause and stop, to vary pace. Use a pause for dramatic effect, but don't overuse it.
- In a group show rehearse with your fellow performers. Concentrate on your cues: be spot on, don't miss them or your 'mark' (where you should be physically in the performance space at the beginning and end of each 'speech').
- Study master performers, eg: singers or storytellers. Notice their delivery, the shape and length of their set. Try to gauge the precise point a song or tale finishes and be the first one to clap.
- Observe successful comedians and how they use timing.
- Learn to read the atmosphere of a room or place. When is a good time to tell a story, when is a bad time? Choose your moments carefully, then seize the day!

Checklist ✓ T
THE WARM-UP

It is essential to warm-up before a show for a number of reasons. As with vocal warm-up (see **Voice of the Wind** exercises) you risk straining yourself if you do not limber up, as any athlete will know. If your show is to be an especially physical performance this is essential, but even if you are going to remain seated throughout, it is important to 'loosen up', otherwise you may have tension trapped in your body that will manifest in your posture and voice, and inhibit your performance. There are inevitably nerves and tension immediately before a show, so a physical warm-up routine will help to release a certain level of it (although you should remain fully alert, like a coiled spring). We should seek to avoid what the inventor of the Alexander Technique calls 'the bad usage of self': clenched shoulders, stooped neck, tight stomach muscles, fidgety hands, strained expression, etc. We also want to raise our energy levels and our spirits, so we are ready to give out something good in our performance. We may have come from a bad day at work, a traffic jam, a dismal wet evening – you have to leave that all behind as you walk upon the stage. You have to ensure you are fully present, that you are centred, as James Roose-Evans explains, in his description of 'teachers' (of which Bards are one kind): "The true teacher of any spiritual discipline will be in themselves a centred person, while their physical strength and calm will proclaim the strength and calm within. Such a person is a whole person, in whom every gesture becomes, quite naturally, meaningful." In the last moments before you are to begin, you need to clear you mind of all clutter. Don't try to remember your entire set. All you need to do is remain calm and centred – then the rest will come. Raising the Awen is an excellent way of focussing and feeling empowered. If it helps, visualise a safe place where you feel relaxed and alert. If you ever encounter difficulties during the performance, then just picture this place: you are there, all is well. Then take a deep breath and plunge in. Let the tale tell itself, your tongue will remember what to do. Ask for Awen and it will give you all you need to stand up there and shine.

The Physical Warm-Up:

In a suitable space (large enough, out of the way) stand with your legs planted firmly on the ground, shoulder width apart. Working upwards we are going to relax the body:

- Shift your balance onto your right side and lift your left foot, shake it. Keeping it raised, tense and relax your left ankle and calf. Then raise your thigh so it makes a right angle with your body and, maintaining your balance, rotate your left foot in a clockwise and anticlockwise direction. Lower gently and relax.
- Repeat with your right foot and leg.
- Shake your hands, forearms, upper arms. Now swing backwards and forwards. Now sway left to right from the pivot of your hips, sinking slightly by bending your knees.
- Delineate circles with your arms by swinging them completely over. Try in the same direction, then in opposite directions (a test of co-ordination!)
- Stretch your arms sideways as far as they will go, with fingers held together in a flat point. Breathe in and tense your arms, breathe out and relax. Turn your palms upwards and repeat.
- Lift up shoulders, tense and then release. Roll shoulders in joints, both directions, and relax.
- Rest your head upon your chin and very slowly rotate your head in a clockwise direction, rolling it over your shoulders in a full circle. Repeat in opposite direction.
- Jump up and down.
- Slow your breathing. Take deeper breaths. Centre yourself, perhaps closing your eyes for a minute if you feel stable. Feel calm, centred, ready.
- Try practising a couple of the symbolic movements or postures from the show.
- Have a **walk through** (see next part).

Checklist ✓ U
THE WALK THROUGH AND WARMING UP THE SPACE

The big day has arrived and you have arrived at the venue – ideally with plenty of time to spare: to set up, to relax, and to have a walk through. This involves simply pacing through the set in rapid succession, topping and tailing each story, song or poem (reciting the first and last line) just to remind yourself of all the cues and marks. This is essential if you are doing a group show with quick change-overs or choreography (see **Working in a Group**). It also familiarises you with the feel of the performance space so that you acclimatise and 'claim' it. Make sure there are no corners or sections of the stage that you don't feel comfortable in, or feel that are not 'yours': all the stage is yours as a performer, including the auditorium – don't create invisible barriers or thresholds for yourself. Make sure there are no obstacles between you and the audience, ie: a significant drop in height if you're on a big stage with a small audience needs to be avoided, as does any clutter at the front of the stage (PAs, cables, etc.). Break any lines: the 'barriers' in front, between and around the audience – venture along aisles, walk amongst the crowd, even run around them (if appropriate). After you have claimed the space in this way you need to warm it up.

Warming up the Space

When you first encounter an audience they are 'cold', that is why there are warm up acts, even warm up guys in TV shows with a studio audience, to prime the crowd for the main event. Bards rarely have such luxury. So we have to be our own warm up acts. Start with a crowd-pleaser, something to get the audience laughing, feeling relaxed and reassured that they're in for a good time. Damh the Bard is adept at this, soon getting the crowd into the palm of his hand in his seemingly informal way, before introducing 'deeper' material. If you have an opportunity, raise the Awen in the space you are to perform in. If you cannot do this beforehand, you can incorporate it into your introduction or even get the audience to help you at the start of the show, as I have done. Other techniques include getting the audience to clap, to sing a song, to lend their energy in some way. I have seen two black storytellers who were great at this: Jan Blake came on singing a Creole song and got the audience to clap along with her as she swayed onto the stage. TUUP (The Unprecedented Unorthodox Preacher) invoked the blessing of different saints, elementals, ancestors, relatives, etc., like a medicine man, asking for contributions from the audience as he poured a little libation from his bottle of water with each name, blessing the space, and raising the energy at the same time. This took up half of his set, but it was definitely electrifying to watch! Fire Springs start their Eco-Bardic epic of Greek Mystery Myth, *Return to Arcadia* with an invocation to the Muses, in Greek: we walk on ritualistically, incantating the 'fumigation to the Nymphs', whilst wafting incense over the audience. This immediately initiates the audience into the 'story space', asks for inspiration and blessing and establishes the mood. The atmosphere is created: the show can begin.

Checklist ✓V
AUDIENCE PARTICIPATION

Storytelling, like improv comedy, relies upon audience participation. Without their 'participation' the stories wouldn't happen at all for it is a co-creative act. The vitality of the story hinges completely on the imagination of the audience. Of course, this is 'fired up' by a good performer, but the story really only comes alive in a Third Space between teller and listener. The engagement and reciprocation of the audience is fundamental to a successful performance: a teller depends upon it. A great story can be completely derailed by a dead auditorium, by stony faces, or unnerving blackness. That is why eye contact and being able to see the audience's expressions and reactions is key. The Bard is always casting out lines and trying to reel in his audience, like Ogma who chained people to his tongue with eloquence. Remember, the Bard is the listener's guide to other worlds – he or she needs to check they are always with them, 'holding their hand' as it were, and not straying from the path, as they are taken through weird and potentially treacherous territory.

There are many ways of checking whether an audience is still 'with you,' – essential tools in the teller's repertoire. The most classic audience participation technique originates in the Afro-Caribbean tradition. The teller would go "Crick!": the audience respond "Crack!" It's as simple as that, but surprisingly effective: it can be used to punctuate a telling, designating the end of a section, and making sure the audience is staying alert, as they have to respond quickly – as the teller plays a little game with them, trying to catch them off-guard. I have seen it used to brilliant effect to 'kick-start' a story and performance: the exchange is repeated three times, then the teller begins straight away – this instantly raises the energy of the room and gets the audience caught up in the tale. It is almost like the crackle in the air before a thunderstorm.

I have used variations of this over the years. During a week at the Royal Armouries Museum as part of their 'Once and Future King' exhibition I was telling Arthurian stories. In one tale, referring to the legend of the King sleeping under the mountain, waiting to return in the time of the country's greatest need, I would call out: "Is Arthur awake yet?" and the audience (mainly families with young children) would shout out "Yes!"

In *Return to Arcadia*, with Fire Springs, I tell the story of Aristaios and the Bees. During the sequence when he goes to Proteus to find out why his bees had died and the wily old man changes shape to avoid the answer, I get the audience to repeat the advice his mother gives him: "Hold on tight!" Sometimes I also get the audience to suggest things Proteus turns into, so that it's different every time, and my reactions of incredulity and distress, having to deal with a succession of rhinos, octopus, Mongolian death worms, camels, whales, sharks, anacondas, etc., provides amusement. However, you need to prime an audience to do this, and it's not always possible (it's not when I do the Aristaios tale as part of the tightly-structured *Return to Arcadia* – if I do tell the tale on its own, I can because I can prime the audience before I begin by saying that I'll "need their help").

However, audiences can slip into a passive state, which isn't surprising considering they are sitting there 'just' listening (although listening can be active). If you do not make them expect audience participation they may be caught completely off-guard, which can result in a dismal response. When I do my green man poem *One with the Land* I rehearse the participation with the audience beforehand (basically to repeat the title three times at the end of the poem). The important thing is that I give them a cue, so they know when to come in: a single clap. This, I have found, highlights the hypnotic effect of stories, poems and songs – for when I do the clap it jolts the audience from the semi-trance of listening, and acts as a mnemonic, reminding them when and where they are, like the hypnotist's finger click.

The most amazing audience participation I've witnessed was during Bob Geldof's massive Live8 concert with its global audience of 3 billion. Will Smith, contributing to the American concert in Philadelphia, got everybody in the auditorium (and through a live broadcast, the rest of the viewing world) to click their fingers every 3 seconds to symbolise the death of a child in Africa through poverty. It was simple, successful and incredibly powerful, hearing the vast chorus of clicks break the dead air with regular inevitability.

Getting the audience to repeat a line is the easiest and often the most successful form of audience participation. It is wise to keep it simple and not overdo it. I have been scuppered by attempting complicated songs or poems with audience participation, either because it throws you, or throws them. And once I got an audience to repeat every line of *Sir John Barleycorn* after me, which made it go on too long. Another time, I got them just to join in on the end of each verse, which worked far better. With audience participation, you really don't know if it's going to work until you try it – it's something that is difficult to rehearse realistically, because your fellow performers, even friends and family, are not going to be a 'cold' audience, who don't know you and may not be so obliging. It is worth thinking it through carefully at least!

Tips:
- Riddles are a classic device for audience participation. Otherwise, beginning your tale with a bold, possibly rhetorical question (ie: "Who has not heard of Fionn Mac Cumhail, the greatest hero that ever was?") can act as a hook.

- Songs, chants and rhymes.
- Clapping and stamping.
- Movement, ie: getting the small children to wriggle like little pigs in mud, as I do in the tale of **The Swineherd Prince and the Flying King**.
- Make noises. Animals are always popular, eg: grunting, mooing, barking, howling, etc. Alternatively, noises of things, ie: 'click-clack', the sound of Baba Yaga's loom; or 'clatter, clatter', the sound of her bony knees knocking together as she chased after Marusia.
- Role-playing different characters in the tale.
- Asking their opinions, ie: "What do women want?"
- Asking for suggestions for different elements of the story, especially in Fooling.
- Leaving them with a challenge: "Who will plant the wildwoods anew?"
- Getting them to remember different complicated details of the story.
- Getting them to repeat complicated character, place names or 'runs'.
- Creating sounds of weather (the wind, the rain) or other natural phenomenon (the sea, hail, thunder).
- Sound effects and story elements: whispering, shouting, the sound of battle, astonishment, laughter.
- Ask for their judgement, ie: "Do you think the princess should go with him?"
- Remember, listening is the fundamental form of participation essential to story-telling.

Checklist ✓W
WORKING WITH INTERRUPTIONS

The mark of an experienced Bard is one who can not only deal with disruptions but turn them to his or her advantage, and make a witty remark out of it. This nearly always gets a laugh, because any interruption to the show creates a build-up of nervous tension – as the audience subconsciously wonder if the distraction will 'puncture' the integrity or boundary of the story space – which is relieved by a comic aside or quip. Instantly the audience are reassured the outside *can* intrude without the show stopping: the 'alternate reality' of the tale can be maintained and co-exist with the mundane. A Bard should always be able to walk between worlds in this way, and strive to keep them in equilibrium.

We shouldn't be thrown by intentional disruptions either. They are a way of testing your mettle and skill. Ben Okri, in *A Way of Being Free* offers wisely this advice: "Remember: it is from the strength of your antagonists that you derive your greater authority. They make it absolutely necessary for you to be more than yourself." Remember, you have complete belief in yourself. Your conviction will give you courage. And do not forget, in the face of any heckling, that the audience is normally there to see you, not some drunken idiot, and they *want* you to succeed, want the show to go well because they want to be entertained, they want to have a good time. Thus, most audiences are supportive. This is their quality 'R&R' time and they are choosing to spend it listening to *you*.

Tips:
- **Disruptive Kids:** get them to join in – obviously they are demanding attention, so give it to them. Get them on stage and give them something to do, ie: be the loud monster.

- **Hecklers:** Conflict breeds more conflict. Work with them – be over-enthusiastic and encouraging, or get them on your side by agreeing with them. Like disruptive kids, they want attention. Give it to them – shame them into saying something smart or shutting up.
- **Put Downs:** Comedienne Donna McPhail dealt with an unpleasant heckler in her Edinburgh Fringe show with the withering riposte: "What do you use as a contraceptive? Your personality?" This devastating use of wit relates directly back to the Bard's feared Satire, which could raise blisters on the face of enemies. Fear of mockery or public humiliation alone is enough to quell any snide comments.
- **Off Stage Noises:** Possible distractions such as mobile phones, music, a baby crying, a car horn, a plane flying by, a dog barking, etc., incorporate into your story by mentioning them, or alluding to them in an indirect way, ie: the sound of the monster was like a baby crying. Such asides can often win a smile or a laugh from the audience. They are also being reminded every time you do that, the show is being created live in front of them, in a unique way, with local references, or with allusions to the particularity of that moment in time, just for them. Such references, when assimilated in this way remind people to be fully present, that this is happening now.
- **Watch the Professional:** go and see a top stand-up comic, storyteller, singer or poet and see how they deal with such situations. The true professional is never fazed by such 'attacks', but turns it around into a display of their consummate skill. Often such incidents, especially intentional disruptions 'test' the ability of the shaman-Bard.

Checklist ✓X
MULTI-MEDIA

The modern Bard has many tools at his disposal. Contemporary theatre and performance art uses a wide range of multi-media, and these are also available to any adept practitioner. However, it is wise to remember that the power of the Bard lies in his voice and memory, and its endurability and universality has hinged, I think, on its low-tech 'simplicity': basically, 'have tongue, will travel'. A Bard should be able to perform almost anywhere at any time – coming out with a tale at the drop of a hat without elaborate equipment and setting up. Bearing that in mind, you may want to consider the options below. But before choosing any, always ask yourself – *do you really need it to tell your tale?* Start with the attitude: what can I do without, rather than what can I do with. There is a thrill in seeing how a good performer can keep an audience spellbound by his or her voice alone; or, if a prop is needed, improvising one from the immediate surroundings: a table becoming a boat, a chair, gallows, etc. For in doing so, he or she turns the mundane into the magical and suggests to the audience: Everything is Story. It is also incredibly empowering for the audience, because the more austere the accoutrements of the performance, the more it relies upon the imagination of the audience. Far superior than the biggest budget blockbuster, the best state-of-the-art special FX, is the power of the imagination.

Ideas:
- Digital projectors/laptops
- Backing tracks/audio loops

- Slide projectors on automated carousel
- Smoke machines
- Lighting
- Scent, ie. incense
- Backdrops
- Sets
- Music
- Dance
- Film, ie: Super 8mm projector directed onto a backdrop, screen or performer.
- Live video playback, or pre-recorded material (with which the performer can interact)
- Handouts, ie: printed material/programme, lyrics, background.
- Objects to handle (ie: artefacts relating to the story).
- Circus, either incorporate circus skills (eg: clowning, acrobatics, juggling) or create a narrative structure for a circus show, ie: The Cabaret at the End of the World's 'apocalypse revue', or No Fit State's *Immortal*[2], which depicted lost souls journeying into the afterlife (with the audience moving en masse through the different sets).
- Chainsaws, arc-welders, motorbikes, or customised machinery, eg: Archaos, Mutoid Waste Company, or Kiss My Axe.
- Re-enactment, ie: a tournament, a fencing duel as part of the show (ideal for Living History/heritage venues).
- Wind-up/mechanical automata or puppets (as some street performers use)
- Art installations
- Story walks, using various locations and even characters.

Checklist ✓ Y
RECIPROCATION AND REMUNERATION

In danger of stating the obvious, how you are received can make the world of difference: performance is all about energy. At the end of a show, check if you feel elated or depleted? If you feel the former it is because the energy you gave out was reciprocated. If you feel the latter, it's because you were haemorrhaging energy throughout the show. If an audience is non-commital or even difficult, it can be exhausting continually trying to win them over and 'drag' them along with you, ie: if attentions are wandering and they are being distracted by outside influences. When an audience is with you, it makes you feel buoyed up: their attention, participation and goodwill gives you energy (the collective energy of those gathered) to work with, like a good group ceremony. It can be the best buzz, or the worst feeling in the world, depending on how it goes.

Ask yourself these three questions to gauge how it went: How did you feel before the show? How did you feel during the show? How did you immediately after the show? A show may be technically perfect but if you feel drained after a show, something obviously didn't go right. You can gauge to a certain extent if it's going down well – are the audience laughing, sighing, crying, clapping, cheering, etc. in the right places – although if the auditorium is pitch black, or the audience is too far away sometimes it is difficult to tell. The next step is to consult any fellow performers (see **Closure**), stage crew (lighting technician, stage manager, MC, etc.) and organisers (promoter, host, festival director). You may be simply told directly by an audience member afterwards, or overhear some in the bar, or read them in the comments book (see **Documentation**). Finally, you may get a review, if you're lucky, or comments in a chatroom, or by correspondence (ie: "I saw your show the other week and…").

Do you feel it was worth it, in terms of time and effort? What about remuneration? Any other perks, eg: meals, free tickets, freebies? Use the checklist below when trying to calculate what to charge (when you are at a stage that you are able to). Modern Bards seldom make any money: it's certainly not a road to riches (excluding the notable exceptions, the 'top of their career' performers). You have to do it for the love of it: anything else is the icing on the cake. If your inspiration and motivation is purely commercial, then it will show through in a soulless performance. It has to come from the heart, always. But, of course, Bards have to eat and pay the rent like everybody else. They should be remunerated for their efforts (although the years of training have to be your sacrifice and offering). And, in this money-orientated world, if something is free it is seldom valued, alas (think of all the natural resources in the world which are exploited and squandered). If you charge people to see you, they generally make the most of you – because they want their monies worth. Do it for free in a park, or at a party, and many people will simply ignore and talk over you (happens time and time again to pub bands).

Payment

When gauging what to charge, consider the following:

- Your experience/profile. Are you a beginner or a veteran, a star or a newcomer?
- Development/rehearsal time. Keep a record of the hours you put in. If you are asked to devise a completely new show, this is effectively a commission and should be charged accordingly. If it is a show you have done many times before and don't need to rehearse, then perhaps you can charge a flat fee. If it's one that you need to resurrect with several rehearsals, then you may want to factor that in. It is rare, however, to be paid for R&D time. Day rates normally take into account a certain amount of preparation, ie: a workshop of two hours includes an hour prep time. If it is a new show that has taken a long time to develop, then you need to perform it as many times as possible to make sure the effort you have put in is reciprocated.
- Travel expenses. How far do you have to travel? How long will it take? Is it worth it?
- The duration of the show. Have a sliding scale for different slots, eg: 30, 45, 60, 90 minute shows.
- What's the 'going rate'? What are your peers being paid? What's the 'usual fee', ie: the Arts Council recommended rate for artists is £175 for a full day's work-shop (2006). Story circles may offer a basic £50 for a guest slot, or more depending on their door-charge policy and any funding. Festivals may only offer a free ticket.
- Will you be able to sell your own merchandise, eg: CDs, booklets? This may help to compensate if they cannot offer expenses, or full payment.
- Create a sliding scale or rates, which can be used as a basis for any query. Have it by the phone in case a prospective venue rings and asks for a quote. Sometimes you have to negotiate. Be prepared to be flexible, taking into

account what their budget is, what else is on offer, eg: expenses, meals, accommodation, if it's for charity, how far away it is, if it's a show you have done several times, or a completely new one, whether it is a workshop or performance, or both. And so on.

- Remember to always be polite, professional and precise. Keep track of payments. Be prepared to send out invoices, receipts, reminders, etc. You may want to set up a different bank account for yourself, or your group. If you are going self-employed you need to keep your accounts and declare any earnings.
- Public liability insurance and Criminal Records Bureau checks are standard these days as well – most venues require these, and you will lose out on a lot of work if you don't have them.
- Remember, enjoying your performance and a good response from the audience should be the best reward.

Checklist ✓Z
DOCUMENTATION
It is always good to keep a record of each show you do. This helps you to keep an archive of your performances, for posterity and as useful reminders of a particular set. If you get a request for a particular show from your repertoire, ie: Hallowe'en Tales, then you can simply watch or listen to the recording of it to jog the memory. It is also extremely useful to have evidence of previous performances for prospective venues, some of which request evidence of a 'track record'. If your show has been funded, then documentation may be a condition of the grant (ie: for monitoring and evaluation purposes).

Tips:
- Audio recording
- Video recording
- Photographs. Get a friend or even better a professional photographer to record the show.
- Comments book
- Feedback form (combine with free entry for a raffle to guarantee some response!)
- Demographic Stats, eg: Age, Ethnicity, Disabilities
- Pre-ticket sales and actual bums on seats. Do a head count.
- Scrapbook of clippings, eg: reviews, posters, flyers.
- Folder of venue information, programmes, etc.
- Keep a Bardic log tracking each story, song or poem (see **Repertoire**).

Checklist ✓aa
CLOSURE AND FOLLOW-UP
The show is over. What now? It is important to avoid a sense of anti-climax by making sure there's sufficient closure: you have 'opened' yourself out to the audience in many ways – it's essential to 'close down' properly: the Throat Chakra is especially vulnerable. You would have opened this up for your performance. If you leave it 'open' it can be prone to infection. In the similar way an athlete wraps up after their training, put something

warm on, change into different more comfortable clothes, do whatever you need to become yourself and get grounded. Have a hot drink and a snack, or better still a beer! Time to celebrate, or commiserate, with your fellow performers or peers. It is vital to celebrate the achievement of your performance, however it went, just to acknowledge your effort and not to leave you feeling 'bereft'. One often feels 'emptied' after a show. It is time to replenish the well – initially with food, drink and friendship; later on, in a spiritual way (see **Retreat**). For now, the main thing is to ground yourself. One can often feel light-headed or hyper after a show: this is when accidents occur. Don't just rush off. Whatever you do, don't just jump in a car and drive away. You've only just got back from the Otherworld: you need to fully return to this reality.

Tips:
- Celebrate! You've worked hard. Let your hair down.
- Mingle. Mix with the audience afterwards, let them buy you a drink and tell you how much they enjoyed it. Most people will respect the effort you made even if they didn't completely like the show.
- Packing Up: after the crowd has departed, time to pack up and go home. Do this carefully and methodically (you may want to use a checklist). Don't leave anything behind!
- Winding Down: For the next day or two take it easy. Let the aftermath of the show sink in. You may want to write up how you thought it went, but don't write too much, or do anything too strenuous.
- Debriefing: if you are performing in a group arrange a 'debriefing' session, maybe a week later. It could be informal, over tea and cake, or a glass of wine. Hear everyone's feelings on the show, their high and low points, and take heed of any constructive criticisms.
- Ring the venue – ask how they thought it went. Would they like to book you again?
- If you don't hear from the venue in a month or two, contact them before the start of the next season. NB theatres and festivals programme at least six months in advance. Offer a variation of the old show (if the original was popular) or something completely new.
- In the light of how the show went, what, if anything, do you need to change or add?

Month 12: A Bardic Life

You have reached the last month of your first year as an Anruth, and have made significant progress on your path to being a Bard. As I stated at the beginning, this book will not make you a Bard – only you can do that, through your commitment and belief, but *The Bardic Handbook* should have improved your learning curve significantly and provided all you need to know (outside of an experiential workshop) about becoming and being a Bard. Yet even after nearly a year you have only just begun your journey – for being a fully fledged Bard (Taliesin Grade) takes twelve years, an Ollamh twenty years, and mastering the Bardic Arts a lifetime. Such long-term dedication is not for everyone, but you can still

Eco-poet Helen Moore,
8th Bard of Bath.

benefit from Bardic skills and Bardic wisdom, whether short-term or long-term: as a storyteller, singer, poet, or remembrancer for your community, in public-speaking situations, or in general self-esteem.

I hope you have gained something from this year, if you have stuck at it, or from this book, if you've just dipped into it for inspiration now and again.

For those of you who wish to continue pursuing the path of the Bard it is time to consider what is called in shamanic training 'the Second Revelation' – how to integrate inner work into outer life. I call this the Way of Awen. By now you should be well-acquainted with the flowing spirit – you would have used it for inspiration, for eloquence, for guidance. Now it is time to use it in everyday life. It is essential to 'walk your talk', to live rightly and live lightly.

It is not about making your life a performance, although some people do (ie: pop stars). Rather than play 'the Bard', be real, be yourself, otherwise you'll start to distance those who love or like you.

A Bardic Life is about being sensitive to the Awen at all times: in the way we speak, the way we act, the way we interact with others, the way we lead our lives. This is perhaps the most difficult challenge of the Bard. You have to lead by example and embody the wisdom you convey through your songs, stories and poems.

Having explored the **Elements** you should by now be fairly balanced, and by using the 5-point method of the **Shining Word** (Appendices), you should be able to monitor and maintain that equilibrium in your performance and in your life.

It is about being respectful and responsible – to oneself and to others. Do you look after your body, nurture your mind, and feed your spirit? If you do not have inner health, you will not be able to fulfil your potential as a Bard, and an illness (ie: alcoholism) or dis-ease may affect what messages you give out. It's not about being 'whiter than white' – a dubious notion – but about balance. The more we deny the Shadow part of ourselves (eg: sexuality, prejudices, etc.) the more it will fester and manifest in other ways (a perversion, Freudian slip, shocking remark, or over-reaction). It is best to accept and assimilate. The Id will out, anyway! Honour your dark places and bright. Shadow gives us substance, stops us being anaemic. Let your full Self breathe in the light of day. Express who you are, and accept who you are – not that this is an excuse to be complacent, or to justify ugly opinions or damaging behaviour! We are all works-in-progress. To err is to be human, but don't stop making an effort. Apply the Awen Life Laundry below to leave no part of your life unscrutinised or untransformed.

EXERCISE: the Awen Life Laundry

Think about the different aspects of your life and consider how Awen can inspire and influence them:

Work: Are you happy at work? Are you doing what you believe in, or selling your soul? Are you using your talents or wasting your time? Not many of us are lucky enough to be paid for what we love doing, but if you are not and want to be, rather than bemoan your lot and regret your life, change it – make it the way you want to be, whatever it takes (ie: retraining). Remember: life isn't a rehearsal. But whatever it is you find yourself doing, and life can throw us some curves and we find ourselves doing something we had never intended, bear in mind what that Persian Bard Khalil Gibran said in *The Prophet*, "Make Work Your Prayer".

Relationships: Is Awen flowing in your relationships with friends, family, loved ones? Use it to help foster communication, balance, respect, trust, joy, and the sum of these things: love. In some ways love *is* Awen – the flow of spirit between two people. Work with it, cherish it, and celebrate it. Sometimes the feelings we have for another are nebulous but we know something is there. Explore the connection. Awen, like love, happens in the 'space between' – between two hearts. With some people you feel an instant rapport, others you cannot get on with at all. Explore why that is: often the ones who we come into conflict or confrontation with, the ones who really push our buttons, have the most to teach us. Why are they 'winding you up'? Often it is because they carry an unreconciled part of yourself that they either represent or stir up in you. You don't like them because it is, in fact, a part of yourself you don't like – possibly in a deeply subconscious way, something you don't even know you hate. They make you confront your 'issues'. Use the Three Rays of Awen to throw light on these dark unexplored places. Make a list of the relationships in your life: are they healthy or unhealthy, positive or parasitical? Do you have any 'crazy-makers', as Julia Cameron calls them: people who disrupt and drain your creativity? Or are *you* the crazy-maker? What signals are you sending out, what reality are you creating for yourself? First and foremost, if change is needed, *be* the change. Work on yourself and how you act with people. If there's any dysfunctional relationships (with family, friends, work colleagues) then use the Awen (invoke it and visualise it flowing between you if it helps) to shift any blockages and to mend broken lines of communication. Once I was mending a patchwork blanket, and as I was stitching its squares back together I was thinking about the relationships I had that needed mending: this helped me to take the initiative to do this. Friends, even family, drift apart – if we let them. It takes effort and love to keep the tribe or community together, with little gestures – a phone call, or a birthday card. It doesn't take much to stay in touch. We need to look out for one another: check on the old lady next door, or that friend you haven't seen for a while. Chat to your neighbours over the garden wall, or in the local shop. Think about the people you come into contact with every day: the beggar on the street, the ticket collector on the train, the waitress, the traffic warden – are you polite to them, or rude; friendly or hostile? And how do they react to you? If someone reacts in an unprovoked way, ie: a shop assistant snaps at you, then consider why: they are often 'acting out' a problem, which isn't directed at you – you just provided the trigger. Foster good relationships in your community – get people talking and sharing stories (see **Running a Bardic Circle**, Appendices). This is the best way for people to understand and sympathise with one another.

Play: This is about the freeing of energy, of shedding any preconceptions and expectations about an activity and enjoying it for the sake of it. You can use the idea of Creative Play in all aspects of your life, but don't let it become too purposeful. Remember to always keep some time aside just for 'sacred play', whether it's going canoeing, dancing, surfing, ice-skating, bowling, bungee jumping, or just knocking a ball about in a park, taking the dog for a walk and throwing a stick (dogs certainly know how to play), feeding the ducks, or going to a Fun Fair. It is about getting back in touch with your Inner Child, and 'working' with the archetype of the Fool, with their cleansed perception and renewed innocence, so we can see things as they really are (like the boy in the Emperor's New Clothes) and be in the moment, fully present to the possibilities around us and the wonder of the world. Do something fun today!

Lifestyle: Is there balance and flow in your life: between work and play, company and solitude, consumption and creation, giving something back and nourishing yourself? Think about what you use and how you dispose of it. Recycling is a timely metaphor for the Awen – it is all about balance and the flow of energy. Are you giving back what you take, in terms of the planet's resource (ie: planting trees to balance the carbon emissions of your car)? The less you use, the less you'll need to recycle. None of us have 'zero impact' lifestyles, but we can all learn to live more lightly; and we can use the idea and energy of Awen to help our lives flow better. You may want to draw a Flow Diagram of your life with various boxes for 'Money In', 'Money Out', 'Play', 'Friends', 'Home', 'Community', 'Travel', and so on (alter size according to importance, and use colouring to represent health or status) to see how your life 'joins up'. See your life as an ecosystem – is it functioning properly, or are there imbalances, dead ends and diseased parts? The energy, or Awen, should be flowing around it, being 'recycled'. Balance things out by reprioritising. What are your Wants (non-essentials) and Needs (essentials)? Could you want less and appreciate what you already have more?

Beliefs: Is there Awen in the way you see the world, in your ideas and core beliefs? Do you tolerate other beliefs, listen to other sides of an argument, and accept different viewpoints? How can you use the Awen to help your community to integrate and flow better? Could you set up an Interfaith Group, a Speaking Circle, or even a MultiFaith Festival? Do your politics match your path as a Bard, or are they at odds with it? Do you need to be greener, more liberal? Which party or political system has the most Awen? Certain politicians seem to, however they use or misuse it. Is your religion or belief system one that allows things to flow, or is it dogmatic, intolerant or extremist? How much Awen is in your heart, in your Soul?

Health: Without our health we have nothing, or very little we can enjoy. All the things we take for granted go out of the window. Depending upon the illness, we could be physically, mentally or emotionally disabled, or a combination of all three (often a problem has a holistic cause). Your whole life can become derailed. Every day people overcome disabilities in the most amazing courageous ways, but it's better if we take care of ourselves in the first place, and whatever our state of health and ability, we should never take it for granted. Diet and exercise go hand-in-hand. One can never cancel out the need for the other, so be wary of faddy fix-all 'miracle' diets. Just eat healthily and exercise regularly. Listen to what your body needs. How do certain foods make you feel? If fried foods make us feel greasy inside, and raw foods make us feel 'fresh', what does common sense tell us? Of course, we have weaknesses and weak moments, when comfort foods call us. Treat yourself now and again by all means, but don't make it a crutch you rely on (to compensate for a dysfunctional love life or job, for instance). If you need a carrot and stick approach to motivate yourself, don't make the carrots bigger than the stick! A chocolate biscuit every now and then won't kill anyone, but cigarettes, alcohol, and Class-A drugs will! If you must have a vice, make it a healthy or at least harmless one, ie: buying books. But if it is something unhealthy then remember this equation: the worse the thing you put in your body, the more exercise and detoxing you'll need to do. If you are prepared to honour this 'contract', fair enough. If not, your health will suffer, and your body can only take so much.

Fortunately, exercise can be enjoyable, sometimes even exhilarating (ie: a good run). It oxygenates your body, releases endorphins, raises adrenalin and clears the mind. If Awen is about energy, in essence, then exercise (or any physical activity, such as sport or dancing) frees up anything stagnant and gets it flowing again. We return to our work, to our homes, to our partners and friends, better inside and more alive.

So, the Bardic Life is about attitude and action as much as belief and effort: deeds, not 'just' words. In what other ways can Awen enable your life to flow better?

A Year and a Day: Accepting Your Bardic Chair

By now, if you have worked through this book sequentially and thoroughly, you should have followed the Way of Awen for an entire circuit of the **Wheel of the Year**, learning all you need to know to set you on your Bardic Path. So now it is time to claim your chair: this is not to claim you are a fully-fledged Bard after only twelve months, but an Anruth of the Hare Grade, and have honoured your oath and fulfilled your obligations. For the last year you have been like Gwion Bach, stirring the Cauldron of Inspiration. You have tasted of its wisdom and have been transformed. You are ready to move on, into the next stage of your bardic development. With the ears and alacrity of the hare you must venture into the public arena, listening all the time to your community, to the Awen and to your heart. Speak or sing your words with eloquence and passion, and be in the moment, poised and lightning-witted.

Create a simple rites-of-passage ceremony to mark the transition into the Grade of Hare, ie: the Crossing

The Bardic Chair of Caer Badon, made by Rob Miller and Miranda Young.

of a Threshold. You may want to actually make your own Chair (with spaces for each of the grade-icons to be added over the years), or some other symbol of office (eg: a robe, amulet, silver branch, or laurel crown). After a year and a day have passed, go back to the place where you had declared your intent (see **Declaring your Chair**). Wear your finest Bardic regalia. Make offerings of incense, libation and the fruits of your toil – take along your journal, copies of poems or songs, or something symbolising your repertoire, eg: an embroidered cloak of tales or a story bag. Cast a circle. Invoke the Quarters and invite the Spirits. Raise the Awen, chant the Gorsedd Prayer, then state your purpose, along the lines of: "It has been a year and a day since I stood here and declared my wish to commence my Bardic training and follow the Way of Awen. I have now come to claim my Chair, as Anruth of the Hare Grade, unless any here object". If no one does, and no one in their right mind should, commence with the next stage. Accept your graduation, ideally from a Chief Bard or Druid (otherwise, ask an elder of your community). Use the handing over of the **Certificate** below (in a variation of the **Anruth Ceremony**) to officially mark your graduation. Have witnesses present, either friends, members of your community, or other Anruths – this may be their 'Bard-day' as well, if they embarked upon the Way of Awen at the same time as you. Open the Gorsedd and speak from your heart: recite one of your poems, songs or stories; then pass the Talking Stick or Poet's Wand for others to share. Finally, offer around bread and mead (don't forget some for the Spirits of Place). Close the circle, thanking the gods and elementals before sending them on their way in peace. Clear the site. Have a photograph taken for posterity and celebrate! Write up in your journal. Do you feel different? Complete the **Final Feedback Form**, and make plans for your Year of the Hare.

Repeat this format for each graduation, as you go through the transformations of Taliesin to become a fully-trained Bard. Each time include a new element to symbolise the new grade, connected to the animal or symbol (eg: hare, greyhound, salmon, otter, wren, hawk, etc.). You may want to tell part of the Tale of Taliesin each time, or re-enact it in some way, using it in your ceremony – so that you become Gwion being chased by Ceridwen, the initiatory Goddess, metamorphosing into different forms (or states of consciousness) and attuning with different totems and icons as you weave along the Way of Awen.

So, rise and take your place in the Gorsedd of the Silver Branch as an Anruth of the Hare Grade. You are part of this Fellowship of Bards now, and I suggest joining **The Silver Branch Bardic Network** if you have not done so already, for it serves as a peer support network and forum, with a programme of events throughout the year. If you are lucky, your local Gorsedd or Grove will provide some of this. If one does not exist, then you may want to consider creating your own. A circle has to start somewhere (although in reality it has no end or beginning). As more and more Anruths become initiated (and you may want to facilitate some, having gone through it yourself) then your circle will widen and your Gorsedd will grow. You may wish to facilitate a regular Bardic Circle, or even establish an Eisteddfod. See advice in the appendices on **Running a Bardic Circle** and **Setting up and Running a Bardic Chair**.

Author on Adam's Grave, Vale of Pewsey, Wiltshire, 2004.

If you need further help or guidance then contact the author via a letter to the publisher or email: **bard@tallyessin.com**

See you along the Way of Awen!

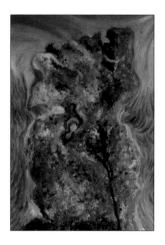

Quarterly Review

You have completed your final element. Let's take stock.
You should have looked at and completed the following:

- ❖ Spirits of Earth: write a winter solstice poem;
  write a mummers' play; hold a midwinter celebration
- ❖ Month 10: Your Bardic Debut
- ❖ The Bladder Stick – using humour
- ❖ Story: Bolverk and the Skaldic Mead
- ❖ The Crane Bag: *Briamech Smetrach* – the uses and misuses of satire
- ❖ Voice of the Earth
- ❖ Sitting Out: A Night on Bard Mountain
- ❖ The Crane Bag: *Dindsenchas* – stories of place. Research and tell a local folk tale
- ❖ Month 11: The Tongue That Cannot Lie. Personal prophecy exercise
- ❖ Voice of the Ancestors. Personal ancestor exercise
- ❖ The Crane Bag: Stone upon the Belly. Sleeping on it exercise
- ❖ Voice of the Stars. Starsinging and star quality
- ❖ On Being a Twenty-First Century Bard
- ❖ Voice of the World – relevance and motivation
- ❖ Checklist
- ❖ Month 12: A Bardic Life. Awen Life Laundry
- ❖ Claiming your Chair
- ❖ Quarterly Review
- ❖ Final Feedback Form
- ❖ Certificate

Final Review

Harvest of learning I have reaped,
Fruits of many a lifetime stored,
The false discarded, proven kept,
Knowledge that is its own reward –
No written page more true
Than blade of grass and drop of dew.

Hollow Hills, Kathleen Raine

Having completed all of the above, it is time for your final exercise: to reflect upon what you have learnt over the year. At the beginning of the training programme I asked you to complete a **self-evaluation form**. Dig it out, read it, and then fill in the **final feedback form**.

Final Feedback Form

At the end of your first year of Bardic training, how do you feel?

What have you most enjoyed about the training programme?

What have you least enjoyed?

What do you need to work on?

What would you like to focus on next?

How much commitment are you prepared to make…?
    On a daily basis:
    On a weekly basis:
    On a monthly basis:

What goals do you set yourself in the coming year?

Where do you want to be, Bardically…
    In a year's time:
    In five year's time:
    In ten year's time:

How do you see the Way of Awen manifesting in your life?

Have you joined The Silver Branch Bardic Network yet, and are you planning to go to any events, workshops, performances, camps, etc.?

WELL DONE! MAY THE AWEN ALWAYS FLOW

Way of Awen participants at Bedd Taliesin,
Ceredigion, 2004

CERTIFICATE OF BARDIC GRADUATION
NB: Photocopy onto coloured card (ideally, blue for Bard).
Fill in using a fountain or calligraphy pen.

THE SILVER BRANCH BARDIC COLLEGE

THIS IS TO CERTIFY THAT

....

HAS SUCCESSFULLY COMPLETED

ONE YEAR OF BARDIC TRAINING

Date............/.............../............

AND IS HEREBY AWARDED THE BARDIC NAME OF

....

You are now a Bardic Initiate (Anruth),

....Grade, and a member of the

GORSEDD OF THE SILVER BRANCH

Appendices

(i) The Wheel of the Year - BY SHEILA BROUN

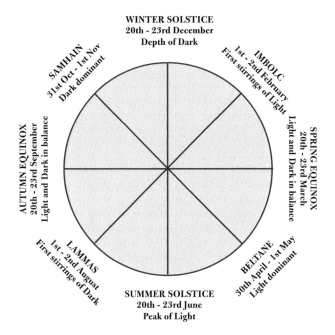

WINTER SOLSTICE
20th - 23rd December
Depth of Dark

SAMHAIN
31st Oct - 1st Nov
Dark dominant

IMBOLC
1st - 2nd February
First stirrings of Light

AUTUMN EQUINOX
20th - 23rd September
Light and Dark in balance

SPRING EQUINOX
20th - 23rd March
Light and Dark in balance

LAMMAS
1st - 2nd August
First stirrings of Dark

BELTANE
30th April - 1st May
Light dominant

SUMMER SOLSTICE
20th - 23rd June
Peak of Light

SAMHAIN: marks the beginning of winter and the Celtic New Year. A time of death and rebirth – the fruit has decayed and the seed is left, holding the pattern of next year's cycle.

WINTER SOLSTICE: celebrates the turning point of the sun at midwinter. From this time onwards, light increases. Frost spreads across the land and everything is strengthened through rest.

IMBOLC: here are the first stirrings of life. Shoots of the first flowers come through the earth. The early lambs are born, and the cockerel joins the hens and they begin to lay again.

SPRING EQUINOX: day and night are of equal length. A time to celebrate the beauty of dawn. The earth is awake and seeds germinate and burst into life. The mating season begins.

BELTANE: marks the beginning of summer. This is the merry month of May when everything blossoms. It is a time of fertility and rapid growth.

SUMMER SOLSTICE: a time of maximum light and the longest day of the year. A time to enjoy golden summer days. From this time onwards the light decreases.

LAMMAS: first fruits of harvest. A time of abundance and celebration. A time of giving thanks to the earth for our food, and of working together.

AUTUMN EQUINOX: day and night are of equal length again. The harvest is finally gathered in with thanksgiving. A time to celebrate the beauty of dusk.

(ii) Bardic Reading List

Bardic Tradition

- *Bards and Heroes*, Carl Lofmark. Llanerch 1989
- *Celtic Bards, Celtic Druids*, Robin Williamson and RJ Stewart. Sterling 1996
- *Tales of the Celtic Bards*, Claire Hamilton. O Books 2003
- *Taliesin – Shamanism and the Bardic Mysteries of Britain and Ireland*, John Matthews. Aquarian 1991: reprinted as *Taliesin – the Last Celtic Shaman*. Inner Traditions 2002
- *Taliesin Poems*, trans. Meirion Pennar. Llanerch 1988
- *The Bardic Source Book*, ed. John Matthews. Blandford 1998
- *The White Goddess*, Robert Graves. Faber & Faber 1961

Celtic World

- *Celtic Heritage*, Alwyn & Brinley Rees. Thames & Hudson 1961
- *Celtic Myths and Legends*, TW Rolleston. Senate 1994
- *Mabon and the Mysteries of Britain*, Caitlin Matthews. Arkana 1987
- *Pagan Celtic Britain*, Dr Anne Ross. Cardinal 1974
- *The Ancient Celts*, Barry Cunliffe. Penguin 1999
- *The Celts*, Nora Chadwick. Penguin 1997
- *The Encyclopaedia of Celtic Wisdom*, Caitlin & John Matthews. Element 1994

Storytelling

- *Celtic Fairy Tales*, Joseph Jacobs. Senate 1994
- *Fables of Aesop*. Penguin Classics, 1964
- *Folktales of the British Isle*, ed. Michael Foss. Book Club Associates 1977
- *From the Beast to the Blonde: on fairy tales and their tellers,* Marina Warner. Vintage 1995
- *Gods and Fighting Men*, Lady Gregory. Colin Smythe 1976
- *Greek Myths*, Robert Graves. Penguin 1960
- *Italian Folktales*, Italo Calvino. Penguin 1982
- *Kalevala, The Land of Heroes*. The Athlone Press 1985
- *Magical Tales*, RJ Stewart. Mercury Publishing 1990
- *Metamorphoses*, Ovid, trans. Mary M Innes; or Ted Hughes' version. Penguin
- *Myths and Legends of the British Isles*, Richard Barber. Boyden Press 2004
- *Myths of the Sacred Tree, Crystal Tales, Women in Celtic Myth*, etc., by Moyra Caldecott
- *Sample of British Folktales*, Katherine M Briggs. Routledge & Kegan 1977
- *Storytelling and the Art of the Imagination*, Nancy Mellon. Element 1992
- *Storytelling Scotland*, Donald Smith. Polygon 2001
- *The Brothers Grimm*, Collected Stories. Various editions
- *The Complete Illustrated Stories of Hans Christian Anderson*. Chancellor Press 1983
- *The Fisher King and The Handless Maiden*, Robert A Johnson. Harper 1993
- *The Guizer*, Alan Garner. Hamish Hamilton 1975
- *The Mabinogion*, trans. by Lady Charlotte Guest, or J Gantz. Penguin Classics, 1976
- *The Maiden King*, Robert Bly and Marion Woodman. Element 1999
- *The Norsemen*, HA Guerber. Senate 1994
- *The Odyssey; The Iliad*, Homer. Penguin Classics, various editions
- *The Penguin Book of Scottish Folktales*, ed. Neil Philip. Penguin 1995
- *The Secret Rose and other stories*, WB Yeats. Papermac 1982

- *The Uses of Enchantment,* Bruno Bettelheim. Penguin 1991
- *The Voyage of Argo*, Apollonius of Rhodes. Penguin Classics 1971
- *The Way of the Storyteller*, Ruth Sawyer. Penguin 1977
- *Tree and Leaf,* JRR Tolkien, or 'On Fairy Stories' in *The Monsters and the Critics.* H C 1997

Voice

- *The Healing Voice*, Paul Newham. Element 1999
- *The Sacred Word*, Helen Watling. Capall Bann 2002

Harp and Song

- *Earth, Air, Fire, Water: pre-Christian and pagan elements in British Songs, Rhymes, and Ballads.* Skelton & Blackwood. Arcana 1990
- *English and Scottish Ballads*, ed. Frances James Child. Dover Publications 2003
- *Music Theory and Arranging Techniques for Folk Harps,* Sylvia Woods. Woods 1984
- *One Hundred English Folk Songs: for medium voice,* ed. Cecil J Sharp. Dover, 1975
- *The Singer of Tales*, Albert B Lord. Atheneum 1976
- *The Small Harp*, Alison Kinnaird. Kinmore Music (ideal for beginners)
- *Three Ravens and Other Ballads,* Suzanne Guldimann. West of the Moon 1999
- *Where is St George?* Bob Stewart. Moonraker Press, reissued by Blandford Press 1988

Poetry

- *Beowulf*, Seamus Heaney. Faber & Faber 1999
- Blake, William, Collected Poems. Various editions
- *By Heart,* ed. Ted Hughes. Faber & Faber 1997
- *Dart*, Alice Oswald. Faber & Faber 2002
- Hardy, Thomas, Collected Poems. Various editions
- *Nursery Rhymes*, Iona & Peter Opie. OUP 1992
- *Psychic Poetry*, Jay Ramsay. Diamond Press 1990
- Raine, Kathleen, *Hollow Hills,* and others
- *Sounds Good*, ed. C Reid. Faber & Faber 1998
- *The Candle of Vision*, AE. Prism Press 1990; *Song and its Fountains*. Macmillan 1932
- *The Sleeping Lord,* David Jones. Faber & Faber 1975
- Thomas, Dylan, Collected Poems. Various editions
- Watkins, Vernon, *Selected Poems.* Faber & Faber 1967
- Yeats, William Butler, Collected Poems. Various editions

Fiction

- *A Glastonbury Romance,* John Cowper Powys. Penguin 1999
- *Bard*, Morgan Llewellyn. Century 1985
- *Beyond the Fields We Know*, Lord Dunsany. Pan 1972
- *Burning your Boats,* Collected Short Stories, Angela Carter. Vintage 1996
- *Don Quixote,* Cervantes. Wordsworth 1993
- *From the Isles of Dreams* and *Within the Hollow Hills*, ed. John Matthews. Floris 1993/4
- *Guardians of the Tall Stones*, Moyra Caldecott. Arrow 1986
- *His Dark Materials* trilogy, Philip Pullman. Scholastic Press 2001
- *Little, Big,* John Crowley, Fantasy Masterworks. Millennium 2000
- *Lord of the Rings,* JRR Tolkien. Harper Collins 1991
- *Monkey*, Wu Ch'ng-ên, trans. Arthur Waley. Penguin 1961

- *Greenmantle, Moonheart,* Charles de Lint. Pan 1982, 1990
- *Mythago Wood* cycle, Robert Holdstock. Grafton 1985, republished under Legend
- *Parzival and the Stone from Heaven*, Lindsay Clarke. Voyager 2001
- *The Circle and the Cross* (*The Wanderers* trilogy), Caiseal Mor. Earthlight 2000
- *The Dark is Rising* series, Susan Cooper. Puffin 1994
- *The God Beneath the Sea, The Golden Shadow*, Garfield & Blishen. Corgi 1975
- *The Never-Ending Story*, Michael Ende. King Penguin 1984
- *The Princess Bride*, William Goldman. Bloomsbury 1999
- *The Stone and the Flute*, Hans Bemman. Penguin 1987
- *The Storyteller*, Mario Vargas Llosa. Faber & Faber 1991
- *The Weirdstone of Brisingamen, The Stone Book Quartet*, etc., Alan Garner. Various eds.
- *Thomas the Rhymer*, Ellen Kushner. VGSF, 1992
- *Turlough*, Brian Keenan. Jonathan Cape 2000

The Ritual Year/Festivals
- *Celtic Rituals*, Alexei Kondratiev. New Celtic Publishing 1999
- *Stations of the Sun*, Ronald Hutton. Oxford University Press 1996

Environmental
- *Earth Tales From Around the World,* Michael J Caduto. Fulcrum 1997
- *EarthCare: World Folktales to Talk About*, Margaret Read MacDonald. Shoe String Press 1999
- *Of Wolves and Men,* Barry Lopez. Touchstone 1995
- *Stories that Crafted the Earth*, Adrian Beckingham. Gothic Image 2005
- *Storytelling and Ecology: reconnecting nature, community, and human soul*, Anthony Nanson. Oracle SFS 2005
- *The Passionate Fact: Storytelling in Natural History and Cultural Interpretation.* Susan Strauss Fulcrum 1996

Magazines/journals
- *Pagan Dawn*, BM 5896, London WC1N 3XX
- *Pentacle*, Editorial, 78 Hamlet Rd, Southend-on-Sea, Essex, SSI 1HH
- *Storylines*, Society for Storytelling, PO Box 2344, Reading RG6 7FG
- *Tooth and Claw*, Philip Shallcrass, British Druid Order, PO Box 1217, Devizes, Wiltshire, SN10 4XA
- *Touchstone*, Order of Bards, Ovates and Druids, PO Box 1333, Lewes, BN17 1DX

(iii) Contacts

Organisations
- Council of British Druid Orders, c/o Liz Murray, Liason Officer, BM Oakgrove, London, WC1N 3XX
- Fellowship of Isis, Lady Olivia Robertson, Fellowship of Isis, Clonegal Castle, Enniscorthy, Wexford, Eire. **www.fellowshipofisis.com**
- Gorsedd Caer Wyse (Exeter), c/o Mark Lindsey Earley, Sandside, Mill Quay, Stoke Gabriel, Totnes, TQ9 6RD.
- Gorsedd of the Bards of Caer Badon (Bath) c/o The Scribe, The Cauldron, 7 Dunsford Place, Bath, Somerset BA2 6HF.

- Order of Bards, Ovates and Druids (OBOD) PO Box 1333, Lewes, BN17 1DX
- Pagan Federation, c/o The Secretary, The Pagan Federation, BM Box 7097, London, WC1N 3XX (include SAE) Website: www.paganfed.demon.co.uk
- Society for Storytelling, PO Box 2344, Reading RG6 7FG Website: **www.sfs.org.uk**
- Tales in Trust, The Northern Centre for Storytelling, Church Stile Studio, Grasmere, Cumbria, LA22 9SW, Tel:015394 356641 **www.taffythomas.co.uk**
- The Druid Network, PO Box 3533, Whichford, Shipston-on-Stour, Warwickshire, CV36 5YB email: **office@druidnetwork.org**
- The Silver Branch Bardic Network, (see advert at back of book)

Courses

- Emerson College: 7 week 'Storytelling as a Performing Art' and other courses. Forest Row, East Sussex. Tel:01342 822 238 **www.emerson.org.uk**
- Introductory Foundation Course for Performance Storytellers (tutor: Ben Haggerty) email: **epicstory@aol.com**
- Order of Bards, Ovates and Druids, PO Box 1333, Lewes, BN17 1DX
- Storytelling with Kevan Manwaring MA. University of Bath, Claverton, Bath. 10 weeks, Oct-Dec. Bookings Tel:01225 826552
- Tales at the Edge – Wenlock Edge residential course, Tel:01939 236 626
- The Silver Branch Bardic Network – various Bardic Mysteries workshops (ibid)

Festivals and Camps

- Awen Camp, July, Welsh Borders, FFI: **www.druidnetwork.org**
- Bardic Festival of Bath, weekend before Winter Solstice – centred around the annual competition for the Bardic Chair of Caer Badon. Email: **bard@tallyessin.com**
- Beyond the Border International Storytelling Festival, early July, St. Donat's Castle, South Wales. Box office 01446 799 100 **www.beyondtheborder.com** email: **boxoffice@beyondtheborder.com**
- Cape Clear International Storytelling Festival, Ireland, first weekend in September. **www.indigo.ie/-stories/** email: **stories@indigo.ie** Tel:00:353(0)28 39116
- Festival at the Edge, late July, Wenlock Edge, Shropshire. Tel:01939 236 626. **www.festivalattheedge.org** Email: **info@festivalattheedge.org**
- Lammas Games, First Saturday in August, Braziers Park Wallingford, Oxfordshire, The Druid Network (see advert for Eisteddfod at back)
- Samhain Salutation, end of October – annual competition for the Bardic Chair of the Avalon Marshes. Year round programme of tales. Peat Moors Centre, Shapwick Rd, Westhay, Somerset, Tel:01458 860 697
- Sting in the Tale, East Dorset Storytelling Festival, FFI: Tel:01202 639 012
- The Linking of the Chain: The Lakeland Festival of Storytelling, third weekend of September, Tales in Trust, Tel:015394 35641
- West Country Storytelling Festival, late Aug, Hood Manor, Dartington, Devon Tel:01803 863 790 email: **info@weststoryfest.co.uk**

Websites

- Bardic Chair of Caer Badon: **www.bardofbath.freeservers.com**
- British Druid Order: **www.britishdruidorder.co.uk**
- Caer Feddwyd, a resource for those working within or researching the polytheist Brythonic traditions and the Bardic lore: **http://homepage.ntl.com** – **Caer Feddwyd**

- Dreampower (RJ Stewart site): **www.dreampower.com**
- Fire Springs Storytelling Company: **www.firesprings.co.uk**
- Gothic Image Publications: **www.gothicimage.co.uk**
- Gorseth Ynys Witrin (Bardic Council of Glastonbury): **www.bardic.org**
- Gorseth Kernow (Organisation promoting Cornish culture): **www.gorsethkernow.org**
- Hallowquest (John and Caitlin Matthews site): **www.hallowquest.org.uk**
- Living Myths (harper and author Claire Hamilton's site): **www.livingmyths.org.uk**
- Mythstories (Storytelling Museum, Lake District): **www.mythstories.com**
- National Eisteddfod of Wales: **www.eisteddfod.org.uk**
- Order of Bards, Ovates and Druids: **www.obod.co.uk**
- Robin Williamson, master harper and storyteller: **www.pigswhiskermusic.com**
- Tallyessin, 3rd Bard of Bath (author site): **www.tallyessin.com**
- The Clarsach Society: **www.clarsachsociety.co.uk**
- The Druid Network: **www.druidnetwork.org**
- The Scottish Storytelling Centre, Netherbow, Edinburgh: **www.scottishstorytellingcentre.co.uk**
- The Silver Branch Bardic Network **Yahoo! Group: the-silver-branch**
- Helen Moore, eco-poet: **www.natures-words.co.uk**
- Storytelling-and-Listener: **storyteller-and-listener.blog-city.com**

(iv) A Brief Bardic Glossary

Anruth a trainee bardic initiate.

Awen Inspiration, literally 'flowing spirit'. Called the 'Holy Spirit of Druidry' (Shallcrass).

Awenyddion Welsh, pl. An 'inspired one'; speaker of tongues and seer, akin to an Ovate.

Bard a poet, storyteller, musician, lore keeper, teacher, remembrancer of the tribe — of 12 years experience and training. A winner of a Bardic Chair.

Bardic Chair annual tide awarded to the most proficient poet, singer &/or storyteller of a certain region, either through competition or claim (following a public declaration a year and day prior). Always fixed to a physical location — normally an ancient site, ie: Solsbury Hill — hence, the Bardic Chair of Caer Badon. Sometimes an actual chair and robes are awarded (as in Bath). The Bard must perform a public role for their time in office, promoting the Bardic Tradition, and encouraging entrants in the following year's heat.

Brighid Celtic Goddess of poetry, healing and smithcraft, associated with Imbolc.

Caer Welsh n. Fort, but more loosely any ancient settlement/gathering place, ie: Caer Myrddin/Camarthen. Often the site of the Gorsedd and thus usually associated with a Bardic Chair.

Cauldron vessel of inspiration, healing, plenty, rebirth. The Proto-Grail. The womb of the Goddess. Heroes are initiated by searching for it, drinking from it or winning it.

Ceridwen the Crooked One, the Hag Goddess of Initiation and Inspiration, who cooks the Potion of Inspiration for Afagddu. She chases Gwion Bach through various shape-changes until finally eating him and giving birth to him as Taliesin, the Twice-born.

Chief Bard head of an Eisteddfod, or Gorsedd, usually elected from peers.

Cyfaredd n. Welsh. Enchantment

Cyfarwydd n. Welsh. Storyteller.

Dark Speech language of Bardic initiates and Druids.

Druid oak Priest/ess of the Celts, and modern day followers of druidry. MCs/law-makers/shapechangers/magicians.

Eisteddfod (pl. Eisteddfodau) Literally 'a seated session' or gathering. A festival of the Bardic Arts often with competitions for the Bardic Chair in different fields, eg: singing, poetry, harp.

Filidh pl. (Fili: singular) Irish equivalent of the Welsh Bard.

Gorsedd (pl. Gorseddau) Literally 'high seat'. Traditionally a sacred or historical mound symbolizing the spiritual heart of an Eisteddfod, eg: Gorsedd Arbeth, or Primrose Hill.

Gramarye magical language and the magic of language.

Imbas Irish n. Inspiration, akin to Awen.

Imbolc from the Gaelic 'oi melc' (ewe's milk). Eve of February. The poet's festival, dedicated to Brighid. With the first thaw Spring begins, snowdrops appear and lambs are born.

Imus magical poetic quality.

Ogham Celtic tree alphabet, aka 'Beth-Luis-Nion' after the first three letters; birch, rowan, ash. Called the Secret Language of Poets. A sign language and runic script. Named after Ogma.

Ogma Celtic God of eloquence, who acquired the Ogham from the Wheel of Taranis, in an act of self-sacrifice similar to Odin on the World-Tree. It is said a chain links listeners' ears to his tongue, so spell-binding was his speech. Epithets: Sun-face; Honey-tongued; the Strong.

Ollamh senior poet — a doctor of verse. A Bard of 20 years training and renowned merit.

Ovate Sooth-sayer and natural philosopher. One of the 3 equal grades or paths of Druidry, along with the Bard and the Druid. The Vatic path is associated in modern practice with the healing arts and environmental issues.

Penbeirdd head, or chief bard, as in Pendragon. An acknowledged master. Title used exclusively for Taliesin. In the context of the Way of Awen, a lifetime's achievement award.

Salmon the 'poet's fish', because it is said to eat from the hazel nuts which fall into the mythical Well of Segais at the bottom of the sea, and thus embodies deep wisdom.

Seanachie Irish n. Storyteller.

Silver Branch sign of the poet's office. Key to the Otherworld. Features in many myths.

Taliesin Primary Chief Bard of Albion. 6th Century Welsh bard, and semi-mythic recipient of Ceridwen's Potion of Inspiration. His name means 'Radiant or Shining Brow'.

The Three Illuminations divinatory methods of eye, mouth and hand: *Imbas Forosnai* (light of foresight); *Teinm Laida* (composition by song) and *Dichetal do Chennaib* (finger incantation).

The Tongue that Cannot Lie the gift of prophecy, which Thomas of Ercildoune won from the Queen of Elfland. His 13th Century poems contain his prophecies.

Twice-Born an initiate, who has been reborn into a new and deeper awareness.

Way of Awen the path of the Bard living in harmony with Spirit and All That Is.

(v) The Shining Word

'He who gives no light will never be a star'

MAKE YOUR PERFORMANCE SHINE WITH THIS 5-POINT METHOD

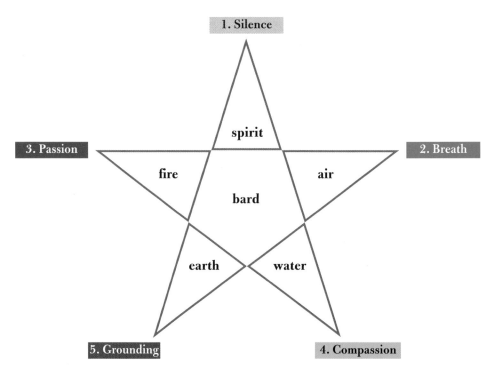

1 **Silence.** Listen to your heart, to the Earth, to Spirit, to the Universe. What does it want you to say? Meditate. Invoke the Awen and ask for inspiration. Consider the Endless Sound: the silence between the words.

2 **Breath.** Breathe from below (the belly). Warm-up the vocal chords with voice exercises, eg: humming, toning, chanting. Deep breaths to relax and to keep your lungs filled. Speak slowly and clearly. Project.

3 **Fire in the Heart.** Speak from the heart and say it loud and proud, with passion, with sincerity, with energy, but do not 'scorch' – temper with…

4 **Ripples in the pond.** After passion comes compassion. Be sensitive to your audience, your words and yourself. Imagine dropping pebbles in a pond with your words – let each one have its impact. Be aware of the energy you are raising/atmosphere you are creating.

5 **Bringing it down to earth.** Make sure your message reaches home by manifesting it fully. Use body language, movement, props, costume, drums. Establish and use the space. Use humour and spontaneity. Take the audience on a magical healing journey there and back again.

(vi) British and Irish Gods and Goddesses

This is just one pantheon you can work with, although it is also wise to work with the tutelary spirits of the country in which you are residing. So, when in Rome, use Roman Gods – in Britain, use British ones (although some indeed have been imported through waves of invasions and migration, eg: Mithras or Orpheus). Gauge what resonates in a particular locality, ie: if there was a Roman Temple there, then it would be legitimate to work with one of its deities, (and some are composites of native and alien gods, ie: Sulis-Minerva); the same goes with Mithraic, Nordic, Saxon, Christian, Jewish, Hindu, Sikh, Afro-Caribbean and Sufi pantheons and cosmologies. I haven't included more details because I think it is important to research them yourselves: find their sites, spend some time there, meditate, visualise, invoke and give voice to – always in a respectful way. Remember, these are powerful beings, work with and honour them wisely.

Andraste	Gog/Magog	Nuada
Arianrhod	Gwydion	Nodens
Badb	Gwynn ap Nudd	Oengus Mac Og
Balor of the Baleful Eye	Jack-in-the-Green	Ogmios
Crom Cruach	Lleu Llaw Gyffes	Ossian
Bel	Lugh/Lamfhada/	Olwen
Bladud	Samildanach	Rhiannon
Blodeuwedd	Mabon	Robin Goodfellow
Boann	Mab/Madb/Maeve	Scathach
Bran	Manannan Mac Lir	Sulis
Brighid	Manawydan	Tailtiu
Cailleach	Merlin	Taranis
Ceridwen	Modron	Twrch Trwyth
Cernunnos (Herne)	Morgan le Fay	Washer at the Ford
Cucullati	Morrigan	Wild Herdsman
Dagda	Nemetona	Wayland
Danu, Dana	Niamh	
Elen of the Ways	Nimue	Find and add your own…

A good place to start would be John & Caitlin Matthews' *British and Irish Mythology*, Diamon Books, 1995; and RJ Stewart's *Celtic Gods and Goddesses*, Blandford 1990.

(vii) Eco-Bardic Principles

DEFINITION:

Ecobardic– an evolving artistic approach that recognises the centrality, in our time, of the relationship between humankind and the global ecosystem and harnesses certain qualities of ancient and modern Bardic art: the inspiration of Nature, acknowledging the existence of the spiritual, making potent political comment, remembrance of the past, respectful engagement with the audience, and rigorous training and craftsmanship.

Anthony Nanson, *Storytelling & Ecology*. Papyrus, 2005

Ecological Awareness – fostering a positive sense of Earth stewardship; of humanity's impact upon the planet, its finite resources, the fragility of its ecosystems, the connectedness of Life's Web, its cycles, riches and lessons.

Creative Responsibility – being aware of the effect and impact of what we create – the messages we send through our work, deeds and words. Acting with awareness. Using our creativity for healing the planet and its peoples. Bringing peace, wisdom and beauty into the world. Ben Okri says our stories should be "oxygenated with a sense of responsibility".

Non-competitive Co-operation – as opposed to 'survival of the fittest'. Sharing information, opportunities and resources.

Mutual Empowerment – giving one another permission to fulfil one's potential, and the freedom to fail.

The Primacy of the Imagination – as a tool for social change, a midwife of the Divine, for emancipation of Spirit, and for re-enchanting the world.

Honouring the Past – respect what has gone before, but innovate Tradition where necessary for the needs of the present.

Strength in Diversity – inclusiveness and encouraging fresh ideas.

Respect – for the material (stories, songs, poems) we use, the peoples and places that inspire us, and those who have gone before us.

The Ennobled Individual – within the web of community and ecosystem. Allowing people to shine, to find and fulfil their 'role' in the world.

Honour and Humility – in all things.

A Sense of Awe and Wonder – what Keats called 'Negative Capability': "…that is, when man is capable of being in uncertainties, mysteries, doubts, without any irritable reaching after fact and reason" (from a letter from John Keats to his brother, 1817). A restoration of the Sublime in Nature, in human nature.

Devised by Fire Springs (Hartsiotis, Manwaring, Metcalfe, Nanson, Selby) 2005.
For further elaboration and information on Eco-Bardic shows: **www.firesprings.co.uk**

(viii) Eisteddfod

In the contest, everything is revealed
Taliesin

The Eisteddfod, (pronounced: eye-steth-fod) a Welsh word meaning literally 'a sitting, or session', is at the heart of the Bardic path. It is the most public expression of the skill of the Bard, where they compete with peers and win renown. Philip Shallcrass, Chief of the British Druid Order, describes them as: "meetings of professional poets and musicians, concerned with maintaining the standards of their craft" (from document on the revival of the British Bardic Chairs, Council of British Druid Orders 1992). It is a way of encouraging and rewarding excellence. Although a Bard should avoid rivalry, friendly sportsmen-like competitiveness within the parameters of the Eisteddfod can foster camaraderie, community and development of the craft.

The modern Welsh Eisteddfod is a vast affair, with National and International versions, and has been called the 'largest cultural festival in Europe'. It has been going annually since 1861, but the first recorded Eisteddfod was held over Christmas 1176 at Cardigan Castle, when Bardic Chairs were awarded to the best poet and musician. However, there is a custom which predates it. The 10th Century Welsh King Hywel Dda's Law Code states: "a seat at court in the Prince's Hall was always reserved for the chief poet who was elected to the position by means of a poetic contest". And, to this day, the idea of the Bardic Chair has stuck. Shallcrass explains further: "The Bardic Chair is both an honour awarded for outstanding ability in the Bardic arts and an actual chair given as a trophy in token of the honour". The holder of a Bardic Chair has the title of *Cadeirfardd*, or Chaired Bard, from the Welsh *Cadeir*, a 'Chair of Honour'. In the modern Welsh Eisteddfod the Bardic Chair is awarded to a poet excelling in metrical verse, while a Bardic Crown is awarded for composition in freer verse.

Yet the Bardic Chair need not be an actual chair. In 1637 John Jones records an Eisteddfod where a silver harp was awarded to the best musician, a silver tongue to the best singer, and a silver chair for the best bard – exalted times! – and in the Twenty-First Century the Lammas Games Eisteddfod, organised by the Druid Network, offers the Spear of Lugh to the winner, who becomes spear-holder for a year and a day. Thus, the Bardic Chair can be a moveable feast. And Shallcrass argues that the Chair need not be fixed to a specific location. He suggests they are, in fact: "...an honour bestowed on an individual. In the Period of the Princes, they entitled the individual to a place of honour in the Prince's court, but when the court moved, the Bard and the place of honour moved too". This may have been so in medieval times, yet this contradicts the central concept of the Eisteddfod: its spiritual heart is the Gorsedd, and the Gorsedd, by definition (a high seat or mound) is traditionally attached to a particular location. The ancient list of **British Bardic Chairs** (see Appendices X) gives specific locations, nearly all of which are hill-forts or ancient sites: certainly, sacred hills are the common factor. It is essential to maintain this connection with the Earth and make a commitment to a particular location, with its genius locus, heritage, rare species, etc. – what Common Ground call 'local distinctiveness'. By creating new Bardic Chairs, associated with a Site of Special Scientific Interest, or an Area of Outstanding Natural Beauty, we, as Bards, can help to preserve, promote and celebrate a place – by re-enchanting it with our words and maintaining it with our deeds (eg: tree-planting, litter-picking, restoring springs).

Other customs have accrued around the Eisteddfod, many of them inventions of Iolo Morgannwg, such as the robe colour scheme (blue, green and white were first worn officially in 1894) and use of a sword. However, these can be imbued with meaning in a modern context, however spurious their origin. Storyteller Gordon MacLellan describes: "the Bards in blue, [as] symbolic of celestial love", which is a good enough reason, but it is intriguing to note that blue is also the colour of the Throat Chakra, fundamental for a Bard in 'traditional' Eisteddfodau. No weapons were allowed to be drawn, thus the legacy of the ritual of the half-sheaved sword, symbolic of Peace. In a world torn by conflict, asking for peace, and swearing to stand 'heart to heart, and hand in hand' (The Gorsedd Prayer, recited for the first time in 1855) is more significant and relevant than ever.

So, although the Eisteddfod has ancient roots, the form we know it in today has relevant recent origins. The first Eisteddfod of the modern era was held at Corwen in Wales in 1789, and it was not until 1928 that the Cornish Eisteddfod, Gorseth Kernow, was established at Boscawen-Ûn stone circle. So the idea of a revival of the Bardic Chairs of Britain is not unprecedented and should not be seen as invalid or separate from the Welsh, Breton and Cornish initiatives. Colin Murray, of the Golden Section Order, first mooted the idea in the Seventies. Liz Murray, his widow, proposed it to the Council of British Druid Orders in 1991. The following year the council sent a petition to the Queen requesting the establishing of an annual English Eisteddfod at Stonehenge (mirroring the Semi-National Eisteddfod held at Torquay in 1922). However visionary (and, to be realistic, unlikely in the present climate with its dearth of the imagination) this grand plan is, the pathway to it is just as, if not more, important. The re-establishment of the ancient Bardic Chairs of England would provide the necessary stepping stones to this ultimate goal – although they are just as valid and worthy of initiating in their own right. The idea is that each Gorsedd selects an annual Chaired Bard, and one day – when the English Eisteddfod is established – the Chaired Bards of each region could compete for the coveted title of Primary Chief Bard of Logres. And, who knows, maybe one day all of the Gorseddau of the British Isles (Lesser and Greater Britain) will join together in competition and fellowship, realising that they are all part of the same Tradition and branches of the same tree.

Bardic Awards, The Circus, Bath 2005.

(ix) Setting up and Running a Bardic Chair

1   Check the **list of Bardic Chairs** to see if there is one in your area and whether it is active or not. Check with the British Council of Druid Orders for updates, and to notify them of your intent: this is not just asking permission (although it is respectful to acknowledge the groundwork of the Council) but also so that any Bardic Chair can be registered and monitored. If a Bardic Chair has already been set up in your town or city, then you should not attempt to establish a rival one, for such infighting is self-defeating to pagans in general and Druids in particular. Either join forces and lend your energy and good will to the established Chair, or look elsewhere. If your area is not on the list, then you could try to establish a new one (with approval from the Druid Council) but you need to ensure you have the following: a Gorsedd Mound (this could be an ancient monument such as a barrow, stone circle or hill fort, or a decent grove or public space), a Druid willing to be MC, judges, willing entrants, and a groundswell of local support.

Tim Sebastian, Arch-Druid of the Secular Order of Druids, and founder of the Bardic Chair of Caer Badon.

2   Choose a date for the Eisteddfod. A year and a day before your proposed contest, publicly declare your intent in the location where it is to happen. Have witnesses present and ideally a local newspaper photographer. Send a press release to the media announcing it. Make the occasion ceremonial: wear robes, cast a circle, invoke the Awen, speak the Gorsedd prayer and declare the resurrection of or creation of the Bardic Chair. State that a contest will be held a year and a day hence in that place open to poets, storytellers and singers in the area: if any wish to challenge you to the right to be Holder of the Bardic Chair to come forward and make themselves known, otherwise for the Chair to go to you. Mention that a theme will be set and further details, including conditions of entry and **Roles and Responsibilities of the Bard**, to be publicised nearer the time. Toast the 'birth' of your Bardic Chair.

3   Monitor media reaction and be prepared for response from the public having made your details known as the contact for the contest. You may want to set up a PO Box or new email to ensure your privacy is maintained.

4   Promote the idea of the Bardic Chair at every opportunity. Be prepared to give talks about it to raise its profile (do your research – if necessary ask the Druid Council, the Druid Network or the Silver Branch Bardic Network for support and guidance). You may wish to give examples of Bardic skills in public performance to illustrate what a Bard is and does. You could organise a talk by someone with experience or knowledge of the Bardic Tradition/Bardic Chairs.

5   Halfway through the year set the theme and the deadline, find good judges (Druids, academics, experienced storytellers, poets, teachers, actors or writers) and draft the Conditions of Entry (see example below) and publicise the contest through flyers and posters in all public places. Send another press release to the local media. Be willing to give interviews. Spread the word.

6   Hopefully you will now start to get some entries in. If the response is poor, then re-advertise. All you need are two entries (yourself and another) for a contest; otherwise the Chair goes to you (but only if you have followed the necessary steps in registering, announcing and promoting it publicly). Of course, the more the merrier. Even just half a dozen entries will make an exciting contest.

7   Book a suitable venue (ie: community hall) and design posters and flyers to advertise the 'Battle of the Bards' – the first contest for the Bardic Chair of your area. If you get no entries then, fair's fair, you will be announced the Holder of the Bardic Chair for that year. Sometimes this is necessary just to get the ball rolling. The main thing is that it's done publicly and democratically.

8   Send any entries to the judges in advance. The exact criteria is up to you, but you should be judging the contest on the content, the performance and the audience response at least, although you may want to include a 200 word statement of intent as well, in which the contestant sets out their plans if they were to win the Chair.

9   The big night has arrived. Wear your finest Bardic regalia. Have friends help you with the door, with serving drinks, with stewarding and security. All the contestants and judges should be there. Make sure you have a photographer on hand – invite the local press and any VIPs you can persuade – make it a glitzy occasion. Bardic Contests are often tense and exciting. Prepare the space, ask for protection (cast a circle or summon threshold guardians), raise the Awen, and shine!

10   The judges must decide who is the worthy winner of the Chair – often a difficult decision. Get the MC (Chief Druid or Bard) to announce it. Let the winner step forward and receive their prize, either symbolically (a scroll will suffice) or an actual chair. Thank everyone involved and congratulate all who entered. Encourage them to re-enter next year and remind them they are now part of the Gorsedd of the Chair. Celebrate!

Jordan Ashley-Hill, 9th Bard of Bath, reading winning poem at the annual contest for the Bardic Chair of Caer Badon.

(x) British Bardic Chairs

"A list of thirty one sites which…represented at one time the seats of the chief Druids of Britain, centres of Druidic learning, places of worship, Bardic colleges, and places of public assembly, each of which has as associated Gorsedd mound."

Philip Shallcrass, based upon Rev RW Morgan's list of supposed Gorsedd sites in his book *British Cymry* (18th Century, unknown source). *Active* sites as of Spring 2006.

SEATS OF THE THREE ARCH-DRUIDS OF BRITAIN

Caer Troia –	London (aka New Troy/Trinovantum): Primrose Hill*, Parliament Hill, Penton, the White Mount (Tower of London), Tothill
Caer Evroe –	York
Caer Leon –	Caerleon (possible site of King Arthur's Round Table)
	*Primrose Hill, Gorsedd of the Bards of Britain, 1792, Iolo Morgannwg.

SEATS OF THE CHIEF DRUIDS OF BRITAIN

Caer Badon –	Bath *active*
Caer Caint –	Canterbury
Caer Cei –	Chichester
Caer Ceiont –	Caernavon
Caer Ceri –	Cirencester
Caer Coel –	Colchester
Caer Don –	Doncaster
Caer Dur –	Dorchester
Caer Glou –	Gloucester
Caer Gorangon –	Worcester
Caer Gourie –	Warwick
Caer Gwrgan –	Cambridge
Caer Leil –	Carlisle
Caerleon ar Dwy –	Chester
Caer Lear –	Leicester
Caer Lleyn –	Lincoln
Caer Membre (or **Caer Bosca**) – Oxford	
Caer Meini –	Manchester
Caer Merddyn –	Carmarthen
Caer Muncip –	St Albans
Caer Odor –	Bristol *active*
Caer Peris –	Porchester
Caer Sallwg –	Old Sarum
Caer Segont –	Silchester
Caer Urnach –	Wroxeter
Caer Wydr –	Glastonbury *active*
Caer Wyse –	Exeter *active*
Caer Wyn –	Winchester *active*

MODERN (20TH CENTURY) REVIVALS:

Boscawen-Ûn –   Cornwall (Gorseth Kernow)
Côr Gawr –   Stonehenge
Caer Abiri –   Avebury

(xi) Case Study of a Modern Bardic Chair:
GORSEDD OF THE BARDS OF CAER BADON

Gorsedd of the Bards of Caer Badon at
Rocks East Woodland.

The Bardic Chair of Caer Badon (Bath) was resurrected from the ancient list of the Bardic Chairs of Britain by Tim Sebastian, Arch-Druid of the Secular Order of Druids in 1996 when he announced his intent to claim the chair at a midsummer ceremony attended by King Arthur Pendragon, among others. After a year and a day no one had come forward to challenge Tim and so he became the first chaired Bard of Bath.

Since then, there have been ten chaired Bards, among them Tallyessin (Kevan Manwaring) who was chosen in the first competition resulting from more than one contender coming forward. His epic poem *Spring Fall: the story of Sulis and Bladud of Bath* was deemed the winner by four top academic judges (Ronald Hutton, Graham Harvey, Michael York and Marion Bowman). That year (1998) also saw the first Bardic Festival of Bath, launched on William Blake's birthday (November 28th) and lasting for three weeks up to the winter solstice when the annual Eisteddfod and chairing of the Bard takes place. The winner receives a beautiful carved chair and robe for a year and a day.

The Chaired Bard's role is to promote the Bardic Tradition through talks and performances, and set the theme for the next year's competition. Each Chaired Bard has added his or her own contribution to the Bardic Chair, eg: a residency, a website, a poetry night, short films, etc. – raising the profile of the Chair and reaching out to a different section of the community.

So far, the Chaired Bards have been young and old, male and female, black and white – performers whose style and medium varies from the traditional to the contemporary: storyteller to pop poet, writer to singer-songwriter. The competition is open to any resident of the Bath and North East Somerset area.

In 2000 a Millennium Grove was planted at a local woodland based upon the Celtic Tree Alphabet and this has served as the Gorsedd grove ever since, although many ceremonies take place in the heart of the city of Bath, in The Circus – the circular urban temple designed by Georgian Druid-architect, John Wood the Elder.

The Gorsedd also has a Vatic Chair, which is held for three years, to promote the healing and divinatory arts; and a Druidic Chair, lasting seven years. The Bardic Chair receives regular coverage in the local press and the annual 'Battle of the Bards' and subsequent winner are widely publicised. Over the years the Gorsedd has campaigned for the restoration of local heritage, promoted green issues, cross-cultural links (as in the 'Coming Together' Druid-Maori Camp in 2004) and equal access to the arts. All are welcome to attend the free monthly Bardic circle, run by Tallyessin and other local Bards, upstairs at The Raven pub on Queen St, Third Monday of the Month, 8pm – where stories, poems and songs are shared (performed from memory, not read). Future plans include *The Book of the Bardic Chair* and a Young Bard of Bath competition. The website is: **www.bardofbath.freeservers.com**

(xii) The Role of the Chaired Bard

EXAMPLE CRITERIA
BY THE GORSEDD OF BARDS OF CAER BADON (BATH)

1   The winner of the Bardic Chair of Caer Badon (BCCB), having been awarded the title after an open competition at midwinter, will receive the actual Chair and Robes – these they will keep along with the title for a year and a day, or until the next Bardic Chair finals, whichever comes sooner. The Chaired Bard will pledge to take due care of the Chair and Robes, maintaining them (ie: dry cleaning, dusting) as necessary, to return them in a pristine state at the next award ceremony.

2   The Chaired Bard is responsible for choosing an appropriate theme for the next year's contest (to be held on the weekend immediately prior to the winter solstice). This theme and the criteria of the competition is to be announced publicly (by Press Release, flyer, poster, interview, etc.) by no later than September 21st. If the Bard is unable to do so for any reason the Gorsedd will take the initiative. The Gorsedd has the right to alter or dismiss any unsuitable theme.

3   The Chaired Bard is obliged to promote the Bardic Tradition (basically, any form of spoken word performance) throughout their year in office whenever possible by performances, talks, writings, and by example.

4   The Chaired Bard is entitled to use their award to promote themselves, as long as they acknowledge where it originates (in the Celtic Tradition, generally; and in particular, the Bardic Chair of Caer Badon established by Tim Sebastian in 1996, under the auspices of the Council of British Druid Orders).

5   The Chaired Bard is to, where possible, promote the Celtic Tradition and its wisdom. This does not cancel out their own – in fact, different manifestations of the Bardic Tradition are encouraged, but it is important to remember the context of the Bardic Chair movement.

6 All Bardic Chairs are connected with a specific geographical location. The Gorsedd (high mound) is the spiritual heart of the Eisteddfod (the festival) and is always associated with a particular hill or ancient monument. In Bath the Gorsedd is linked with both Solsbury Hill (Caer Badon itself), and The Circus. Thus, an awareness of this is important, and a celebration of Bath's landscape and heritage is encouraged.

7 All faiths and paths are welcome to enter the Bardic Chair competition, but the Chair must not be used as a platform for proselytising, or for propagating sexism, religious or racial hatred of any kind. In fact, a message of tolerance, peace and inclusiveness is actively encouraged.

8 The Chaired Bard is responsible for making the arrangements for the annual contest, including securing a venue, publicity, invites and programme. Illness, accident, bereavement or 'acts of God' exempt the bard from any or all of the above obligations, but the Gorsedd must be notified and given explanation.

9 The Chaired Bard must select a suitable panel of judges, which will comprise the following: the Chaired Bard, two experts in their field (ie: a poet and a storyteller) and the holder of the Druid Chair. The judges will be vetted by the Gorsedd. In the event of a draw, or an inability to reach a decision, the holder of the Druid Chair (currently Tim Sebastian) will have the casting vote.

10 The conditions of entry for the Bardic Chair competition will be clearly stated on the publicity.

(xiii) Running a Bardic Circle

Anthony Nanson, founder of the Bath Storytelling Circle,
setting imaginations alight. Courtesy of *The Bath Chronicle*.

A regular showcase is a great means of practising and sharing material, socialising with fellow wordsmiths, and promoting the Bardic Tradition in an inclusive, accessible, and enjoyable way. You could do this publicly or privately. If you would rather start small, then why not hold a private 'Gorsedd' around your house with a small group of Bardic friends to begin with? If you feel there is enough potential for a public Circle in your community, (ie: a 'critical mass' of performers – a dozen would be enough, and sometimes such initiatives can draw people out of the woodwork) then use the following guidelines:

- Find a suitable venue, such as a back room or upstairs of a pub. Make sure it is pleasant, centrally situated, ideally disabled accessible and smoke-free, with little or no noise pollution, eg: juke box, TV sports, etc.
- Negotiate with management for the best deal, ie: free hire, provided punters buy drinks.
- Come up with a name and identity that captures the spirit of what you are trying to achieve. It can be quirky (ie: Flying Pigs storytellers) as long as the general public know what it is at a glance. Sometimes, simplicity is best, ie: Bath Storytelling Circle.
- Advertise: design a poster and flyer, print and distribute (try local shops, libraries, colleges, bookstores, cafés, friendly pubs, Tourist Information Centres, hostels and hotels).
- Send a press release to the local media announcing the launch. Make sure you get across that the Circle is for adults and that you don't have to perform – just come, listen and enjoy.
- Link up with the Society for Storytelling – great for sharing publicity and information. Get listed in their Story Diary. Why not time the launch with National Storytelling Week for maximum impact (late January-early February)? It is always best to launch in Autumn or Winter, as in Summer numbers tend to be affected by the holidays.
- Prepare a couple of stories, songs, poems, riddles, jokes or anecdotes, to set the tone and fill in the gaps between contributors.
- Create a circular seating arrangement if possible: no stage or 'stars', equal and informal.
- If safe, use nitelites or candles to create an atmosphere – place in the centre of the circle if possible to symbolise 'hearth'.
- Before you commence take a list of willing contributors at the beginning: name of teller; story, song or poem; overall mood (eg: comic or spooky), and estimated duration (5-10 minutes max. is best).
- Remind people that you encourage contributions to be performed, not read – to preserve the Oral Bardic Tradition.
- Start off with any housekeeping, eg: toilets, fire exit, format. Make people welcome.
- Tell a story, song or poem to set the mood, ideally a seasonal or topical one. Keep it light.
- Pick next teller, either at random, or select, if you think they will follow well. For variety, alternate: male/female, story/song/poem, comic/serious, short/long. Keep the mood up and the pace sharp. Another way is to ask tellers to pitch in if inspired, keeping the thread.
- Break at half time, perhaps with any announcements (other arts events, courses, etc.) before or after interval.
- Encourage people to put their names on the mailing list. Set up an email group to keep people notified. Social events may spiral out of the Circle, but respect people's privacy and do not share personal details without permission.
- If the Circle develops and is going well, why not organise a showcase of local talent (perhaps a group of the best tellers) during a local festival. You may want to give your group a name, eg: Off the Wall Storytellers, or Fire Springs. Such events will raise awareness about the Bardic Circle. Always encourage new people to come. Get regulars to spread the word and bring a friend. Share the Awen around.

(xiv) The Dialogue of the Two Sages
VERSION BY ROBIN WILLIAMSON

Celtic Beard-pullers. Adapted by George Bain.

About the time of Christ, when the king of Ulster was Conchobhar mac Nessa, Adna the Ollamh of Ulster died. His place was bestowed on the poet Fercheirtne, whose experience and mastery made him a more than likely candidate. But Adna's son Nede, being away to study in Scotland and unaware of Fercheirtne's appointment, learned of his father's death from the sound of the sea waves as he strolled the shore. He returned at once to Emhain Macha, capital town of Ulster, to take his father's place. The first man he met on entering the halls of Conchobhar was Bricriu, a man who loved to stir up conflict whenever he could. Bricriu undertook to bestow the ollamh position on Nede, accepting in return a valuable gift, remarking only that Nede as a beardless youth was hardly suitable. Nede plucked a tuft of grass and, uttering a verse of power, placed it against his chin, where it at once took on the appearance of a luxuriant beard. And Nede seated himself in the ollamh seat and about him he wrapped the robe of three colours: the middle part of it many bright feathers of birds, the lower part of it white bronze in colour, the upper part of it bright gold.

Now chuckling to himself, Bricriu set out to tell Fercheirtne how Nede had stolen his ollamhship, and Fercheirtne, in a fury, set out for Conchobhar's palace to deal with the interloper. But when he beheld the youth who sat in his chair, Fercheirtne was taken aback by his poise, and addressed Nede with some civility stating, however, that he was occupying the chair awarded to Fercheirtne. Nede replied with equal politeness and formality pointing out Bricriu's malicious jest, but nevertheless requesting that Fercheirtne should satisfy himself that the boy who had unwittingly usurped an already given position was, in fact, most worthy to be Ollamh of Ulster. In establishing this, Fercheirtne addressed Nede thus, as the bards relate:

A question, O child of education
where do you come from?

to which Nede replied.
    not hard to answer
    from a wise man's heel
    from a confluence of wisdoms
    from perfection of goodness
    from brightness of sunrise from poetry's hazels
    from splendour's circuits
    from that state where truth's worth is measured
    from that measure where truth is realized
    from that reality where lies are vanquished
    from where all colours are seen
    from where all art is reborn

and you, my elder, where do you come from?

to which Fercheirtne replied:
    not hard to answer
    from the width of the pillars of the age
    from the fill of the rivers of Leinster
    from the length of the hall of the wife of Nechtan
    from the reach of the arm of the wife of Nuadu
    from the extent of the country of the sun
    from the height of the mansions of the moon
    from the stretch of a babe's umbilical cord

a question, o youth of instruction what is your name?

to which Nede replied:
    not hard to answer -
    minuscule and muckle I am
    dazzling and highly hard
    entitle me Fire's flame
    name me Fire of Word
    or Noise of Knowingness
    or Fountain of Riches
    or Sword of Canticles
    or Ardent Verity of Genius

and you, my elder, what is your name?

to which Fercheirtne replied:
    not hard to answer
    of seers most sure
    I am chief revealer
    of that which is uttered
    and that which is asked
    Inquiry of the Curious

Weft of Deftness
Creel of Verse am I
and Abundance of the Sea

a question, o young man of learning, what art do you practise?

to which Nede replied:

not hard to answer
I bring blush to face
and spirit to flesh
I practise fear's erasure
and tumescence of impudence
metre's nurture
honour's venture
and wisdom's wooing
I shape beauty to human mouths
give wings to insight
I make naked the word
in small space I have foregathered
the cattle of cognizance
the stream of science
the totality of teaching
the captivation of kings
and the legacy of legend

And you my elder, what art do you practise?

to which Fercheirtne replied:

not hard to answer
sifting of streams for gold of wisdom
lulling of hearts from the fires of anger
captaincy of words
excellency of skill
putting feathers in kings' pillows
I have acquired a thirst that would drain the Boyne
I am a maker of shields and wounds
a slicer of pure air
an architect of thought
I can say much with few words
I can sing the long miles of great heroes' lives
I am a jeweller of the heart

a question, O young exalted man, what are your tasks?

to which Nede replied:

not hard to answer
to cross life to the mountain of youth
to rise to the hunting of age
to follow kings to the tomb
to pass between the wick and the flame

between the sword and the terror

and you, my elder, what are your tasks?

to which Fercheirtne replied:
　　not hard to answer
　　to scale from honour to honour
　　to attain the conversation of the wise
　　to suckle at the breast of poetry
　　to wade the wide rivers of the world
　　to make music for the ferocious demon
　　upon the slope of death

A question, o wise man of young face, by what path have you come?

to which Nede replied:
　　not hard to answer
　　by way of a king's beard
　　by way of the forest
　　on the back of the ploughman's ox
　　upon a nourishment of acorns
　　upon the barley and milk of the mother of song
　　on one grain of wheat
　　by way of the most narrow river crossing
　　upon my own two legs

and you, my elder, by what path have you come?

to which Fercheirtne replied:
　　not hard to answer
　　by way of the whip of the many-skilled Lugh
　　by way of the sweet breasts of women
　　by way of the letters cut on the staff
　　by way of the spear head
　　and the silver dress
　　upon a chariot without a wheel
　　upon a wheel without a chariot
　　upon the three things unknown to Mac Ind Oc
　　The son of the young

and you, young man of manly understanding, whose son are you?

to which Nede replied:
　　not hard to answer
　　I am the son of Poetry
　　Poetry son of Looking
　　Looking son of Thought
　　Thought son of Learning
　　Learning son of Curiosity
　　Curiosity son of Seeking
　　Seeking son of Great Wisdom

Great Wisdom son of Great Common Sense
Great Common Sense son of True Understanding
True Understanding son of Insight
Insight son of the Three Gods of Poetry

and you, my elder, whose son are you?

to which Fercheirtne replied:
not hard to answer
son of the fatherless man
buried in the womb of his mother
blessed after his death
married to his own death
my father is the first cry of the babe
the last cry of the dying
Ailm is his name

A question, Nede:
What news do you bring?

to which Nede replied:
not hard to answer
I bring good news
seas of fish
fullness of lakes
glad countenance of glades
wood at work
fruit boughs bending
barley bearded
bees swarming
joyful land
peaceful peace
merry weather
soldiers paid wages
kings sitting in sunlight
war distant
art present
men boasting
women sewing
thorn trees spiky
caskets of gold
a bravery for every boast
enough thread for every stitch
every good thing I sing
for ever
there is none greater
than the Great Creator
the same who revealed
at first

The Shining Lord. Oil on canvas.

the nine hazels of poetry
who made also
the rank of Ollamh
for in the world I have
three real fathers
my father in flesh
Adne who is dead
my father in Art
Eochu Horsemouth
who is in Scotland
and my father in years
Fercheirtne

Then Nede rose from the ollamh seat, handing as he did so the poet's many-coloured robe to Fercheirtne

and Fercheirtne said:
great poet, wise young man
son of Adne
may you get glory from men and gods
may you be the greatest treasure
of Emain Macha, Ollamh of Ulster

and Nede replied:
may that same glory be yours Ollamh of Ulster

From Irish tradition (English version by Robin Williamson)

Index

Italics: books, films, plays • 'Quotes': titles of poems, stories and songs • **Bold**: illustration

The Silver Branch Bardic Network

OPEN TO ALL INTERESTED IN THE BARDIC TRADITION:

✤ **Storytellers**
✤ **Poets**
✤ **Singers**
✤ **Musicians**
✤ **Actors**
✤ **Celebrants**
✤ **Writers**
✤ **Academics**
✤ **Audience**

**The Silver Branch Bardic Network is free to join.
The intention of The Silver Branch is to:**

Honour the Bardic Tradition
Provide a voice for modern Bards
Create a Community
Share Information/News
Publicise Events/Workshops/Publications
Offer Peer Support
Organise Social Gatherings
Run Eisteddfodau and Showcases
Hold Camps
Acknowledge and Link to other Organisations,
eg: The Druid Network, OBOD, PF, etc.

Register your interest in joining:
subscribe-the-silver-branch@yahoogroups.co.uk

Check out our annual programme of events at
Yahoo! Group: the-silver-branch